# Toward a Wider Vision of Behavioral Economics

By the Same Author:

*Money Matters: A Keynesian Approach to Monetary Economics* (with Sheila C. Dow, 1982, Martin Robertson)

*The Economic Imagination: Towards a Behavioural Analysis of Choice* (1983, Wheatsheaf Books)

*The Corporate Imagination: How Big Companies Make Mistakes* (1984, Wheatsheaf Books)

*Lifestyle Economics: Consumer Behaviour in a Turbulent World* (1986, Wheatsheaf Books)

*Monetary Scenarios: A Modern Approach to Financial Systems* (1990, Edward Elgar Publishing)

*Microeconomics for Business and Marketing: Lectures, Case and Worked Essays* (1995, Edward Elgar Publishing).

*Information, Opportunism and Economic Coordination* (2002, Edward Elgar Publishing)

*Business Economics: A Contemporary Approach* (with Tim Wakeley, 2005, McGraw-Hill UK)

*G. L. S. Shackle (Great Thinkers in Economics Series)* (with Bruce Littleboy, 2014, Palgrave)

*Principles of Behavioral Economics: Bringing Together Old, Newe and Evolutionary Approaches* (2022, Cambridge University Press)

*Beyond Misbehaving: Changing Universities, Pluralism, and the Evolution of a Heterodox Behavioral Economist* (2024, PE:AT Publishing)

Fiction, under the penname Darcy Crick:

*Dealbreakers: Sex, Quiz, and Rock 'n' Roll* (2025, Darcy Crick Books)

# TOWARD A WIDER VISION OF BEHAVIORAL ECONOMICS

(Second Edition)

Peter E. Earl

Honorary Associate Professor of Economics
University of Queensland

Available in eBook and soft cover print editions.
PE:AT Publishing, Westlake, QLD, Australia
Distribution to major online retail platforms via Draft2Digital

# Table of Contents

# Preface

This book is offered as a contrast to Nobel Laureate Richard Thaler's (2015) intellectual autobiography *Misbehaving*, which carried the subtitles *The Making of Behavioral Economics* (on the cover) and *How Economics Became Behavioral* (on the title page). Thaler's book offers a clear and engaging account of how his ideas developed and his role in taking economics in a (particular) behavioral direction. Indeed, it was for these reasons that I set it, instead of a regular textbook, as required reading for my behavioral economics students from 2016 onward. However, I was careful to explain and demonstrate to my students that the portraits of behavioral economics that have been offered by Thaler and the authors of most behavioral economics textbooks are needlessly narrow compared with the vision of behavioral economics that I have been assembling since 1975, when I first encountered the field as an undergraduate student at the University of Cambridge. This book provides an account of how I came to view behavioral economics as I do, the key sources that influenced my thinking, and the opportunities that behavioral economists are likely to miss if they confine themselves to the narrow vision of behavioral economics that has become a standard part of modern economics. The chapters that follow also serve as a prequel to my magnum opus, *Principles of Behavioral Economics: Bringing Together Old, New and Evolutionary Approaches*, which was published by Cambridge University Press in 2022 and was designed to be usable as an advanced textbook, complete with extensive online teaching and learning resources.

The intellectual autobiography that I present in this book contrasts with Thaler's *Misbehaving* not merely in the vision of behavioral economics that it offers but also in the tell-all confessional style that I employ. It is sometimes said that the only negative things that authors of autobiographies reveal about themselves are how bad their memories are. That does not apply here, for I still have a very good memory – even of occasions where I forgot things that I should have remembered – and I use it in this book partly to show how, and why, during much of my career, I did a rather poor job of getting my vision of behavioral economics noticed by those who came into the field from the mid-1980s onward. I use ideas from behavioral economics to explore my under-achievement, and I hope this will help early-career behavioral economists to avoid the kinds of mistakes that I made.

This book both draws on and extends material from a much longer memoir draft that I wrote between December 2021 and May 2023 and published in slightly shortened form in January 2024 under the title *Beyond Misbehaving:*

*Changing Universities, Pluralism, and the Evolution of a Heterodox Behavioral Economist*. That book was mainly aimed at those who brand themselves as "heterodox" economists, as I have long believed that their academic futures would probably be much less bleak if they were to embrace the kind of behavioral economics that I practice and then use it for the microfoundations of their analysis. *Beyond Misbehaving* therefore included detailed analysis of how the academic world has become much more challenging for those who position their research outputs as "heterodox" and seek to teach "heterodox" ideas alongside the conventional textbook wisdom. With behavioral economics now so widely embraced within economics as a whole, the challenge for those who already think of themselves as operating as behavioral economists is different: how to stand out and/or find new areas to research as the field becomes increasingly crowded and mature. So, the present book focuses purely on my behavioral journey and ends with a detailed research agenda chapter that its predecessor did not include.

In deciding to put the present book together, I was partly responding to Geoffrey Hodgson (the founding editor of the *Journal of Institutional Economics*) and my former University of Stirling colleague Peter Bird, who suggested, respectively, that a book of this one's size, or a couple of short books, might be extracted from the original memoir. I am grateful for their encouragement to try to do this. My commitment to the memoir project has been enhanced by much encouragement from John Creedy, and I would also like to acknowledge correspondence with Sheila Dow, Greg Clydesdale and Jason Potts, and feedback from participants at a Zoom presentation that I gave in October 2023 to the University of Witwatersrand's workshop series on economic methodology. My reference in Section 8.9 to Pixar's way of promoting constructive criticism was the result of my wonderful team of high-achieving behavioral economics tutors – Jessica Downing-Ide, Ryan Palfrey, Lillian Rangiah and Edward Watson – giving me a copy of Ed Catmull's (2014) book *Creativity, Inc.* as a memento of our working relationship, after they had the insight to notice how it intersected with what we had been teaching. Finally, it is important to note that the writing of this book has greatly depended on the love and support of my partner, Annabelle Taylor, to whom I owe my apologies for once again inflicting on her a period of my "absent-minded professor" operating mode.

*Changes for the Second Edition (2026)*
The changes that I made for this second edition are minor. The main body of the book has grown by only one page, which is due to the reworking of Section 4.11

at what are now pages 138-40. There, I have improved the accuracy and precision of the account of the "revise and resubmit" stage of my PhD. The account in the first edition was largely accurate but purely memory-based, whereas the revision draws on the relevant documents that I could not locate when writing the original. The rediscovery of these documents was unknowingly facilitated by my brother-in-law, Andrew Gay, when he kindly arranged to ship to me several boxes of things that I had left with my parents almost forty years earlier when I emigrated to Tasmania. The shipment arrived in Brisbane shortly after the original edition was finished and, to my surprise and delight, it included a folder of PhD-related correspondence pertaining to the examination process for the PhD.

The second edition also benefits from the removal of typographical errors that became glaringly obvious to me via the much-improved vision that cataract-removal surgery gave me in the interim. Evidently, as my vision deteriorated during work on the original edition, I had been over-confident about my ability to continue to cope by working in "dark mode" even though, in Microsoft Word 365, issues with my colour vision made it impossible for me to see the underlining of wrongly typed words. Too often, I saw through the mist what I expected to see. However, I had delayed having the surgery for as long as I could on the advice of my ophthalmologist, who was nervous about the collateral risks it might pose for causing tectonic impacts at the back of eyes that had longstanding retinal issues due to the stretching effects of years of very high myopia. In the end, there were no collateral impacts, so it might seem that we had been over-cautious in delaying the procedure. But if one already has compromised central vision and still has items on the "to write list," a safety-first heuristic is the natural one to use.

I have also occasionally reworked sentences to improve their clarity, and I have renumbered items in the Index where necessary to take account of the extra page of text.

# Introduction

This book is an unusual contribution to the literatures of behavioral economics and the history of economic thought. It is the story of life on a less traveled behavioral economics road than the one that led to what most economists, and many professionals in the wider world of policymaking, view as behavioral economics and to Nobel Memorial Prizes for Daniel Kahneman and Richard Thaler. I have been on a journey along this less traveled road since the mid-1970s, i.e., about as long as Richard Thaler has been developing, generating interest in, and applying his Kahneman- and Tversky-inspired way of doing behavioral economics. When I started out, the kind of economics on which I had become hooked was already called "behavioral economics." A few years later, one of its key pioneers, Herbert Simon, was awarded the 1978 Nobel Memorial Prize in Economic Sciences. However, because of their limited vision of behavioral economics, Thaler and those who followed him down the more traveled road found little need to draw upon work by those that I viewed as behavioral economists, and the phrase "behavioral economics" gradually became viewed as synonymous with the work that grew from the seminal contributions by Kahneman and Tversky (1979) and Thaler (1980). Esther-Mirjam Sent (2004) has labeled their work "new behavioral economics" and the kinds of contributions that inspired me as "old behavioral economics," but "evolutionary behavioral economics" is probably a better term for the kind of economics to which the less traveled road has taken me.

The goal of this book is to interest behavioral economists in scope for enhancing their contributions by taking up ideas from the "old/evolutionary" approach. My aim is to promote a pluralistic "horses for courses" way of doing behavioral economics in which practitioners of behavioral economics have both the "new" and "old/evolutionary" versions at their disposal. This is how I have always trained my behavioral economics students to be prepared to operate. I see the two approaches as complementary.

I have set out such a vision of behavioral economics at length in my book *Principles of Behavioral Economics: Bringing Together Old, New, and Evolutionary Approaches* (Earl, 2022). It was my tenth book as an author, my seventh as a solo author. The present book can be viewed as a kind of "prequel" to that volume. It introduces many of the ideas that I have worked with over the years, how I arrived at them, and the main contributions that I made to the field. To that extent, this book works in a similar way to Richard Thaler's (2015) intellectual autobiography *Misbehaving* – except that my story is that of an initial high-achiever who became an "also ran" contributor rather than someone who achieved academic superstardom. However, because of my limited success in cultivating a following for the kind of behavioral economics that I advocate, I decided that it would also be worthwhile to explore in this book how I might have done a better job in developing and marketing the ideas that have captivated me.

Clearly, I run the risk of damaging my reputation by offering an account of my journey as a behavioral economist that also exposes my own academic shortcomings. However, I am prepared to run this risk as a means of promoting the "old/evolutionary" behavioral approach. The fact that I have been prepared to do this instead of proceeding quietly into a comfortable retirement may signal just how passionately I view the benefits of including insights from the "old/evolutionary" approach in the practice of behavioral economics. But I also hope the confessional areas of this book will help other behavioral economists to limit the extent to which they fail to see and/or seize important scholarly opportunities.

The body of this book is divided into eight chapters. The first seven cover, in chronological order, the stages in my life during which I laid the foundations for, and made contributions to, my "wider vision" of behavioral economics.

Chapter 1 covers my school years while growing up in a post-war new town in the south of England in the 1960s and early 1970s. It focuses not merely on formative experiences that I had when I began to study economics at high school but also on how some of the behavior that I saw my parents engage in as consumers, and the hobbies that I pursued, affected my receptiveness to ideas that I later encountered about decision-making and the importance of non-price competition for how the economic system works.

Chapters 2 and 3 cover the period between October 1974 and June 1979, during which I was studying economics at the University of Cambridge. Chapter 2 focuses on the behavioral ingredients that I picked up in my three years as an undergraduate. This period equipped me with two key areas of knowledge of a behavioral kind. One was a perspective on macroeconomics that focused on the significance of uncertainty, investor psychology, and complex, layered networks of financial balance sheets, that prepared me for a world of periodic financial crises. The other was a grounding in behavioral and evolutionary approaches to the theory of the firm and industrial change. It included a significant dose of material on the sociology of organizational behavior and ensured that I was not puzzled when Herbert Simon became the 1978 Nobel Laureate in Economics. I graduated as one of the highest achievers in my year but, instead of seeking to get a scholarship to study at a top North American university, I opted to return to Cambridge to begin research for my doctorate without taking any further coursework.

My Cambridge mentors asserted that the Cambridge BA program in economics was taught at a much higher level than its US counterparts. I believed (and still believe) they were right to make this claim, for a very large proportion of the reading that I did as an undergraduate was from primary sources rather than textbooks, and there was a focus on thinking critically about what one read. However, nothing prepared me for how disappointing Cambridge's PhD system turned out to be, which had nothing to do with the absence of US-style graduate coursework. Chapter 3 begins to explain how, as I began my research on the economics of structural change, I was essentially left to fend for myself with very little supervisory input and very little guidance on what I would need to deliver to get confirmation of candidature and ultimately get my thesis accepted. I say "begins to explain" because what happened at the end of my first year as a research student set in train a series of events that led me to move from Cambridge at the end of my second year as a research student to complete my doctorate remotely, with the whole process of getting my Cambridge PhD taking almost seven years from start to finish.

Chapter 4 explains what happened during the rest of my PhD saga, which took place while I worked as a lecturer (assistant professor) at the University of Stirling in Scotland. As a research student in Cambridge, I had mainly been focusing on coordination processes and the responsiveness of firms to changing market conditions, but during my time at Stirling (July 1979 to May 1984), my research focus shifted to consumer behavior. I was therefore very interested when I saw Thaler's seminal (1980) article shortly after it was published, and I referred to it when writing my very first conference paper in Spring 1981 (which was published two years later: see Earl, 1983c, p. 186). However, the many other works to which I referred in that paper reflected the fact that, for reasons that are set out in Chapter 4, I was already working with a much wider range of sources than Thaler, from areas such as marketing, personal construct psychology, cognitive psychology, sociology, and social anthropology. Indeed, the scene was set for the rest of my career: I would maintain an interest in the kind of work undertaken by Thaler and those who closely followed his lead, but I always employed it as part of a bigger behavioral economics toolkit. In addition to explaining how I arrived at this viewpoint, Chapter 4 highlights some important things that I failed to spot, and opportunities that I was aware of but did not pursue at that stage.

After completing my doctoral dissertation and writing several books at Stirling, I spent the rest of my career working in universities "Down Under." Chapters 5 to 7 are devoted to how my approach to behavioral economics developed there between 1984 and my retirement at the end of 2020, with each of these chapters pertaining to a different university. These far-away institutions each enabled me to enjoy much better material living standards than I would have enjoyed if I had stayed in the UK, but they differed greatly in how conducive they were to me continuing to make original research contributions in behavioral economics and get them noticed globally. However, it will also become evident that what I was able to accomplish was affected by how I managed my career and the lifecycle stages through which I passed.

Chapter 5 covers my work on behavioral economics at the University of Tasmania from June 1984 to June 1991. There, I produced a lot of output that related to behavioral and/or psychological economics but which was not the result of me developing a conventional, tightly focused post-doctoral research program. This had much to do with the wider vision of behavioral economics that I employed and with the fact that, now free of the shackles of the PhD saga, I operated rather too much as "a young man in a hurry." This was made deceptively easy due to some senior scholars reacting favorably to my early works: as a result, I found myself at an unexpectedly early stage working on mid-career kinds of commissioned projects. This doubtless led to me being offered, at the age of 35, a full professor position. It would also enable me to live in one of my wish-list locations, so I accepted it.

However, as Chapter 6 shows, moving to Lincoln University, near Christchurch in New Zealand showed the power of the expression "be careful what you wish for." I ran into major challenges as I tried to incorporate behavioral ideas into the curriculum. The administrative load was much bigger than I expected, too, and for the first eight years of the decade (mid-1991–mid-2001) that I spent there, my original research largely dried up. Although, as I explain in Chapter 6, I then started to get my behavioral economics research happening again, it took a decade for me to rebuild my reputation as someone who could do original research. Hence, in 2002, shortly after I escaped back to Australia from the toxic environment in which I had been working, a referee of a research grant application that I had co-authored was still able to dismiss me as someone "who has not lived up to his initial promise."

My Lincoln decade was a period in which the longer that I spent trying – always mindful of sunk-cost bias – to make the job come right so that I could enjoy life in Christchurch, the more difficult it became for me to move to a less toxic environment. Escaping from it into a well-ranked research-focused institution necessitated going back down the career ladder to where I had been at the end of my time in Tasmania. It also necessitated moving to a city that I liked less than those in which I had lived previously.

Chapter 7 covers how my approach to behavioral economics evolved at the University of Queensland from mid–2001, up to my retirement at the end of 2020. It was a fruitful time for developing my wider vision of behavioral economics, though it took me until around 2007 to appreciate what had happened in behavioral economics, particularly in North America, during my largely lost decade working in New Zealand. It will be evident from Chapter 7 that my work increasingly had an evolutionary dimension that centered on connective structures in complex adaptive systems. It also became more empirical, experimenting with a wider range of research methods. This was eventually aided by success in winning a large competitive research grant, to study the quality of decision-making in the market for cellphone connection services with an emphasis on procedural rationality and the effects of consumers being able to outsource significant chunks of their decision-making processes.

Finally, Chapter 8 brings together themes from the previous chapters to summarize what my "wider vision" of behavioral economics entails in terms of research methods, research opportunities and organizing principles. I have written this chapter in as self-contained a way as possible so that those who are only interested in where I ended up, or only have time to read one chapter, can save time by not reading about the journey that resulted in the perspective that I advocate.

# 1 Beginnings

## 1.1 INTRODUCTION

To understand the origins of how I came to see economics in the way that I do, it is necessary to know not merely about my life prior to my university-level studies but also about what I knew, when growing up, about the lives of my parents. I was born in the UK in 1955. My parents both came from working-class families in the St Pancras/Camden Town and Islington areas of London. They married on Christmas Day, 1945, when my father Eric, at twenty-one, was a private in the Royal Army Medical Corps. He had been drafted after spending most of the war making parts for Spitfire fighter aircraft and had met Julia, my mother, at a dance class. She had only turned eighteen a few weeks before their wedding and had been working in a confectionery factory. Both had qualified for middle ability high schools but Eric's father could not afford to keep him there beyond fourteen, while Julia, too, had ended her education very early due to not going back to school after returning to London following a brief evacuation at the start of the war. Julia's evacuation had taken her to live with a middle-class family in Hitchin, 35 miles north of London, and it gave her a short taste of the kind of life that she ultimately went on to have.

Unlike many in their generation, my parents delayed starting a family. Soon after they married, my father broke his leg badly in a motorcycle accident in his army camp at Tidworth in Wiltshire: he told me that it happened because an army truck unexpectedly turned out in front of him, and he had ridden his army motorcycle straight into it rather than swerving into a group of marching soldiers. To make matters worse, his leg had to be re-broken after being poorly set. After his slow recovery and demobbing, my parents were allocated a small, modern apartment in a public housing scheme not far from where they had grown up, and my father returned to working in a machine shop. However, my mother caught tuberculosis, probably from her father (who eventually succumbed to it, aged only 49). She was admitted to Grove Park Hospital in Lewisham, which had been a workhouse prior to World War I and had been acquired by the Metropolitan Asylums Board in 1918 for use as a specialist hospital for tuberculosis patients. At that time, tuberculosis had no drug-based cure and long-term resting in bed was the best hope for surviving it. On seeing how many fellow patients were succumbing to the disease, my mother decided to discharge herself and try to recover at home. With my father caring for her, she lived to tell the tale, but even once she had recovered, they delayed starting a family as she remained weak. Shortly after I was born, while she was pregnant with my sister, she caught tuberculosis again, but this time newly developed drugs provided the cure.

My mother's periods of illness affected the family finances, too, not merely by keeping her out of the workforce but also because my father's pride limited the extent to which he was willing to claim "national assistance" when he took periods of unpaid leave while she was ill. During these periods, they lived on their savings. When they told me about this in the late 1960s, as they belatedly began to accumulate a house deposit, it was my first lesson on principles-based behavior.

If I had followed in my father's footsteps, I would have become an engineer by working my way up from tea-boy in a small engineering works, becoming a skilled machine-tool operator and toolmaker, and eventually being promoted to a junior management role in a large factory. However, my parents were keen not merely to take their own lives up into post-war Britain's middle class; they also expected that my sister and I should both get the best educations that we could and have much better careers than themselves. From an early age, I realized that they seemed much more aspirational about me and my sister than most of my uncles and aunts seemed to be about my cousins. I am sure that noticing this was a major factor that led me to want to understand differences in how people operate, rather than accept the usual practice of economists that entails focusing on "representative" economic agents.


## 1.2    THE TOWN THAT MADE ME

Two years before I was born, my parents marked their aspirations for a better life by moving to Stevenage, about 30 miles north of London and 30 miles south-west of Cambridge. Stevenage was one of the rapidly expanding satellite towns that were being built about thirty miles from London under the 1946 New Towns Act, as part of the post-war planning and reconstruction process. When I was about ten years old, my parents investigated the possibility of emigrating to Australia, but they decided against doing so because they feared that what they viewed as a dusty land would exacerbate my problems with asthma. Otherwise, they showed no sign of considering moving elsewhere while I was growing up. Stevenage was thus the only town in which I lived before going to university, and it was in Stevenage that I got hooked on economics. These days, it is not a town that is seen as a great place to live, but in the early post-war period, it was seen very differently.

The decision of my parents to move to Stevenage was the result of a conversation between my father and a workplace colleague who was about to leave to take up another job. The colleague said that he was going to work in a factory in a new town that was being built in the countryside with clean air (unlike smog-prone London, prior to the implementation of the 1956 Clean Air Act) and plenty of new houses to rent at reasonable rates. My father made inquiries about what might be available, and within weeks, he and my mother followed suit. Instead of being socially embedded in living close to the rest of their families, my parents had been very keen to move away.

As I grew up, I witnessed with great interest a ten-fold growth in my hometown's population. This experience helped me to get a sense not merely of the payoffs to planning but also of how planners could get things wrong due to deficient foresight. What particularly struck me was how the planners seemed to envisage that, if they equipped Stevenage with an extensive network of cycle tracks, the town's residents would make great use of them for commuting. The planners seemed to fail to appreciate the extent of the motorization that would take place in the post-war decades, with people (including my father) switching to commuting by car as they became more affluent. Motorization resulted in suburban streets becoming increasingly clogged by parked cars – partly because most houses were not built with off-street parking, let alone their own garages, but also because vehicle ownership spread to spouses and then to teenagers. In Stevenage's main industrial area, there was a long period of disruption as the key arterial road was remodeled to cope with the growing volume of traffic. But at least Stevenage will not suffer the disruption that other cities face in attempting to retrofit cycle tracks into their transport systems to enable people to take a greener and fitter approach to commuting.

Stevenage was also a wonderful venue for observing Schumpeterian processes of evolution in the context of retailing. The "old town" had been a coaching town on the main road from London to York. Much of its high street was therefore unusually wide, allowing coaches to pull into the many inns. When work on the new town began, the old high street initially served as the main shopping area. Except for a large Woolworths variety store and a Boots pharmacy, health and beauty store, chain stores were absent. As growth increasingly sprawled away to the south and east of the old town, the new suburbs were built with their own small strips of shops, but from the late 1950s a new, state-of-the-art pedestrian shopping precinct was built as the "town center." This attracted much larger shops than the old town could offer, including major supermarket, clothing, furnishing and electrical appliance chains. However, from the early 1980s, the town's motorized population increasingly had alternatives to shopping at the town center, such as larger supermarkets built on its periphery, and the emergence of "big box"-style retailers, while, in other towns, urban redevelopment involved building climate-controlled indoor malls that in ensuing decades have come, via processes of competitive refurbishment, to have interiors that resemble marble palaces. Stevenage town center thus ceased to be a modern marvel and evolved into a decaying monument to post-war brutalist design. Attempts to refurbish it with new pavers and other external cosmetic changes seemed in the early 2000s to be failing to address its obsolescence. It makes a great **case study** if one is teaching a course on the evolution of economic systems and/or needs tutorial material for a behavioral and/or evolutionary analysis of retailing. The changes that I observed as I was growing up were not conducive to taking seriously models of competition that were based on static equilibrium analysis.

My parents' decision to move to Stevenage, coupled with the cohort into which I was born, gave me the educational opportunities that enabled me to achieve a place at the University of Cambridge. I had the good fortune to be in one of the last cohorts of school children whose academic abilities determined which high schools they were able to attend. Because of this, as a very weedy-looking, bespectacled eleven-year-old, I was one of five boys from my junior primary school who started their high school education in the autumn term of 1966 at what was then known as Alleyne's Grammar School. Located at the northern end of old Stevenage, Alleyne's had been founded in 1558, the year that Elizabeth I became Queen of England, and it had a proud academic heritage. It often recruited teachers with degrees from Oxford or Cambridge and its senior staff knew how to place top students at these elite institutions in the face of strong competition against students from elite private schools (which are known, confusingly, in the UK as "public schools"). It is now known as The Thomas Alleyne Academy.

After excelling at Alleyne's in my first couple of years, I was offered the chance to compete for a Hertfordshire County Council scholarship to study at Harrow, Rugby, or Winchester, outside the state system. The only academic concern about my chances of success if I gave it a shot was that I might not have enough Latin, as I had only started taking it in my second year. In the event, I declined this opportunity because of a demand-side deal-breaker: I did not want to go to a boarding school. Despite their aspirations for me, my parents did not put any pressure on me over this decision, and I never regretted it. At that stage my vocabulary did not include the expression "deal-breaker," but it would later become a key ingredient in my approach to behavioral economics.

Later in this chapter, I will explain the role that Alleyne's played in starting me on the road that I took as an economist. But first, I reflect on the non-academic side of my personal development and how it fed into the economics that I went on to do.

## 1.3 FORMATIVE EXAMPLES OF QUESTIONABLE CONSUMER BEHAVIOR

I have a very rich set of memories about the evolution of the lifestyle of my parents while I was growing up in Stevenage. The vividness of these memories is a result of the fact that from a very early age I watched closely what my parents did and listened intently to what they told me or what I heard them saying to each other about their choices. What I observed primed me to be skeptical about models of rational economic agents when I encountered them as an undergraduate. Later, these memories contributed significantly to my openness to the idea of taking a psychological approach to consumer behavior, particularly in relation to the role of emotions and the management of cognitive dissonance. They also helped to make me receptive to the work of Thaler and others whom Mehta (2013) has accused of "pathologizing" consumers. However, whereas Thaler-style behavioral economics portrays *humans in general* as being, by nature, prone to "misbehave" in the sense of taking account of "supposedly irrelevant factors" and making sub-optimal choices, I was from the outset much more interested in the relative success of *different* consumers in making the most of their opportunities. There was much about my parents' behavior that seemed crazy to me when I was growing up, and their behavior got even more bizarre as they got older. But my "case study" of my parents' behavior played no role at all in stirring my interest in the challenges that consumers face in dealing with complexity and how they try to cope with them.

My father was almost 47 when we moved, early in January 1971, into a five-year-old semi-detached chalet bungalow on a small private estate near the northern end of Stevenage old town, very close to my high school. Although my parents said that taking so long to get a foot on the property ownership ladder was a consequence of the impact of my mother's bouts of tuberculosis on their ability to save up a house deposit, I have often wondered whether, in the first couple of decades of their marriage, they had even seriously entertained the idea of becoming homeowners. Their track record in spending suggested their priorities lay elsewhere. This was not surprising, given that before they moved to Stevenage, the only time that either of them had entered an owner-occupied home had been when my mother was evacuated from London at the start of the war; on moving to Stevenage, they had ready access to affordable modern rental housing provided by the Stevenage Development Corporation that the government had set up to administer the creation of the new town. In 1957, when my sister was born, they upgraded from a two-bedroom house to a much more spacious three-bedroom house. Moreover, at that stage, inflation rates were low and there was no sense that delaying getting on to the property ladder could be a regret-inducing error.

While failing to save for a house deposit, my parents did manage to save up for modern consumer durables, rather than using emerging hire purchase opportunities to get these products sooner. By the time they moved to Stevenage, they already had not merely a standalone radio (in a huge wooden cabinet) and a radiogram but also the television that made it possible for them and their neighbors to watch the coronation of Queen Elizabeth II in June 1953. Around the time that I was born, my father acquired a 1932 Austin Seven car and was trying, unsuccessfully, to pass his driving test. The Austin was sold after he failed the test a second time, which was also around the time that my mother was again diagnosed with tuberculosis. My father was also learning to play the piano and had replaced his original, old-fashioned Brinsmead (which had candlestick holders and must have been bought second-hand) with a brand-new Zender. Around 1960, a refrigerator was purchased, and my mother started to shop at the new supermarkets in the town center (using my sister's stroller as the means to transport the shopping home) instead of making near-daily trips to the local shops.

Even though I was then very young, it was hard for me not to notice this sudden transformation and the exciting new environment of Sainsbury's supermarket, whose shopping trolleys I so keenly wanted to push. The following year, my parents had a telephone installed but they canceled the service within a matter of months after repeatedly getting misdialed calls intended for a restaurant whose number was quite similar. They found this first telephonic experience so disconcerting that they did not bother to have a telephone service again until they retired to Polperro in Cornwall in 1987, even though there was already a wall-mounted phone in the entrance hall of the house that they purchased in 1971. Because of this, all telephone calls had to be made from a payphone and were only made when absolutely necessary. I thus grew up without developing any skills in handling telephone calls.

The first instance where I wondered about the quality of my parents' decision-making was in respect of what they did when the sales of domestic tape recorders started to take off in the early 1960s. I had barely been at school a year when my parents joined the tape-recording bandwagon and recorded me reciting the child's poem about how "Incy wincy spider climbed up the spout." However, they did not join the bandwagon by purchasing the kind of reel-to-reel recorder that we had seen on a visit to London to see some of my mother's relatives, who keenly showed off their new toy. Instead, they economized by buying a "Gramdeck." It was the first grown-ups' product whose packaging grabbed my attention, as the various modules each came in a bright red box with an embossed brassy label that contributed to the product's air of quality despite it being targeted at those who wanted to reduce the cost of experimenting with tape recording.

As can be seen from videos posted on YouTube by collectors of vintage electronics products, a Gramdeck did not have an electric motor for driving the tape and the tape reel spindles. Instead, it piggybacked on the motor of a record player's turntable, over whose spindle it was mounted. It also lacked a power amplifier and loudspeaker, with the signal from its pre-amplifier module being fed into the power amplifier of the record player or radiogram whose turntable power it was using. It delivered comparable sound quality to a typical tape recorder of its time but inevitably it was hardly ever used in a household that primarily wanted to listen to records rather than tape recordings. It might not take long to unbox and set up, but a behavioral economist would today view this hurdle as enough to be a deterrent to its use by consumers who are naturally prone to suffer from availability bias and to engage in quasi-hyperbolic discounting. My parents' choice seemed crazy to me at the time, even though I was only six years old: it seemed obvious that the Gramdeck was hopelessly cumbersome to use and would be what I later learned to call a "white elephant." This unwise purchase resulted from a visit by a door-to-door salesperson and was my first lesson in the value of having the confidence to say "No" and to think carefully about products before buying them. The experience of seeing my uncle's tape recorder and the Gramdeck led to a memorable case of confusion some months later, when I turned seven and moved from my infants' school to the adjacent junior school: my teacher, Miss Claxton, told the class that we would be able to start learning to play the recorder, but of course it was the wind instrument, which I had not encountered before, not what I thought she meant.

A year or so before the Gramdeck was purchased, my father had given me what was probably the first demonstration I received of technological progress: he had the original 78-rpm record turntable in the radiogram replaced by one that could play a stack of 45-rpm singles or 33-rpm albums. The first 45-rpm single that he purchased was one of my first tastes of something Australian, namely Slim Dusty's hit, "A Pub with No Beer." The song's lyrics puzzled me at one point, for without any notion of a dingo in my memory, the best I could make of the phrase "wild dingoes call" was "wilding goes cool." I imagined that "wilding" referred to what I latter came to know an Australian refers to as "the bush." Little did I know then, or subsequently with my confusion about "recorder," that I would later spend a lot of my time dealing with the significance of our views of the world being personally constructed (Kelly, 1955) and memory-dependent (Hayek, 1952), as this instance neatly illustrates. Nor did I anticipate that, on a road-trip vacation over half a century later, my partner Annabelle and I would find ourselves disappointed that we could not eat at the hotel in Ingham, Queensland whose beer shortage story inspired the song. This time, the pub had plenty of beer, but neither of us wanted to drink alcohol; the problem was that it offered neither gluten-free nor vegan food.

Around 1967, my father decided to upgrade from the radiogram to a stereo system (without any form of tape recorder). Again, he seemed to make a mistake, despite this time being prepared to say "No" to a salesperson. He arranged a home demonstration of a Bush Arena component hi-fi system by the local hi-fi store, Stevenage Record Center. However, he decided against it under some pressure from my mother. Her concerns that the Bush system did not function as a piece of furniture were then addressed via the purchase of an elegant but sonically less capable stereogram from another store.

I was very disappointed, as it was clear to me that stereograms were becoming obsolete and that the component system that my parents had rejected would be easier to upgrade and, in any case, already sounded better. The upgrading issue was on my mind because it was clear that when the radiogram's turntable had been replaced, this had very obviously entailed replacing some of the elegant, polished wood in the cabinet with a sheet of plywood to accommodate the new turntable's mounting requirements. Any such transplant looked like it would be very problematic on the stereogram due to its very different cabinet configuration. It was also clear that the stereogram's integral speakers resulted in a compromised aural experience, given where it had to be put to fit in the lounge, whereas separate speakers would have given the flexibility to get the best stereo separation. It was not clear that my mother really understood what stereophonic sound was all about, but she saw the teak stereogram as a nice piece of furniture that included storage space for their growing collection of records.

The stereogram served them well for a decade before it was given away and replaced by a Rotel component hi-fi system that included a cassette tape-deck. This time, my mother could not veto a component system by questioning where it, and the LPs that had been stored in the stereogram, might be put: my father had already built a set of low cupboards that also served as a modern-looking stand. This was one of several rather IKEA-like items of furniture that he made by using second-hand melamine-faced panels that he purchased from a stall in Hitchin market that sold parts of kitchen units that had been salvaged rather than simply being tossed into skips when homes were being renovated.

All in all, the stereo saga seemed to be blighted by short-term thinking. If they had bought the Bush Arena system, they could readily have upgraded the turntable (and added a stereo FM radio tuner) without any custom installation being needed, and the amplifier and loudspeakers of the system would probably have served them for many decades. The saga was my first practical lesson on why it could matter whether systems were integrated or modular, an issue that would later become one of my enduring interests via Simon's (1962, 1969) work on the evolutionary significance of system architecture.

My parents' car choices provided other food for my thinking on consumer behavior. After selling the Austin Seven, my father continued cycling to work until early 1964, when he bought a 1954 Standard Eight from a colleague, who also taught him to drive well enough to pass the test this time around. Never again did family holidays necessitate traveling by coach or train. However, at the end of 1964, the Standard Eight was replaced by a brand-new Monaco-red Ford Anglia Deluxe. I was disappointed that my father did not buy from the same dealer the one-year-old Anglia Super that he also considered. The latter had a bigger engine and a sportier look, as it was finished in white with a dark green roof and side stripes. However, my mother vetoed the latter car on the basis that "Bottle green is unlucky." This superstition-based decision rule left me wondering about her sanity, but she is not a lone example of someone having this affliction, particularly in relation to cars – as is readily evident if one Googles "dark green unlucky" and examines the search results.

Unlike the blue Ford Anglia of the Weasley family in the Harry Potter movies, my father's red Anglia did not fly. Indeed, it suffered from terrible stalling and juddering when he took delivery of it from Zenith Motors in Stevenage, and it continued to operate as if it were powered by what my father called "kangaroo petrol" until its woeful one-year warranty had expired. At that point, Zenith's mechanics seemed finally able to diagnose what was causing the problem, namely, a porous carburetor casting. This was the first situation I encountered that looked like it was an example of what Williamson (1975) labeled as "opportunism" – i.e., a possible case of guileful, self-serving behavior by Ford's dealer, exploiting my father's lack of knowledge about their previous "efforts" at diagnosing the problem.

It is to be hoped that these days Zenith Stevenage (which went on to become a local institution and is still the town's Ford dealer) would operate in a more Marshallian manner and treat its customers with what are now referred to as post-warranty "goodwill gestures" and fix problems without charge if they become evident shortly after the expiry of vehicle warranties. However, the earlier failures to diagnose the carburetor problem may have been a case of incompetence, for other encounters with Zenith's service department drove my father to start to service the Anglia himself.

The last straw was when legislation was introduced requiring all new cars to have front seat belts (from January 1, 1968) and my father wisely decided to have some retrofitted even though the Anglia's December 1964 registration meant that it fell short of the compulsory retrofitting for cars made from 1965 to 1968. He asked Zenith to install the belts that he had purchased via a mail-order offer he had seen in *The Sun* (which had become our daily newspaper when it succeeded *The Daily Herald*, whose last year or so of output provided my first experiences as a newspaper reader). However, pre-fitted seatbelt mounts had not been made compulsory until the year after my father's car had been manufactured, and Zenith's staff clearly had no idea about where to mount the seatbelts: when my father collected the car, he found that they had anchored what should have been the door-pillar mount to the rear floor so that, as my father put it, "Even a deformed dwarf wouldn't have been able to use them."

But although my father sought to overcome the risk of opportunism and incompetence by servicing the Anglia himself, he was over-confident about his own capacity to do the job. As a result, one Monday morning, my father and I had to push the Anglia to a local garage due to his service efforts the previous afternoon leaving it unwilling to fire properly. He was late for work that morning but fortuitously I was offered a lift by my form teacher who happened to be passing as we reached the garage. The Anglia thus provided my first experience of the economics of outsourcing versus do-it-yourself.

Despite not having accumulated a particularly high mileage, the Anglia was replaced around Easter 1970 by a brand-new Morris 1300. By this time, my mother had at last re-joined the labor force, greatly improving our family finances. However, trading up to the Morris had all the signs of being an unduly panicked reaction to the first signs of rust on the Ford. The Morris was purchased only eight months before they bought their first house and it chewed up a significant part of the house deposit that they were trying to accumulate. As a result, their first couple of years as homeowners involved needless mortgage stress. But they were happy to leave Stevenage new town and felt they had done so in the nick of time. This was not simply because of the increase in inflation of housing prices, but also because of their racial prejudices: they were concerned that, as the oldest part of the new town, the area in which we had lived was absorbing a disproportionate number of "immigrants" as those who had been there moved on to newer public rental homes further from the town center or, like my parents, became homebuyers.

With front-wheel drive and a "hydrolastic" suspension system, the Morris 1300 was mechanically much more complex than the Anglia and my father outsourced its servicing. However, he opted to have it serviced by an independent local garage close to where we lived, rather than by the authorized dealer from whom he had purchased it. This strategy also left us wondering about service quality. The most spectacular case was when one side of the front suspension collapsed one evening when my father was driving into our estate. More costly was the fact that the engine and gearbox wore out unexpectedly quickly, with my father having a reconditioned engine and gearbox installed when the car was barely six years old. His decision to authorize this rather than scrap the car was probably another mistake, for two years later he got a terrible trade-in deal due to the major rust problems that had emerged. But perhaps he was misled about the prospective costs of attending to the rust problems, for he spotted the car running, with new sills, a year or so later. At that point, I had not yet come across the classic article on credence goods by Darby and Karni (1973), but my father's experiences with motoring ensured that I was very conscious of both the importance of trust for the functioning of markets and the problem of knowing when a supplier was trustworthy.

My father's behavior in respect of the car with which he replaced the Morris provided my first experience of a factor that rational choice theory would view as irrelevant in choice, namely, a product's country of origin. (Note that, for all her racial prejudices, my mother was willing to buy and eat fruit that people of color had grown and harvested.) The car in question was a brand-new Honda Civic, which my father sold, after only two years, in as-new condition (without even having removed the clear plastic film that covered the doors' interior trim) and with a very low mileage. Soon after selling the Civic, he told me that this was because he just didn't feel comfortable having a car that came from Japan, "given what the Japs did to our forces in World War II." He felt that he really should have bought a British car and hence traded the Civic against a brand-new Ford Fiesta. I was rather peeved that he had done so without offering me the chance to buy it from him. Given the maintenance costs I had run into on my first car, I would have been interested in such an opportunity. Even so, I refrained from immediately telling him that his "British" Ford was actually made in Spain. His behavior in respect of the Civic left me wondering how many people allow the country of origin to affect their choices. I subsequently encountered many other instances of this sort of behavior (most recently in relation to people using a "nothing from China" rule) and I noted examples of it in some of David Lodge's novels (see Earl, 2011). However, I have never sought to investigate it via a systematic empirical study.

The choices that my father made in relation to getting his cars serviced seemed, over-confidence aside, to have far more reasonable foundations than those that he and my mother made in relation to house maintenance. There, they displayed a dysfunctional reluctance to have tradespeople come to fix things that needed to be fixed. My father would instead do his best, as with bodged work on replacing rotting windowsills and the garden gate on the house they bought. If that strategy failed, the problem would be left as it was if they felt they could "live with it." An example of the latter was their willingness to keep flushing the upstairs toilet by taking the cistern lid off and fiddling with the mechanism: they never showed me or my sister the knack for doing this and they lived with this situation from the day they moved in until the day they moved out over sixteen years later following the retirement of my father.

Their move to a brand-new bungalow in Cornwall left them without such problems for a while, but gradually more and more issues became evident each time that I or my sister visited, such as a sagging kitchen ceiling and failed bathroom taps. At one point, the failure of the sound on the lounge TV was addressed by purchasing a cheap portable black and white TV and sitting it on top of the problematic TV as a source of sound, rather than by calling a TV repairer to see if the problem could be fixed.

Whenever I or my sister commented to them about things that they were neglecting to get fixed, their replies revealed that the issue did not seem to entail concerns about the risk of opportunistic over- or under-servicing that they might reasonably have had after their vehicle maintenance experiences, and they did not seem to have an exaggerated view of my father's capacities as a handyman (as opposed to his engineering expertise being applicable to servicing a car). Rather, both my parents were simply wary of having outsiders come to the house to do any work, as they suspected that those who came might gather information that might later be used for house-breaking and theft. How they came to hold such fears was not clear; however, if it were the result of having seen a news report about an instance of such behavior, we might wonder about their skills in forming probability estimates or whether they were grossly overweighting the significance of very low probability events as they worked out their strategy, consistent with Kahneman and Tversky's (1979) prospect theory.[1]

Fear also underpinned my parents' reluctance to outsource food preparation: they completely resisted any idea of eating out, except for getting fish and chip takeaways when we went on vacations. My father would try to dispose of any suggestion that they might dine out by questioning the point of doing so on the basis that my mother was a wonderful cook (which was not the case), without any recognition that she might deserve to be treated to some "chef's relief" from time to time (since he did none of the cooking). However, persistent probing revealed that the real issue was their concern with kitchen hygiene where someone else was preparing food out of sight, unlike the case in fish and chip shops. This concern had nothing to do with my father's wartime duties in the Royal Army Medical Corps having been focused on hygiene in army camps. Rather, my mother explained that in one of their early holidays she had discovered cigarette ash in a café sandwich and had no intention of having an experience like that ever again.

## 1.4   THE SOCIAL SIDE OF CHOICE

Formative experiences in my life also came in relation to my parents' behavior in social settings and via things they told me about their workplace experiences. Although they were quite early adopters of many consumer durables of the early post-World War II era, I never got a sense of them being keen to "show off" how well they were doing by engaging in conspicuous consumption. They socialized very little, visits by relatives were rare, and I can only recall a handful of non-relatives ever being invited into the house. Even so, they seemed concerned

---

[1] Memories of my parents' choices in relation to car servicing and house maintenance provided plenty of food for thought when I served as principal advisor for a University of Queensland PhD by Ti-Ching Peng (2009), who is now a professor in the Department of Real Estate and Built Environment at Taiwan's National Taipei University. Ti-Ching's PhD project was a study of the decisions of property renovators in Brisbane. It used primary data from a large-sample mailed questionnaire to explore the empirical payoffs to adding proxies for psychological factors when modeling over-capitalization and choices to renovate via do-it-yourself versus hiring contractors.. Ti-Ching and I later (Earl and Peng, 2012) labeled this kind of work as "Trojan horse pluralism," for at first sight it can look like conventional applied econometric analysis, but it has potential to draw orthodox economists (and journal referees) into being open to alternative lines of thinking. When analyzing household choices between do-it-yourself and outsourcing of renovation work, Ti-Ching also applied ideas from the literature on vertical integration by firms, using both Williamson's (1975, 1985) transaction cost analysis and Richardson's (1972) capabilities-based perspective.

about how others might view them when they were out in public. My mother was always determined to be well-presented and this, combined with her good looks, did not endear her to her female colleagues when she returned to the workforce. I rather got the impression that my academic success was their main status symbol with their acquaintances. Whenever I visited them after they retired to Cornwall, I would often go walking on the coastal path with them and was always embarrassed by the way that they introduced me when they encountered people that they knew.

Mostly, my parents preferred not to attract attention. I remember a tense evening when I was about fifteen and away on vacation with them at a caravan site near Polperro in Cornwall, minutes away from where they eventually ended up living. On the occasion in question, I probed them about why they were, not for the first time, not taking to the venue's empty dance floor despite their love of ballroom dancing. They would wait, and wait, until another couple did so. In replying, they explained that they did not want to have everyone looking at them and thinking they were showing off. The incident marked the start of my teenage rebelliousness: I found their attitude very strange and vowed never to be concerned about what strangers thought of me.

However, the dance floor episode contrasted sharply with my mother's workplace behavior, which was characterized by a pride in doing her job well regardless of social pressures to conform to workplace norms. I became aware of such pressures via one of my father's bedtime stories about his early workplace experiences in Stevenage. He told of the retaliation meted out to a colleague who was both conspicuously productive and who – unlike almost everyone else – already had a car. The poor fellow sometimes had to contend with sabotage that took the form of sugar being poured into the car's fuel tank.

What happened in the case of my mother was very different. When she returned to the workforce, she readily got a job as an assembler of industrial instruments at a US-owned company called Taylor Instruments. She proved to be very good in this role, often being used as a rate setter by her managers. After about six years, she was promoted to the role of instructress. She soon discovered that she hated this more socially interactive role and asked if she could return to her former role. As with her glamorous presentation, her productivity had not endeared her to her colleagues, and her request provided them with an opportunity for payback: she did get to "go back on the bench" but the union dictated that she could only do this if classed as a new employee. When the firm put this proposal to her, she accepted it, little realizing that it would soon prove costly. A year or so later, the firm's US parent company decided to close the factory. Because she was formally a "new" member of staff, my mother received a much smaller redundancy pay-out than her actual years of service would normally have yielded.

I should probably add, on a happier note, that adjacent to the Taylor Instruments factory in Stevenage's industrial area was the building that gave me my first example of a trade association and inter-firm cooperation and which comes to mind whenever I think of Richardson's (1972) work and Hodgson's (1988) analysis of market institutions: the building had FIRA written on its side in huge letters, signifying the Furniture Industry Research Association. FIRA remains based in Stevenage, though Stevenage has no history as a UK furniture-making town.


## 1.5    INSIGHTS FROM TEENAGE HOBBIES

The three hobbies that I had in my high-school years were ones that I pursued seriously, and they could have led me to take career directions that were very different from economics. Yet they each had consequences for my economic thinking.

One was ornithology, which I picked up purely because my first-form desk partner at Alleyne's was a member of the Young Ornithologists' Club (YOC), the junior offshoot of the Royal Society for the Protection of Birds. I pursued ornithology very seriously for about five years, but I ultimately realized that my eyesight was a major constraint on how adept I was at identifying birds in the field.

Four decades later, my limitations as a birdwatcher had an impact on my contributions to behavioral economics, for they primed me to be receptive to Hayek's (1952) book *The Sensory Order*, in which he sets out a theory of how the mind works, and to appreciate the relationship between Hayek's theory and Kelly's (1955) *Psychology of Personal Constructs*.

As a young birdwatcher, I was certainly fitting Kelly's notion that people may usefully be viewed "as if" they are scientists, for birdwatching entailed a set of expeditions in which I tested my capacity to spot birds, especially ones that I had never seen before, either at all or in the environment in question. To do this successfully, one needs two things. The first is the capacity to spot birds as patterns against the background of their environment; the second is to have a set of memorized templates of bird types and specific bird species to test for their match with the pattern that one has inferred. In other words, cognition is an active process that involves finding a pattern and then finding a match between it and patterns stored in one's memory: the birds that one is trying to observe do not tell us directly what species they are, and after going through this process we are left with conjectures (in Kelly's terms, "personal constructs") about what we have seen.

Hayek's analysis of cognition brings out the first stage more explicitly than Kelly, who is clearer on the second stage. As a short-sighted, somewhat colour-blind birdwatcher, I would often not be able to spot a bird quickly enough or clearly enough, that others had noticed and whose features they had registered. If I did spot a bird that was available only for a fleeting glimpse, I would, other things equal, have a smaller chance of identifying it correctly. However, because I had spent a lot of time reading field guides for birdwatchers and memorized the templates for many birds, I would have a good chance of identifying birds if I got more than a glimpse and could confirm with others whether, say, the wading bird that I was looking at had red or green legs.

On occasions when I did get a "good enough look" at a bird, I sometimes had the experience of being able to narrow down the range of possibilities very quickly based on what ornithologists refer to as a bird's "jizz" (or "gizz"), i.e., a simplified pattern comprised of its silhouette and style of behavior or movement that serves as a kind of signature. I picked up the "jizz" notion very early in my time as an avid birdwatcher, but three decades were to pass before I started to think about it in relation to economics and marketing (see Section 6.6), a decade before I at last read *The Sensory Order* (see Section 7.5).

My second formative hobby was slot-car racing, which I pursued from Christmas 1965, when my parents gave me a Scalextric set, until mid 1977, though it was very sporadic in the last four years of this period due to me and my enthusiast friends being away at university. It grew out of my long-standing childhood fascination with cars, that as a child I could only address in a hands-on manner via models, and, as with birdwatching, I went on to take it very seriously. Here, too, it primed me to become the kind of economist that I became, but it could readily have led me to a career in the automotive sector or at least in engineering if I had not become captivated by economics.

In my third year at high school, I moved beyond ready-to-go Scalextric slot-cars and small tracks at home, up to the club level. This entailed transitioning to much faster slot-cars and racing on very large 4–6-lane tracks. My first club-level cars were kits from the USA, but they were soon followed by my own creations with elaborate hinged chassis frames made from soldered-together pieces of brass and piano wire. The bodies were purchased in clear-plastic form and then painted in one's chosen colours on the inside of the shell.

The market for the clear plastic body-shells provided my first lesson about the role of product cloning in the competitive process. The body-shells were mainly purchased by mail-order and I had read that they were made by a vacuum-forming process whereby heated sheets of thin plastic were sucked on to a mold. From the mid-1960s to the mid-1970s, the leading UK supplier was a company called GT Models, whose name reflected not Grand Touring but the fact that its proprietor was Gordon Tapsell, a leading figure in the Electric Car Racing Association (ECRA, of which I became a member). I noticed that, when GT Models released new body-shells, a raceway store in Southend-on-Sea often followed rapidly with its own-brand equivalents. The latter were slightly cheaper, and their shut-lines and window frames were sometimes not quite so sharp, but otherwise they looked identical to those from GT Models.

The idea that product piracy was happening came when, with my classmate and fellow slot-car enthusiast, Ian Reid, I compared the rival firms' versions of a Buick Riviera body-shell, a popular choice in the large sedan class. It was evident that the one from Southend-on-Sea even replicated the rather poorly executed rear bumper in the GT Models version. From this, we deduced that the store in Southend-on-Sea might be making its products via molds made from the original GT Models products. This led us to run an experiment to see if we could do likewise and even go as far as making a body-shell.

Ian's father made a surprisingly accurate cast from the inside of one of our Buick Riviera body-shells by using concrete rather than plaster, after which Ian and I made a very primitive vacuum molding system that entailed a small electric heater, a vacuum cleaner, and a large metal biscuit tin. We punched holes in the top of the tin and cut a larger hole in its side for the vacuum cleaner's hose. The concrete mold was placed on the top, followed by a sheet of plastic that we melted with the electric heater from above. As it got softer, we started to pull it down, around the mold, on to the biscuit tin until the suction through the holes around the mold pulled the plastic tightly on to the mold. The quality of definition that we achieved was not as good as on the clone from Southend-on-Sea, but our crude system was a proof-of-concept indication of how easy it would be to enter this market via product piracy if the leading firm did not, or could not, attempt to sue for breach of copyright.

Slot-car racing was booming as an adult leisure activity in the second half of the 1960s. In the USA, the bowling alley equipment manufacturer AMF took note of this and got into the business of producing huge six- or eight-lane model raceways at commercial venues, A few AMF tracks were even installed in the UK, but serious slot-car racing in the UK mostly took place on large hand-built tracks at community centers or corporate social clubs. Stevenage was no exception: it had two slot-car racing clubs, one at Pin Green Community Center and the other at the local Kodak factory's sports-ground. Nearby, Hatfield had one (at what was then the Hawker Siddeley aircraft factory, previously de Havilland) and Luton had two (at the Vauxhall car factory and the Electrolux appliance factory, at both of which my team-mates and I would do our best, as early teenagers, to compete against adult teams in six-hour endurance races).

It was via competing in club-level slot-car racing that I learned how "creative destruction" worked, long before I heard of the term and the work of Schumpeter (1943) – and I am not referring here to the destruction, in high-speed crashes, of the models that we created. The pace of innovation was intense, just as in the full-size world of carmakers and racing teams, and those who took part eagerly awaited the latest magazine issues to find out what was being tried and how well it worked. I funded the parts for my first creation, a 1:32-scale Oldsmobile Tornado, by selling my model railway equipment to one of my father's workmates, for model trains had none of the allure of model cars. The Tornado consisted entirely of my choice of state-of-the-art, off-the-shelf parts and was a huge step up from the kit models that I already had. But within a few months its chassis design (which had an inline motor at a right angle to the rear-drive axle) had been rendered obsolete by what was called an "anglewinder" design, which had the motor mounted as transversely as possible to the rear axle, permitting much more stable cornering. I took the Tornado to pieces and built my first own-design chassis, reusing all the other parts except for the main drive gear. Within a few months, the next chassis innovation came in: hinged chassis sides known as "bat-pans," so I again set to work with the soldering iron. The process continued relentlessly in all areas of the models. Keeping up to date was made more challenging because most people (myself soon included) raced in three or four different classes. Those of us who were relying on pocket money or newspaper delivery earnings to pay for our upgrades found it difficult to keep up with the adults who had bigger budgets to play with, and we tried to save money by recycling parts in new combinations as far as we could, or sometimes by buying second-hand cars from adults.

Eventually, ECRA decided to make things fairer in competitive terms by introducing a standard "Formula 32" class for models with identical off-the-peg chassis and motors. The regulated competition of the Formula 32 standard was successful in enabling youngsters to achieve high rankings when competing with older players but, by the time that my cohort had finished at high school, it started to seem that slot-car racing at the club level faced an existential threat from another kind of innovation: affordable, larger-scale radio-controlled model cars that could be raced on outdoor tracks. I could hardly have wished for a more compelling case study than this to get me thinking about competition as an evolving, dynamic process.

From 1970 onward, I added a new area of interest to my leisure commitments, namely music. It rapidly became, and remains, the dominant leisure activity in my life, but in embarking on it I had absolutely no idea how important it would become or where it would take me. My parents had not encouraged me to take music lessons, even though there was a good piano at home that was rarely used (due to my father giving up taking piano lessons not long after my sister was born). I had the good fortune to learn at junior primary school how to read music, but I soon gave up the recorder. There was a school orchestra at Alleyne's but none of my classmates seemed to be in it or taking lessons on an instrument of any kind. Alleyne's provided a weekly class in which we were introduced to classical music via recordings and by the teacher, George Partridge (who also taught me architecture and English literature) playing the piano, but these, too, included no attempt to nudge students into taking up an instrument. Otherwise, for most of my childhood and early adolescence, I had little involvement with music beyond listening to whatever my parents listened to, which tended to include what was in the singles charts at the time. In 1970, however, curiosity and social demonstrations led me to start listening to the album-focused rock music of my time, and to decide that I wanted to see if I could learn to play the guitar.

Classmates started bringing LPs to school to lend to each other; this was followed by acoustic guitars that were played during break times. I then discovered that BBC Radio 1 had started a weekday early evening program called "Sounds of the Seventies" that was devoted to albums, and I set out to use it to get some knowledge of what lay beyond the singles charts. Without even having touched a guitar or really knowing anything much about any guitarists, I announced to my parents that it was a guitar that I would like for my fifteenth birthday. They must have been very surprised but nonetheless gave me £10 to get one.

My birthday occurred during the summer vacation. So, on the morning in question, I was able to head off to the Stevenage Record Center, which offered a small stock of acoustic guitars and was at the time the only place in Stevenage where a guitar could be purchased. My budget constraint was enough to buy the cheapest steel-string guitar but not a nylon-string guitar of the kind my classmates played, which started at £12. It would prove a tougher way to start but probably accounts for the fact that I went on to become focused on rock and jazz guitar rather than folk or classical. As with my other leisure pursuits, I built my knowledge in a proto-academic manner via library books and, from September 1970, I became an eager reader of the weekly music newspaper *Melody Maker*.

In August 1971, my parents allowed me to purchase an electric guitar for my sixteenth birthday, with a much bigger budget that may have reflected both the evidence that my interest in the guitar was no passing curiosity and the swag of good O-Level results that I had achieved. The guitar was a second-hand, mint-condition Watkins Rapier 33 that came with a five-watt amplifier that was likewise a product of the British firm Watkins Electronic Music (WEM).

Before the 1970s came to an end, events in the global electronic musical instrument industry would help to inform my understanding of the dynamics of the competitive process, just as slot-car racing had done, and decades later I would write a teaching case study on these events, including what happened to WEM. What I observed during the 1970s was a growth of knowledge process that transformed the guitar market. Japanese luthiers shamelessly copied classic US guitar designs and forced lower-tier firms such as WEM out of the market by undercutting their prices. The US firms sued, to keep the Japanese copies out of the USA, but the Japanese firms kept selling their "lawsuit" models in other markets, with their quality coming to match that of the originals. The Japanese firms then moved up-market by creating their own designs and selling them at premium prices, competing head-on with the US firms.


## 1.6    HIGH-SCHOOL ECONOMICS

A few weeks after starting my half-century-plus journey into the world of electric guitars, I was back at school, engrossed in my first classes in economics. The event that most aroused my interest in economics had occurred nearly four years earlier, on November 18, 1967. That was when I saw the televised address in which Harold Wilson, the UK Prime Minister announced the devaluation of Sterling but claimed rather unconvincingly that it would not reduce the value of the pound in one's pocket. However, despite thereafter taking an avid interest in news reports about the struggles of the UK economy, I did not initially take any other steps to learn more about economics. At the time of Wilson's address, I was in the second year of my high-school education at Alleyne's Grammar School. By the time that I began to study economics there, it had been renamed simply as Alleyne's School, for county grammar schools had been abolished and it was now admitting students of all abilities. Economics was only offered as a subject in the sixth form.

In 1971, at the end of my fifth form at Alleyne's, I had no hesitation in deciding that I was going to work toward A-Levels in economics, geography and history when I went into the sixth form. Although I greatly enjoyed chemistry and biology, with the latter, like geography, being one of my top subjects, I did not for a moment consider taking A-Levels in any of the sciences. I also gave hardly any thought to the idea of doing mathematics instead of history at A-Level, despite having not done poorly with mathematics up to that point; I just opted to study what interested me most and presumed that if I needed more mathematics to accompany economics, I would be able to pick it up from courses at university or by teaching myself from textbooks. I have never regretted that decision.

Those of us who intended to take A-Level Economics were encouraged to get a sense of the subject over the summer vacation between the fifth form and lower-sixth by reading Michael Stewart's (1967) *Keynes and After*, and G. C. Allen's ([1939] 1970) *British Industries and Their Organization* and/or his (1968) *Monopoly and Restrictive Practices*. These books had a major impact on the kind of economist that I became. Stewart's account of the context in which Keynes's ideas emerged, what they were, and the impact that they had, was essentially what I would later learn to call a "Post Keynesian" view: as a member of the Department of Economics at University College London, Stewart was an enthusiastic Keynesian and at the time his book appeared he was a senior economic advisor to the Cabinet Office of the Labour Government led by Harold Wilson. Allen's books gave me empirical foundations for an evolutionary view of firms and industries and an interest in structural change.

The A-Level Economics training that I received covered far more material than a typical first year of a university degree in economics, and I supplemented what we did in class by reading extensively from the impressive economics section in Stevenage Central Library. One of this public library's recent acquisitions was a copy of the Collected Works edition of the first volume of Keynes's *Treatise on Money* (Keynes, 1971), which, not surprisingly, I gave up reading after finding it very tough to follow. A much more engaging book at that early stage was Alchian and Allen's (1967) *University Economics*, which offered a much richer view of markets than I had found in either the textbook being used at school (Stanlake, 1967) or the one that I had bought in a local bookstore in my initial attempt to find something better (*Benham's Economics*, by Paish, 1964). What I particularly appreciated in Alchian and Allen were the accounts of how speculation was supposed to smooth out price disturbances. However, I then moved on to reading Lipsey's (1966) *Introduction to Positive Economics* after picking up a just-superseded second edition at a bargain price from a bookshop at the London School of Economics on a class trip to attend an inaugural lecture delivered by Alan Prest. In the upper-sixth, for applied material, I gleaned much from the fourth edition of Prest and Coppock (eds)

(1972), a copy of which I purchased with a prize voucher for my achievements in the previous year.

Stevenage Central Library's collection included many publications by a right-wing think tank, The Institute of Economic Affairs (IEA). They included ideas associated with the "Austrian" view of economics and provided plenty of material for generating classroom debate with the senior of my two economics teachers, Les Ransley. Les was a graduate of the University of Birmingham and was clearly a Labour voter. At that stage, in the UK's climate of terrible industrial relations, my microeconomic inclinations were very much in the Conservative direction, and they remained that way until Margaret Thatcher was elected and showed just how dogmatically neoliberal her party had become. As far as macroeconomics was concerned, however, nothing in the IEA's pamphlets shook my admiration for Keynes's ideas. Baiting Les Ransley with IEA-style policy ideas was one of my responses to comments by teachers in my Autumn 1971 school report about me being "quiet" and "reticent" in class despite displaying promise in my written work. Les took it all in good spirit and thereby provided me with my first role model in pluralistic teaching.

The other economics teacher was a recent London School of Economics graduate, John Rushton. He strongly encouraged my wider reading. This was especially the case at the end of the lower-sixth year. At that time my class had been required not merely to attempt to add O-Level Economics to our credentials; we were also required to sit a multiple-choice examination as part of a project being undertaken by a team at Heriot-Watt University in Edinburgh on the performance of high-school students of economics versus those taking first-year university courses in economics. I was one of two students in my class who scored exceptionally well in the Heriot-Watt test, and John was advised of the results just before the end of the school year. As I walked back to the sixth-form building from the final school assembly of the academic year, he came up to me and said, "You've got something here, so don't waste the summer." So, while many of my classmates found themselves a source of income via a summer job, I spent much of the time continuing to work through the economics section in Stevenage Central Library.

Not long after the 1972–1973 upper–sixth commenced, John Rushton gave me my first taste of what has been one of my key sources over many years, namely, George Richardson's paper on cooperative methods of business coordination and the significance of capability differences between firms for making sense of the division of labor between firms. Richardson's paper had just been published in the September 1972 issue of the *Economic Journal*. In those days, Stevenage Central Library did not merely supplement its economics books with the reviews published by the major banks (which I read avidly), it also received copies of the *Economic Journal* after they had been circulated among the local high-school teachers of economics. After explaining that he had come across the article by this means, John went on to give some examples from it. I cannot recall for sure whether I read the paper first-hand at that stage, but I certainly did not remember who had written it; five years later, when I was reading it after seeing it referred to by Loasby (1976), I suddenly recognized it as the paper to which John Rushton had referred. It is hard to imagine material from recent *Economic Journal* articles being fed into high-school classes in this kind of way in the 2020s.

Messrs Ransley and Rushton were not the only sixth-form teachers who played a formative role in my life as an academic economist. Much credit is also due to one of my geography teachers, Roger Luxton, a Cambridge graduate. It was through his economic geography classes that I began to get interested in development economics and it was he who introduced me to Myrdal's work on cumulative causation and the relevance of the idea for regional policies. The classes in which this occurred were just before the entire sixth form was treated to a "general studies" class at which the guest speaker was Professor Peter Bauer (who would become Lord Bauer during the Thatcher years). In essence, he presented the core of the arguments in his then-new (1971) book *Dissent on Development*, which presented a conservative critique of Myrdal's (1957) view that poor countries needed foreign aid in order to develop, since they were trapped in a vicious circle whereby their low incomes prevented them from restraining consumption and accumulating capital. Bauer maintained that failures to develop were due to motivational shortcomings, which handouts from overseas would only made worse. In effect, his contention seemed to be that economic systems in poor countries contained enough slack for their populations to improve themselves if they were determined to do so. He argued that even a poor natural resource endowment can be overcome if attitudes are conducive to doing so, and he pointed to Hong Kong as an example of this.

In the ensuing weeks, Bauer's presentation sparked heated but inconclusive debates in class. For me, this was not merely a wonderful early experience of pluralism; the clash between a mechanical feedback system generating vicious circles versus potential to find an escape route via some form of slack if one were sufficiently motivated (as embodied in the maxim "Where there's a will, there's a way") also became a key theme in my thinking. However, at that stage, it did not occur to me that one might apply it to industrial dynamics; five years later, I would discover this application, via Downie's (1958) analysis of the competitive process.

Toward the end of my lower-sixth year there was another formative experience, namely an "industrial tour" for my economics cohort. It was not my first opportunity to view the internal workings of production systems, for there had previously been a school trip to the Fidelity Radio factory in Stevenage's industrial area, a factory that, in terms of today's standards, was rather cluttered and poorly lit. However, the industrial tour proved to be my equivalent of the industrial tour that Ronald Coase took while visiting the USA on a study scholarship to the University of Chicago in 1931–1932. In my case, the tour to which our class was treated visited memorable sites in the West of England and South Wales, with our accommodation being at the University of Bristol's Churchill Hall. Three of the sites that we visited were especially thought-provoking. The first was the W. D. & H. O. Wills cigarette factory in Bristol, an example of ethically challenged private enterprise, whereas the others were at the time parts of state-run industries.

The Wills factory overlooked the bonded warehouses where its tobacco supplies were stored. Inside, the aroma of tobacco was pervasive, and I found it nauseating. I suspect that my strong anti-smoking sentiments and new-found non-reticent mode of operating led me to ask something about business ethics in the question-and-answer session at the end, but I cannot recall this with certainty. However, what really hit me was the sight of the cigarette-rolling machines, which we were told were made by the Molins Machine Company, one of only a few in the world that had the capacity to make this type of machinery. The machines were astonishingly quick at what they did but it was the only thing that they could do. They provided a perfect example of what I would come, via Williamson (1985), to know as "asset specificity." I later realized that the challenge of making such machines would be a useful ingredient in a situation such as the German hyperinflation of 1923 in which cigarettes became a better store of value than the German currency, for if the supply of such machines could not be increased rapidly, neither could the supply of cigarettes.

Later in the tour, after a morning talking with town planners in Cwmbran, the Welsh equivalent to Stevenage new town, we spent an afternoon at the British Steel Corporation's Ebbw Vale steelworks. We observed the steelmaking process from start to finish. This, too, was replete with asset specificity, this time of a heavy-metal variety. Our guide stressed that the key to keeping costs under control was to keep the process running without interruption so that the in-process steel did not get a chance to cool down. However, disaster struck as we were walking the length of the final stage, the rolling and coiling process that turned slabs of hot steel into coils of sheet steel ready for car factories. The long sheets of thin steel that emerged from the rolling mill hurtled down a conveyor system before being coiled on reaching the end, but we witnessed an instance where the leading edge of the tongue of steel got stuck as it entered the coiling equipment. The jamming of the coiler caused the rest of the steel to concertina to a noisy halt. What then happened was remarkable: men immediately appeared, like ants, seemingly out of nowhere, to clear the wrecked new sheet of steel and unjam the coiler. Everybody performed their emergency roles as if they had been drilled for such an occasion. Shortly after, during refreshments, a somewhat embarrassed manager told us that although they had succeeded in sorting out the problem rapidly, it would probably have cost a six-figure sum in terms of the cost of keeping steel hot at earlier stages. What my classmates and I had witnessed was an example of internalized economic coordination that was a wonderful preparation for getting to grips with the transaction cost approach to industrial organization that future Nobel Laureate Oliver Williamson was working on around this time.

The third memorable segment of the industrial tour was a visit to the huge British Rail engineering workshops at Swindon. This left me wondering about the extent of overstaffing in large organizations. Whereas the British Steel Corporation's emergency response team seemed to appear from nowhere and could justify their annual salaries in an hour or two, there seemed to be many men in the railway workshop who were conspicuously not doing much at all, and I remember noting the latter in a report on the industrial tour that I wrote for the school magazine. The spectacle did not align well with the idea of cost minimization.


## 1.7   THE UNIVERSITY ENTRANCE PROCESS

The process of getting a university place to study economics was the first occasion on which I faced a choice environment in which I was conscious of the problems of information overload and quality uncertainty, and the need to behave strategically.[2] However, I was able to choose effectively because I did

---

[2] Clearly, the decision would have been even more complicated if I had started it with an open mind about which field to study, or even whether to aim for tertiary-level studies at that stage, and if I had been focusing on the pecuniary returns to different types of careers. This more open question was the focus of a University of Queensland PhD by Mary Hedges (2010) for which I served as the principal advisor. Mary was then a teaching-focused economics lecturer based in Auckland, and she did most of the work for her PhD remotely. She was keen to understand how students in New Zealand made their tertiary education choices, and she saw this as an opportunity to conduct a pluralistic study that explored both the rational choice-based human capital

not operate alone and could call upon the expertise of my teachers: it was a case of what Austrian economists call "extended cognition" (cf. Dekker and Remic, 2024). On the demand side, the academic staff who had to decide which applicants should receive offers faced similar challenges, and the decision rules that they used were not always reliable.

Early in the upper-sixth year, I had to decide what to do about applying for university entrance. In the UK this necessitated applying through a central clearing house system (managed by a body known as UCCA) on a form that allowed applicants to nominate specific degree programs at five institutions. My success by the end of the lower-sixth year led me to be advised to consider trying for Oxford or Cambridge. However, since at that time it was rare for "Oxbridge" colleges to make offers subject to the attainment of a particular set of A-Level grades, the best strategy was to delay an Oxbridge application until the 1973 round and stay on at school for the Autumn 1973 term to study for, and take, the "Oxbridge" entrance exams, even if by that point I was already armed with a stellar set of A-Level grades. In the meantime, I should apply for 1973 university entry to other institutions, so that I would have a fallback position if the A-Levels did not go so well as hoped. It was also emphasized that placing high-ranking universities below the second preference would probably result in them sending an immediate rejection. Which five universities should I select, and which should be my top two preferences?

If I had tried to make the choice purely on my own, I would have had to do so via the hard-copy prospectuses in my school's careers room, with no obvious means of ranking rival institutions. But the task was simplified by the advice that my teachers gave, that the next best thing to Oxford or Cambridge was seen to be Durham, Bristol or one of the best University of London colleges. Given this, the top two emerged readily. The University of Bristol was eliminated despite being in a city that I found appealing and whose Churchill Hall student accommodation had been a very pleasant base for my school's industrial tour. The problem was that Bristol required A-Level Mathematics for entry to economics: this was a no-trade-off zone. With Bristol eliminated, I needed to eliminate one from Durham, University College London and the London School

---

perspective and behavioral ideas that took account of social pressures, norms, and social embeddedness. Her study employed primary data from a questionnaire and, unusually in economics, made use of factor analysis. Mary showed the value of adding behavioral proxy variables to orthodox models. However, because the project centered on students in New Zealand, where there were only a few universities, her domestic subjects faced a far simpler choice than international students or those in other advanced economies once they had grappled with the more basic choice of whether and what to study.

of Economics. UCL appealed to me because of Michael Stewart's presence, whereas the LSE had recently been getting a lot of publicity for demonstrations led by left-wing student activists, so I felt it would not be a good choice given the political views that I held at the time. Durham and UCL thus became my top two, with the remaining three being Birmingham, Aberystwyth, and Sussex for no particular academic reasons and without me really having thought I might need offers from them anyway.

I duly received invitations to interviews at UCL and Durham on adjacent days. This was very exciting, as it was my first trip away from home on my own and involved staying overnight in Durham. The UCL experience was very straightforward though, to my disappointment, my interview was not with Michael Stewart but with Professor John Spraos, with whose work I was completely unfamiliar. We talked more about current affairs, particularly the Northern Ireland troubles, than about economics but he explained that what UCL typically did with someone who looked likely to be an Oxbridge contender was to take the pressure off them by making the lowest offer that was possible, i.e., two E-grade passes at A-Level. Clearly, I had a very strong reference letter from my school, and precisely this offer was what I received a few days later, and I reciprocated by making UCL my back up option the following year.

After the UCL interview, I caught a late-afternoon train to Durham, to stay in Grey College overnight. The following morning, I was interviewed by John Creedy. He is now well known as a remarkably prolific scholar in the areas of labor economics, public finance and the history of economic thought, but at the time he interviewed me, he was only 23 years old and on a one-year contract at Durham. (He returned to Durham as a full professor of economics shortly before he turned 30.) To say that the interview went badly would be to make a major understatement, and my subsequent interview at Grey College did not go well either. At the start of the following week, my bemused headmaster summoned me to his office and asked me to explain why, whereas UCL had immediately made the two-Es offer, Durham had equally rapidly rejected me outright, saying that I appeared to be arrogant and that my knowledge of economics did not match up with the reference my school had provided.

At the time, the heart of the problem seemed to me to be that John Creedy simply did not believe that I had been doing the amount of reading on economics that I said that I had been doing. He then seemed to decide to test my economic knowledge by asking me to "draw the diagram of the theory of the firm." His request completely flummoxed me. I did not think of the firm as something that could be reduced to a diagram. The picture that I had picked up of the economics of the firm was multifaceted. It included elements such as the idea that firms might grow via merger activity as part of a process of industrial restructuring (as I had learned from reading G. C. Allen's account of the industrial consolidation that produced the UK chemicals giant, ICI). I explained to him that I had never seen a diagram with such a name. He then said that what he wanted was the diagram for a perfectly competitive firm, which I duly drew despite merely viewing it as a diagram showing the theory of how a firm in a competitive market chooses its output. But I felt that, by then, the damage was done. Years later, it occurred to me that he had probably been hoping to see instant recall of thinking in the tradition of Edgeworth (on whom he became a leading authority) and Walras, whereas I was on the track that led from Marshall to Penrose and Chandler. In time, I would eventually have my own favorite diagram of how a firm addressed competitive challenges, but it would be the one offered by P. W. S. Andrews in his (1949) book *Manufacturing Business*, a diagram that came with a very different backstory from the one that John Creedy expected me to draw.

Nearly fifty years later, some months after the previous paragraph was drafted, John Creedy sent me a long, pleasant, and helpful email after enjoying a paper I had co-authored to mark the fiftieth anniversary of the publication of Duncan Ironmonger's (1972) book *New Commodities and Consumer Behavior* (Earl, Markey-Towler and Coutts, 2022). At the end of the email, he wrote "To change the subject ... didn't we meet once in Hobart ... when you reminded me that we met even earlier ... in Durham?" John's memory was spot-on, for he had visited the University of Tasmania to present a seminar at the time I worked there, shortly after he had taken up the Truby Williams Chair of Economics at the University of Melbourne. Before his seminar, I was a member of the group that took him to lunch at the staff club. On the way back to the department, I quietly told him that he had interviewed me at Durham and that despite Durham not being impressed with me I had ended up getting a double-first in Cambridge. On hearing this, he looked as though he remembered interviewing me, but we did not have any time to talk further. Minutes later, he graciously began his presentation by acknowledging the department's invitation and adding that I had just reminded him that we had met many years earlier.

It turned out that John Creedy had indeed remembered that interview in Durham. When I replied to his email, I confirmed his memory about our previous encounters. The following morning there was a further email from him, which included the following:

Perhaps I could add a few comments on my perspective of your Durham experience. One reason I remember it is that it was unique. My attitude was that I didn't really care how people interviewed. I felt that, in that situation, I would be very nervous and would not come over well (I never did have any interviews to get to Bristol or Oxford, and was terrified during my first-ever interview, for an ESRC grant). So, I always thought it was fairest just to recommend a "standard offer" – if they got the grades, that was sufficient and one shouldn't really ask for more. During your interview, you certainly did not seem nervous at all, but even though I took my usual approach (no "trick questions" … basic things to get going …), we could not somehow get "on the same wavelength." Then when the college telephoned (and they always took interviews much more seriously), it was immediately clear that they wanted to reject (Creedy, email to Earl, September 2, 2022).

If Durham's standard offer to economics students was pitched at the right level to achieve a balance between available places and candidates who would go on to meet the required set of grades and want to study at Durham, Creedy's empathy-based heuristic for viewing interviews seems perfectly reasonable as well as fair.

Apart from the disconcerting experience at Durham, the second year of my A-Level studies went smoothly, and I duly achieved the three A-grade outcomes that my teachers had expected. As with other potential Oxbridge applicants in my cohort, I also sat two, more difficult, S-Level papers. (Only two were allowed and, of my three A-Level subjects, I opted not to take S-Level in history.) The S-Level papers had originally been designated Scholarship Level, for their role in the 1950s in allocating university scholarships but by the 1970s they were simply referred to as Special Papers and provided candidates with the opportunity to demonstrate how they fared with more challenging, unexpected questions based on the same curricula as their corresponding A-Levels. As such, they should indeed have assisted Oxbridge admissions assessors, for this was precisely the style of assessment that was core to the Oxbridge approach. Those who passed at S-Level could receive a 1 (as I received for geography) or a 2 (as I received for economics).

The results that I received probably reflected the fact that, paradoxically, I felt much better prepared for the economics paper and ran into a problem of choice overload. Normally, when faced with papers that gave a free choice of four essays from 10–12 questions, I did not scan the entire question menu before choosing what to do; rather, I simply worked down the menu until I encountered a question that I anticipated being able to do well and got to work on it, finished it, returned to the menu and continued down the list, and so on, only returning to the top of the menu at a later stage if I got to the end of the menu without finding four questions that instantly grabbed my attention and about which I felt confident.

Though this approach may seem unwise in terms of a view of choice that sees rationality in terms of taking account of all available options, it served me well, as I was usually able to spend almost the entire examination time writing my answers. I never made notes mapping out my answers in the way that many students do; rather, I formed an overall vision of how a good answer might work and got swiftly into the "flow" (cf. Csikszentmihalyi, 1990) or "the zone" of writing. It was a way of choosing that Gigerenzer and his colleagues (Gigerenzer and Goldstein, 1996; Gigerenzer, Todd and the ABC Research Group, 1999) would categorize as a "fast and frugal" decision heuristic. But in the S-Level economics paper I felt I ought to be careful about my choice of questions to attempt, given that they were supposedly more difficult. I therefore gave the overall paper my attention before choosing. The trouble was that I realized, somewhat to my surprise, that I could do pretty-well any question on the paper, and I then delayed my start on my first answer by trying to think which would be the best one to do first. The issue of how I would choose the others then loomed as I wrote.

Armed with these results, I faced a different choice problem from the previous year when I came to make my serious university application in autumn 1973 while most of my classmates headed off to begin their university experiences based on the fit between their A-Level grades and the offers they had received after their 1972 applications. There were three issues to resolve.

First, I had to decide whether I was going to apply for Oxford or Cambridge: both would be oversubscribed with well-qualified applicants, so only one's first preference between these rival institutions would be taken seriously. My second preference on my UCCA form would therefore be my UCL fallback plan. I had no trouble deciding that I would try for Cambridge, and the choice had nothing to do with the convenience of its location, a direct one-hour rail trip from Stevenage. Rather, I knew it was where Keynes had written his (1936) *General Theory of Employment, Interest and Money* and I therefore presumed his legacy there would be something that Oxford could not offer. This presumption was largely because I had become aware, via the biographical note in her *Economic Philosophy* (which I had seen in Stevenage Central Library), that Joan Robinson had worked in Cambridge in the 1930s and was still there. Fortunately, my presumption proved to be well-founded.

The second issue was which college I should apply to enter, for although Cambridge was part of the UCCA clearing house system, prospective students also had to apply directly to Cambridge and indicate their preferred college, and they would then be interviewed for admission to their preferred college by fellows of that college. This was a matter that my teachers knew had to be addressed very carefully. Each year, Alleyne's usually managed, from its pre-comprehensive intakes, to place a handful or so of its top students with Oxford or Cambridge, so it had a track record relationship with some colleges that might help its latest applicants to be taken seriously. The reason that I ended up applying to Queens' College – a choice that I believe was pivotal in getting me started along the behavioral economics track – came about because of this concern about these relationships but this was despite there being *no* recollection at my school of anyone having been sent previously to Queens'.

My destiny was determined by the fact that I loved geography as well as economics and, on looking for a way of studying in Cambridge that might enable me to do economics without altogether abandoning geography, I came across the possibility of following Part I of the Economics Tripos with a Part II in Land Economy. Because the number of students who studied land economy was much smaller than for economics, not all colleges had fellows who were members of the Department of Land Economy. My school arranged for me to go to Cambridge to talk about the land economy program with Mike Turner, who was the Director of Studies for students in land economy at both Emmanuel (where the school had a track record) and Queens'. The meeting with Turner was very pleasant, rather as though we were gently interviewing each other, and at the end I asked him how Emmanuel and Queens' compared. His reply was frank and accurate: "If you go to Emmanuel, you'll probably have to live in lodgings in the second year, whereas Queens' undergraduates usually get rooms in college for all three years, but the food in hall at Queens' isn't very good." I was prepared to put up with poor food to avoid the isolation of living outside college (and the greater distance from lecture theatres and libraries that would likely come with it). My mentors at Alleyne's thought that it would probably be safe, now that the seeds of a new connection had been sown, for me to make Queens' my preferred college.

The third issue was which two subjects I should take for the Cambridge entrance examination. In addition to economics, I chose history rather than geography as it seemed likely to be easier to figure out what additional material I needed to study to cope with very wide ranges of questions that were set to accommodate applicants who had studied different syllabuses. I returned to Alleyne's for an additional term during which I studied an extra century's worth of British and European history and read further in economics. This did not entail going into school every day and, when combined with one-on-one meetings with teachers, it was very like studying as a university student. In addition to the November examinations, the selection process included college interviews. Because I had already met with Mike Turner, I was not required to be interviewed by either of the economics fellows at Queens', but my experience at Durham resulted in me being very cautious when I had my general interview, which was with tax lawyer John Tiley.

In the event, I won a place at Queens'. My next puzzle was what I might do with the first eight months of 1974. I soon found myself in a role that at the time was not uncommon for those in my situation: I was given what was formally a "student teacher" role, initially to fill a one-term gap between the departure of one of the geography teachers at Barclay School (a former "secondary modern" high school adjacent to Alleyne's) and the arrival of his successor. After teaching geography to second- to fourth-form classes and teaching fourth-form geology, I was then retained for a second term to teach CSE Economics (i.e., really basic economics for students of low academic ability, which included a visit to the Vauxhall car factory in Luton) and remedial reading. Finally, during the summer vacation, I was hired to help oversee use of the school's swimming pool.

During the summer of 1974, my view of the world became larger and much clearer. This was due to my short-sightedness having become bad enough to enable me to have contact lenses fitted via the National Health Service, for a mere £9. Wearing contact lenses instead of thick-lensed spectacles seemed to slow the progression of my myopia as well as greatly improving how well I could see. My improved vision soon proved to be vital for dealing with distant blackboards in large lecture theatres.

# 2 Cambridge Undergraduate, 1974–1977

## 2.1   INTRODUCTION

This chapter covers the development of my behavioral economics perspective during my three-year BA in Economics at the University of Cambridge (henceforth usually referred to simply as "Cambridge"). The way that I picked up my initial behavioral foundations was highly context- and path-dependent, so I need first to explain how the Cambridge teaching system works and convey how its economics program worked in the mid-1970s.

By modern "student-centered" standards, it was a very odd way of acquiring a degree in economics, not least because students such as myself worked long hours reading for assignments that "counted for nothing," with much of the reading being from primary sources rather than textbooks, even in the first year of study. The final examinations tended to be full of unexpected analytical tasks, rather than being venues for demonstrating that one could replicate set-piece technical exercises. The system seemed to be geared toward producing graduates who could readily move into jobs that required them to be able to apply economic concepts to whatever problems were thrown at them and write reports that explored the debatable nature of the lessons that economic analysis could be used to generate. Quite a lot of the system that I experienced continues to this day, though not the highly unconventional organization of macroeconomic and microeconomic material that prevailed in the 1970s, and teaching is now much less pluralistic as very few heterodox economists remain (for an account of the processes by which this happened, see Saith, 2022).

Cambridge blended – and still blends – both centralized discipline-based faculties (such as The Faculty of Economics and Politics, which henceforth I shall simply refer to as "the Faculty") and a set of affiliated colleges (such as my college, Queens', which was founded in 1448). Lectures were provided by members of faculties, and final examinations were set and marked by faculty members, whereas "supervisions" (the Cambridge term for tutorials) of very small groups of students (in my time, usually two, but sometimes as many as four) are conducted by "fellows" of the colleges, research students (not necessarily from the same college as their supervisees) and members of faculties or research units (for example, the Department of Applied Economics) who were not college fellows. In the 1970s, the annual intake of undergraduates in Economics seemed typically to be around 170 students, of whom about a dozen would be at Queens'. Some colleges had far fewer economics students.

The supervision system was highly decentralized. It did not operate along the lines of a franchise system in the way that is common today, where a course coordinator determines not merely the lecture program but also all the tutorial assignments, reading lists and final examination questions for all students taking a particular course unit. Moreover, each course unit, or "paper" in Cambridge terminology, typically had several lecturers, sometimes five or six, whose lectures were usually based on their research interests. With one's weekly work focus being on writing essays for supervisions, much would depend upon which topics and readings one's supervisor chose to set. I believe that the fact that I was a member of Queens' College was key to my becoming a behavioral economist, because of the set of tasks that I ended up having to do under the supervision of Ajit Singh, the Director of Studies in Economics at Queens'.

Ajit conducted many of the second- and third-year undergraduate supervisions and recruited other supervisors, but he was not involved in the supervision of my PhD. The story of Ajit's life has been told at length by Ashwani Saith (2019), who was my third-year supervisor for development economics; there is also a less detailed account by Scherer (2017). Ajit was the leader of the far-left political faction within the Faculty. I got on very well with him despite arriving at Queens' with pro-market views and joining the Cambridge University Conservative Association. He was very widely read and strongly committed to keeping Queens' around the top of the list of colleges in terms of the attainments of its economics students. If he could find a way of getting us hooked on reading economics seriously, he seemed content to see us having a pluralistic view of competing approaches even if we did not adopt his political standpoint.

Each undergraduate degree in Cambridge consisted of only two parts despite being known as a "Tripos," for the "Tripos" terms seemed to have come via the three-legged stool that students sat on while being examined orally in medieval times. Attainment levels in both parts of the Economics Tripos in the 1970s were based purely on final examination grades, and written work for supervisions was usually returned merely with feedback comments and without even an indicative grade. Hence, it was hard to know how well one was doing, but there were no marks at stake if one wrote experimental pieces for weekly tutorials to extract the reactions of supervisors.

I did not stick to my plan to spend my first year taking Part I Economics and then take the two-year Land Economy Part II to complete my Bachelor of Arts. Rather to my surprise, I achieved not merely first-class honours in Part I Economics but the second-highest first in my year. When Ajit told me about the latter achievement, he said he presumed that I would now continue into Part II

Economics. After I confirmed this, he said it was a wise move, as Land Economy was for those from very wealthy families who had large estates to manage. This may well have been true at the time. However, the Department of Land Economy has increasingly been focusing on ecological economics and the impact of climate change. It also became the place where research on the behavioral economics of property speculation and herding behavior was conducted by Michelle Baddeley (e.g., Baddeley, 2010), who has written one of the most successful behavioral economics texts (Baddeley, 2013).

My first in Part I meant that I felt I was under a lot of pressure to perform just as well in Part II. However, although I took my academic work very seriously and put in long hours on it, I also frequently attended debates at the Cambridge Union Society and meetings of the Cambridge University Conservative Association. I was also musically very active, playing electric guitar not merely in rock bands but also in review bands. I managed to deliver academically, ending up with a coveted "double-first." But, in my hands, this credential did not set me on track for a stellar academic career.

## 2.2   MAKING SENSE OF KEYNES'S *GENERAL THEORY*

There were no optional or elective papers in Part I of the Economics Tripos when I "went up" to Cambridge in October 1974: everyone had to take two economics papers, along with a paper on the "Practice and Principles of Politics in Modern Britain," a paper which then carried the rather parochial title "English Economic History" and an introductory statistics paper entitled "Elementary Quantitative Economics" that focused mainly on index numbers and getting used to using official statistics. Taken together, these papers were conducive to viewing economics in terms of processes rather than a succession of equilibria. Those of us who had not taken A-Level Mathematics at high school also had to pass an extra paper in mathematics to qualify for entry to Part II of the Tripos. I took this paper, despite my plan to do Land Economy, so as to leave my options open. In this section, I will focus purely on the two economics papers as they were extremely demanding by first-year standards. They were called "Macro-Economic Theory 1" and "Macro-Economic Theory II" and thus covered only macroeconomic/monetary theory and policy.[3] Yet, despite microeconomics being kept for the second year,

---

[3] Half a century later, Part I Economics has a similar no-choice five-paper structure, except that one of the economics papers is on microeconomics and begins with what would normally be taught as "intermediate" microeconomics, so A-Level Mathematics, or an equivalent credential, is required for entry.

the work that I did for the economics papers included some elements that I later came to view as part of behavioral economics.

There were very early signs that, in contrast to common practice, first-year Cambridge economics was not going to be a re-run of high-school macroeconomics. The supervisor for the economics papers was Brian Van Arkadie, a development economist who was also a fellow of Queens' College. When I and other members of the new Queens' economics cohort had our introductory meeting with him, he told us that we should each buy a copy of Keynes's (1936) *General Theory of Employment, Interest and Money*, as the first term's reading would be built around it. Brian assured the sole member of our cohort who had not previously studied economics that he should not worry about this since it meant that he was "unencumbered by books and knowledge."

We then spent seven weeks trying to get to grips with Keynes's own words. It soon became clear to those of us who had done A-Level Economics that we had been given a very simplified picture via the "income–expenditure" model that did not draw attention to scope for shifting expectations to impact on the value of the multiplier, or the significance of the role of money as a hedge against uncertainty, or why flexible wages and prices could not be relied upon to prevent economic systems from suffering major depressions. The essay topics from weeks 6 and 7 offer a sense of what we were wrestling with in trying to understand where Keynes offered original insights:

> "For Keynes, the rate of interest was a reward for lending; for 'the classics' it was a reward for abstinence. But for both it was the cost of investment." Discuss.

> "If wages and prices were perfectly flexible, there would not be any problem for long with unemployment or over-full employment." Discuss.

After much struggling, we came to understand why lending does not necessarily increase to an offsetting degree if the desire to spend decreases, and why Keynes argued that highly flexible money wages could *exacerbate* instability rather than lead an economy with deficient aggregate demand back to full employment with lower levels of prices and money wages.

In wrestling with such assignments, our focus was on getting a clear picture of the macroeconomy as a complex system of interacting parts and the feedback relationships between these parts. We thereby came to appreciate that a "fallacy of composition error" was being made by those who presumed that wage cuts would reduce unemployment at the macro level by making it possible for firms to offer their output at lower prices and sell more, which they would produce by hiring more workers.

The error results from taking what I learned three years later (via Coddington, 1976) to call a "reductionist" perspective: it views macro-level phenomena as simple aggregates of micro-level phenomena that have been considered in isolation from one another, typically by focusing on a "representative" unit and making an "other things equal" assumption.

If firms as a group cut money wages, they were also cutting the purchasing power of workers, so aggregate demand in monetary terms would fall, too. If firms were oblivious of this and expected to sell more, they might indeed hire more workers and produce more output to sell at lower prices. But Keynes believed that, if they did so, they would be likely to be unable to sell as many units as they expected, for the rehired workers might only have fractional marginal propensities to consume. The latter matters in a monetary system because unspent income may simply be held as cash (likely in Keynes's time when many workers did not have bank accounts) or (more likely today) as pre-existing bank deposits rather than cause an equal amount of extra lending to occur to offset the extra saving. Hence, the employers *as a group* would fail to recoup in revenue all that they were paying out to those workers to produce the additional output. To appreciate the latter view, one needs to view the economy as a system of interacting components and be mindful of the operating rules of the institutions that facilitate these interactions.

Although we were not introduced to the notion of reductionism at this stage, the process of getting to grips with Keynes's thinking set me on a non-reductionist pathway whereby I never presumed that macro-level phenomena were simple aggregates of micro-level outcomes predicted by viewing the micro units as if they functioned independently of each other. This perspective affected my economic thinking and helped turn me against the Conservative Party's austerity policies that were based on Margaret Thatcher's view that the macroeconomy should be managed like a household and "live within its means." Although I had shared Thatcher's concerns about the strength of trade union power in the UK in the 1970s, the non-reductionist view of the economic system that I picked up from Keynes ensured that I took seriously the possibility that, in situations of deficient aggregate demand, unemployment could be involuntary, leaving those who could not find work with a justified sense of being powerless.

## 2.3 "ANIMAL SPIRITS," SOCIAL INTERACTION AND THE CONSUMPTION FUNCTION

Although much of those first seven weeks was concerned with getting a clear sense of the economic system in terms of changing stock levels and output flows as new financial assets were issued and output was produced and transactions took place, we also discovered how Keynes thought about the expectations that underpinned risk-taking by speculators and businesspeople. What he had to say about this (especially in Keynes, 1936, chapter 12) was non-reductionist, too; but it was also very psychological. He saw risk-takers as being acutely aware that the outcomes of their financial gambles would depend upon the financial bets that others placed. Hence, the key to forming one's expectations was to figure out what other players expected about what the rest of the market would expect to happen. If such expectations were very difficult to form with any confidence, players could be wise to hold back from taking risks and to exercise "liquidity preference" until things became clearer.

There was no presumption in Keynes's analysis that market participants would form the same expectations even if they had access to the same set of information. Rather, relative prices of assets would commonly be the result of the distribution of different expectations about future relative prices that led people to choose different portfolios for holding their wealth. Markets could behave in dangerous ways if there was widespread convergence in expectations about the scope for particular asset prices to rise or fall. Sometimes, both those who avoided particular assets, fearing that their prices were likely to fall, and those who bought these assets, expecting their prices to rise, could be mistaken, as the balance of their different expectations might for a time hold the prices stable. But it seemed unlikely that such situations would last, as falsifications of expectations would provoke rethinking how the future might unfold. All this pointed toward viewing asset markets as inherently restless.

Market participants who undertook major financial gambles in the face of major uncertainties would be making leaps in the dark that Keynes saw as being driven by "animal spirits," i.e., urges to action that are not underpinned by careful, evidence-based, probability-weighted calculations. Sometimes, even seasoned financial gamblers will exercise liquidity preference in conditions of great uncertainty. But obviously, it is rather hard to identify oneself as a "market speculator" or "entrepreneur" if one becomes chronically unwilling to make financial gambles. We may thus wonder when the urge of such players to act in line with such self-images will kick in to generate some excitement and help to kick-start a recovery from a depression.

In effect, Keynes's highly psychological view of risk-taking was where I first read something that could be viewed as a behavioral perspective. But at the time – 35 years before Akerlof and Shiller's (2009) book *Animal Spirits* was published as an aid for understanding the 2008 Global Financial Crisis – I did not know this; in my mind, it was simply "animal spirits" and the psychology of the crowd. Over the next few years, I learned that senior economists who adhered to the kind of first-hand view of Keynes that I had picked up branded this perspective as "Post Keynesian Economics" to distinguish it from the more common textbook-style "Keynesian" approaches that focused on equilibria rather than uncertainty and restless expectations. However, Keynes's work would eventually be thoroughly dissected to demonstrate just how much his thinking can be viewed as taking a behavioral approach: see Pech and Milan (2009), Baddeley (2017) and, especially, the book by Schettkat (2022).

More behavioral macroeconomics was lurking in the reading for the week 9 supervision (with week 8 having focused on the Harrod–Domar extensions of Keynesian ideas to growth theory in the late 1930s and early 1940s). The week 9 essay posed some questions about the saving behavior of different types of consumers, and we were expected to answer them after we had familiarized ourselves with the alternative theories of the consumption function that emerged in the early post-war period.

In setting out his thinking about the propensity to consume, Keynes had included some psychological content, mainly to make the case for a fractional marginal propensity to consume when income changes. However, much of the work that sought to develop the consumption function idea proceeded without psychological inputs and instead adopted a rational, optimizing agent perspective. It was easy to see what the suggested modifications to Keynes's consumption function ideas were trying to achieve, and they seemed to contain some grains of truth. The underlying thinking seemed to be that people know better than to make their consumption a simple function of their current income and will tend to smooth out their consumption through time in light of what they know about the likely ups and downs of their income in the short-term and their income trajectories in the long term. If they expect their incomes to rise in the long term, they could borrow to increase their current spending, later repay the loan as their income rises and then save so that they could maintain their spending after retiring. If income went above (below) its trend trajectory they would initially hold back from spending more (from cutting their spending) and wait to see whether their long-term prospects had shifted to a new trajectory.

However, I had trouble reconciling this view fully with how I sensed that people behaved if they received a windfall, such as some kind of unexpected "bonus" or a legacy: unless the amount were very large, it did not seem to me that they would consume it in tiny amounts over the rest of their lives. Rather, it seemed likely that they would have a temporary splurge in their spending as a "treat" or to buy something by which to remember the person from whom they received the legacy. Here, my suspicions were similar to those of Thaler (see Thaler, 2015, chapter 9) but, unlike him, I did not then have the great idea that saving and spending more generally could be shaped by consumers' "mental accounting" rules (Thaler, 1985).

The key reading that we were given to get us started on our consumption function assignment was a survey article by Farrell (1959), a member of the Cambridge Faculty, who died in 1975, aged only 49. However, Brian Van Arkadie told us that a textbook by Ackley (1961) had a very good survey chapter on the consumption function, and I therefore added the book to my rapidly growing collection. He was right about the chapter in Ackley's book: it is far more comprehensive than subsequent macroeconomics texts and, unlike Farrell's article, it included the social psychology-inspired "relative income hypothesis" proposed by Duesenberry (1949) whereby concerns about maintaining social standing via conspicuous consumption produce a kind of "ratchet effect": when incomes rise, people increase their spending to "keep up with the Joneses" but they try to avoid cutting spending if their incomes fall. Given its social psychology influences, it is not surprising that Duesenberry's book ended up being ignored within mainstream macroeconomics (see further Mason, 2000; Drakopoulos, 2021), but it should be an essential source for behavioral economists.

Ackley's chapter was also unusual in mentioning, at least briefly, the work of psychologist George Katona, a colleague of his who ran the University of Michigan's Survey Research Center and pioneered consumer sentiment surveys and, in effect, extended Keynes's ideas about the importance of confidence from the realm of business investment to that of discretionary spending by affluent consumers (see Katona, 1960). However, this did not register with me at the time: I only noticed it after accidentally discovering Katona's work three years later, during my first year as a research student. This discovery was the result of my gaze being drawn to the PhD-based book by Ron Smith (1975) while I was looking for something else in the Marshall Library. Ron had been a superb lecturer for the statistics paper in my second year, but I had not previously been aware of the book, which was on the demand for cars in the USA. In it, he explored, among other things, the significant role of consumer sentiment. Katona's (1960) book *The Powerful Consumer* was shelved nearby and sometime after reading it, I checked to see if I had not registered seeing it being referred to in Ackley's chapter.

This experience was a lesson to me in how easy it is for economists to fail to pick up contributions they should be taking seriously, and from my first publication in 1982 onward, I have sought where possible to draw attention to Katona's emphasis on the shifting *willingness* of consumers to spend on discretionary items: having the ability to spend is necessary but not sufficient to ensure that people will spend as much as they could spend. I even made Katona's contribution the subject of the first lecture that I had to present, which was when I was a participant in a training course for rookie lecturers in 1979. But it has been frustrating in the years that followed to see how little such ideas have been taken into the economics curriculum, despite major banks coming to make serious use of indices of consumer sentiment. (For useful papers on Katona's career, contributions, and his unjustly limited impact, see Wärneryd, 1982, and King, 2016; for an excellent, related survey of the psychology of saving, see Wärneryd, 1999.)

In the remaining two terms of Part I of the Economics Tripos, there was nothing that would later become part of my behavioral toolkit except for the anti-monetarist perspective on inflation that Cambridge's Jackson, Turner and Wilkinson (1972) offered. In their view, a spiral of wages and prices was a manifestation of incompatible claims for wage and profit shares in the national income. These incompatible claims seemed to reflect rather sticky aspirations, with representatives of trade unions and firms being unwilling to make tradeoffs. At this time, it was also hard not to be aware that some levels of unemployment were viewed as more significant than others and that people seemed to habituate to key levels (most obviously, one million unemployed) after they had been exceeded.


## 2.4 EARLY WORRIES ABOUT ORTHODOX CONSUMER BEHAVIOR THEORY

Although I knew that I would need to work hard to have a chance of getting a first in Part II of the Economics Tripos, the Prelims year of Part II was the most relaxed of my three years as an undergraduate. The Prelims year only entailed four papers, and it left time for wider reading. There were two compulsory Economic Principles papers (with no division between microeconomics and macroeconomics) and a compulsory paper on Economic and Social Statistics. There was a very limited choice for the fourth paper, and I chose Comparative

Economic Development (an economic history paper that covered Japan, the USA, and Western Europe, with more development theory than there had been in the Part I economic history paper) rather than the alternative, a paper on sociology and political science. Better still, in those days, the examinations at the end of the Prelims year did not count towards one's final grade in Part II. I was thus able to do more reading and to read beyond readings suggested for the weekly supervision essays.

We spent the first Prelims term looking critically at the dominant constrained optimization approach to microeconomics and its welfare implications. We did this in a way that was utterly different from how today's students in a typical university would learn the material. The lectures were delivered brilliantly (but very arrogantly) by Professor Frank Hahn, one of the best-known general equilibrium economists of his time, via both graphical and mathematical techniques. However, the weekly supervisions were purely essay-based and did not entail arriving at particular numerical answers to "problem set" questions after demonstrating along the way that we could do the necessary calculus. At most, they would entail using graphs as means of illustrating what we were saying about the kinds of results that one could extract via such theory, and what we were saying about its limitations. The first assignment got me thinking seriously about economic method, particularly about why economists were prepared to make assumptions that seemed to be very unrealistic. Its topic was as follows:

> "The Hicks–Allen model of consumer behavior is utterly useless because it yields no testable hypotheses." Discuss.

The original sources of the Hicks–Allen model – which remains the dominant model of consumer behavior taught in intermediate microeconomics – are Hicks and Allen (1934a, 1934b), but Ajit Singh recommended studying it via the coverage in Hicks's ([1939] 1946) book *Value and Capital*. I duly bought a copy of the slightly revised paperback edition and studied it with a close eye not merely to the theory itself but also to anything Hicks said to justify it.

This question appears to have been inspired by the introduction to the article in which Lancaster (1966) sets out his "characteristics-based" approach to consumer behavior and ends with an attempt to provide some testable implications of his "new" approach. Ajit did not tell us this at the time and saved Lancaster's theory until a Part II supervision in which we were discussing the notion that "non-price factors" lay behind the UK's declining performance relative to international trading partners such as Germany and Japan. But even without knowing the background to the contention that we were required to discuss, there were major issues to raise, such as:

- Was the statement correct in relation to the theory having "no testable hypotheses" and, if so, why? Thus, one could begin by showing why the theory does not predict that a reduction in a commodity's relative price will necessarily result in an increase in its sales, as income effects may be either positive or negative without violating the assumptions about preferences being convex, and a positive income effect might be large enough to outweigh the substitution effect. However, one might then argue that the theory does predict that the sign of the substitution effect is always negative. Ajit conceded this, but he then told us that, empirically, substitution effects at the level of the product category were small relative to income effects, as shown in Houthakker and Taylor (1970).

- Insofar as the theory did have any predictive power, could we identify any anomalies? What concerned me at that point was that it seemed at odds with situations in which a person says that they are not willing to consume a particular product at any price, for example, cigarettes, "because I'm not a smoker" or beer, "because I don't drink alcohol." The theory could accommodate not consuming any units of a product at current prices via a "corner solution" with a set of indifference curves that intersected with the vertical axis that represented the other good under consideration and which did so with slopes that were shallower than that of the prevailing budget line. But, so long as the indifference curves slope smoothly downward to the right, the theory predicted that there would always exist lower prices at which the negative substitution effect would be observed. At this point, proponents of the theory would be likely to point out that the theory is about a "representative agent" rather than something intended to apply to all agents, with the representative agent's set of choices amounting to a $1/n$-scale version of the mix of things consumed by all the $n$ consumers in the economy as a whole. Such a defense typically will include the claim that economists need only to concern themselves with what happens at the level of the market rather than with individuals whose choices collectively determine market-level outcomes. But, in the years that followed, I increasingly realized that there might be policy lessons to be had from studying behavior in a much more disaggregated way, to understand why some people do not participate at all in some markets for reasons that have nothing to do with price.

- Can a theory be useful even if it has no testable hypotheses, and, if so, how? (For example, can the Hicks–Allen theory be used as a foundation for

statistical analysis of patterns of demand or for analyzing the welfare impacts of rival economic policy proposals?)
- Could the Hicks–Allen theory be viewed as useless for reasons other than its (limited) ability to offer testable hypotheses? For example, could it be misleading due to being based on unrealistic assumptions, or does the way it is constructed limit its domain and preclude it from being used to frame important real-world issues, such as how new products come to be adopted?

Picking apart the question word by word may seem redolent of how members of a debating society go about constructing their speeches, but it was great for developing analytical skills. Having to contend with these types of questions and address them in this way promoted a much deeper kind of learning than one would get from undertaking a technical exercise built around the same piece of theory.

The question for that first Prelims supervision was as much a question about economic method as a test of how well one had grasped the theory and could explain how it was arrived at and where its strengths and weaknesses originated. Little did I realize that I would go on to spend much of my career focusing on alternatives to the Hicks–Allen theory of consumer behavior.

Having begun Prelims in this way, I hoped to see alternative approaches in lectures given by John Eatwell (on Post Keynesian and Neo-Ricardian alternatives to orthodox thinking) and Bob Rowthorn (on Marxian economics). But neither of them said much about consumer behavior and my classmates and I were left merely with a sense that they felt that patterns of demand had a lot to do with the impact of advertising, social norms and interpersonal competitive pressures – factors that the "given preferences" method of the Hicks–Allen approach ignored but which Galbraith (1958) and Veblen (1899) were mentioned as taking seriously.

## 2.5　FIRST ENCOUNTER WITH THE "BEHAVIORAL" APPROACH

Toward the end of the first Prelims term, I had my first encounter with some economic analysis that was referred to as taking a "behavioral" approach. This was when I was reading for an assignment that Ajit Singh had set on alternatives to the profit-maximizing approach to theorizing about firms. That week's reading focused on the "new theories of the firm" that proliferated in the period from 1958 to 1964. It included Machlup's (1967) critical methodological reflection on these contributions, the Marshall Library copy of which had been defaced with the phrase "sexist pig" (or other words to that effect). This was at the point where Machlup (1967, p. 21) was considering Williamson's (1964) model of top managers who use their discretionary control over resources to maximize their utility at the expense of shareholder returns. They could do this by pursuing "pet projects" and/or enjoying perquisites that might include, as Machlup put it, a "lovely secretary." That issue aside, Machlup's paper stands up well as a thoughtful defense of "as if" profit-maximizing models; it was a very helpful introduction to alternatives to such models, with careful reflection on the contexts in which they might be useful. I also read some of the contributions reprinted in Archibald (ed.) (1971), which included a list of "non-maximizing" approaches to the firm but reprinted none of them. Finally, I read Simon's (1959) survey on models of decision-making, which included his aspirations-driven "satisficing" view of search and choice that was central to what was being called the behavioral approach to the firm. It seemed very different from the other "new theories of the firm," for the latter were essentially modified version of the dominant profit-maximizing approach in that they were models of constrained optimization in which imperfections in product and capital markets afforded senior managers the discretion to maximize something other than profits, such as sales revenue (Baumol, 1959, 1962), the rate of growth of the firm (Marris, 1964), or, as in Williamson (1964), managerial utility. However, at this stage, I did not start reading Cyert and March's (1963) book *A Behavioral Theory of the Firm.*

Those who advocated the behavioral approach sought to build models based on what was known about real-world behavior. However, Machlup suggested they were succumbing to the "fallacy of misplaced concreteness" because their research program produced more complex models from which it could be difficult to glean predictions. I could accept that any model must be a simplification, but I was wary of the idea of building models based on assumptions which are clearly false. Hence, I thought I should remain open to Simon's attempt to take account of the realities of managerial decision-making even though I did not yet have a sense of where I might use his satisficing perspective.

Ajit Singh noticed my interest in Simon's work and, more generally, my growing resistance to the sets of assumptions that lay behind orthodox economics. But I also made it clear to him that I was disappointed with what I had seen of the microeconomic content of the Marxian and Neo-Ricardian alternatives. As a result, he suggested that I should read Janos Kornai's (1971) book *Anti-Equilibrium* during the Christmas vacation as something that might appeal to me more. This was a very important suggestion, for although I have not referred frequently to Kornai's book over the course of my career, it had a big impact on my view of economics.

Kornai is best known for his work as an economic planner in Hungary, but *Anti-Equilibrium* was an attempt to challenge static equilibrium analysis and build a framework for understanding how an economic system evolves as product lifecycles unfold when innovation happens, and as decision-makers use norms and simplifying rules to cope with the complexities of their changing environments. Kornai seemed to be signaling that economists should build a synthesis between the behavioral approach of Simon (1947, 1959) (and of Cyert and March, 1963, whose approach to the theory of the firm was one of those considered in Machlup, 1967) and the evolutionary approach of Schumpeter (1943). This was, in effect, what Nelson and Winter (1982) later delivered in their remarkably influential book *An Evolutionary Theory of Economic Change*, with no reference to Kornai as a precursor to their work.

The excitement of the first term of my Prelims year led me to commit further to economics by joining the Royal Economic Society in early 1976. This meant that I received personal copies of the *Economic Journal*, which in those days published a far more eclectic range of articles than one would find there today, and whose book reviews I found very useful. The very first issue that I received included a paper by Paul Mosley (1976) that applied satisficing ideas (including the notion that decision-makers tend to give "sequential attention to goals" rather than arriving at trade-offs between them) to understand the making of macroeconomic policy in the UK's "stop–go" decades. (The approach was latter extended in its temporal coverage and to the US economy: see Mosley, 1984.) However, this was the only Simon-inspired work that came my way during the second and third terms of the Prelims year, for the focus of supervisions led me to concentrate on uncertainty and coordination problems in economic systems.


## 2.6    ECONOMIC COORDINATION PROBLEMS IN THE REAL WORLD

During the first Prelims term, Ajit Singh had tried to ensure that we were aware of the many assumptions that were necessary for building models of general competitive equilibrium. As part of this, he explained in supervisions the essence of the strange institutional arrangements that the general equilibrium economists employed when trying to show how an entire economy might achieve equilibrium even in the presence of uncertainty. Then, early in the second Prelims term, for supervisions with Vladimir Brailovsky (a member of the Department of Applied Economics), I read Leijonhufvud (1968) and articles by Clower (1965, 1967) reprinted in Clower (ed.) (1969) that attempted to make sense of Keynesian economics by aggregating up from general equilibrium microfoundations with an eye to how the institutions of the real world differed from those assumed in pure theory. While this work helped me firm up my macroeconomic perspective, it was also significant because it got me more interested in the problem of economic coordination under uncertainty at a micro-structural level. The latter led me to view the question of how entrepreneurs figure out whether to try to enter or remain in a market as fertile ground for behavioral research.

Ajit had explained that, in the original general equilibrium models devised by Edgeworth and Walras, production only went ahead after a price vector had been found that would clear all markets given what economic agents were prepared to demand or supply based on their preferences, endowments and technological possibilities. The set of market clearing prices in these fantasy worlds would be found by a process of "recontracting" (in effect, shopping around without making binding commitments until it became impossible to find better quotations) or via some kind of gigantic simultaneous all-market auction process in which an auctioneer kept calling for buy and sell offers at different price vectors and adjusted the set of relative prices in light of excess supply or demand until a set emerge that cleared all markets.

Modern general equilibrium theory had attempted to incorporate uncertainty into such models by assuming that contracts for the delivery of specific goods or labor services only applied if a particular state of the world eventuated. Uncertainty could supposedly be dealt with by making multiple contracts, each specific to different states of the world. However, the scale of knowledge problems (and the inconvenient question of how to incorporate economic agents who had not yet been born) makes it impossible to pre-reconcile everything via forward contracts, even those that have masses of fine print to cover different contingencies, for such contracts cannot handle states of the world that have not yet been imagined. In the real world, there is an inherently experimental dimension to investment decisions – not just those taken by firms and government agencies but also those taken by consumers who make commitments to current-generation products, often of uncertain quality, without knowing what future-generation iterations will offer.

In the absence of anything equivalent to a Walrasian auctioneer, much of what is produced in the real world is produced speculatively rather than to orders placed by end-consumers. This enables buyers to delay their purchasing decisions until they have a better idea of what the state of the world is, what they want, and what products are avail (including innovations that were not previously available or foreshadowed) and at what prices. Moreover, workers are paid in money; they are not paid in terms of titles to (some of) what they produce, that they can exchange for titles to other forms of output. Taken together, these ways of doing business ensure that levels of employment depend on how entrepreneurs form and adjust their expectations amid uncertainty about what the correct market-clearing prices and quantities should be, in light of data about actual sales at prices that have been set experimentally for quantities offered without advance sales having been achieved. The process plays out in real time, whereas, in the general equilibrium models, all transactions are decided before production occurs. If expectations are falsified, it will not necessarily be obvious how far to adjust them, and the prices at which one is prepared to pay or accept. But, as Leijonhufvud emphasized, sluggish adjustments due to inelastic expectations may result in the build-up of stocks and losses of income and spending if workers are laid off rather than being retained after having their wages cut in sectors where sales have been disappointing.

One interesting aspect of these attempts to look at the microfoundations of macroeconomics in terms of a neo-Walrasian mindset was that they did not assign central roles to Keynes's concerns about inter-temporal coordination of saving and investment and the significance of a fractional marginal propensity to consume as a barrier to the capacity of money wage reductions to reduce or eliminate involuntary unemployment. Rather, the root of the problems of involuntary unemployment seemed to be a kind of "Catch-22" problem associated with the payment of wages in terms of money. Clower seemed to be saying that the issue was that workers could not make their "notional demand" for output "effective" if they did not have income, which they would only get if prospective suppliers were confident that effective demand existed for the products that they were thinking of supplying. This way of thinking was rather like treating a production economy purely as an exchange economy, except for the presence of money getting in the way of hours of labor time being exchanged directly for output. The problem was not that workers would not signal the future demand that they would finance by drawing on their savings; rather, the problem was that they could only signal their demand by making purchase offers if they could sell their labor services or obtain credit despite not yet having employment.

From a Clower-like standpoint, coordination failures could result in unemployment even if no attempts to save were being made; all that was required was a lack of confidence on the part of entrepreneurs that, if they paid wages ahead of selling their products, what they paid out would, directly or indirectly come back to them as revenue. As in Keynes, this was a theory in which money played a key role, but the whole story could be told without any reference to the problem of a fractional marginal propensity to consume or to prospective returns on investing in durable assets such as buildings, plant and machinery. Failures of effective demand could occur simply due to uncertainty about the relative *near*-future sales prospects for different types of products if tastes were fickle, if new products could appear or if the economic system could be subject to short-term external shocks.

The idea that I needed to think about inter-sectoral and/or within-sector coordination issues started to dawn on me when I was reading for a supervision essay for Vladimir Brailovsky that required discussion of the claim that "The reason for creating a planned economy is that the market cannot give effect to individual preferences." In exploring arguments for economic planning, I came across the work of Vera Lutz (1969) who was writing about "indicative" planning methods used in some capitalist economies as a means of dealing with the coordination problems that central planners in socialist systems tried to circumvent. Lutz examined the French planning system in which government planners got together with industry representatives to work out how much capacity growth was needed in each sector to deliver desired rates of growth of final outputs. In contrast to the Soviet system, in which enterprise managers were given directives about how much to produce, indicative planning systems left it up to individual firms to make their investment decisions mindful of the targets that had been worked out for their sector. As Lutz realized, unless everyone attempted to expand at the rates that had been announced for their sectors, there could be problems if too much or too little capacity was created via the plans that the firms arrived at without knowing what their competitors were going to do.

My concern with coordination problems then led me to write a very different essay from what I knew I was expected to write for one of two supervisions that Ajit Singh arranged for Ken Coutts to provide on Sraffian economics. The essay task involved discussing a quotation from Ricardo about the significance of commodities being in some cases produced and in other cases being non-reproducible. This was a task for the Easter vacation, so I wrote it not in my room in Queens' but in Stevenage Central Library, armed with my copies of Sraffa (1960) and Sraffa's edition of Ricardo's *Principles* (Ricardo, 1951). However, despite having invested in these books, I did not allow sunk-cost bias to drive me to write the Sraffa-focused essay that I knew I was expected to deliver. Instead, I approached it mindful of a remark by Joan Robinson in one of her Prelims lectures (which she echoed in Robinson, 1977) that had also related to the significance of economic activity involving both produced and non-reproducible goods: she had started the lecture by brandishing a letter that she had just received from Robert Clower and saying that it was clear that his way of trying to rewrite Keynes's thinking in Walrasian terms meant that he ended up missing much of what made a production economy different from a pure exchange economy. Her remark had helped me to arrive at the perspective on Clower's work that I outlined earlier in this section, but I now started to reflect on its relevance to the essay that I needed to write.

As I did so, it occurred to me that those who invest in systems to produce goods and services face more uncertainty than those who try to make a profit by purchasing and reselling non-reproducible assets. The latter's returns depend on what others turn out to be prepared to pay to get control over those assets and on the reservation prices of owners of substitute non-reproducible assets, if any such assets exist. By contrast, the profits achieved by those who invest in production systems depend not merely on the demand for the output of the product to which their investment contributes but also on the extent to which others invest in the same supply chain or in producing the same type of output.

This is because the investment that others make will determine the costs of inputs that they need and, depending on how much capacity gets created, the price that their output will fetch, given the demand for the product in question. As entrepreneurs consider adding to production capacity by investing in reproducible goods, they must contend with the fact that their payoffs are mutually interdependent, as in Lutz's concerns about the limitations of indicative planning. To eliminate such uncertainty, they would need to be able to make forward purchases of their inputs and forward sales of their output over the lifespans of their investments. But, as noted earlier, there are good reasons why, in the real world, comprehensive forward markets are conspicuously absent.

From there, my mind moved to scope for coordination failures of the kind encapsulated in the "cobweb diagram" analysis of price and output instability that I had discovered during A-Level Economics. In the cobweb diagram, firms were portrayed as ignoring the mutual interdependence of their returns and as if they made their supply decisions by assuming that the price realized in the current period would be the price next period. Reflection about this led me to a further concern: if there were no entry or exit barriers in product and factor markets, there was potential for the economy to operate completely chaotically in real time as investors and workers tried to chase opportunities based on current prices.

The implication seemed to be that some so-called "market imperfections" are necessary to enable orderly adjustment of supply to changes in patterns of demand in a production system. Some of these barriers to entry may be physical, such as a lack of suitable sites, but movements of factors of production can also be impeded by psychological and knowledge-based issues. Shortfalls in awareness, know-how and/or willingness of entrepreneurs to pursue profit opportunities outside their existing market habitats will limit the risk of boom–bust episodes. I made the idea that less than perfect mobility can have desirable consequences the basis for the essay that I wrote for Ken Coutts. It seemed to be an idea that aligned nicely with Keynes's view that impediments to wage flexibility could be good for macroeconomic stability.

Ken commented that my essay was "very interesting" and suggested that I might enjoy the Marshallian view of market processes that he had recently seen in a University of Stirling discussion paper by Brian Loasby (later published formally as Loasby, 1978). I looked at the Loasby paper but did not follow up any of its references at the time. Hence, I failed to discover that I had just reinvented ideas that are central to George Richardson's (1960) book *Information and Investment*. During the 1976 long vacation between Prelims and Part II, I expanded the ideas from my essay into an article-length entry for Cambridge's annual Adam Smith Essay Competition. My entry came third, earning me an "honorable mention." In the longer term, however, the significance to me of this view of what was necessary for orderly structural change to occur was that it pointed toward seeing entrepreneurial studies as a fertile field for behavioral analysis of what determines the opportunities that get noticed and taken up by entrepreneurs. We should also be mindful that impediments to labor mobility can actually help ensure orderly structural adjustment in contrast to the chaos observed during, say, a boom–bust "gold rush" or when economic migrants flood into regions that lack the infrastructure needed to support them.

## 2.7   BOUNDED RATIONALITY AND FUNDAMENTAL UNCERTAINTY

My reflections on the differences between idealized general equilibrium worlds and the real world set me on a track to having a wider view of the challenges of real-world decision-making than even Herbert Simon seemed to be acknowledging. Simon presented humans as operating with "bounded rationality" in the sense that they want to avoid wasting resources but are forced to employ cognitive shortcuts because they cannot process all the information at their disposal in the time that they have available, and they are likely to sense that they risk making mistakes if they overload their information processing systems. To me, this seems very much a cognitive psychology perspective inspired by computing analogies.

From this standpoint, bounded rationality seems to arise due to (a) a surfeit of potentially accessible information in contexts where there are many options that differ in many ways and/or because (b) there is uncertainty in the sense that decision-makers are aware that some or all options are associated with ranges of possible outcomes due to recognized scope for variability in how products perform and/or for different states of nature to eventuate. In the latter kinds of situations, knowing all the relevant probabilities makes figuring out the value of any single option akin to dealing with a mass of options whose outcomes are not in any doubt. Given human computational limits in terms of processing speed and working memory capacity, it is easy to see why people would end up choosing by searching locally until they found an option that seemed sufficiently likely to meet aspiration levels that they set experimentally and adjusted in light of attainments.

The door to a wider view of the problem of choice was opened to me in the spring of 1976 when I found time to read George Shackle's (1967) book *The Years of High Theory*. It had been listed for some of Brian Van Arkadie's Part I supervisions, but I had not read it at the time. However, I remembered the title and realized that it might also be relevant for Prelims. It led me eventually to read many of Shackle's other works and turned my growing interest in problems of knowledge and uncertainty into my focal concern in relation to how the economic system works.

Shackle presented the essence of Keynes's theory of employment in terms of material from chapters 12 and 17 of the *General Theory* and from Keynes's (1937) summary article in the *Quarterly Journal of Economics* (which I read via the reprint in Clower, ed., 1969). Shackle also used ideas from Townshend (1937) to build his view of the radical departure that Keynes's work represented. He thereby supercharged the view that I had been forming during Part I of the Economics Tripos about the need to focus on the significance of poorly anchored expectations, rather than on given behavioral functions, when trying to understand how the economy works. For Shackle, dealing with uncertainty was not about the challenges of processing complex sets of *known* probabilities (though I later discovered he had developed a theory of attention-focusing that could be applied to this issue: see Shackle, 1949, 1969; Earl, 2023b); rather, it was about *gaps in knowledge* that could not be resolved in the time that was available for choosing.

Keynes (1937) viewed this kind of situation in terms of people being unable to calculate probabilities with any confidence, and he then proposed essentially a heuristics-based view of how people choose if they "simply do not know," whereby they assume present trends will continue or outsource their views of the future to those who seem to know more than they themselves know. Also, his view of choice entailed a liquidity preference aspect: when there is great scope for being taken by surprise, people will favor assets that seem likely to be easy to dispose of to finance the purchase of other assets that suit better the events that transpire (see Keynes, 1936, chapter 17, and Townshend, 1937). This was significant for Keynes's theory of employment insofar as the assets that hold their value and enable people rapidly to switch to other assets may not be those that can readily be reproduced by employing people and investing in machinery.

Much of the uncertainty that drives preferences for liquidity and reluctance to make commitments is a result of people being aware of gaps in the information they can access and in what they can know – gaps that are often associated with scope for innovation and the extent to which the future depends to some degree on events that have not yet taken place and choices that have not yet been made. There is often no guarantee that structural change will not take surprising forms, so one cannot confidently infer probabilities in an inductive manner by looking at evidence of the past frequencies of particular classes of events.

These "fundamental" kinds of uncertainty and the idea that people use simple rules and heuristics for dealing with them called into question the underlying idea in general equilibrium theory that relative prices are firmly underpinned by supply and demand functions derived from given sets of preferences, agents' initial endowments, and given sets of technological possibilities. In the radical interpretation of Keynes's *General Theory* that Townshend (1937) offered, ways of coping with knowledge gaps could in some cases entail following conventions, but in other cases could entail taking cues from people whose opinions were respected even if they departed from conventions. There was potential for resource allocation patterns to be shaped by questionable relative values that were being distorted by whirlpools of speculation. But it was problematic to say what the right set of values was, given that the potential for structural change called into question the notion that there is an ideal set to be inferred by modeling based on what are commonly referred to as "market fundamentals" that reflect past conditions and behavior. Townshend summed up his interpretation of the implications of Keynes's analysis in a way that I found memorable and useful: he asked his readers to consider the difficulties of knowing what relative values ought to be if everyone woke up one day with no memories of what relative prices had been, and he suggested that, in essence, the market system is held up by its own bootstraps, with prices generally being anchored by conventions but with scope for speculation sometimes to dislodge them from established reference points.

## 2.8  MINSKY'S MODERNIZATION OF KEYNES

The final key work that I read in my Prelims year was Hyman Minsky's (1975a) book *John Maynard Keynes*, which adds the complexities of modern, multi-layered financial systems to the fundamentalist Keynesian perspective. I studied Minsky's book very soon after seeing it on display in Heffers Bookshop in Cambridge following its 1976 UK publication by Macmillan. Monetary aspects of Keynes's *General Theory* are set out largely via a simplifying focus on choices between bonds, equities, cash, and durable assets, as alternative ways of holding one's wealth. Minsky recognizes that most money balances are not held as cash but as deposits in financial institutions, so he proceeds with due consideration of the complex balance sheet nexus between banks, non-bank financial intermediaries, firms and households, and the significance not merely of short-term illiquidity risks but also of insolvency risks and their system-wide ramifications. His work thus played a key role in ensuring that I developed a non-reductionist, systems-based way of viewing the economy.

Minsky also adds weight to the signals that Keynes offered about the importance of being mindful of the psychological drivers of behavior in financial markets. He introduces the idea that market bubbles can be associated with speculators starting to experience feelings of euphoria – i.e., widespread over-confidence and a misplaced belief that "the sky's the limit." Minsky seemed implicitly to be suggesting that, from time to time, the norms that Townshend's paper had seen as playing key roles in enabling the economic system to work in an orderly manner could cease to apply as system-wide reductions in liquidity preference took hold.

My appreciation of Minsky was enhanced during my Part II year, via Tony Cramp's lectures on money and banking, where emphasis was given to the tendency of financial systems to become increasingly fragile as people move from their familiar financial market habitats into unfamiliar areas that have started to seem less risky, and as complex multi-layered structures of interconnected balance sheets emerge. In his lectures, Cramp occasionally quoted from his correspondence with Minsky, notably about why the financial system was resilient enough to ensure that "the sky did not fall" during the banking crises around the world in the mid-1970s (see Minsky, 1975b). He also explained how, in the UK secondary banking crisis, financial regulators had found it difficult to keep up with the innovative ruses that were being used by some of the players. This seemed fertile territory in which to keep in mind Simon's emphasis on the limited information processing capacities of decision-makers in relation to fathoming complex problems, especially where people are short of what we now call "financial literacy." But the role that shifts in expectations and risk assessments played in Minsky's analysis also seemed related to how fundamental uncertainty leads to an absence of firm foundations for expectations that people form about prospective asset yields and which they may suddenly change if there is a change in the "state of the news" (Shackle, 1974).

Given that I had picked up these fundamentalist Keynesian/Minskian foundations during my undergraduate years, I was rather underwhelmed by Akerlof and Shiller's (2009) *Animal Spirits*, which appeared over thirty years after I graduated. In the interim, I had used Minsky's ideas, with upfront credit to Minsky, whenever I was writing about macroeconomics and the financial system, sometimes with case study material (see, for example, Dow and Earl, 1982; chapters 11 and 12; Earl, 1990, chapter 12; Earl, 2022, chapter 12; and Earl and Wakeley, chapter 13). Like other Post Keynesian economists, I did not bury references to Minsky in endnotes or try to portray him, as Akerlof and Shiller did, merely as an economic historian.

## 2.9  THE BEHAVIORAL ECONOMICS OF FIRMS, PRODUCTIVITY AND GROWTH

Part II of the Economics Tripos was a busy time for me. Normally, it consisted of six papers, three of which were freely chosen from a reasonably large list, or four papers, with a dissertation instead of two of the elective papers. However, I chose an additional elective, Russian Economic History (for which I had no supervisions and simply relied on lectures and reading) in case I found the Economic Theory elective too technical (which did not turn out to be the case), with the best three electives to count to my final grade. My remaining electives were the paper on Money, Banking and Public Finance, and Economic Development. What I read for the latter on the chronic problems of Latin American economies did much to heighten my interest in impediments to economic change and poor responsiveness to changes in market signals. Of the other three papers in Part II, two were compulsory Economic Principles and Problems paper and the other was either Labor Economics or The Modern Business Enterprise and Social Structure. I chose the latter, and it played a vital role in shaping my view of behavioral economics.

Much of the focus of the Part II Principles and Problems papers was on the policy challenges associated with the UK's slow rate of per-capita income growth and its declining economic performance relative to countries such as Germany and Japan. However, the initial supervision tasks for these papers required us to explore the nature of the problem from a macroeconomic standpoint. This was done primarily by contrasting Denison's (1967) neoclassical empirical analysis of growth as being constrained by growth in supplies of factors of production, and Cripps and Tarling's (1973) Keynesian view that the UK's problems resulted from the absence of consistently strong effective demand needed to stimulate the investment that was required to raise output capacity and productivity.

Denison's approach was not convincing, for it was based on an aggregate production function with constant returns to scale and assumed that factors of production received their marginal revenue products. The relative contributions of growth in supplies of capital and labor were weighted according to their shares in national income. It was here that the seeds of my skepticism about the wisdom of always assuming the possibility of substitution were sown, for Denison's use of the relative shares of profits and wages in national income to measure marginal products of capital and labor assigned capital growth a far less important role than it gave to growth in the supply of labor. Worse still, it implied that if there were no new capital equipment there would still be economic growth if the supply of labor grew, with more workers somehow making use of the existing capital stock. To be sure, sometimes extra shifts might be run, but the idea that workers might simultaneously use equipment that had been designed for one operator seemed laughable. That issue aside, there was also the problem that the residuals in Denison's regressions were substantial, with this being ascribed to the significance of factors such as technical progress as a source of productivity growth. This was something that the neoclassical approach was not well equipped to handle, and it begged the question of why nations might differ in the technological dynamism of their firms, or in whatever else it was about their firms that affected productivity and was buried in Denison's residuals.

The behavioral view of firms offered a way of understanding this, for it did not presume that firms necessarily behave in the same way even in a given market context, let alone in different countries. Differences in how aspiration levels were set and adjusted in response to attainments could affect the effort that went into searching for better ways of doing things and the kinds of quality control standards that were pursued. With marginal products being hard to identify, returns to stakeholders could vary depending on how bold staff were and on how pushy people were during organizational bargaining, or in making contracts for the supply of inputs. The returns potentially available to the various stakeholders would differ not merely due to differences in the quality of equipment or scale of production but also due to the sets of rules and routines that firms used. Furthermore, the ways in which, as a rule, managers and other personnel in a firm saw external threats and opportunities could affect how they reacted: for example, if hubris has taken hold, we would be unwise to assume that potentially grave long-term threats will be recognized as such or that new ways of doing things that have been devised in other organizations will be taken as seriously as in-house proposals or routines that have hitherto served the firm well.

None of the Part II lecturers systematically set out such a view, but it was where I had broadly arrived by the end of Part II. I then got a clearer vision of it during my first year as a research student, especially after discovering the "Japanese way" of doing business via Adams and Kobayashi (1969). Key ingredients came from the lectures that Alan Hughes contributed to the Modern Business Enterprise and Social Structure. Three sources from his reading lists proved to be especially formative.

The first was Silberston's (1970) superb survey article on the price behavior of firms, which emphasized the diversity of economic perspectives on how firms behave as competitive conditions change. It offered a bigger view than I had got from Machlup (1967) of what a behavioral approach constituted, for it included analysis of behavioral studies on pricing (that pointed toward a rule-based view of pricing in which prices were set by adding a mark-up to "normal costs") as well as considering the essence of Cyert and March's (1963) *Behavioral Theory of the Firm*. I found their notion of "organizational slack" especially interesting. Their idea was that the various stakeholders in a firm could not be sure how far they could improve their positions at the expense of other stakeholders but were aware of the risk of ending up worse off if they pushed their luck too far and caused some other stakeholders to exit for better deals elsewhere. Given this risk, the hypothesis was that they would not push their luck so long as they were meeting their aspirations regarding what they got from their membership of the coalition that constituted the firm. If they raised their aspirations less rapidly than their attainments, it would become possible for other stakeholders to capture the surplus from them by bargaining more assertively. There could thus be a buffer that would enable some stakeholders to get back to achieving satisfactory returns if they bargained harder after finding they were unable to meet their aspirations.

In relation to pricing, this could mean, for example, that managers might find they could get away with passing increased costs on to their customers, despite not having dared to charge higher prices before their costs increased. But it seemed also to point to scope for managers to keep a firm going in the face of tougher external competition by cutting their mark-ups and reducing dividends to shareholders and/or squeezing the real wages of their employees, so long as these parties had been getting more than their "transfer earnings," i.e., more than the minimum that they would tolerate rather than move elsewhere. For a time, then, it might be possible for the firm to keep going in the face of tougher competitive conditions without doing anything more fundamental, such as developing new production methods or better products.

The second formative source was Salter's (1966) analysis of how competition worked in industries where firms operated with different "vintages" of equipment. Even though investments in new technologies with lower average total costs would depress market prices as output from them came on-stream, it would not necessarily force the overnight abandonment of all the older, less productive technologies, only those whose average non-sunk costs per unit exceeded the market price. Of course, when production systems with historic average total costs per unit greater than the market price eventually wore out, they would get replaced by more modern technologies, but the process whereby old technology vintages were retired could take many years. There seemed to be even more potential for processes of structural change to be protracted if one took account of Cyert and March's ideas about the uptake of organizational slack, as managers of older production systems could have potential to push per-unit operating costs down if they could get away with bargaining more aggressively with their employees and other suppliers of inputs.

Thirdly, there was Downie's (1958) book, *The Competitive Process*, which is a precursor to Salter's analysis but in some respects goes beyond it (and in doing so is a precursor to Nelson and Winter, 1982 – see further Nightingale, 1997, 1998) by taking account of the feedback relationship between profits and productivity, with an emphasis on the relationship between market share and unit costs. Downie was concerned about the future of competition if a "transfer mechanism" was operating, whereby firms with bigger market shares enjoyed lower unit costs than their smaller rivals and could plough back more into investing in new products and processes that would enable them to take even more market share and further squeeze the smaller players. However, he acknowledged that this feedback process might be held in check by an "innovation mechanism," whereby existential threats concentrated wonderfully the minds of staff in firms whose profit margins were being squeezed, with the result that they were able to come up with innovative production methods or products. Implementing such innovations would require them to be able to invest enough, despite facing a squeeze on their retained profits.

If the innovation mechanism had enough power, Downie's thinking pointed toward a view of industries as operating rather like sporting leagues whose teams occupy changing rankings as the years go by, rather than becoming dominated by a single team that is able always to hire the best players. However, in light of Salter and of Cyert and March's notion of organizational slack, it seemed to me that it was an open question whether potential existential threats were perceived as such and did produce this sort of pattern: on the one hand, if such threats provoked creative thinking, then taking up organizational slack might facilitate getting the resources necessary to put new ideas into practice; on the other hand, as noted earlier, taking up organizational slack might simply provide a means of keeping afloat temporarily without making any fundamental changes. The compounding effects of feedback processes could mean that denying the gravity of a competitive threat could result in delays in making changes that, if implemented earlier, could have prevented the crossing of tipping points beyond which a firm's demise becomes inevitable.

These lines of thought were amplified in my mind when Ajit Singh encouraged me to read Leibenstein's (1966) first paper on the notion of "$X$-inefficiency," a paper to whose empirical content Ajit had contributed as a doctoral student at Berkeley while working as Leibenstein's research assistant. Leibenstein argued that, due to their habit of assuming that firms maximize profits, economists had limited themselves to talking about inefficiency only in relation to deadweight losses associated with market imperfections that distorted relative prices. Moreover, in assuming that, given the prevailing set of prices, production costs were as low as they could be, economists ended up underestimating the efficiency impacts of market imperfections. In Leibenstein's terms, firms whose unit costs were needlessly high were suffering from "$X$-inefficiency." He saw considerable potential for firms to achieve lower costs and higher productivity if they were better managed and under stronger competitive pressure. As he saw it, firms were often failing to use best-practice methods and managers often allowed workers to make the most of vagueness in employment contracts and get away with less industrious behavior than they would be prepared to offer if pushed harder or given tighter job specifications.

It seemed to me that there was a good deal of overlap between Leibenstein's $X$-inefficiency notion and Cyert and March's idea of organizational slack.

Leibenstein seemed to be recognizing potential for applying better knowledge to improve or bolster returns to stakeholders, and to be taking the view that this knowledge would be found and applied if there were external pressure to find ways of reducing unit costs and/or if more capable managers with higher performance aspirations were appointed by firms that were underperforming. However, he seemed to be oblivious of the distributional consequences of his arguments: he seemed to focus purely on scope for cutting costs, without any concern for the impact that this might have on employee welfare via workplace restructuring that led to workers being retrenched or workers having to work harder. By contrast, distributional issues were central to Cyert and March's view that returns to stakeholders depended on their success in bargaining, although Cyert and March seemed to be underplaying the potential for raising productivity by applying better knowledge as opposed simply to working harder (if one kept one's job).

Leibenstein's vision of workers guilefully exploiting vagueness in their job descriptions and inadequate monitoring by managers pointed toward efficiency-enhancing policies based on tightening up employment contracts and investing in more supervisors to monitor compliance with these contracts. Such policies did indeed become part of managerialist thinking during the 1980s, but I could see that a more carefully considered behavioral approach was necessary. This was partly because during Part II I read Coase's (1937) analysis of the nature of the firm, which Gordon Hughes had mentioned in his lectures for the Economic Theory paper and which I had seen referred to by Goodhart (1975) around the same time. As Goodhart noted, Coase had shown that firms emerge as means of reducing transaction costs that arise when people are beset with uncertainty. It can be futile or very costly to try to organize production by complex labor-hire contracts to cover all possible contingencies, or by negotiating successive short-term contracts to deal with contingencies as they arise. However, if entrepreneurs or managers hire workers via incomplete employment contracts, then, as contingencies arise, they can simply provide instructions about what the workers need to do and try to ensure that it gets done.

In a world based around contracts that specify precisely what workers deliver, there would be no need to incur the costs of having managers, but there could be major costs of forming contracts and litigating over alleged failures in their implementation. Having managers plus loosely specified employment contracts is a cheaper way of getting things done in a world of surprises that require adaptive behavior. Leibenstein seemed oblivious of this, whereas anyone who was familiar with what happened when trade union members "worked to rule" would be able to appreciate the hazards of trying to organize production via contracts with clauses that preclude flexible behavior that managers might prefer to see from their workers as a means of keeping output flowing amid unexpected problems.

My doubts about the wisdom of using more detailed job contracts and more supervision as means of raising productivity also came partly from D. K. Lee, the final figure who played a key formative role in my interest in how aspects of internal organization affect the productivity and resilience of firms in changing environments. Lee lectured on the "sociology of organizations" for The Modern Business Enterprise and Social Structure. He was something of a mystery figure: I cannot recall his first name (if indeed he supplied it) and I have not been able to find any trace of him during research for this book. If I recall correctly, he said he drove up from Colchester to give his lectures, so he may have been from the University of Essex. I did not feel that we were being short-changed by lectures on this topic being outsourced, for it showed that those who designed the Economics Tripos had a clear vision of the lecture content that we needed to be provided with, recognized a gap in local expertise, and were not unwilling to seek assistance from someone who had the requisite knowledge. I found Lee's lectures fascinating.

I appreciated the behavioral theory of the firm better via what Lee said about March and Simon's (1958) book *Organizations*, with its detailed analysis of the impact of individuals' sub-goals and its emphasis on organizations having "persistence" tendencies (which most behavioral economists would nowadays call "sunk cost bias") that resulted in them failing to abandon projects in the face of unexpectedly poor performance or dramatic cost over-runs. More importantly, via what he said about the work of Selznick (1957), I started to develop a sense of how the "culture" of an organization could shape how its members viewed the external environment and in turn shape the organization's internal modes of operation, for good or ill, sometimes keeping it within a predictable behavioral "groove" for decades. It was from here that I started to see that the cultures of business organizations are rather like scientific paradigms in the way they affect how the world is seen and the kinds of changes to which people are open.

I do not recall learning anything from Lee (or anyone else, at that stage) about Chester Barnard's (1938) emphasis on managerial authority being granted by those who are being managed, rather than coming automatically via being given a specific managerial role. That Lee did not cover Barnard is not surprising, for Barnard had written his analysis based on decades of experience as a practicing executive, not as an academic sociologist. Nor do I recall being introduced to Herbert Simon's (1947) extension of Barnard's thinking via the notion that the "docility" of workers is necessary for organizations to run smoothly and adapt to changing conditions. However, I picked up these notions via Lee's exposition of what Gouldner (1954) observed in an ethnographic study of a gypsum mine where attempts by a new manager to run a tighter operation to deal with health and safety issues were resisted by the workforce whose behavioral norms were being challenged, with this resistance increasing as even more supervisors were put in place to try to ensure compliance.

At the end of his series of lectures, Lee discussed Joan Woodward's (1965) work on the importance of firms aligning their preferred type of organizational system with the type of operating environment they face. This helped me to appreciate better the difference between Leibenstein and Coase in relation to contractual incompleteness, and it reinforced my sense that Leibenstein's view was rather simplistic. Woodward saw a formal, bureaucratic organization as well suited to a surprise-free environment in which jobs entail limited sets of operations (as with, say, workstations on a production line). Such a situation might indeed be one where the more tightly specified contracts that Leibenstein seemed to view as desirable might raise productivity by keeping workers better focused on their jobs; moreover, if the attention of managers was not frequently being captured by surprises, they could focus on monitoring whether workers were doing their jobs in the ways that they were supposed to do them. By contrast, Woodward saw the need for workers to be given the right to use their expertise as they saw fit, without first getting permission from higher authorities, if they were working in environments in which surprises could have very expensive consequences if they were not attended to promptly (as in, say, a nuclear power plant or in the cockpit of an airliner). Trusting professionals to do the right thing and hiring them via vague contracts that left them with considerable discretion seemed to align well with Coase's way of thinking about the nature of the firm.

Yet, in a sense, the way that Lee presented Woodward's vision of trusted professionals implied that we might extend Coase's notion of the firm as a loosely specified pool of resources to be allocated contingently, for it admitted the possibility that workers could be left to figure out for themselves how to change what they were doing as their situations changed, without managers needing to be present to decide what needed to be done and give them the corresponding instructions. A workforce of intrinsically motivated professionals could function effectively with minimal need for managers so long as everyone was careful to consult with their colleagues to avoid coordination problems. That possibility seemed to get ignored in the era of managerialist organizational reforms that commenced soon after I left Cambridge. Instead of accepting the presence of a few slackers as the price of getting the benefits of trusting everyone with professional capabilities to use their skills with pride, managers have applied simplistic views of organizations and slack as a basis for treating everyone as if they are not trustworthy and work in demotivating roles.

Such managerialism has been particularly evident in the university sector (for a study in the Australian context, see Lafferty and Fleming, 2000), which historically had operated with minimal spending on managers and little monitoring of the performance of academic staff. From the 1980s, universities commonly turned increasingly into untrusting bureaucratic systems with more and more layers of management and massive manuals of policies and procedures to keep everyone in line and thereby supposedly increase their productivity. The productivity of academics working "at the coalface" has thereby increased according to some measures, but we may wonder what percentage of the gains has been captured by the additional layers of managerial staff.

## 2.10   FROM UNDERGRADUATE TO RESEARCH STUDENT

In the Lent term of 1977, I decided that I wanted to continue studying economics after completing my Cambridge BA, rather than move on to a graduate-entry job in the corporate sector or public service. This decision had the advantage of greatly simplifying my life as I concentrated on consolidating my knowledge ahead of the Part II examinations. Unlike many of my peers, I did not have my time chewed up by preparing job applications and attending interviews. I filled in just four application forms and only had to attend one interview. There was no requirement to send a detailed research proposal with any of the forms; at most, I just had to give an indicative topic and write a paragraph about what I had in mind. I applied to enter the Cambridge PhD program and, for a back-up, to one-year coursework master's programs at the LSE, UCL and the University of York, each of which could lead to doctoral studies at these institutions.

I was aware that, from the standpoint of the behavioral economics that I had so far encountered, what I was doing might seem to be a case of satisficing with needlessly low aspirations and local search. I knew that if I got a first in Part II, I probably had a chance of winning a postgraduate scholarship wherever in the world I wanted to study: John Eatwell provided a role model for such a pathway, for after studying as an undergraduate at Queens' he had done his PhD at Harvard. Taking that route would require me first to take a GMAT examination, and a typical modern behavioral economist would no doubt see my reluctance to follow in Eatwell's footsteps in terms of hyperbolic discounting and present bias regarding the hassle of meeting the GMAT requirement. But I had some more basic issues about studying in North America, each of which I viewed as a deal-breaker in its own right. One of them was the kind of program that would be entailed. All I really wanted to do was to get straight into research, with the aid of world-leading library facilities, without any further coursework.

Cambridge ticked those boxes. I did not want to go to a top-tier department in the USA to take courses that would improve my technical skills for doing mainstream economics; rather, I simply wanted to get on with doing the kind of economics that excited me, a mixture of behavioral, evolutionary, and Post Keynesian economics. I had no plan to get a PhD as a stepping-stone to an academic career, or to any other career; I just wanted to get a better understanding of how the economic system worked. It was as simple as that. Working out what career I wanted to pursue was something I could do later.

My attitude toward US postgraduate economics would probably be viewed by mainstream economists as presumptuous. It was not based on careful research, merely on Ajit Singh's assertion that what my classmates and I had learned even in the Cambridge Prelims year went conceptually beyond what one would do in a well-ranked US postgraduate program before being allowed to advance to a PhD. This was the great advantage of focusing on methods and concepts, often via primary sources, rather than on mastering techniques required for solving closed problems set out in advanced textbooks. My position was, and remains, that rigorous economic thinking does not have to be based on formal models, and formal models may be precise on their own terms yet be built on logically questionable foundations.

When I asked Ajit what an economics PhD entailed, his answer was simple. In essence, he said, "You spend three years writing a book in which you make an original contribution to economic knowledge." I imagined that, before I came to write my thesis, I would spend a lot of time reading critically what others had written and looking for clues about the kind of contribution I could make. However, I had not ruled out the idea of doing empirical work as a major part of my thesis and I presumed that I would be able to pick up relevant empirical techniques if the need arose.

Clearly, I needed a fallback position in case I failed to do well enough to get a scholarship to stay on in Cambridge. I hoped that my application to the UCL master's program would provide one for me. This time, Michael Stewart interviewed me and once again UCL was willing to serve as my fallback; I do not recall pursuing the LSE or York applications any further once the UCL offer arrived.

In the end, I got a first in Part II and a PhD place in Cambridge. On graduation day, I returned to my former room at Queens' and found a note pinned to the armchair instructing me to ring John Llewellyn immediately. John held the position of Assistant Director of Research, which meant that he managed the Cambridge PhD program in economics. I went down to the porters' lodge and phoned him. It was a very short conversation. He told me that he had one fewer Social Science Research Council PhD scholarship than he had suitable candidates. (The number of scholarships was either three or four, rather fewer than I had imagined Cambridge would get.) He then asked, "Do you want one of these scholarships? Yes or no, now!" I said "Yes," thanked him and went back to my room to continue getting ready for the graduation procession.

# 3 Cambridge Research Student, 1977–1979

## 3.1   INTRODUCTION

During the years that I worked toward my Cambridge PhD, my focus as a behavioral economist shifted away from firms, other organizations, and fundamentalist Keynesian macroeconomics to the analysis of consumer behavior. This change of focus took place in my third year of research. By that time, problems with my initial attempt to get confirmation as a doctoral student had set in motion a train of events that had resulted in me ending my period of residence in Cambridge as a research student at the end of my second academic year and becoming a remote research student based at the University of Stirling in Scotland. This chapter covers what happened up to that point, following my return to Cambridge in October 1977 in my new role as a research student. Chapter 4 covers the rest of my PhD saga, which ran for my entire stint at Stirling. While I regard my experience as a Cambridge undergraduate as a valuable privilege, it will be evident from this chapter and Chapter 4 that my experience as a Cambridge research student was frustrating and needlessly protracted. I only got through it due to having considerable reserves of personal resilience. What follows in this chapter and Chapter 4 is both a Cambridge horror story as well as an account of how I continued my behavioral economics journey.

My horror story is far from unusual, but it at least had a better outcome than the sagas of many other Cambridge research students. The problems that I and others experienced despite being very industrious and having previously been very high achievers were rooted in the system in which we tried to arrive at finished dissertations that would satisfy examiners. It was a system that badly needed to be modernized with a focus on risk-management issues.

At that time, the process of doing a PhD in Economics in Cambridge was essentially the same as it was exactly a quarter of a century earlier when Brian Loasby, my mentor-to-be, had embarked upon his own attempt to get a Cambridge doctorate. (Like me, he had achieved first-class honours in the Economics Tripos and previously attended a public-sector grammar school whose staff knew how to place its top students in Cambridge.) About the only difference was that the Wrenbury Scholarship that I was awarded by the University in 1977 was worth far less than it had been when it was awarded to Brian in 1952, as it had not been indexed to inflation. Hence, the great bulk of my funding came from my Social Science Research Council Scholarship.

The essence of the system was that research students had just one supervisor, with whom they met very infrequently; otherwise, they operated very much by themselves. They were free to attend any of the Economics Tripos lectures, but the general view in the Faculty seemed to be that there was no need to put on advanced coursework for PhD students since the level at which undergraduate teaching took place was far more advanced than elsewhere. That view might seem arrogant and hubristic, but to me, given what I had experienced as an undergraduate, it seemed perfectly reasonable at the time. Where research students needed to learn new techniques, they taught themselves, sometimes in collaboration with fellow students whose needs were similar (as Duncan Ironmonger, a late 1950s Cambridge PhD student, recalled in an interview reported in Earl, Markey-Towler and Coutts, 2022).

In contrast to a well-run graduate program in the 2020s, Cambridge's research students in Economics were not provided with handbooks that detailed the process of getting a PhD, or templates for their PhD confirmation document or final thesis, and there were no requirements to make public presentations of one's work at annual "review milestones." Hence, it was a case of feeling one's way forward in the dark, with no role models except for what could be inferred from books based on PhD dissertations.

Of course, there was potential for supervisors to share their experiences with their supervisees, but if supervisors were both elusive and had not themselves obtained PhDs, there was potential for research students to flounder for want of strategic advice about how to get through the program successfully. As a result, a significant proportion of research students failed to complete and submit dissertations. Many of those who managed to submit were required to revise and resubmit, as happened in my case. Some only ended up with an MLitt (as in the case of Brian Loasby) or failed outright.

Cambridge was not the only institution to have terrible completion and pass rates for its doctoral students: by the time I was well into my saga, things had been recognized to be so bad in the UK's research higher degrees system that questions were being asked about the amount of money the Social Science Research Council was wasting through its research scholarships. The Conservative government that was elected in 1979 was also hostile to social science disciplines such as sociology. Two major inquiries were therefore conducted: see Rothschild (1982) and Swinnerton-Dyer (1982), after which the SSRC was given an expanded remit and renamed as the Economic and Social Research Council. It was indeed fortunate that, in those days, it was still possible to build an academic career even if one did not achieve a doctorate.

## 3.2    GETTING STARTED AS A RESEARCH STUDENT

After an induction that was nothing more than a morning tea for my cohort, my first task was to find myself a supervisor. In contrast to common practice today, the application process had not required applicants to have enlisted support from a supervisor prior to submitting an application. Given the size of Cambridge's Faculty of Economics and Politics, it was reasonable to expect that finding a suitable supervisor should not be a problem. In my case, however, the difficulties I had in getting supervision set the tone for the rest of my experience as a research student.

At the time that I applied for a place in the PhD program, my tentative project title was "A Keynesian Approach to Structural Change." What I wanted to study was how an economy achieves coordination at the sectoral level as patterns of demand change and as innovations occur. I was concerned that the price system had shortcomings as a signaling mechanism (as I had explained in my entry for the Adam Smith Essay Competition) and that, given what I knew from behavioral economics and organization theory, firms might not be as responsive or adaptable as the proponents of the market mechanism seemed to presume. I called it a "Keynesian" approach because it was related to what Keynes had addressed at the level of the economy as a whole via a focus on the saving/investment coordination problem and possible failures in market signaling mechanisms.

In my "Keynesian" vision of the challenges that structural changes pose, the possible failure of firms to respond effectively and in an orderly manner to changing conditions played a role that was analogous to how Keynes saw the possible failure of money markets to prevent deflationary or inflationary gaps in his aggregate-level analysis of the problem of avoiding unemployment and/or inflation. Moreover, as Goodhart (1975) had pointed out via Coase (1937), firms and money are institutions that emerged due to transaction cost problems: both exist to provide cost-effective ways of dealing with contingencies as they arise and for employing better knowledge if and when it becomes available. Neither firms nor money have any role in the idealized static, transaction cost-free world of general equilibrium theory, in which there are no macroeconomic problems or problems of structural adjustment because production does not commence until contingent claims contracts that address all possible states of the world have been concluded for the purchase of inputs and outputs.

Given that my thinking about structural change and coordination had been triggered by the roles that Ajit Singh, Ken Coutts and Alan Hughes had played in my undergraduate studies, it might appear that I was spoiled for choice when it came to finding a supervisor. But this was not the case. Ajit had not volunteered to be my supervisor and I felt it was not wise to ask him to serve in the role given that one of my key ideas clashed with his claims about the policy implications of his work on de-industrialization (Singh, 1977). The issue harked back to the clash to which I had been introduced at high school between Myrdal's view of cumulative causation and Bauer's view that vicious circles can be broken, given determination to do so, because systems usually have some slack. Ajit was very much in the Myrdal camp and hence saw a strong case for import controls and other government intervention to help firms in the UK recover lost ground against their overseas rivals, particularly firms in Germany and Japan. I was less sure what was needed, for I recognized that although slack provides a basis from which recovery or development may be possible without assistance, it may instead be used as a means of carrying on with outmoded ways until it is too late to recover.

Alan Hughes therefore seemed a better choice as a potential supervisor, for it was he who had introduced me to the industrial economics equivalent of Myrdal versus Bauer, namely Downie's (1958) analysis of the "transfer mechanism" versus the "innovation mechanism." But Alan was still enrolled for a PhD himself, which meant that he was precluded from being a PhD supervisor. The same applied for Ken Coutts. I think it was John Llewellyn who then suggested that Richard Goodwin might be interested, given his work on economic dynamics and because he had supervised Paul Stoneman's PhD on the uptake of computers in the UK (published in slightly revised form as Stoneman, 1976). I went to see Goodwin, but he was not interested.

The only other person who was suggested to me was James Trevithick, my monetary economics supervisor for Part II. He did not have a PhD and had not been in Cambridge very long, but he seemed to be gaining some traction as a Keynes scholar as well as for his work on inflation: my Part II supervisions with him had entailed traipsing out to Fitzwilliam College, but now he was a fellow at King's with a room in the magnificent Palladian-style Gibbs Building. Although much of what I intended to do was not in his zone at all, the "Keynesian" tag was enough for him to agree to take on the role. It is possible that I was his first research student and that he felt some pressure to accept the role as part of the process of getting a firm foothold in Cambridge.

Aside from finding a supervisor, the only initial formal task was an interview with senior members of the Faculty of Economics and Politics. A few weeks after term started, John Llewellyn's secretary asked if I would be able to come in for a Saturday morning chat with some of the staff. She did not give any indication that when I was shown into the room, I would be the only research student present and would find myself facing David Champernowne, Phyllis Deane and Frank Hahn, along with John Llewellyn (and one or two others that I do not recall with certainty). Very soon it became clear that this was not a welcome but an interview. I was asked to explain what my research topic was and my key ideas, and John Llewellyn then invited the senior staff to question me in turn. I have no recollection of the questions or my replies, but what I do recall is that when it was Frank Hahn's turn, he declined to ask me anything and said, to the others, "He's clearly an economics poet."

Hahn's arrogant put-down seemed less insulting after I heard him used the same phrase on my next encounter with him. The latter occasion was about a year later at a meeting of the Political Economy Club (for high-flying undergraduates) held one evening at Hahn's house. I attended it to support Chris Chaloner, the star Queens' undergraduate, who was giving a paper about the role of slack in economic systems. The paper was based on sources on the behavioral theory of the firm and economic coordination that I had fed to him during Prelims supervisions. This time, "economics poet" was applied to Brian Loasby, whose thinking figured in Chris's paper. So, I was in good company when it came to being an "economics poet"! I also warmed to Hahn on that occasion because it was clear that he was listening with interest and knew of the behavioral theory of the firm and the notion of $X$-inefficiency: when Oliver Hart was having trouble getting his head around what Chris was saying about the nature of organizational slack, Hahn cut in and said, "No, he's perfectly right on this."

As my first term as a research student progressed, I began to wonder whether I should have continued searching rather than agreeing to have Trevithick as my supervisor. On the rare occasions that we met, his focus seemed to be on me fitting in with his research activities rather that serving as a mentor to me in relation to what I was proposing to do. I realized that I was probably going to have to fend for myself when he suggested I should read a recent neo-Keynesian book by Barro and Grossman (1976): it had nothing to do with what I was proposing to do but it was one of two books that were the subject of a review article he was preparing (published as Trevithick, 1978). My next task was to comment on his draft, which he probably viewed as a good research training activity, something that I would not have had to do as an undergraduate. However, I now think that the key issue underlying our failure to develop an effective, regular working relationship was probably that neither of us had a clear sense of how we should be interacting, especially given that I was concentrating on reading things that mostly were in fields outside his comfort zone.

The feeling of isolation that my supervisory situation produced was compounded by a decision that I made in the first week: I was not going to work in the research students' room below the Marshall Library and would instead carry on working in the library itself just as I had as an undergraduate. I realized that it would limit my chances of getting to know other research students in economics, but using the room came at the price of having to put up with cigarette smoke, whereas the library was a smoke-free zone. I thus had no idea about what kind of supervision experience my peers were having. At one point, I went to see Ian Gosling, one of my Alleyne's classmates, who had returned to Emmanuel College after getting a double-first in mathematics and physics, to see how he was faring as a research student in electrical engineering. Sadly, his situation was rather like mine.

It might seem that another reference point would have been my Queens' contemporary, Andy Vickerman, with whom I was sharing the supervision of the Queens' Prelims students in Economics. But I did not get a sense of how he was faring. Unlike me, Andy lived out of college, so it had been decided that he would use my room as a venue for holding his supervisions of Queens' Prelims students. Andy was a smoker, as were some of his students. Each time I returned to my room after they had been there, it reeked of tobacco smoke, despite the "No Smoking" reminder I had chalked on my blackboard before heading off to the Marshall Library. Never very close as undergraduates, Andy and I were now barely on speaking terms. Unfortunately, his PhD experience was to prove very like mine, with his thesis listing in the Cambridge University Library even having the same approval date as is listed for mine, namely, July 13, 1984. (A version of his thesis was published as Vickerman, 1985.)

My first day in the Marshall Library in my research student role had also been very disconcerting. I had planned to begin by reading Brian Loasby's (1976) *Choice, Complexity and Ignorance.* I had seen it on display in Heffers Bookshop during Part II, and I had sensed that it might bring the perspectives of Shackle and Simon together. However, I had decided to delay reading it until I was free from the essay-writing treadmill. A minor surprise was that the Marshall did not have a copy listed in its card catalogue. That was easily remedied: I pointed out the gap to Mr Finkel, the librarian, and he said he would get a copy from Heffers right away. But there was a big shock at the point in the catalogue where I had expected to find Loasby's book, namely a card that referred to a recent discussion paper that he had written. Its title was "On imperfections and adjustments" (Loasby, 1977, which eventually led to chapter 6 of Loasby, 1989). My heart sank: I correctly surmised that I was going to learn from it that what I had argued in my Adam Smith Essay about the coordination problem and the beneficial aspects of so-called "market imperfections" as facilitators of orderly structural adjustments had already been argued by someone else. Day one of my PhD thereby became the day that I discovered George Richardson's neglected (1960) book *Information and Investment* and that I had reinvented what is now known, by those who know about its origins, as "the Richardson problem."

The discovery that I had reinvented Richardson's core idea meant that one aspect of what I hoped to write about in making my "original contribution to knowledge" had evaporated. But on seeing that Richardson had developed his analysis of the investment coordination problem into a PhD-length book, I got a sense of confidence about my critical and creative thinking capacities: it showed what I might have been able to do if he had not done it already. There was also a sense of relief that I was not alone in worrying about the standard view of how the market mechanism works. But it was also a lesson that I should proceed very carefully in developing my knowledge of the literature to ensure that the ideas that I had for my thesis were original.

In the absence of online citation tracking tools or the kind of powerful search engine that a modern academic library offers, this was a much more challenging task than it is for today's doctoral students. I realized that I was going to have to be vigilant in following up sources from reference lists and footnotes.[4] The task was going to be like that of a detective, always on the lookout for new leads and clues. I soon saw the significance of self-citations for nudging readers to explore the genealogy of one's ideas, and that, by publishing in a restricted set of journals, one could make it easier for others to find one's more recent contributions if they latched on to one's earlier publications. Further clues about relevant sources could come from carefully reading prefaces to books and acknowledgment footnotes in articles. But the whole process could be accelerated if one had a supervisor who had extensive knowledge of the area in which one had chosen to conduct research.

As I did not have such a supervisor, the foundations for my first year of research came from the reference lists in Loasby's *Choice, Complexity and*

---

[4] For example, it soon became apparent that I could have discovered Richardson in my Prelims year: on re-reading the section of Leijonhufvud (1968, pp. 69–70) that had triggered my interest in the impact of uncertainty on market coordination, I discovered footnote references to Richardson. Moreover, on looking through my notes from Alan Hughes's Part II lectures on industrial organization, I discovered that *Information and Investment* was on his reading list. Alan had been one of the assessors for the Adam Smith Essay Competition, so this discovery left me with the uneasy thought that he might have wondered whether I had plagiarized Richardson's analysis.

*Ignorance* and Williamson's (1975) *Markets and Hierarchies*, and – as had happened in my discovery of the latter – by delving into books that were adjacent on the library shelves to works that Loasby and Williamson cited. I also came to see the need to be determined to track down sources that were missing from the Marshall's shelves (as was the case with Richardson's *Information and Investment* whenever I tried to find it there), even if this meant making a trip to the University Library. It could be hazardous to tell oneself that "I'll get to it later" because of the risk of forgetting to do so. Trying to make do with a review of an absent book could be hazardous, too, if the reviewer failed to convey the key messages correctly.

## 3.3    LOASBY'S APPROACH TO ECONOMICS

My plan to start my research by reading Brian Loasby's *Choice, Complexity and Ignorance* had major consequences, both via its impact on my view of behavioral economics and for my career. Given this, it is appropriate to provide some background material at this juncture about Loasby's own career and view of economics. These days, he is probably best known to evolutionary economists, particularly via his books *Equilibrium and Evolution* (1991) and *Knowledge, Institutions and Evolution in Economics* (1999) (which was a joint winner of the 2000 J. A. Schumpeter Prize), but his prolific output (which I have catalogued in Earl, 2023d) has a remarkably consistency ever since his first publications in the mid-1960s. He has never styled himself as a behavioral economist; instead, beginning with an early paper (Loasby, 1967b), "management economics" has been his preferred term for the kind of economics that he does, and when the University of Stirling promoted him to a chair in 1971, he requested that his title should be Professor of Management Economics. An understanding of what Loasby means by management economics is essential if one is to appreciate the wider vision of behavioral economics that I advocate. This is most readily attained via knowledge of Loasby's career up to 1967, the year he became a lecturer in economics at the newly opened University of Stirling.

Loasby was born in 1930 and grew up in Kettering, Northamptonshire, UK, where he attended Kettering Grammar School. Kettering experienced rapid growth in the second half of the nineteenth century because of the impact that the invention of the sewing machine had on the economics of what became its main industry, the manufacture of boots and shoes. By the time that Loasby was a Cambridge undergraduate, it was clear to him that Kettering's boot and shoe firms operated in a market that was chronically out of equilibrium, as were its constituent firms: there was considerable entry and exit, with much of the entry coming from businesses set up by former employees of existing firms. These entrepreneurs had typically either been "clickers" (who cut leather parts as economically as possible from hides) or had been involved in the marketing of shoes – in other words, they had the key capabilities needed for success in this sector. This industry was easy to reconcile with Marshall's (1890) analysis of the firm but when Loasby was a Cambridge undergraduate (1949–1952) he realized that it did not align with the equilibrium-focused view of firms under "imperfect" competition that Joan Robinson (1933) had proposed and on which she lectured. Moreover, Loasby could not see how managers of real firms could acquire the knowledge needed to attain equilibria of the kind that Robinson postulated, whereby prices and outputs were arrived at by finding where marginal costs and marginal revenues were equal.

Loasby's concerns were similar to those held by P. W. S. Andrews, a member of the Oxford Economists' Research Group, whose book *Manufacturing Business* (Andrews, 1949) offered an alternative, neo-/post-Marshallian perspective that was not beset by such problems. Andrews had based his analysis on studies of actual firms, with his data even including interviews with managers who ran some of Kettering's shoe-making firms. He argued that prices were set without reference to marginal revenue by adding a mark-up to "normal costs," with the size of the mark-up being limited by the managers' fears that, if they were too greedy, they would attract new entry – particularly from those who (as in the Kettering case) had acquired key capabilities as employees of incumbent firms, or from established firms diversifying across from industries based on similar technical and marketing capabilities. Andrews argued that, having set their offer prices, firms would supply the volume of output that customers wanted to buy at those prices. Failures to reach target levels of sales would trigger investigations and experimentation with new marketing strategies.

Andrews found that firms typically operated with a greater capacity than the targets they set for their sales. This was so that they could accommodate unexpectedly large numbers of new customers without being unable to serve their established ones. Changes in the population of customers and failures of rival firms to manage adequately their goodwill relationships with customers ensured that opportunities for picking up new customers often arose. Hence, well-managed new firms could hope to see their market shares growing as they succeeded in developing goodwill relationships with more and more customers who gave them repeat business so long as their prices did not drift out of line with those quoted by rivals and they could be counted on to meet delivery deadlines and quality requirements.

Mark-ups could differ between firms, for entrepreneurs did not necessarily have the same view about what constituted a safe profit margin, partly because they differed in their knowledge of the production and marketing processes and hence in the normal costs that they could attain. This was in sharp contrast to Joan Robinson's theoretical world of firms with identical costs and identical ways of responding to changed market conditions.

Andrews's analysis became a major ingredient in Loasby's view of the competitive process, and thereby in mine. However, its adoption by Loasby was delayed because Andrews's work was treated with disdain in Cambridge during the 1950s. Loasby did not start to engage with it seriously until the 1960s after Andrews (1964) had published a critique of the dominant wisdom.

In the interim, Loasby made his unsuccessful attempt to earn a Cambridge PhD. Here, he switched to economic history because he could not see how he might produce a thesis on economic theory, and his dissertation was on "The Economic Development of Kettering, 1850–1914." He produced his thesis under a succession of supervisors, none of whom seem to have pulled him up for not building his analysis around an economic model (for which Andrews's analysis could have served as a starting point if anyone had encouraged him in that direction). The thesis seems to have been completed while he was holding a three-year position at the University of Aberdeen (1955–1958), where he taught economic history. However, the absence of an economic model of Kettering's transformation process was viewed as a major flaw during the examination process, so he was awarded his MLitt without being given an opportunity to revise and resubmit his dissertation.

The dissertation had drawn not merely on archival material but also on interviews with managers of long-established Kettering businesses. The experience that Loasby had thereby gained in interviewing businesspeople helped him get a research fellowship at the University of Birmingham (1958–1961) to study how firms were dealing with location policies that made it very difficult for them to expand to new premises unless they did so by relocating to one of the UK's peripheral "development areas" (i.e., relatively depressed industrial areas) or to one of the new towns (e.g., Stevenage) that were being built as part of the post-war reconstruction process.

This work was pivotal for Loasby, for it brought him back to economics and led him to start to construe managerial decision processes in ways that had similarities with ideas that Simon, Cyert and March were developing around the same time into a behavioral view of the firm. Loasby discovered that many firms ended up avoiding the need to relocate, or found that they could eliminate the downsides of growing by relocating, by searching and finding ways of reorganizing how they operated their businesses. What they discovered often could have been discovered much earlier but they had not been looking for it (Loasby, 1967a). In Simon's terms, we could say that they had been satisficing and their first response when they ran out of space was often to search locally for bigger premises.

So, before discovering the work of Simon, Cyert and March. Loasby thereby came to recognize a key issue that underlies Simon's work on bounded rationality, namely, that attention is a scarce managerial resource and the economies that firms achieve therefore depend on the questions that their staff attempt to answer. Hence, a key aspect of research on the behavior of firms should be on the process of "problem finding," i.e., on what causes managers to notice the things that they classify as problems, why they classify them as such, and why they deem them worthy of attention.

Next, Loasby worked at the University of Bristol (1961–1967), beginning as a tutor in management. This role was another opportunity for him to use his experience in interacting with managers of firms, for the program at Bristol involved a sandwich arrangement with classroom elements either side of a practical component in each student's normal place of work. This was at a time when it was not easy to find academic staff with the skill sets needed for teaching executives in business schools, and Loasby was given the opportunity to spend the 1965–1966 academic year in the USA as an Arthur D. Little Fellow to develop his expertise in executive education.

This was the transformative year of his career, both via its impact on how he viewed decision-making and because it triggered a series of events that led him to get to know one of his key influences, Charles Suckling (an industrial chemist who was a senior executive at ICI) and culminated in him being offered a lectureship at the University of Stirling in Scotland. The Arthur D. Little Fellowship entailed attending courses at both Harvard Business School and MIT (which he perceived to have very different ways of operating and were capable of helping executives acquire different sets of capabilities), as well as being involved in Little's management consulting work. Even so, it left him time to visit Carnegie-Mellon University and meet with the pioneers of the behavioral theory of the firm, whose work had aroused early interest among those involved in the management program at Bristol.

It was during this period that he recognized that the problems that managers found and sought to address were often unexpected consequences of their previous attempts to solve other problems. He thus came to be skeptical of attempts to construct equilibrium-based models of the growth of firms, for (as in Penrose, 1959) the growth of firms seemed to be driven by growth in what their staff knew, which came about via their participation in problem-solving processes. He embraced with enthusiasm the "decision cycle" notion employed by both David Clarke, one of his senior colleagues at Bristol, and Bill Pounds, the then-director of the Sloan School of Management at MIT. (The latter did so in a paper eventually published as Pounds, 1969.)

From the decision cycle standpoint, decision-making is viewed as a kind of helical process wherein problem recognition –> search for solutions –> evaluation of potential solutions –> choice –> attempts to implement the preferred option –> hindsight review –> problem recognition, and so on, with decision sub-cycles commonly being nested within the various stages of each main cycle. It is the ongoing processes of change, that results from humans being unable fully to foresee the future and the implications of their choices, that Loasby has in mind when he refers to evolution in economic systems. When changes are made, they typically entail the application of new rules, new ways of organizing, thinking about, and doing things.

This view of management enabled Loasby (and, via his *Choice, Complexity and Ignorance*, me) to be comfortable about adopting Andrews's view of the firm even though Andrews was highly critical of the behavioral theory of the firm (see Andrews and Brunner, 1975, p. 1), as he felt that it (like other "new theories of the firm" that were proposed in the period 1958–1964) paid insufficient attention to the pressure of competition, both from external rivals and between promotion-hungry colleagues. Andrews saw such pressures as ensuring that managers tried to maximize profits in the long run. To him, satisficing behavior required a slack competitive environment. However, satisficing behavior is not inherently a manifestation of poor motivation and a "that will do" mentality such as that of a student who is capable of getting a distinction but aims merely for a pass.

Even if one is very keen to find ways of trimming costs and increasing sales, the fundamental challenge is to know how to allocate one's attention effectively. Defining whether problems exist via the use of targets and external reference standards is a means for allocating attention when operating under pressure and without knowledge of the bounds of what might be achievable. In hotly contested environments, potential entrants need to be confident that they can meet performance targets that will be high enough to enable them to survive and grow, while incumbents will need to keep aiming higher if they are to remain competitive. The problem is to know how high it is reasonable to aim in any performance area, as over-ambitious targets may result in the diversion of management attention into trying to deal with "problems" that they cannot solve, away from areas where they might have been able to get better outcomes if they had set more ambitious targets that were actually feasible.


## 3.4   FIRST ATTEMPT TO OBTAIN CONFIRMATION AS A DOCTORAL CANDIDATE

Research students in Cambridge were initially enrolled merely as master's students. To claim to be a PhD student, one had to get one's candidature confirmed as such. This may sound like what commonly happens in the 2020s, where students in well-designed research higher degree programs are commonly required to survive a set of milestone tests held at roughly twelve-month intervals on the way to submitting their dissertations for examination. In such systems, confirmation of candidature is the first milestone, followed by mid-term review, and thesis review. However, the system that I experienced did not have any further progress review stages.

Confirmation recommendations were made to the Board of Graduate Studies by an independent committee but any understanding of what the committee expected had to be arrived at with little advice from the program coordinator and without any resources such as a program handbook or document templates. The confirmation process was based purely on a piece of written work, the "thesis proposal." Hence, there were no confirmation presentations by other students that one might attend as a means of getting an idea of what was expected. This amplified the need for an experienced and committed supervisor.

I do not recall being given any instructions on what a thesis proposal should look like or the criteria in terms of which it would be assessed. In the absence of effective guidance, my path to confirmation of candidature as a PhD student proved to be far longer and more troubled than that which a modern student is allowed to experience.

*Attempt 1 (1978): A Keynesian Approach to Structural Change*
Before getting to the confirmation stage, there was another fuzzy requirement: one had to submit, by the end of April in one's first academic year as a research student, "a substantial piece of work" as evidence of what one had been doing. So, toward the end of March 1978, after six months of reading, I began to type my "substantial piece of work" on a manual Smith Corona typewriter. The ensuing five weeks were grueling both for my fingers and for the typewriter. The latter had hardly been used in the decade or so since my mother had

purchased it to see whether she could learn to type. After four weeks, the machine was showing signs that it was not an office-grade tool, for the paper roller was giving trouble, but it had enabled me to produce a 147-page document (and a carbon copy) entitled "A Keynesian approach to structural change." I was happy with it, but in the absence of any guidelines, I had produced a piece of work that was far too substantial. By this stage, John Llewellyn had left to take up a position in Paris as a senior economist at the OECD. His replacement as Assistant Director of Research was one of my Part II supervisors, Geoff Meeks. Just before I finished my tome, I saw Geoff and reported on my progress. He was alarmed to hear how substantial my document was, and he said that he would never be able to get anyone to agree to read it at that length. He therefore directed me to spend the remaining week before the submission deadline writing a version of it that was no more than about thirty pages in length.

I managed to deliver it on time. However, given that the typing experience left me fearing that I might damage my fingers, it was the last thing I ever typed on a manual typewriter. As luck would have it, an Adler electric typewriter came my way in time to use a couple of months later when I was preparing my thesis proposal: a fellow Queens' postgraduate asked me to mind it for him while he took a year out from his studies.

The feedback on my "substantial piece of work" was not extensive and I cannot recall that it proved to be of great use when I wrote my thesis proposal document. Again, there was little advice on what was required beyond a summary of what one had done during the first year of research and what one planned if one achieved confirmation. The document that I submitted consisted of ten, single-space pages, the first six and a half of which summarized and neatly categorized the reading that I had been doing. My thoughts on what I might do next amounted to slightly less than two pages, and the remainder of the document consisted of the list of references. I suggested two possible research projects as sequels to what I had done so far.

The first project would have been reasonably straightforward to undertake, namely, a study of the impact that switching to an organizational structure based on mini-firms-within-the-firm "profit centers" had on the performance of firms in the UK context. In a PhD-based book, Channon (1973) had detailed how firms in the UK had adopted this "M-form" kind of structure, often in the process of following advice from the McKinsey consulting group, but he had not explored the effect that the change had on their financial performance or productivity. The fact that it seemed an obvious opportunity made me nervous that it might not be substantial enough for a PhD and that other researchers might also be attempting to do it. My caution turned out to be justified, for very soon after, in the

September 1978 issue of the *Journal of Industrial Economics*, Steer and Cable published a paper that reported the results of a study that did something akin to what I had envisaged. It was indeed useful to be mindful of the Richardson investment coordination problem in the market for contributions to economic knowledge.[5]

My second project proposal was spelled out at much greater length. It was essentially an extension of my original "Keynesian approach to structural change" idea, presented with a closing emphasis on Leijonhufvud's (1969, 1973) urging of economists to study why multiplier processes usually do not work explosively, and what role system buffering plays in damping these processes. However, this time it was framed explicitly as aiming to test Ajit Singh's contention that unorthodox policy measures were necessary to prevent the further de-industrialization of the UK economy that was otherwise inevitable because of cumulative causation processes having taken hold (Singh, 1977). Rather than framing my thinking in terms of Downie's transfer mechanism versus his innovation mechanism, I stressed the need to study the different learning curves that UK firms and their overseas rivals were on, and the responsiveness of UK firms to growing existential threats: the slower their responses, the more challenging their performance turnarounds would be insofar as differences between them and their overseas rivals became amplified by differences in their learning curves.

To conduct the latter empirical investigation, I would need firm-level data, and therein lay the key problem, for unlike Downie, I was not a public servant who could get access to raw data from the Census of Production. I therefore tentatively suggested that I might be able to get data via bodies such as the Business Ratios organization that enable firms to learn where they stand in the pecking order for their line of business, and from industry-level development agencies such as those whose reports on structural change I had read.

My attempt at confirmation was not successful. In looking at it from the standpoint of my later PhD administrator roles, I have no hesitation in saying that Phyllis Deane and her committee were entirely right in deciding not to recommend me for confirmation as a PhD student, even though the process did not provide any opportunity for me to discuss my proposal with them, defend my position by addressing any questions they might have, or discuss any ideas they might have about how to extend what I had been doing into a viable study. In a well-run modern system, a student would get all of these opportunities.

---

[5] Many years later, I wrote a paper (Earl, 1995b) about the relevance of Richardson's idea in relation to academic work, which was presented at a colloquium held at St John's College, Oxford in Richardson's honour.

With hindsight, I think that there were two kinds of things that I could have been encouraged to consider on structural change and corporate responses to increasingly challenging external conditions. One possibility would have been a more case study-based approach in which I examined differences between firms that managed to "dig themselves out of a hole," versus competitors that "went to the wall." This would have been a precursor to works such as Erica Schoenberger's (1997) book *The Cultural Crisis of the Firm* and Clayton Christensen's (1997) PhD-based book *The Innovator's Dilemma*. In a sense, my 1984 book *The Corporate Imagination: How Big Companies Make Mistakes* went in this direction: it used much of the reading on which this attempt at confirmation was based, supplemented by case study work taken from business history. That book took a scientific paradigms-/research programs-based view of firms and the difficulties that they often have in adapting to change, which was very much a precursor to Schoenberger's analysis. I had picked up from Loasby (1976) the idea that novel industrial products were prone to face skepticism and resistance similar to that faced by new scientific paradigms (which Loasby had picked up from a Stirling PhD on technological economics and which he illustrated with reference to resistance to Halothane, a new anaesthetic). However, I did not arrive at the corporate strategy-level version of this view until late in the autumn of 1978.

The other possibility that I can now see probably would not have been feasible back in 1978 due to limited computing resources: there was scope for developing a multi-firm simulation model to explore how an industry evolves when firms experience different rates of learning-by-doing and differ in their responsiveness to falling attainments.

## 3.5    UNEXPECTED CONSEQUENCES OF A CHANGE OF SUPERVISOR

The failure of my first attempt at confirmation led me to reflect seriously on my future as a research student. Given that I was not focusing on macroeconomics, it was clear that James Trevithick was not the right supervisor for me. Perhaps we might have developed an effective working relationship if I had opted to go down the road of mining Keynes's *Collected Writings*. I readily could have done this: I had already read (and referred to in my first confirmation attempt) a loose-leaf draft of what was then catalogued in the Marshall Library as "Volume 14b" but which eventually appeared as Volume 29 (Keynes, 1979), and between October 1978 and February 1979, I wrote three papers on Keynes, money, and unemployment, the first of which used ideas from that loose-leaf volume. These papers were never submitted for publication but ideas from them were eventually used in Dow and Earl (1982, especially chapter 8) and Earl (1990b).

My concerns about the Richardson problem applying with academic research investments seemed relevant in this area, too, and once again they were justified: Roy Rotheim soon went down the track that I imagined taking via a "Keynes (1936) chapter 17" view of the theory of value, augmented via material from Volume 29 of Keynes's *Collected Writings*, and he did so to very good effect (see especially Rotheim, 1981). But a more fundamental reason why I did not become a Keynes scholar was that I felt I had got enough out of Keynes already and that my biggest interests centered on structural adjustments and the efficiency and evolution of firms. Given this, I felt that I needed either to get a new supervisor or to call it quits as far as a PhD was concerned and pursue my interests in the more hands-on world of management consulting. I decided to arrange a meeting to put this to Geoff Meeks before heading off to spend my summer break back at home in Stevenage.

Geoff immediately gave the impression that he would do whatever was necessary to deter me from pulling out. He did not start thinking aloud about whether he might himself be the supervisor I was looking for. This was despite the fact that he might have been a potential supervisor, given that I had liked his recently published PhD-based book on the impact of mergers on corporate performance (Meeks, 1977). Nor did he ask why I was not suggesting having Ajit Singh as my supervisor. Instead, he said that it was possible to arrange an external supervisor if an appropriate case could be made. He then asked me to name the person I would like to have, given that possibility. Without hesitation, I said, "Professor Brian Loasby, of the University of Stirling." Geoff told me to leave the matter to him and he would see if this could be arranged.

A few weeks later, during my break back at home, I was reading *The Economist* in Stevenage Central Library and noticed an advertisement for a teaching assistant, two lecturers (assistant professors) and a senior lecturer at the University of Stirling. I contacted Geoff to see whether he thought it would be appropriate for me to apply for the teaching assistant position or even for a lectureship as a means of working alongside Loasby if he became my supervisor. Geoff advised me only to apply for a lectureship and pointed out that even if I did not get the job, I might at least get an expenses-paid trip to Stirling for an interview and thereby get to meet Loasby. I took his advice and did indeed get an interview – despite sending only a very brief application letter in which I named my referees, mentioned what my potential areas of interest in teaching were and that I was a research student, without even saying how well I had performed as an undergraduate.

The interview at Stirling did not take place until late October or early November 1978. In the meantime, I ploughed on without any supervision or sense of where I should be trying to go as far as the PhD was concerned. I decided that it might be useful to get my thoughts clear on the intersection between unemployment associated with deficient aggregate demand and unemployment associated with coordination failures as the structure of aggregate demand changed and new technologies were introduced. This resulted in the first of my three Keynes-related papers, and much of it sought to confront Keynes's views with those of Hayek, mindful of material in the "Volume 14b" draft about the distinction between a monetary economy and a barter-style system in which workers shared entrepreneurial risks. The technology side of the paper was inspired by a Part II lecture by Michael Posner on whether it made sense to provide financial support to factories on Merseyside that made telephone exchange switchgear that had been rendered obsolete. After consulting with Geoff Meeks, I sent the paper to Brian Loasby so that he could get a sense of what I could do. His reaction to the paper turned out to be a sign of how things were going to be with him as my supervisor.

I spent the morning before my Stirling job interview talking to Loasby. After explaining that he was on sabbatical and therefore was not part of the hiring process, he turned to my paper, saying that, coincidentally, he, too, had recently been reading some of the Hayek works to which I had referred. He then launched into a monologue that began with his thoughts on Hayek. Then, after also noting my interest in system buffering, he started drawing connections with some of his favorite sources. It was like being treated to a live improvisation in the broad area of *Choice, Complexity and Ignorance*. But in the weeks that followed I received no written feedback from him on the paper that I had sent to him, and I ended up simply filing it away. On re-reading it during the research for this chapter, I realize that I probably should have submitted it to the just-established *Journal of Post Keynesian Economics* to see what feedback I got, as it was by no means a terrible paper despite being my first attempt to write something in the journal article format.

Unlike my Saturday morning grilling by the senior Cambridge economists a year earlier, my Stirling job interview was an enjoyable experience. Indeed, I was so relaxed that I even dared at one point to offer a reply that would initially have seemed very flippant. When the chair of the interview panel, Professor Chuck Brown asked how I would teach second-year macroeconomics, I confessed my ignorance of how the first-year macroeconomics was taught and asked what I could take for granted. On being told that it was a standard treatment in the Lipsey or Samuelson vein, I replied, "In that case, I'd be inclined to start again from scratch!" But looks of concern rapidly evaporated when I went on to explain that I would like to present macroeconomics of the kind that I had learned from reading Keynes first-hand, and I thought that Leijonhufvud (1968) had been correct in arguing that, in many ways, the standard textbooks were misrepresenting what Keynes had argued in his *General Theory*.

Within a couple of weeks, I was offered a tenurable lectureship, with only a two-year probationary period. However, I did not immediately accept the offer, as a salary at the bottom of the scale did not look particularly enticing given my current income from my SSRC scholarship and from supervising undergraduates. Furthermore, as one of two Munro Scholars at Queens', I now enjoyed spacious, rent-free accommodation and the right to dine free at high table once a week. The Munro Scholarship had been awarded to me based on the reputation I had rapidly built for my teaching in my first year as a research student (and it was the only teaching award I received in my entire career), but it only lasted for two years, and it was not clear that I would then be able to move up to the next step, a college research fellowship, to see me through to the completion of my PhD.

My delay in reaching a decision resulted in a message in my pigeonhole at Queens' porters' lodge asking me to call Professor Chuck Brown, chair of the Stirling interview panel. Because my application letter had been so brief, he had no idea of what the Munro Scholarship entailed, and after I explained the details to him, he revised the offer two points up the salary scale. He also said that, if I performed well, there were good prospects for me to be given accelerated promotion up the lecturer scale (which had 14 levels beyond the revised offer). I accepted this revised offer, but it turned out initially to leave me feeling poorer than I had been in Cambridge.


## 3.6   SECOND ATTEMPT TO OBTAIN CONFIRMATION AS A DOCTORAL CANDIDATE

Although I accepted the job at Stirling and Brian Loasby became my external supervisor, I had to complete two years of full-term residence in Cambridge as a research student before I could move to Scotland and take up the position. This kept me in Cambridge until June 1979. In March 1979, I submitted my second attempt to get confirmed as a PhD candidate. This time, my proposal focused on economic method. Just after my Stirling interview, I had started to think about the potential for applying Kuhn's (1962) thinking on paradigms and the structure of scientific revolutions to the ways that firms (and, I started to realize, individuals) operated. I therefore thought it would be a good idea to read further on economic method and the philosophy of science. This took me to the work of Lakatos (1970), Feyerabend (1975) and Latsis (ed.) (1976) but not to a proposal to write a thesis under the title that I later gave chapter 5 of my (1984) book *The Corporate Imagination*, namely, "The Structure of Corporate Revolutions." Instead, I abandoned any thoughts of an empirical study of the competitive performance of UK firms.

*Attempt 2 (1979): Progressive and Degenerating Research Programs in Economics: A Lakatosian Appraisal While Applying Lakatos's Methodology of Scientific Research Programs to the History of Economic Thought*

I proposed instead to study whether Lakatos's (1970) methodology of scientific research programs could be used to make sense of the preference of economists for continuing to employ the deterministic, equilibrium-focused approach to economics despite the existence of a body of economic thought that took seriously the open-ended nature of problems that real-world decision makers have to address. To make this project work, I would need to construct a picture of the latter as a scientific research program and then compare its empirical content with that of the orthodox approach. This proposal can to some extent be viewed as intending to go from the first attempt to apply Lakatos's thinking to economics, namely Latsis (1972), to the reappraisal of it eventually offered by Nightingale (1994), while dealing with thorny questions about the kinds of useful empirical content that economists can generate and the problems of specifying what constitutes efficiency in a world in which slack in systems can be welfare-enhancing.

The proposal was partly a consequence of a few letters that Brian Loasby and I exchanged, which resulted in me taking my reading on methodology beyond the work of Kuhn (1962). The proposal's date was March 3, 1979, which was several weeks before the purchase dates that I wrote on my copies of Lakatos (1970) and books on economic method by Hutchison (1938, 1977) and Latsis (ed.) (1976) that I expected to use frequently if the project gained approval. However, I do not recall any detailed discussion with Loasby about the proposal. Given that it was not until February 5, 1979, that I finished the third of my three papers organizing my thoughts on Keynes, money and unemployment, the obvious inference is that this second proposal was cobbled together in haste, possibly to meet a submission deadline. That is not the way to prepare this kind of document.

Late in the afternoon on the day before my candidacy was due to be considered, an envelope was posted under the door of my room at Queens'. It contained a card that read, "Good Luck with the Philistine!" The card was from a student in one of my Part II supervision groups. The members of this group were not from Queens', and we had all become good friends. I had mentioned to them my upcoming milestone and my concern that my progress might once again be thwarted by Phyllis Deane and her committee. The greeting raised an interesting cognitive puzzle: should I view it as indicating wit or as the result of the sender trying (with English as her fourth language) to make sense of what I was saying, without her having ever encountered Deane as a lecturer?

Once again, however, my proposal was rejected. I have been unable to find any written record advising me of the outcome, and it is possible that I simply received verbal notification from Geoff Meeks. My recollection was that I was advised that a methodological thesis would be challenging to present as a contribution to knowledge, and that Phyllis Deane was not convinced that I would be able to demonstrate the existence of a coherent alternative scientific research program in economics along the lines that I outlined. This recollection was confirmed when I discovered in my files a carbon copy of a letter that I had written to Professor Elizabeth Brunner at the University of Lancaster, dated January 29, 1980, seeking clarification about several aspects of her work with P. W. S. Andrews. I explained that I was attempting to piece together what I called a "disequilibrium" approach to economics using elements from "Post-Marshallian industrial economists" (specifically, Andrews, Brunner, Downie, Lamfalussy, Penrose and Richardson), "subjectivists" (here I mentioned Austrians, Keynes, Shackle, and practitioners of the LSE approach to costs epitomized by the papers in Buchanan and Thirlby, eds, 1973), along with American institutionalists and behavioral economists. I mentioned the difficulties I was having with my PhD confirmation and noted that:

The reaction was that:

(a) A methodological work, even one attempting to operate on the additional level of appraising Lakatos's theory of the growth of knowledge as applied to economics, would not contribute [enough] to knowledge given the high standard required in Cambridge.

(b) Phyllis Deane took an unreasonably narrow interpretation of Lakatos and said that because some of the disequilibrium economists attacked each other their work could not conceivably belong to the same research program.

On revisiting my proposal with the benefit of over four decades more experience, I think that the committee rejected the proposal for the wrong reasons but was nonetheless right to force me to have a further rethink. To say that economists cannot be thought of as members of a group because they do not agree on every aspect of how to view the economy is rather like saying that a particular political party is a sham because it is made up of several factions. The key issue for the coherence of a group is whether its members' views of the world intersect in core areas. In the case of the group that I had in mind, these core areas entailed the recognition of uncertainty, that people use rules to cope with the challenges of real-world decision-making, that economizing activity takes place amid events that unfold in historical time, and so on. The relationship between the ideas of Andrews and those of the proponents of the behavioral theory of the firm, considered at the end of Section 3.3, illustrates this issue well: despite making rule- and target-based behavior part of his analysis, Andrews seemed to have failed to appreciate that his approach was not inherently at odds with Simon-style thinking once one recognized how problems of knowledge impinge on attempts to decide how to try to maximize profits.

The real problem with my second proposal was that it was far too ambitious for a PhD, as it was promising to get into challenging territory in terms of comparing the empirical content of research programs that have very different implications about the kinds of predictions that are valuable, and it would have entailed a major effort (not just one major chapter) to stitch together and justify the synthesis comprising the alternative research program that I envisaged. Therein lay the basis for my third attempt at confirmation.


## 3.7    PROGRESS REVIEW

If I had been a modern-day research student enrolled in a well-run graduate school, the position that I had arrived at by the end of my second academic year as a research student in Cambridge would have resulted in my candidature being terminated. I had failed two attempts at getting confirmed as a PhD candidate, and although my first year of research had been highly focused and had advanced my knowledge of behavioral approaches to the firm, my second year of research had not been focused with reference to a specific research question. But the fact that I seemed to be floundering could be viewed as reflecting shortcomings in the supervision process, rather than proof that I did not have what it would take to make a PhD-style "contribution to knowledge." Although I had lately exchanged a few letters with Brian Loasby, I had not had any formal meetings with a supervisor for well over a year.

Unless I could find a way of drawing extensively on my research on the behavioral approach to the firm, I seemed to be in a situation where I needed essentially to start again from scratch. When I arrived at the University of Stirling on Monday July 2, 1979, I had three calendar years and just under three months remaining within which to get a topic confirmed, do the remaining research, write it up as a thesis and submit it to Cambridge's Board of Graduate Studies. It did not seem to me to be an impossible task, even amid thoughts about the demands that having to write lectures and mark examination scripts might place on my time (as opposed simply to running tutorials instead of the many supervisions I had been enjoying running during my time in Cambridge as a research student). However, although I was about to start working with a supervisor who shared my interests and my way of thinking about economics, and whose office would be only a few steps away, I still lacked a research question on which to focus, Moreover, I  would soon discover that my new supervisor's gifts for pinning down the shortcomings  of works by leading economists did not translate into a supervisory style that provided ample and timely feedback, thoughtful strategic advice, and evidence of determination to ensure that I got the job done successfully.

# 4 University of Stirling, Scotland, 1979–1984

## 4.1    INTRODUCTION

The University of Stirling (which henceforth I shall normally refer to simply as "Stirling") was a much smaller, much poorer institution than the University of Cambridge. Yet it had a beautiful campus, spectacular surroundings, and was the university at which I most enjoyed working during my career. I found it easy to be productive there as a researcher and, although the students were not, on average, as academically capable as those in Cambridge or those at the institutions at which I later worked in Australia, they were a pleasant, memorable bunch who displayed none of the air of entitlement that I increasingly encountered later in my career. Although my time at Stirling was shorter than at any of the universities at which I subsequently worked, it was the place with by far the biggest number of colleagues who became lifelong friends.

When I started my job at Stirling, there were about twenty teaching and research staff in the Department of Economics, plus several research fellows. A disproportionate number of staff had studied at Oxford or Cambridge, and I was one of eight lecturers who were working on their doctorates. At not quite 24, I was by several years the youngest lecturer. There was a generally pleasant air of pluralism, with mainstream and heterodox economists often co-teaching courses and usually almost everyone attended seminars and workshops, at which the atmosphere was constructive rather than combative. It was a very nice place at which to work.

Yet I did not stay there. The realities of Thatcherism that I experienced in the early 1980s led me both to rethink my political stance and to apply for jobs in Australia when an end to my PhD saga came into sight. I had been right to be concerned about the economics of living outside of a college on pay near the bottom of the lecturer scale: it was initially quite a challenge to service a mortgage, keep warm in winter and deal with a succession of expensive motoring bills, especially when monetarist policies entailed a rise in interest rates of four percentage points. Then, in 1981, Stirling was dealt a savage funding cut by the University Grants Committee, with the Department of Economics being required to shed around one-third of its established staff. No compulsory redundancies were necessary: I was part of an exodus of staff who simply were not replaced.

This chapter is disproportionately long relative to the length of time that I worked at Stirling versus where I worked subsequently. This is because it was at Stirling that I acquired pretty much all of the post-Cambridge key foundations for my view of behavioral economics. This had much to do with the fact that Cambridge's Board of Graduate Studies requested that, for my first year at Stirling, I should have a light teaching load. It consisted of half a dozen tutorials per teaching week and, frustratingly for me, no lectures, while my administrative and service roles were negligible. Hence, I had just as much time for research as I had enjoyed in Cambridge except for the weeks when I had to mark end-of-semester examinations.

During my first year at Stirling, the seminal modern behavioral contributions by Kahneman and Tversky (1979) and Thaler (1980) became available, and they did not go unnoticed by me. Indeed, it was me who purloined the sample copy of the first issue of the *Journal of Economic Behavior and Organization* (in which Thaler's paper appeared) when it completed its process of circulating among members of the Department of Economics. In the next few years, my knowledge of research on heuristics and biases in decision-making was enhanced via Hogarth and Makridakis (1981) and Nisbett and Ross (1980). However, other sources that I studied around the same time exerted a bigger pull on my attention. This was despite the fact that, in my first three years at Stirling, I switched from focusing on industrial and corporate change to focusing, like Thaler, on consumer behavior. Thus, although I was interested in how people may end up making poorer decisions than they might have made (just as I viewed my parents as doing), my view was not dominated by the heuristics and biases perspective. What particularly fascinated me was why people differ in how they operate even despite sharing operating heuristics that are part of human nature.


## 4.2    GOING BEYOND REDUCTIONISM

When I started my lectureship at Stirling in July 1979, I was in the process of considering the implications of two books that I had been reading in my last few weeks in Cambridge. One was *The Innovating Firm*, by Stirling alumnus Neil Kay (1979). It seemed an essential purchase for me when I noticed it in Heffers Bookshop, both because of its subtitle – *A Behavioral Theory of Corporate R&D* – and because browsing in it revealed to me that it was based on Kay's Stirling PhD. The other book that I was trying to digest was *Beyond Reductionism*, a volume edited by Koestler and Smythies (1969) from what was known as the

1968 Alpbach Symposium. I discovered the latter book via a reference that Kay had made to one of its contributors.

### Top-Down Rule-Based Resource Allocation

Kay's book was my first encounter with material on the theory of the firm that accused mainstream approaches of being reductionist and suggested that the way ahead for analyzing how firms allocated resources to research and development was to view firms as hierarchical systems.

A reductionist approach to resource allocation within a firm would view all potential uses of its financial, physical, and human resources as mutually rivalrous, i.e., as substitutable for each other: a dollar not spent on one form of investment could be used in any number of alternative investments, or in alternative advertising strategies, staff training or recruitment programs, and so on. From a reductionist standpoint, the amounts committed by a firm to generic categories are simply the totals arrived at by summing the amounts committed to the individual projects that are approved in each category. Optimal resource allocation reduces to an all-embracing trade-off of expected yields from marginal dollars in any area against what they could yield in other areas in which they might be spent. But from Kay's standpoint, it is misleading to view resource allocation in this way. For one thing, it is cognitively too challenging to do this, but there is also the problem of how one compares alternative uses of resources in the presence of fundamental uncertainty of the kind faced by, say, a pharmaceuticals corporation that must choose which new drugs to try to develop. Managers in such a firm are not in a position to know even as confident probabilities the marginal returns to allocating funds to one drug project rather than another.

Kay contends that firms therefore allocate resources in a top-down manner that begins by making allocations between broad generic categories and then gradually gets down to more detailed sub-categories. Thus, spending on marketing may be traded off against spending on research and development in general terms to derive budgets for the marketing and research departments, but subsequent choices of how these budgets get deployed do not involve comparisons of specific uses of resources on advertising against specific uses of resources on research and development. Similarly, competing uses of research and development budgets between "research" and "development" may be traded off to give separate budgets for these two categories, but once this has been done, specific research projects are not compared with specific development projects. In other words, just as firms have hierarchical organizational structures, they also allocate resources to departments and, ultimately, to individuals by hierarchical processes that refer to abstract notions before getting to the level of specific activities and projects.

Allocating resources in this way proceeds without managers necessarily knowing relative marginal payoffs to giving a bigger budget to one use at the level in question at the cost of giving less to rival uses at that level. In the absence of such knowledge, decision-makers can use long-established rules and industry norms that were arrived at by trial and error, and which are adjusted experimentally if there are reasons to believe that this is necessary. So, for example, there may be norms in particular sectors about what percentage of revenue should typically be spend on R&D or marketing, just as, at the nation-state level, attempts may be made to allocate particular percentages to defense (for example, two percent of GDP if one is a member of NATO), foreign aid, and so on. Of course, those to whom the budgets are being allocated will always try to push for bigger budgets in their own areas, so we should not neglect the significance of shifting coalitions, rather than definitive changes in knowledge, as drivers of the allocations that are agreed to at each level. We should also be mindful that those involved in such decisions are likely to use external reference standards – in the form of any intelligence they have about what rival organizations are doing – as they make their claims for resources.

Many years later, it struck me that the allocation of research grants to academics can be viewed similarly, with rules being applied in relation to the track records of grant applicants and grant reviewers, as proxies for the probability that funds will be well spent if allocated to one project rather than another. However, track records in business and academia are not static, so the relative credibility of project advocates and critics will change through time. Two papers that I wrote much later with Jason Potts (Earl and Potts, 2013, 2016) explore the process of allocating resources to individual projects in relation to tidal shifts in the balance of power between "creatives" and "bean-counters."

*Systems of Systems*
The 1968 Alpbach Symposium volume opened a wider vista of the world as a system of systems that were usefully to be viewed as functioning holistically, with a focus on how outcomes depend on linkages between component parts. I had been introduced to this idea at high school in the context of biology via some classes on ecology, but I was now being introduced to notions such as systems having "emergent properties" (for example, life, resilience, or the capacity to fly) that may only be present if specific sets of system elements are present, and the idea that cognitive processes could be based on "gestalt" configurations. The latter reminded me of the notion of "jizz" that I had encountered in ornithology.

This was not the kind of thinking that would be conducive to accepting Margaret Thatcher's famous reductionist claim that "There is no such thing as society." She was well into her time as prime minister when she made that claim (in an interview published in *Woman's Own*, October 31, 1987). However, in mid-1979, as I studied *Beyond Reductionism*, I had been intrigued to see that Thatcher's guru, Friedrich Hayek had been listed as one of the participants at the Alpbach Symposium. The book did not include a paper by him, so I was left wondering why he would have been there. My only idea was that it had something to do with his view of market systems producing spontaneous order as a kind of emergent phenomenon. (Years later, I had another idea about why Hayek was a participant: see Section 7.5.) At that time, Marshall's way of viewing the economic system seemed to me to have more obvious parallels than Hayek's had with anti-reductionist ecological thinking in biology.

It gradually became apparent to me that the Marshall-inspired works of P. W. S. Andrews (1949, 1964; Andrews and Brunner, 1951, 1975; and papers by Andrews that were among those later reprinted in Lee and Earl, eds, 1993) that I had been trying to get to grips with for the past couple of years made a lot more sense if one thought about them as an interlinked set that had not been written from a reductionist standpoint. Andrews seemed to think holistically rather than in relation to equalization at the margin. For example, in analyzing investment in the steel sector, Andrews and Brunner (1951) did not present steelmakers as considering great arrays of projects with marginally different capital requirements. Rather, firms would consider very limited sets of specific proposals in terms of their prospective *overall* net rates of return on the capital that would be invested in them. They would exclude dominated alternatives, rank the un-dominated projects in order of their respective overall rates of return, and then implement all the projects that seemed to offer a big enough return to cover the rate of interest required to finance them. In other words, an entire project whose overall return only just matched the required return would be "marginal" – there would be no equalization of the return on a marginal dollar of capital investment with the cost of obtaining a marginal dollar of funding in the way that reductionist thinking would presume.

Likewise, Andrews did not see pricing of manufactured products as entailing the equalization of marginal costs and marginal revenues, with prices emerging and being adjusted according to the transactional interplay between individual producers and consumers who are all simply looking for the best spot deal at that moment and who would not think twice about dealing with someone else next time. Rather, he assigned major roles to long-term goodwill relationships between suppliers and their customers: he emphasized that customers were often other firms within a supply chain, not end-consumers. The existence of such relationships meant that trading was not about maximizing returns on individual transactions; what counted were the net returns that one enjoyed over the long run, with negative returns on some transactions being the price that was worth paying to achieve greater positive returns on others in the long run. The analysis of pricing therefore should not be reduced to the competitive interplay of those currently demanding and supplying the product in question, for in the long run suppliers would always need to be mindful of the threat of entry by those who are not currently competing for business but have the capacity to start doing so.

In respect of retailing, Andrews's non-reductionist way of thinking led him to focus on the importance of being competitive at the level of the "basket" (in modern terms, the "shopping trolley load") of goods that customers typically bought, because shopping was too complex and time-consuming if approached on a reductionist basis with a focus on getting each commodity from the cheapest supplier. He also recognized the structural complexity of purchasing and retailing processes that act to structure or generate demand, such as how the pressure of competition is increased by people's lives entailing mobility (so that having to travel to conduct some kinds of activities provides scope for shopping for other things on route, which limits the market power of local suppliers) and how stocks of one kind of product may induce sales of other products to buyers drawn in by the prospect of finding the former product. A similar emphasis on the rich web of relationships that shapes how the competitive process works, including how coordination failures can be avoided, was evident in the work of Richardson (1972) and, much earlier, in Marshall (1890) (see also Loasby, 1978).

## 4.3   TOWARD A HIERARCHICAL VIEW OF DECISION-MAKING

The process of reflecting on Andrews's non-reductionist way of thinking played a very significant role in my shift of focus away from the economics of the firm. I had a sense that Andrews's views about the behavior of shoppers reflected his Marshallian sensibilities and that there was scope for expressing them as an alternative to the dominant Hicksian approach whose limitations had been the focus of my first supervision essay in my Prelims year in Cambridge. Unlike my subsequent work on consumer behavior, my first attempt at devising an alternative approach was framed in the goods space rather than focusing on choices made in characteristics space. It was partly inspired by Hicks's (1976) confession that, with hindsight, he felt that the Marshallian approach that his analysis had displaced was the more realistic of the two. Marshall's (1890) view did not portray people as considering all feasible substitutions simultaneously. Rather, his idea was that people decided whether to buy something according to whether the marginal utility they expected to derive from it was no less than the marginal utility of holding on to the money they would have to part with to get it. It thus seemed to be a kind of liquidity preference approach to demand, which seemed applicable to situations such as where a consumer is deciding how expensive a product to buy in a market crowded with products that differ both in price and how much value for money they offer.

However, the picture of demand that I had been getting from Andrews (1964) acknowledged a prior stage in the choice process, namely, that the consumer would not look at all products within a particular category and would instead only attempt to equate the marginal utility of spending in the category and the marginal utility of money in respect of products whose prices fell within a particular range that had upper and lower bounds. This seemed to require a theory of budgeting that grappled with the sequential nature of attention to budgetary categories and uncertainty about how much would end up being spent within each range that was set for the various budgetary categories. I could see that perhaps (in line with Keynes's view of saving as a residual) the total of the set of upper budget ranges would be constrained not to exceed the consumer's total spending capacity, with any residue from spending somewhat less in some categories then being saved. But how would the lower bounds of budgets be set?

I presented this perspective as my first departmental workshop, emphasizing that I had no idea whether there was any literature on household budgeting that looked anything like this, and I noted that this top-down way of allocating household resources was in some respects like Kay's (1979) non-reductionist view of the allocation of resources to research and development in firms. Ron Shone's feedback was especially helpful, for he introduced me to the "utility tree" literature particularly associated with the work of Strotz (1957) that is sometimes presented as lying somewhere between good-space and characteristics-space modes of thinking due to budgetary categories ultimately being based on differences in the sets of characteristics that their respective products offer or the wants that they enable consumers to meet. However, I was not left with a sense that this literature captured the sequential aspect of spending processes or the idea of double-sided budget ranges.

Not long after my workshop presentation, I had a "lightbulb moment" that led me to question a key idea in the orthodox theory of rational choice, namely, the "axiom of Archimedes" or "principle of gross substitution." In the standard goods-space view of choice, indifference curves that slope downwards to the right at a decreasing rate guarantee that changes in relative prices produce a substitution effect. Likewise, in Lancaster's (1966) characteristics-space analysis of choice, not only can substitution always be induced by a price change of some magnitude, but weaknesses of products in some areas may be offset by suitably strong performances in other areas.

In Cambridge, I had sometimes sensed that there might be some cases where this did not apply. This was particularly the case when I read Stout's (1977) report exhorting UK manufacturers to be mindful of the impact of "non-price factors" in international trade, but Michael Posner argued soon after in his lectures (and in Posner, 1978) that "If you can't sell good goods, sell cheap goods," i.e., that with an exchange rate depreciation and/or improvements in production efficiency, a country's firms should be better able to survive competition from overseas rivals whose products they cannot match in terms of design and/or standards of quality. From Posner's standpoint, the key question was whether workers will accept real wage reductions of the size necessary to make possible price reductions that are big enough to offset non-price shortcomings.

My "lightbulb moment" could readily have been the one that led me to resolve, in the New Year of 1982, to become a vegetarian – a resolution that I have not deviated from since then except by becoming a vegan a few months later. In that case, the lightbulb moment came in the departmental coffee room when I was having my lunch with several colleagues. The group included Sue Shaw (who later became Professor of Marketing at the University of Strathclyde), who was doing research on fish marketing and had just returned from visiting a salmon farm. She noticed that I winced as she described how the salmon were harvested via an electrocution tank, and she went on to add that it was a more humane process than what happens in an abattoir. Somehow, this had a much bigger impact on me than that generated by the posters about veganism on the office door of Dr Enid Marshall, Stirling's Reader in Business Law, which I often passed as I came in from the car park. Indeed, what got me thinking that I might as well also give up eating eggs and dairy products was the hassle I soon encountered as a new vegetarian when trying to source cheese made with animal-free rennet (which was often out of stock in the local health-food store) and free-range eggs (which could more reliably be found in a butcher's store).

These dietary changes were clearly at odds with Lancaster's model, as they involved an ethical principle that ruled out consuming food from murdered or exploited animals, and a desire to prevent the process of shopping for food from becoming too fraught. But there was clearly also a growth-of-knowledge process going on as I changed my dietary requirements both in terms of what I was prepared to eat and which meals I knew how to prepare. Indeed, it was attending a talk about veganism by Eva Batt, a vegan cookery writer, at Stirling's vegetarian society – rather than lurking by Enid's door to read small print about "What happens to the calf?" – that sealed my decision to become a vegan. Having not read that small print or tried to figure out for myself what it might say in answer to the question, I had previously been oblivious of the implications of dairy cows giving birth to male calves.

However, while it was that conversation with Sue Shaw that set me thinking about how dietary choices could entail no-go zones, I was, at the time of that conversation, already about two years into thinking about choice in a way that clashed with the principle of gross substitution: it entailed setting priority rankings for characteristics and setting targets for how options must perform in respect of these characteristics in order to be deemed acceptable.

The actual "lightbulb moment" came on a Saturday morning as I was reflecting on how tired I was, just as I had been on quite a few previous Saturday mornings. On Friday nights, many members of the department and some of the postgraduate students usually went to one of the pubs or hotels close to the campus. Most of the group would eventually adjourn to someone's house nearby. These Friday nights were the main element of my social life in my early months at Stirling, but I was losing my enthusiasm for them. This was partly due to the inequities of the round-buying system when I was merely drinking orange juice, and on the lowest pay, while others drank expensive brands of whisky. But there was also the problem that I found myself sometimes getting to bed well after two in the morning, partly due to first driving home, in the opposite direction, Stirling's sole politics lecturer, Kevin Featherstone (later Professor of Greek Politics at the LSE), who was nearly as young as myself and did not yet have a car. As I walked to the supermarket that Saturday morning, I was reflecting on my shortage of discretionary income and time and the problem of budgeting. Something had to go.

In concluding that I would rather spend money on LPs, or petrol to drive out to the mountains, and that I would rather be able to enjoy a full Saturday of leisure without failing to get enough sleep, I realized that I was not thinking along the lines presumed in the utility tree view of budgeting. I was thinking in terms of priorities over separate goals and asking whether I was getting enough in top ranking goals before being willing to allocate resources to ones that I viewed as less important; I was not computing overall scores for rival strategies by weighing together how much I got on different dimensions. To get enough sleep, I must either get up later and lose my Saturday morning, or give up the social Friday nights, which would also leave me with more money to spend on things that I ranked higher than conversing with colleagues. Based on this, I stopped joining my colleagues on Friday nights.

After starting to think about priority-based budgeting between product and/or activity categories, it was a short step for me to start to think about choices between rival products within a category in terms of priority-based tests of adequacy for expected performance in relation to product characteristics. Each of these tests was, in effect, an aspiration level for the characteristic in question, and in some cases a pair of aspiration levels might be involved (for example, a breakfast cereal that was "not too heavy and not too light"). So, I seemed to be adapting Simon's aspiration-based, satisficing view of organizational decision-making into the consumer behavior setting. From this standpoint, the process of choosing looked rather like a hurdles race in which failure to clear a hurdle results in disqualification, with the product that survives the most tests, in priority order, being the one that gets selected, and with simple tie-breaker rules being used if more than one product is deemed adequate for all the characteristics on the buyer's checklist. I coined the phrase "characteristic filtering" to denote this priority-based view of choosing.

I soon discovered that this way of thinking intersected with the marketing literature on consumer behavior. (Section 4.5 explains how I came to read in this area.) There, the idea that consumers might use checklists when choosing was known as a "conjunctive" way of choosing, to distinguish it from what was labelled a "disjunctive" approach in which the consumer is obsessed with getting as much as possible of a single characteristic. However, the marketing literature did not seem to envisage a series of priority-ordered targets as being used to deal with situations in which no option "ticked all the boxes." Rather, reference was made to two other possibilities. One was the use of lexicographic rules that entail a hierarchical ranking of disjunctive wants, rather than targets, with a tie for the maximum offered on the top-priority want leading to a focus on which of the tied products performed best in terms of the next highest-ranking want, and so on; the second was Tversky's (1972) notion of "elimination by aspects." The latter does entail the use of characteristic targets, but they are not prioritized; instead, the order in which they are applied is probabilistically grounded and triggered by contextual factors.

These approaches were categorized in marketing as "non-compensatory" ways of making decisions, in contrast to "compensatory" or "expectancy value" methods that were the marketing equivalent of Lancaster's (1966) analysis of choices in characteristics space. Some of the compensatory models that were popular in marketing seemed to go beyond Lancaster by (a) recognizing that cognitive constraints could limit the number of characteristics that were considered, (b) offering plausibly simple ways of incorporating uncertainty, and (c) recognizing that consumers may weigh their personal assessments against how they think their social referents would view them if they selected the products under consideration (most notably in the model offered by Fishbein and Ajzen, 1975). In contrast, the non-compensatory approaches seemed much less well developed, especially in relation to uncertainty about how products would perform for some or all characteristic axes. I set out to remedy this shortcoming by extending my analysis with elements adapted from Shackle's (1949, 1958, 1969, 1979) non-probabilistic theory of investment decision-making.

The fact that I came to be reading this area of Shackle's work in late 1979 was purely the result of the manager of the campus bookstore notifying me that he had received a copy of Shackle's (1979) book *Imagination and the Nature of Choice*, which he thought might be of interest to me. This was excellent service, to say the least, and (on November 23, 1979) I duly purchased the book. I then went on to read earlier books in which Shackle (1949, 1958, 1969) had set out his theory in more detail and I began to see how it could be fitted into a hierarchical view of wants.

I realized that people could be viewed as dealing with uncertainty about whether an option would meet their target for a particular characteristic by asking themselves (a) whether the options seemed to have any potential (or, in later versions of my analysis, enough potential) to meet a "gain aspiration," and (b) whether it did not seem to have any potential (or, in later versions, not have too much potential) to result in an outcome worse than their "loss avoidance aspiration," i.e., a shortfall that they viewed as too big relative to the target that they were uncertain the option could meet. If it seemed OK on both counts, the option would be deemed an acceptable gamble in respect of the characteristic in question, with the decision-maker then considering how it fared in terms of the next most important characteristic.

Ideally, consumers would hope to find a product that seemed to offer a good enough chance of meeting all their aspirations – i.e., as we now commonly say, a product that "ticks all the boxes." But from a satisficing standpoint, we would expect search processes to cease when an option was found that seemed to get far enough down consumer wish-lists, with consumers potentially differing in the characteristics that were on their wish-lists, how they were ranked, their aspiration levels for particular characteristics, and how far down their characteristic wish-lists was "far enough" for them to cease searching.

## Ignorance of Precursors

For much of my time at Stirling, I was unaware of the fact that, in coming to view choices as based on hierarchically ranked, satiable wants, I had, in effect, arrived where Duncan Ironmonger had arrived almost twenty years earlier in his Cambridge PhD, belatedly published in slightly extended form as Ironmonger (1972). Unlike me, Ironmonger had presented a formal analysis that used linear programming. But this had entailed not addressing the question of how consumers handle uncertainty. Though I was oblivious of his analysis, I sensed that the graphs that I drew to understand household budgeting processes aligned somewhat with linear programming, for I had learned some of the basics of linear programming when I read Baumol (1972, chapter 5), during the 1975 long vacation, as part of my preparation for the Prelims year of Part II of the Cambridge Economics Tripos. However, although I worked through all Baumol's exercise questions, I never went on to make any formal use of the technique. Instead, I included a less formal graphical analysis of priority-based budgeting in my first attempt to write a paper about the characteristic filtering perspective, which became my first solo discussion paper (Earl, 1980a).

When I later saw Ironmonger's analysis, I thought to myself, "Well, at least I have gone beyond it by addressing uncertainty." But here, too, I was not as original as I assumed myself to be.

The double-sided test that I suggested as a means for judging the acceptability of a gamble over an uncertain characteristic outcome seemed cognitively simpler than the process that Shackle set out in his books. Sure, Shackle's view did involve simplification, for the theory of attention embodied in his "ascendancy function" generated a "focus gain" and a "focus loss" for each of the options that were under consideration. But it then entailed a convoluted process by which these focal pairings came to be ranked for rival options: his view seemed less plausible when a decision-maker was dealing with many decision dimensions rather than merely financial gains and losses.

However, what I did not discover until over three decades later (around 2012, when writing a book on Shackle for Palgrave's "Great Thinkers in Economics Series," published as Earl and Littleboy, 2012) was that Shackle had developed his ascendancy function and theory of focusing after originally proposing an approach that had similarities with mine, as well as predating Simon's work on aspiration levels and satisficing. What is particularly strange about all this is that in late-1981–early-1982, while I was writing my first solo book, *The Economic Imagination* (Earl, 1983a), I corresponded with Shackle about my adaptation of his work and at no point did he refer me to his earlier contributions.

My scholarly failing here was that I did not pursue the genealogy of Shackle's thinking in the way that I had pursued the genealogy of the ideas of other scholars whose work excited me. For example, when I discovered Richardson's (1960) *Information and Investment*, I made it my mission to find all the steps in his published work that led to it, and everything he published subsequently, even though there was no Google Scholar to speed up the process. In Shackle's case, I did not bother to see whether his 1949 book *Expectation in Economics* had been preceded by articles, and I only came across one such article (Shackle, 1943). That discovery occurred purely by chance when I was looking for a paper by Alfred Schutz (his name spelled as Schuetz on this occasion) that I had seen referenced in Garfinkel (1967)[6] and which happened to be in the same issue of *Economica*. But there were earlier papers, and they would have been easy to find.

If I had taken the trouble to look for earlier papers by Shackle, I would have discovered then, rather than in 2012, that Shackle had initially seen investment projects as being ranked using cut-off rules. First, he suggested that an entrepreneur would take the best outcome that seemed "perfectly possible" as a "working hypothesis" about what will actually eventuate and then choose the scheme with the largest prospective "best" outcome "so long as the worst is not too bad" (Shackle, 1940, p. 46). Shackle (1941) then suggested that entrepreneurs might focus on whether their prospects of meeting an upside target if they chose a particular plan did not seem too difficult to believe, and their prospects of not falling below a tolerable downside target were not too difficult to disbelieve. In other words, what I arrived at was very similar to what Shackle had envisaged before developing his "ascendancy function" view of how the attention of an entrepreneur gets focused.

## 4.4    PEOPLE AS SCIENTISTS

By the time that I took up my position at Stirling, I had become a member of the Scottish Economic Society and thereby a subscriber to the *Scottish Journal of Political Economy*. This resulted in me seeing a personally significant paper as soon as it was published, a paper that I otherwise might never have noticed. The

---

[6] I had read Garfinkel's book due to a conversation with a sociologist, Keith McLennan, who, like me, had recently started working at Stirling and lived in "Dalnair," a large, old, university-owned house in Bridge of Allen in which I lived for my first couple of months there. Keith and I had talked about our respective interests, and when I said I was interest in economic methodology, he told me about the field of ethnomethodology in sociology.

paper in question was by Andrew Skinner (1979) from the University of Glasgow. Skinner was a leading Adam Smith scholar, whose work Brian Loasby greatly admired. The paper explored similarities between how Kuhn's (1962) paradigms-based view of the history of science, Shackle's (1967) *Years of High Theory* account of the imperfect competition and Keynesian revolutions, and Adam Smith's ([1795] 1980) posthumously published work on the history of astronomy. The last of these remains little known in economics despite Skinner's attempt to draw attention to it. But, for Brian Loasby and I, Smith's foray into astronomy is a remarkable contribution for what it says about how humans in general operate.

Smith saw human action in general, like that of astronomers, as a scientific activity: people marvel at things they cannot immediately fathom and they give their attention to attempting to figure out what makes them possible. On this view, life is a knowledge-generating process in which people construct frameworks for making sense of things that intrigue (or threaten) them, and they modify these frameworks to accommodate anomalies. As time passes and conditions change or people get data from a wider area, these modifications become more extensive, and they tend to be ad hoc when people find it difficult to accommodate new observations. These frameworks thereby become increasingly unwieldy. But new frameworks that offer different ways of understanding the phenomena in question tend to be resisted until existing frameworks become cognitively too cumbersome to use. At that point, people become willing to incur the upfront costs of getting to grips with a new way of making sense of things that may – once they have got used to using it – prove to be both more effective and easier to use.

A perspective very similar to Smith's was already on my reading list at the time I read Skinner's article, for Brian Loasby had told me (if I recall correctly, in a letter he sent to me in Cambridge a few months before I moved to Stirling) that he had recently been reading George Kelly's (1963) book *A Theory of Personality*. He said he had found it very interesting and strongly recommended that I, too, should read it. *A Theory of Personality* is a short but dense paperback that contains the first three chapters of Kelly's (1955) two-volume magnum opus, *The Psychology of Personal Constructs*, which is built around the proposition that human behavior can usefully be understood by viewing people "as if they are scientists" who are in the business of seeking to predict and control events.

Brian Loasby went on to apply ingredients from Kelly (1963) repeatedly in his publications (beginning with Loasby, 1983) on the behavior of organizations. The fact that he did so is easy to appreciate, as he had learned of Kelly via

Charles Suckling, an ICI executive who was an adjunct professor of management at Stirling. Suckling had said that he had found Kelly's ideas useful for understanding the behavior of people in organizations. As well as echoing Adam Smith's perspective, Kelly's theory of personality has much in common with how Kuhn (1962) and Lakatos (1970) view the role that, respectively, scientific paradigms and scientific research programs play in shaping how academics and research scientists go about their work: although the work of scientists entails creative thinking, it runs along established lines and uses established ways of thinking and unquestioned core assumptions and operating rules that limit the kinds of things they find worthy of investigation, which kinds of evidence they will take seriously when their theories are being challenged, and which of their theories they will be willing to modify or abandon when there are mismatches between predictions and evidence. Kelly arrived at a similar view of how people deal with problems of knowledge ahead of Kuhn and Lakatos, after realizing that there was much in common between the struggles of his postgraduate students and the struggles of patients that he encountered when he was practicing as a clinical psychologist.

Even before reading Kelly, Brian and I were both conscious of the value of thinking about the behavior of firms as if the cognitive processes of their staff or prospective customers could be constrained by established ways of thinking. As I explained at the end of Section 3.4, I first picked up this idea in autumn 1977 from Loasby's (1976) references to resistance to Halothane, a new anaesthetic; by late 1978, I had realized, as a result of reading Alfred Chandler's (1962) *Strategy and Structure*, that the process by which major new ways of doing business are taken up resemble those that Kuhn (1962) had emphasized in the history of science: like scientific revolutions, revolutionary change in the ways that firms operate may be resisted because existing ways of doing business have served managers well in the past and because established ways of thinking get in the way of appreciating the potential of new approaches.

As Kelly had realized, the key problem for changing how we look at the world, whether in science or in the ordinary business of everyday life, is that people can only assess alternative perspectives on what to do from the standpoint of their existing way of thinking. Until those who are trying to promote changes of behavior can find a way of packaging how the alternatives should be viewed that will permeate the established mindset, those who need to change will stick to their old ways. In the meantime, the latter will keep operating in needlessly dysfunctional ways and squander resources.

This permeability problem was central to Brian's presentation to the 1981 conference of the British Association for the Advancement of Science, published as Loasby (1983). It was also a key idea behind my book *The Corporate Imagination: How Big Companies Make Mistakes*, that I wrote during the first half of 1983 in my first sabbatical (for which I stayed at Stirling). It then underlay how I was thinking when I wrote in my post-PhD book *Lifestyle Economics*, soon after leaving Stirling, about consumers who resist change and make mistakes. Ironically, however, these contributions have failed to permeate far into modern behavioral economics.

Readers of the present book might be puzzled about the failure of those works to gain traction with modern behavioral economists. They might think that, if these works emphasized systematically dysfunctional behavior, they were probably taking a similar point of view to a modern behavioral economist who portrays people as if they are, to use Thaler's (2015) term, "misbehaving" in the sense that they fail to do what a "fully rational" economic agent should do and allow "supposedly irrelevant factors" to affect their choices. However, Loasby and I had a different "way" of construing human fallibility from the "way" that human fallibility is seen in the version of behavioral economics that Thaler has done so much to popularize. Moreover, Loasby and I did not presume that optimal choices are knowable; we merely focused on failures to opt for *better* strategies that could have been readily identified by using a different way of looking at the world.

Here, it is important to realize that the "personal" aspect of personal construct psychology makes Kelly-inspired behavioral economics problematic for typical behavioral economists unless the latter are, like me, open to seeing the two approaches as complementary. As in conventional economics, the common practice in behavioral economics is to view economic agents as if they are all the same as each other. Failures to behave as an idealized "econ" would supposedly behave are therefore analyzed as arising due to the use of heuristics from a long list identified experimentally as being genetically programmed into humans. I had, and still have, no problem with the idea of people in general having such tendencies. However, these inherited heuristics are not the only means by which people cope with life: Kelly's message is that people develop hierarchically organized, rule-based *personal* systems for constructing models of parts of the world and deciding what to do. It is the uniqueness of our personal construct systems that makes us the individuals that we are.

Aspects of our personal operating systems *that are not part of our generic ways of being human* can play key roles in shaping how successfully we cope with life's challenges. Our personal "ways" can amplify or over-ride our generic human "ways" of behaving and can initiate behavior. For example, people in general may be prone, as humans, to suffer from sunk-cost bias, but some of them may over-ride that tendency because they have been trained as economists or have otherwise come to see that there is no use in "crying over spilt milk" and/or "pouring good money after bad." Emphasis on individuality clashes with the conventional "representative agent" approach to economics but it does not mean it is impossible to group people, as marketers do, based on similarities in their ways of thinking that produce similar values, just as economic methodologists group economists into schools of thought.

Although Kelly (1963) became one of Brian Loasby's most frequent sources for understanding how people deal with problems of knowledge in economic systems, Brian did not seem interested in doing more with Kelly and did not engage with the wider literature on personal construct psychology to see what it implied about consumer behavior. By contrast, I became captivated with the idea of replacing the notion of utility maximization with a Kellian view of human action in which life is about making sense of the world, increasing one's knowledge (including self-knowledge) and being in control rather than at the mercy of events. For example, I started seeing the activity of watching television as providing many opportunities not merely for gathering knowledge about the world but also for testing, in a safe environment, one's knowledge of the world and ability to anticipate and cope with diverse kinds of events.

When I explored Kelly's (1955) magnum opus and some of the major secondary sources, I was particularly fascinated by the way that emotions were framed in relation to concerns about loss of control and/or scope for damage to one's self-construct if one ventured into unfamiliar territory or acted in a way that was "out of character." Clearly, one's knowledge and ability to control events is not going to advance if, in the process of testing hypotheses (or even in acquiring knowledge from others), one is unwilling to risk getting into situations that are difficult to make sense of and/or in which it is difficult to maintain control. When we recognize this, there seems to be a lot to be said for the heuristic that is commonly attributed to Sir Thomas Beecham, namely, "Try anything once, except incest and folk dancing." It helps to be open to experimenting with things that others view as perfectly normal, even if they are in a minority, rather than limiting oneself to what one already knows. However, how risky an experiment will seem is not determined by the experiment; it depends on the personal construct system that one has constructed, for this will determine the implications that one sees as potentially associated with one's options.

This way of looking at human action seemed to me to have enormous potential for understanding consumer behavior, in ways that utility theory simply could not match. As I set out to see what I could do with it, my only concern was that my lack of life experience might result in me being oblivious of some of its applications. However, I hoped that I might compensate for this vicariously: here, I was encouraged by the new insights it gave me about my parents' behavior and by the way in which some of the novels that I read seemed to resonate with Kelly's analysis.

## 4.5　COMPLEX DECISION CYCLES VERSUS SIMPLIFIED DECISION-MAKING

One of the surprising things that I discovered soon after arriving at Stirling was that being deprived of access to a copyright library (the Cambridge University Library) and a very well-resourced specialist economics library (the Marshall Library) had beneficial consequences for my development as a behavioral economist. This happened because I was able to discover things that I would not have been likely to notice when using the fabulous libraries in Cambridge. Within my first few months of using the library at Stirling, I stumbled upon an area of scholarship that was totally unfamiliar to me, namely, consumer behavior research conducted by marketing specialists in business schools. I discovered books on consumer research purely by chance, while walking past the shelves that housed them, when I was making my way to something nearby related to the behavioral theory of the firm. Soon after, on the racks that displayed new issues of journals, I discovered the *Journal of Consumer Research*, and the other key marketing journals, near to the economics journals in which I routinely browsed. The two accidental encounters led me to recognize that there was much scope for taking a pluralistic approach to the study of consumer behavior, as well as adding further impetus to my pivot toward focusing on a behavioral analysis of consumers' choices.

The stroke of luck that I had in where my gaze landed among Stirling's library book-stacks was truly remarkable, for the first thing that caught my eye was Nicosia's (1966) *Consumer Decision Processes: Marketing and Advertising Implications*. This was a seminal contribution within the marketing literature, and it looked for all the world as though Nicosia had tried to write a consumer behavior version of Cyert and March (1963). This impression was amplified by the fact that the covers of the two books were almost identical. Nicosia presented a boxes-and-arrows version of consumer decision-making as a sequential process. It contrasted with orthodox economic analysis that reduces consumer choice to a single diagram, in just the same way that Cyert and March's view of the operations of a firm contrasted with the one-diagram orthodox approaches to the theory of the firm.

Close to Nicosia's book was a much bigger book, a research-based consumer behavior textbook by Engel, Kollat and Blackwell (1968), in its third edition (Engel, Blackwell and Kollat, 1978), built around a different boxes-and-arrows model that was already well-established as simply "the EKB model." Just as Loasby (1976) had frequently referred to decision cycles in corporations, so the EKB team presented a problem-solving view of consumer behavior built around the decision cycle concept. The EKB team's approach to consumer research was a sign that, contrary to how it is often viewed, marketing is not a "Mickey Mouse subject," for their text is a serious work of evidence-based scholarship. It led me to Dewey's (1910) pioneering statement of the decision cycle process, which considerably pre-dated Loasby's sources on decision cycles.

I saw the EKB model not as something that could be readily tested but as a very useful organizing framework for initiating and considering the potential implications of fine-grained research related to its various modules. If one wanted to test the applicability, in a particular context, of something akin to a single-equation model in applied economics, there was, as Tuck (1976) argued, the model set out by psychologists Fishbein and Ajzen (1975) – which, of course, had rapidly found its way into more recent editions of the EKB team's text. If I had not started to believe that I might be able, via personal construct psychology, to make my own contributions to the analysis of consumer behavior, I could readily have concluded that economists simply needed to look at the work marshalled by the EKB team if they wanted a behavioral view of consumer choice.

It was an article by Olshavsky and Granbois that I discovered in the just-arrived September 1979 issue of the *Journal of Consumer Research* that alerted me to the limitations of the EKB team's approach to consumer behavior even before I had spent much time looking at their work. Olshavsky and Granbois argued that the EKB model and its rivals gave the misleading impression that all consumer behavior entails extended problem-solving, whereas in reality a very large amount of consumption is selected via habits, simple decision rules, and social norms, with little search, evaluation, or consideration of rival offers.

Clearly, a pluralistic approach to consumer behavior was needed, one that embraced both fast and drawn-out decision-making processes, and those between these extremes. I felt that it needed to be done mindful of the possibility that there could be great variety in how different people arrived at their choices in a given context, rather than merely focusing on how decision-making processes differed in a general way between different types of context – though

I remained open to the idea that the context of a choice (for example, how big the range of choice is, how much uncertainty there is, how costly a bad choice might be) could play a major role in shaping how decisions get made.

The Olshavsky and Granbois perspective was challenging for consumer behavior researchers, for what they were arguing reduces to little more than a line of text that has much in common with the institutional economist's view that choice is primarily driven by habits, rules, and norms (as emphasized in Hodgson, 1997). Yet it leaves us with very little to say when teaching or writing about the theory of consumer behavior. Instead, it implies that we should focus on conducting empirical work on the practices of consumers and the norms of everyday life, and then feed these findings into what we write and teach. Behavioral economists may feel rather uneasy about this, as it may seem rather like becoming a sociologist or social anthropologist. It is therefore easy to succumb to the temptation to focus on more complex decision processes about which more can be said from a theoretical standpoint.

Despite the impact that the Olshavsky and Granbois paper had on me at this formative stage, I struggled to write much in this vein a few years later when I fleshed out my view of consumer behavior into my first solo book, *The Economic Imagination* (Earl, 1983a). However, I was pleased that, in its sixth chapter ("Budgets, habits and behavior dynamics"), I did at least attempt to draw attention to simple, rule-based choices. I referred to them as "cybernetic" decisions, in light of the title and third chapter of the book by Steinbruner (1974) that Roland Clarke – one of the most impressive undergraduates that I had supervised while I was a research student in Cambridge – drew to my attention when he visited me in November 1979.[7] It was significant that Steinbruner chose to consider simplified ways of making decisions in the context of high-stakes political choices, not in relation to consumer behavior: there should be no presumption that the more important a decision is, the greater the mental effort people will put into taking it. This point seemed not to have been registered when, in the wake of the critique offered by Olshavsky and Granbois, established consumer behavior texts in marketing – such as the fourth edition of

---

[7] Roland Clarke also commended to me a remarkable then-new book by Hofstadter (1979), which proved to be very helpful for thinking about the challenges to reductionism that were already much on my mind. It also fostered my interest in infinite regress problems and gave me the idea of experimenting with the use of dialogues, one of the aspects of *The Economic Imagination* that readers seem most to remember. Roland's visit to Stirling sticks in my mind in relation to the struggle I was already having in finding enough from my pay to keep my little apartment tolerably warm: he was visibly surprised by how low a temperature I was prepared to tolerate before I turned on the electric radiators, and he made his point by asking if he might take a hot bath as a means of getting a bit warmer.

the EKB text (Engel and Blackwell, 1982) – started to distinguish between "high involvement" and "low involvement" decision-making.


## 4.6    REFEREE REACTIONS TO INITIAL WORKING PAPERS

Within my first fourteen months at Stirling, I produced three working papers and submitted them to journals.

*Wage Stickiness from the Demand Side*
The first paper that I wrote after arriving at Stirling was a joint piece with Keith Glaister, who later had a stellar career as a UK business school academic, specializing in the area of inter-firm collaborative ventures. At the time that we wrote our paper, he was a research fellow on a major externally funded project, led by Chuck Brown, that was examining the impact of taxation on labor supply. Our paper was called "Wage stickiness from the demand side" and it owed much to our mutual interest in the work of P. W. S. Andrews and Elizabeth Brunner (Andrews, 1949, 1964; Andrews and Brunner, 1975). Whereas I had got interested in their work via reading Loasby (1976), Keith's familiarity with it was more direct: his first degree was from the University of Lancaster, where Andrews and Brunner had both worked. However, infusing our paper with their way of viewing competition proved problematic. This was very ironic, since around the time we wrote it and were trying to find a home for it in a journal, I had been reading a recent University of Wollongong PhD entitled "P. W. S. Andrews and the Unsuccessful Revolution" (Irving, 1978) and corresponding with both its author and with A. W. (Bob) Coats, who had been its external examiner and had lent his copy of the thesis to Brian Loasby, whence it came to me.

I had the idea for the paper while Victoria Chick was presenting chapter 5 of her in-process book *Macroeconomics After Keynes* (published as Chick, 1983) at a departmental seminar. Her chapter addressed the microeconomic underpinnings of the aggregate supply function. Naturally, she took account of the kinds of issues that Keynes had viewed as limiting the tendency of workers to try to preserve their jobs in times of falling labor demand by offering to work for less. However, it suddenly dawned on me that the usual presumption was that employers would wish to cut wages if demand fell, so that they could reduce their prices and thereby hope to maintain output and employment. Yet, here we were, with unemployment rising in Margaret Thatcher's Britain, and employers did not seem to be trying to initiate wage cuts any more than trade unions were trying to do so. It occurred to me that this might be due to the employers having concerns that if they initiated cuts in money wages, there could be adverse consequences that went beyond unions retaliating with strike action. Perhaps they were afraid of losing their best workers and/or that productivity would suffer due to employees who had previously been very cooperative now merely doing the bare minimum within the terms of their fuzzy job contracts. I got talking with Keith as soon as the seminar finished, and we decided to write a joint paper about this issue. Before the year's end, a discussion paper (Earl and Glaister, 1979) was released, after our draft had been scrutinized by Paul Hare, who edited the discussion paper series.

We submitted the discussion paper to the *Bell Journal of Economics*, as that was where one of our most recent sources, Williamson, Wachter and Harris (1975), had been published, but the paper was rejected. Then, in July 1980, we submitted the paper to the *Economic Journal*. Before doing so, we tweaked it slightly by adding a recent quotation from a leading Conservative politician, Sir Keith Joseph, as an epigraph. His words epitomized the view that we were challenging, for he presumed that if workers were willing to work for less, they would be able to price themselves into jobs. The policy significance of the paper seemed to us to make it worth sending to the UK's top economics journal, but it was again rejected. We then wrote a less technical, graph-free version and sent it to the *British Journal of Industrial Relations*, where our work fared no better. At this point, we decided that we were getting nowhere and gave up trying to get the paper published. This was probably a mistake, for given the kind of feedback we were getting, we might have stood a better chance if we had submitted it to a heterodox journal such as the newly established *Journal of Post Keynesian Economics*, or the *Cambridge Journal of Economics*. However, the need to get the paper published in a journal seemed to evaporate once I had included the essence of its thinking in the book *Money Matters* that Sheila Dow and I started writing in autumn 1980.

My recollection of the feedback is that the referees were not as bemused by the idea that cutting wages could reduce profits due to productivity being adversely affected, as they were by the literature on which we based our analysis. They seemed to be puzzled as to why we had used sources that were not widely used in economics at that time.

We had stressed, via Coase (1937), that employment contracts do not set out in detail the tasks that workers will be asked to perform, and we drew on the behavioral theory of the firm and the recently published Williamson *et al.* (1975) paper (which I had been familiar with via its inclusion as chapter 4 of Williamson, 1975) to stress the discretionary nature of effort and responses to managerial requests, with workers in particular job categories not necessarily being assigned the same tasks or performing any given task with the same degree of efficiency. We then emphasized that, at the time of hiring workers, employers cannot be sure how well each applicant would perform if hired, whereas, once employed, workers are typically paid salaries rather than being rewarded based on their rate of output. Those who perform better than their colleagues in similar job slots do so in the hope of eventually getting promoted to jobs that have better salaries. Thus, we argued, via Andrews (1958), that "internal competition" normally has a major role in promoting industriousness even though outputs are not specified in detail in employment contracts. If demand for output falls, cutting output and retrenching the weaker performers provides a way for firms to get by without suffering from productivity reductions that could be triggered by driving wages down and then losing better workers – workers that it may be impossible to rehire by restoring wages when demand recovers. We explored this graphically in a pluralistic manner, both for firms that set their prices and outputs by applying conventional marginalist rules and for firms that are, as in Andrews's (1949) analysis, fearful of potential competition, and of wrecking goodwill relationships with customers, and which therefore base their prices on "normal" costs and then supply as much as customers demand at those prices.

I do not recall that our referees trashed the logic of the argument we were making. Rather, they seemed to be rejecting the paper because of its method and the unfamiliarity of its key sources. They seemed puzzled by our pluralistic approach, given that the normal cost perspective was one that had not become standard fare in economics, and by our concern with the internal operations of firms. We were less surprised that our enthusiasm for Andrews's work seemed odd to them than that we were running into difficulties due to being ahead of the game in the belated uptake of Coase (1937) and in employing Williamson *et al.* (1975), and because we had failed to notice that interest in Cyert and March (1963) had collapsed. But what really bugged me was that, in expecting us to argue from well-established sources, it was as if they doubted that arguments from elsewhere could be worth taking seriously and they were therefore not bothering to read and reflect on our analysis carefully. Our analysis was not crazy: all we had done was arrive too early and from left field with an idea that others successfully marketed a few years later as "efficiency wages" (see Akerlof and Yellen, eds, 1986) without committing the sin of using unpopular foundations.

*Characteristic Filtering: Towards a Behavioral Analysis of Individual Choice*
The experience with the wage stickiness paper helped to prepare me for the failure of the next paper that I wrote, in which I attempted to set out my characteristic filtering idea in relation to Kelly's personal construct psychology rather than any notion of a hierarchical utility function, as well as examining budgeting from a priorities-based standpoint (Earl, 1980a). It was rejected outright when I sent it to the newly launched *Journal of Economic Behavior and Organization*, and I realized that it had been a mistake to build it around Kelly's ideas as an alternative to viewing economic agents as utility seekers. It resulted in a presentation of characteristic filtering that was viewed as far too wordy and difficult to understand, yet I do not recall the referees suggesting that I ought to have presented a formal model built around linear programming. Except for some references to Herbert Simon, it is likely that everything I referred to would have been unfamiliar to US-sourced referees if they were economists rather than consumer behavior researchers in marketing. From these experiences, I concluded that I would need much more space to introduce and integrate unfamiliar ideas in a way that sustained the attention of readers.

*A Behavioral Theory of Economists' Behavior and the Lack of Success of Behavioral Economics*
The paper on characteristic filtering was written during the 1980 long vacation. After completing it, I decided that I would have some fun by writing a somewhat satirical paper, to which I gave the reflexive title "A behavioral theory of economists' behavior and the lack of success of behavioral economics." It was inspired by reflection on (a) my experience with the referee reactions to the paper I had written with Keith Glaister, (b) how I had come to know about the sources that informed my work, and (c) the struggle that I had been through with some of these sources (especially with those by Andrews, which entailed multiple readings of them) until I felt confident that I really had "got" what they were saying.

This reflection had left me feeling that the processes that determine the success of contributions to economic knowledge are rather like those that determine the sales of products offered in supermarkets. University libraries offer such vast ranges of products that it is impossible for their customers to become familiar with everything that is being offered that may be relevant to their research and teaching. Choices must therefore be simplified via rule- and routine-based filtering processes that are affected by social interactions. Many books and journal articles may thus fail to enjoy the attention they deserve. This shortage of attention will also affect refereeing processes, partly via its impact on referees' knowledge of cited sources and partly via how much time referees invest in trying to appreciate what authors are trying to do. However, as Irving (1978) had tried to demonstrate in her study of the fate of Andrews's work, the preconceptions of referees can result in them failing to draw the right inferences about what authors are trying to do.

Furthermore, I felt it was unwise to assume that academics were single-mindedly operating as "humble seekers after truth" as opposed to having multiple goals that might be hierarchically ordered, thereby making them intolerant of particular kinds of contributions. Some might be lazy, self-serving folk who prefer "playing with models" to wading through complex prose. As referees, they may fail to give serious attention to works whose styles are not to their taste, especially if they enjoy both the convenience and sense of power of performing a quick hatchet-job rather than ensuring that they "get" what the author is trying to do and then offer constructive criticism. Whether, and where, academic ideas end up getting published and cited may thus have little to do with their benefits for society at large. With hindsight, I would have added that this makes the design of research audit systems very problematic, with the audits having potential to corrupt the ways in which academics operate, to the detriment of society at large.

Although written with satirical intent, my behavioral analysis of academic economics was released as a departmental discussion paper (Earl, 1980b) immediately following the one on characteristic filtering. I therefore decided to submit it to *History of Political Economy* to see whether it would be taken seriously. Somewhat to my surprise, it was. In contrast to the previous two papers, it received some very constructive feedback and an invitation to revise and resubmit. However, although I carefully revised it to take account of the referees' comments, I never resubmitted it. This was due to Alfred Eichner asking if he could build an edited volume (Eichner, ed, 1983) around it. He had been shown the paper by Fred Lee, who had become his doctoral student after spending some time at the University of Edinburgh under the mentorship of Gavin Reid. Gavin was familiar with the work of Andrews and had passed my discussion paper to Fred, thinking he would find it interesting. This chain of events resulted not merely in Eichner's edited volume; it also led to Fred and I sharing our enthusiasm for Andrews with each other, and after more than a decade of correspondence, we edited a volume of Andrews's collected papers (Lee and Earl, eds, 1993).

I realized that letting Eichner have the paper was not my best strategy for enhancing my CV, but I felt obliged, out of collegial duty, to allow him to use the paper: he had given me great encouragement and I felt that my paper could help the book's co-contributors get their related perspectives noticed if other scholars made their way to the book after seeing my contribution being cited. It was the first of many obligational publications that would limit the time that I spent enhancing my list of journal articles in the ensuing four decades.

## 4.7  THIRD ATTEMPT TO OBTAIN CONFIRMATION AS A DOCTORAL CANDIDATE

The first semester of the 1980–1981 academic year had started by the time that the referee reports arrive from *History of Political Economy*. By that point, Sheila Dow and I were co-teaching a master's-level course on monetary economics. We agreed that Sheila would give the first seven lectures, plus a couple at the end, and I would give the rest. My part would include theory and case-study lectures on Minsky as well as weaving in Katona's ideas on consumer sentiment and a cut-down view of wage stickiness from the demand side as ingredients in a very non-reductionist fundamentalist Keynesian perspective and critical analysis of monetarist thinking. However, we faced an unusual situation: the course was going to be discontinued and we had only one student, so the question was how we might get a reasonable pay-off for our efforts in tooling up for it. I proposed to Sheila that we should write a book based on the course and aim to get as much of it written as possible while the course was in process. Initially, she was not keen on the idea, fearing it might unduly get in the way of working on her PhD – and she could also reasonably have pointed out that I should be concentrating on my PhD, too. However, she agreed to give it a go after I argued that if I took near-verbatim long-hand notes on her lectures, it would not take long to transform them into chapters for the book. Meanwhile, I would write my chapters and base my lectures on them. We decided to call the book *Money Matters: A Keynesian Approach to Monetary Economics*. Its writing went largely according to the plan that I had devised: around Easter 1981, the manuscript was ready to send off to publishers.[8]

My attention then returned to the question of how to make progress toward getting a PhD. By this stage, it had become clear that Brian Loasby's approach

---

[8] It was rejected by the first publisher to whom we sent it, as the referee, David Laidler, objected to the inclusion of a methodology-focused chapter on schools of thought in monetary economics He claimed that methodology was a subject for consenting adults to discuss in private, not for students. No such objections were raised when we sent it to a second publisher, who then offered us a contract for it, and we only needed to make minor changes before we submitted the final version for printing.

to PhD supervision was not an active one based on regular meetings for discussing strategies for making progress, with plenty of feedback on things that I wrote, in the manner that today's graduate school deans hope thesis advisors will operate to ensure that research students stay focused on becoming ready for their next progress review milestones. It was not until a year later, when I started getting insistent about the need for feedback as time was getting short, that things got better on that front.

Yet, on the rare occasions that Brian initiated something, the impact was significant: first, there had been his strong encouragement for me to read Kelly's work; next, he had shared with me the copy of Juli Irving's (1978) PhD thesis on P. W. S. Andrews  that had been lent to him;  and then, in Spring 1981, he had said that if I wanted to write a Kelly-related paper to present alongside the one he was writing for the upcoming conference of the British Association for the Advancement of Science at the University of York, then he would try to ensure that Jack Wiseman, the chair of the economics section, would find a place for me in the program, as indeed he did. That, too, had a major impact on my career, for it was at this conference that I got to know George Shackle, Bob Coats, Stephen Littlechild and John Hey, who each helped my career in the ensuing decade.

In my early years at Stirling, the difficulty of extracting significant advice and feedback from Brian Loasby about what he thought of my ideas or what I wrote appeared to be more the result of his social idiosyncrasies and limitations in how he construed his supervisory role than due to him being too short of time to discuss my work with me. Brian quite often would poke his head into my office and then talk about economics in the way that he had done at our first meeting. It was always interesting to hear what he had to say, but sometimes the timing was not ideal. I soon realized that if Brian came into my office and sat on one of my low-level filing cabinets near the door, as he seemed particularly prone to do late in the afternoon, I would not be able to end the interaction by using normal social cues if I needed to get away.

On one occasion this happened when I needed to leave to drive to Glasgow for a performance by Scottish Opera (whose reasonably-priced subscription series were my only indulgence around that time). Because I planned to drive there straight from work and had decided to be dressed for the occasion, I had worn my suit to work that day and had endured a seemingly endless stream of "Where's the job interview?" quips from colleagues. However, until I cut in and said that I really had to go, and why, Brian seemed completely oblivious of what I was wearing and that it, and my other non-verbal cues, signified that he should wind up what he was saying.

I was not the only one to be treated to this, but I probably benefited more than my colleagues did. One, who shall remain nameless, explained to me that he had tried to make his office "Brian-proof" by moving his filing cabinets away from the door, making it difficult for Brian to lean on anything, let alone sit down. The colleague advised me that I had the worst possible arrangement: low-level filing cabinets close to the door.

On one of these occasions, I managed to get Brian on to the question of my PhD and the challenge of knowing what to do to get confirmation. As I did so, I raised a question that had puzzled me ever since I first saw the departmental letterhead, which listed the titles and degrees of the department's professors: I said that I had noticed that he had taken an MLitt in Cambridge rather than a PhD and that I had no idea what an MLitt was. Brian looked very sheepish and said, "It's a failed PhD." All that he then added was what the topic had been. He opened up more about it in 1998 when I interviewed him during the preparation of the introduction to the pair of festschrift volumes in his honor that Sheila Dow and I edited (Dow and Earl, eds, 1999a, 1999b). I now think that the way he went about his role as a PhD supervisor most likely was a consequence of the impressions of the role that he had picked up from how his own supervisors (he named at least three) had operated. Whatever the reason was for the way he played the supervisor role, the consequence was that I essentially continued to fend for myself as I attempted to get confirmation as a doctoral student.

### Attempt 3 (1981): A Behavioral/Post Keynesian Micro/Macro Synthesis

Archaeological activities in my filing cabinets failed to unearth any documents pertaining to my third attempt at winning confirmation, and even the title that is listed above is an approximation. It was, in effect, my response to the reported basis for the verdict on my second attempt: it took the research program idea even further and was based on a book proposal that I had put together after realizing that there was potential for integrating the work I had been doing on consumer behavior (Earl, 1980a) and wage stickiness (Earl and Glaister, 1979) since arriving at Stirling, with the behavioral theory of the firm, Neo-/Post-Marshallian theories of pricing, investment and firm growth, and Post Keynesian perspectives on money and employment.

In its book proposal version, this project failed to generate much enthusiasm when it was sent to Oxford University Press. It also failed as a PhD proposal. Again, Phyllis Deane proved to be immovable. However, Geoff Meeks relayed to me a comment that she had made about it that has stayed in my mind ever since: she had said that it was not suitable for a PhD dissertation since it was "either trivial or a lifetime's work." With hindsight, it seems to me that she was spot-on in her judgment. I still had a long way to go in developing the consumer behavior side of my work, and I had not yet given much attention to the theory of the banking firm (where there was potential for integrating the work of Andrews, Minsky, Coase, and the behavioral theory of the firm). In a sense, my 1990 book *Monetary Scenarios* was my first attempt to do what this proposal had envisaged, but it was well over the length of a PhD. It would indeed be something like a "lifetime's work" before I got closer to where this proposal had envisaged going, namely my (2022) *Principles of Behavioral Economics*, a book that – despite being light on the monetary side – is nearly three and a half times the length allowed for a Cambridge PhD.

Looking back, one might say that my thesis ideas in 1978 were closer to raising the kind of "research question" that I should have used as a basis for a PhD than they had become with my third attempt at confirmation. At the start, my implicit underlying question was an empirical one: "To what extent can non-optimizing theories of business decision-making explain evolving patterns of relative national competitiveness?" Where I had got to with my third proposal was a much more conceptual question, where the value of an answer would be harder to demonstrate: "Is it possible to construct a coherent, unifying approach to economics that takes due account of complexity and fundamental uncertainty?"

The implicit message in Phyllis Deane's comment was that I needed to come up with something that was tightly focused and had depth. However, nothing was coming my way in terms of advice about what a prospective "contribution to knowledge" had to look like to win confirmation of candidature. Yet, by the time that the third thumbs-down was delivered, there was a potential research question that I might have considered based on where I had got to, and it would have provided the basis for a well-defined empirical project: "How significant are the roles that non-compensatory decision rules and personal principles are playing as determinants of penetration of the UK's car market by imported products?" This could have been anchored to Stout's (1977) report on non-price factors in international trade. It could have been based on surveys or focus group-based research with car buyers and could have included interviews with car dealers and marketing executives of carmakers to determine whether they were aware of the possibility that consumers were using intolerant decision rules.

The ingredients were there – Stout's paper had piqued my interest in non-price factors, the potentially catastrophic effects of a single shortcoming for sales of a product were very much "on my radar" via media attention given to catastrophic early rust problems with Lancia Beta cars in the UK shortly after I had started to view choice as a process of "characteristic filtering" and discovered the marketing literature on non-compensatory decision rules, and the story of my father's Honda Civic had got me wondering about principles-based choices – but I failed at that time to make the connections in terms of potential for a research project of this kind. However, even if I had seen the potential of such a project, I would have had little hope of completing it by September 30, 1982, the deadline by which I needed to submit my thesis.

## 4.8    WRITING *THE ECONOMIC IMAGINATION*

The deadline got much closer before I ended up with a more tightly focused project than my third proposal, albeit one that was not focused on an empirical research question. Instead, it offered a psychologically informed behavioral analysis on why people choose as they do. It came about purely by happenstance rather than any deep reflection on how I might be able to win over Phyllis Deane. The chain of events that led to my fourth thesis proposal initially led me to start writing a book without thinking that it might be something that I could turn into a PhD thesis. This section is about the writing of that book; Section 4.9 then explains how the book came to provide the basis for my fourth attempt to obtain confirmation as a doctoral candidate.

One afternoon, toward the end of the first semester of 1981, I went with some colleagues to the University of Edinburgh to attend a seminar. This also gave me my first opportunity to meet Gavin Reid, one of the local attendees. I had hoped he would be there, so that I could thank him for passing to Fred Lee my discussion paper on economists' behavior that Fred had then shown to Alfred Eichner. After the seminar had finished, I introduced myself to Gavin and thanked him for his collegiality. He then told me about his new book, *The Kinked Demand Curve Analysis of Oligopoly* (Reid, 1981). This was naturally of interest to me, given its connection with the Oxford Economists' Research Group. Soon after, I acquired a copy of Gavin's book. It appeared to have been written as a side-project from his PhD and was a short, single-issue book that dealt well with its topic. Later, I often found it very useful when teaching second-year microeconomics. But when I first looked at it, it was its form that got me thinking about whether I might write a short book of my own, a book on the alternative view of consumer behavior that I had been putting together since arriving at Stirling. I saw it as something that could help fill a gap that had become evident with the publication of Eichner's (1979) edited volume, *A Guide to Post-Keynesian Economics*, a book that lacked a chapter on consumer behavior.

The book that I decided to write ended up quite a bit longer than Gavin's one. I gave it the working title "A Behavioral/Post Keynesian Analysis of Choice." It was "behavioral" in the sense that it took ideas from the behavioral theory of the firm and blended them with psychological inputs. It was "Post Keynesian" partly in the sense that it drew on Keynes's views on the significance of confidence and crowd behavior in a world of uncertainty, as well as on related contributions by scholars that Coddington (1976) had called "fundamentalist Keynesians." However, it was published as *The Economic Imagination: Towards a Behavioral Analysis of Choice* (Earl, 1983a), by Wheatsheaf Books, a new economics imprint of the Harvester Press. The main title was the idea of Wheatsheaf's managing editor, Edward Elgar. Edward had conceived the title as ideal for a book that had a strongly subjectivist flavor, as mine had, that he had thought he might one day be able to get someone such as Jack Wiseman to write.

The subtitle's first word signaled that I viewed academic research as a satisficing process and hence I did not view any of my work as definitive. Clearly, scholarship must involve satisficing behavior, for there is insufficient time to read everything that might be relevant to what one is considering writing. But this begged the question of how much is enough where scholarship is concerned, a question whose answer might not be the same for a book that might attract some attention (as *The Economic Imagination* initially did), as for a PhD, or for a book that would have a big impact. This would turn out to be a rather important issue.

By the end of 1981, I had a contract with Wheatsheaf and *The Economic Imagination* was well on its way, not least of all because I was able to salvage and extend material that I had written for the consumer behavior section at the front of the partially written book that had led to my third confirmation attempt, and I had also written some of what became the final chapter as part of my paper for the meeting of the British Association for the Advancement of Science (published as Earl, 1983c). In the remainder of the writing of the book there were two areas that proved challenging: one was the treatment of budgeting; the other was how generally applicable I should present characteristic filtering as being as a way of thinking about deliberative choices.

*Issues in Budgeting*
The manuscript of *The Economic Imagination* that I submitted to Wheatsheaf included a graphical analysis of hierarchical budgeting. However, just before the

book finally went to press, I removed the graphical material and revised the surrounding text despite it not having led to any objections from the two referees. The reason that I ultimately did not even offer a graphical approach to budgeting, let alone try to re-learn and then apply linear programming to this area, was that I noticed that some of the budget lines might not be linear, due to complementarities or negative externalities between different activities that affected attainments for multiple targets. Drawing and explaining hierarchical budgeting with a mix of linear, concave and convex budget lines, and showing how they could move due to changes in income or relative prices was quite a challenge, even for budgeting between just two categories. I felt that I should limit what I wrote to what seemed simple enough to be plausible.

My experience in using graphs to conduct a hierarchical analysis of budgeting provides a good example of how traditional economic tools can lead one to miss what people really do in the area that one is analyzing. If one wants to present such an analysis, the obvious strategy is to show budgeting between two categories on a graph whose axes show the amount allocated to the respective categories. A linear budget line with a 45-degree downward slope can be drawn from the maximum that can be spent in the category represented on the vertical axis to the maximum that can be spent in the category represented on the horizontal axis. One can then successively work down the hierarchy of wants, considering what are the cheapest sets of combinations of the two product categories that will enable the first-priority want to be met. In some cases, this will only entail spending in one of the product categories; if so, this can be represented by a line perpendicular to the spending axis for that category of product at the amount that needs to be spent to satisfy the want.

In other cases, where combinations of the two product types can serve a want, we may get an efficiency frontier that is a straight, convex, or concave line from one axis to the other. We can then show what happens to the efficiency frontier as the consumer moves on to consider combinations of spending that enable the second priority to be met without compromising the first, and so on for the third and subsequent priorities. As we stack on further layers to show combinations of what will need to be spent to meet goals of successively lower priority, the shape of the efficiency frontier may become a complex set of segments of lines and curves that moves progressively towards the budget line and eventually starts to cross it. Sooner or later, we will arrive at a point where the next priority cannot be met without the entire efficiency frontier being to the right of the budget line, so we then have to retreat to the efficiency frontier arrived at for the previous priority and examine the feasible set of allocations that remain, some of which may have a residual amount that can be used to get some way toward meeting the next priority. The allocation between the two product categories that will be selected is the one that will take the consumer closest to meeting the next priority.

Clearly, this is challenging to generalize beyond two dimensions, but the way the graph gets constructed even for two dimensions has a more fundamental problem. In the process just outlined, we began with a blank graph and worked toward the budget constraint by extending spending, where necessary, to cover successively less important wants. To derive the efficiency frontier for any set of $n$ hierarchically ranked wants, we proceed as if the consumer explores all possible combinations beyond the frontier previously arrived at for $n$ -1 wants, computing the total cost of each combination of spending in the two categories. However, real-world consumers seem more likely to reflect on budgetary allocations at points in historical time, after experiencing changes in prices or income, to address questions about how to limit the impact of tighter budget constraints or not miss opportunities presented by easier budget constraints. Given their starting point for budgeting, people will only consider a limited set of new allocation strategies, due to their cognitive constraints, and will stop devising and considering alternatives once they conclude they have found a good enough way of limiting attrition (or advancing, in the case of an easier budget constraint) in the priorities they expect to be able to meet in their current planning period. Instead of considering a comprehensive range of possibilities, people will operate rather like organizations do when budgeting, with routines for seeing where cuts might be possible without unnecessarily compromising the attainment of high priority wants, and with wish-list projects to implement if financial slack appears.

In other words, contrary to the impression that graphical analysis fosters, people who are considering what they can afford do not need to reflect on their options as if budgeting from scratch. Rather, they are typically considering an addition to what they consume, financed by running down their financial reserves and/or making a specific reduction in another area of spending. Hence, the key issue is, "If I spend on what I'm currently considering, to meet a goal that I am not currently meeting, will this prevent me from meeting any more important goals that I will be able to meet if I don't do the spending that I am contemplating?" They thus look back from less important to more important wants in an "other things equal" manner, and if the way they are thinking of adding to the spending and financing that spending leads them to think of *any* presently-met wants that will be compromised, the idea of such spending is then ruled out. This is a kind of marginal adjustment, but it works in a hierarchical sense, not in terms of maximization of an additive utility function.

However, a year before I decided to abandon my graphical analysis of budgeting, I had begun to have a different kind of concern about how people figure out what they can afford. I realized, via Steinbruner (1974, chapter 4) and from my own experience in wrestling with budgeting problems, that cognitive processes could limit how carefully consumers think through the implications of choices that were being driven by temptation associated with prospects of meeting hitherto unmet goals and/or desperation associated with difficulties in continuing to meet more basic priorities.

By March 1981, increases in my pay should have been helping me to restore my discretionary spending by offsetting the increased monthly mortgage payments that monetarist anti-inflation policies had triggered. Yet I was having trouble saving up for anything because I had experienced a string of expensive bills for my 1972 Ford Cortina. I thus began trying to figure out whether I might be better off if I took out a bank loan to buy a much newer car that would, at the cost of increasing my non-discretionary outgoings (i.e., via monthly payments to the bank), enable me to reduce or eliminate the risk of such bills, thereby making some saving possible as I repaid the loan even though the loan would finance a depreciating asset. After rejecting the idea of buying a new or very recent small car on the basis that I would lose the high-speed cruising capabilities that the two-liter Cortina provided, I ended up trading the Cortina against an ex-fleet Vauxhall Cavalier Coupé that was five years younger, a generation more modern, more luxurious, and more stylish. But I made the decision with little idea of the comparative probabilities of repair bills on the two vehicles: by that stage, the Cortina had many new parts so it might then have given several years of trouble-free motoring, but there was still a lot that could go wrong and rust was starting to concern me; the Cavalier had a full service history and came with a one-year warranty that covered some major components (and was duly honored when the Cavalier's water pump failed soon after I purchased it) but I had no knowledge of when maintenance might start getting expensive.

Amid that uncertainty, I could tell myself that upgrading the car was possibly a means to improving the predictability of my finances. It did indeed prove much cheaper to maintain than the Cortina had been. However, it is less clear whether I ended up reducing my motoring cost over the rest of my time at Stirling, given the interest charges on the loan and the Cavalier's depreciation. It is not clear whether rust would have prevented me from keeping the Cortina going until the end of April 1984, the time at which I was preparing to leave Stirling and sold the Cavalier. A further conundrum is the extent to which having to repay the loan on the Cavalier may have resulted in me forcing myself to save more than I otherwise would have done, for when I sold the Cavalier, it was still worth half of what I had paid for it, which was considerably more than the Cortina would have been worth by that point if it were still roadworthy.

A cynic might argue that, at the time I bought the Cavalier, it was more clearly a means to meet less-basic goals and thereby give me a sense that I was getting somewhere. As I reflected on my decision, I could appreciate Garfinkel's (1967, pp. 113–114) contention that the human mind attempts to provide an illusion of rationality by concocting convenient stories to justify actions that the mind has already decided upon by means that might not be clear to the person in question. For some, this might result in dangerously weak-willed behavior in pursuing low priority goals, accompanied by an "I'll cross that bridge if I come to it" attitude in relation to how they will pay bills related to more basic needs.

### Pluralism and Behavioral Economics

There is a rather inconsistent look to the way that I practiced pluralism in relation to behavioral economics during my years at Stirling. On the one hand, I rejected a one-size-fits-all view of consumer behavior in favor of a view that embraced both extended problem-solving and extreme simplification. Furthermore, in my analysis of economists' behavior, I criticized Pickering (1976, p. 622) for suggesting, in his review of Andrews and Brunner's (1975) *Studies in Pricing*, that they had failed to offer a "sufficiently general" theory of the behavior of oligopolies, as though a theory should apply very generally within the context it purports to address. But prior to 1983 (including in *The Economic Imagination*, which I had completed by mid-1982), I was prone to try to "sell" my "characteristic filtering" view of choice as a general way of viewing what people do when choosing between a wide range of options that offer many characteristics. This is especially evident in the dialogue that I wrote for section 4.9 of *The Economic Imagination*. Yet, in all honesty, I did not really believe it applied generally in that sort of situation. So, why did I write as though my approach was generally right and the marginal trade-off approach was generally wrong, rather than preach the need for pluralism?

My concern was that, if I accepted that people might differ in the ways that they take their decisions in a particular context and that some people's behavior might align well with the received wisdom, then I would be unlikely to attract an audience for my non-mainstream perspective: allowing that there could be more than a grain of truth in the orthodox perspective could result in me getting no traction due to orthodox economists not being open to pluralistic thinking. If so, there was the risk that they would respond by asserting that their approach was "sufficiently general" to use as "the" way to view behavior in that context.

They would also be likely to present instances where their view does not seem implausible as means to dismiss the credibility of arguments that I raised to suggest their theory could not accommodate other instances. In other words, they might adopt the rhetorical strategy of saying that if one dug deeper, or bigger changes in incentives had been applied, then cases that I raised to illustrate non-substitution would be revealed as ultimately reducing to cases where "everyone had their price," as in any instances where I accepted the substitution principle. Given the risk of such a reaction, it might be better simply to use strong-looking examples of non-substitution wherever possible and not mention examples where people do indeed seem to make trade-offs along the lines envisaged by Lancaster. Of course, orthodox economists might react by digging up such examples and accusing me of presenting a very one-sided view, but perhaps they might start to advocate the case for a pluralistic approach if, on reflection, my non-substitution examples seemed plausible.

In advocating a "characteristic filtering" view of choice to the exclusion of both the conventional good-space view and Lancaster's characteristics-space view, I thus failed to be as pluralistic as I was in my later writing but naively hoped to promote pluralism in others, to which I would of course be able to accede.

A few months after *The Economic Imagination* was published, Mark Blaug visited Stirling in his external examiner role. After the departmental examiners' meeting, I talked with him in the coffee room. He told me that he had greatly enjoyed my book and that, in writing it, I had been "very courageous." I had merely thought that I was doing what academics are supposed to do, i.e., facilitate the growth of knowledge by challenging the conventional wisdom. However, later in the 1980s, I was told that an external assessor for a job that I had applied for at the University of Auckland had dismissed my application by saying that I was "a brash young man by all accounts."

My lack of life experience was certainly an issue when I wrote the book, for I had simply not done enough shopping or read enough product reviews, or talked enough with others about their purchasing decisions, to be able to offer copious illustrations of intolerant and/or checklist-based decision-making. I also should have made much more use of applications of Lakatos's (1970) methodology of scientific research programs to economics (such as Latsis, 1972, and Remenyi, 1979), to highlight the intolerance of the "positive heuristic" and "negative heuristic" (i.e., the "do" and "don't" rules) of mainstream economics for specifying acceptable forms of behavior within economics. In the event, although *The Economic Imagination* was reviewed quite widely and often more sympathetically than I had expected, no debate ensued about the relative applicability of substitution-based and non-substitution-based views of choice, and the book achieved virtually no citations in mainstream literature.

I would have had a better chance of gaining traction if I had been able to show economists, via empirical work in contrasting contexts, how propensities to choose in particular ways differ between contexts, why this is so, and why it matters for policy. By such work, I might have argued that a better way ahead for everyone is empirically-grounded pluralism, which accepts that rival ideas may each apply to some degree and which attempts to study relative incidences of applicability in both a broad context (for example, how people decide whom to approach via online dating sites) and within variants of that context (for example, whether the applicability of a particular view of such choices varies according to how much information an online dating site displays on a page of search results – cf. Lenton and Stewart, 2008). Such empirical research could perhaps have provided me with a basis for a PhD if I had started working in this area back in 1977. However, a more realistic view is that it was something for which the role-model needed to be provided by a well-resourced team of researchers. This was eventually delivered by Payne, Bettman and Johnson (1993).

## 4.9    FOURTH ATTEMPT TO OBTAIN CONFIRMATION AS A DOCTORAL CANDIDATE

In the second half of 1981, as I worked on writing what became *The Economic Imagination*, I did not give much thought to how I might revive my PhD prospects. The pressure to get a PhD seemed rather diminished since I had completed my two-year probationary period at Stirling and was now a tenured lecturer. I was enjoying writing books and I wondered if I might be able to be as productive on that front as John Hey and Mark Casson, whose new books I kept seeing, along with signs of their career progress, in publishers' catalogues. Had I known at that time that Casson had been a casualty of the Cambridge PhD system and that Hey, too, did not have a doctorate, their role-model impacts might have cemented further the idea that one did not need to complete a doctorate to enjoy a successful academic career, even in the 1980s.

My decision to have a further shot at getting my PhD candidature confirmed was triggered on January 23, 1982. This was the day that George Shackle came to Stirling to deliver the Scottish Economic Society's annual Shell Lecture. I was tasked with being his minder for the day, which included picking him and Catherine Shackle up from Stirling station and the disconcerting experience of seeing that there had been no warning that George was on a special diet and that there was virtually nothing that Catherine deemed he could safely eat. However, my minder role did not prevent me from spending some time catching up with Neil Kay, whom I had first met a year or so previously when he visited Stirling to give a seminar. Neil was now working at Heriot-Watt University in Edinburgh but he had been one of the very first economics students when the University of Stirling was established, after which he completed his PhD there. It had resulted in his book *The Innovating Firm* (Kay, 1979), which I discussed in Section 4.2.

On the day of Shackle's presentation, Neil and I talked about PhDs. In his case (as he had noted in the preface to his book), Brian Loasby had been a source of "initial encouragement," but he ultimately got his thesis safely completed mainly under the supervision of Richard Shaw.[9] After listening to where I had got in my PhD saga, Neil urged me not to give up on getting a doctorate. "It's your travel ticket," he said. I decided to accept his advice.

*Attempt 4 (1982): A Behavioral Analysis of Choice*
My fourth proposal necessarily had to be quickly assembled and had to propose something that would be quick to complete, as the conversation with Neil Kay took place with just over eight months remaining for me to submit a thesis. What I proposed to submit as "A Behavioral Analysis of Choice" consisted essentially of *The Economic Imagination*, minus the second chapter "Pricing Choices," with a revised and extended 60-page version of my discussion paper "A behavioral theory of economists' behavior and the lack of success of behavioral economics" (Earl, 1980b) added at the end as a case study of decision-making involving a rule- and template-based filtering process. This time, Phyllis Deane would not be a potential impediment, as Geoff Harcourt had replaced her on the committee. Better still, two years previously, Geoff had provided some encouraging comments on the original discussion paper version of my study of economists' behavior.

In May 1982, over four and a half years after commencing as a research student, I received a letter from the Board of Graduate Studies informing me that my candidature as a PhD student had been confirmed. The letter included the unsurprising reminder that my candidacy would be terminated if I failed to submit my thesis by September 30, 1982.

---

[9] Like Brian Loasby, Richard Shaw was a Cambridge alumnus, and he, too, worked on the competitive process mindful of the work of Andrews and the US behavioral theorists. Richard was then a senior lecturer at Stirling but his excellent people-skills and management knowledge later enabled him to become the Principal of the University of Paisley (Now the University of the West of Scotland.

## 4.10   SUBMISSION AND ORAL EXAMINATION

The short window between the confirmation of my candidature and the date by which I needed to submit the finished thesis did not seem to me to be a problem, even allowing for several weeks of exam marking, a few weeks of vacation, and a week or two for getting the copies bound and delivered, for what I intended to submit was essentially ready to go aside from some editing and splicing. By the time of my oral examination, its ingredients were "in press" as accepted publications: *The Economic Imagination* had been refereed for Wheatsheaf Books by Professor Mark Blaug and Professor Stephen Littlechild, and endorsed by Shackle, and Eichner had confirmed that he had got a contract for the edited book that he had built around my paper on economists' behavior. Given that economists of some note had liked my work, there was potential for me to be over-confident about my chances. However, I was mindful that Geoff Meeks had warned me that a doctoral thesis is assessed in terms of different criteria from those used for monographs and chapters in edited books. One thing that I felt I had in my favor was that the case study chapter showed more substantial evidence of scholarship than the shorter version eventually published in the Eichner volume. But the basic problem was that I still did not know which criteria my examiners might use to assess whether my work was a sufficiently big contribution to knowledge to be worth a doctoral degree from the University of Cambridge. It really was a case of wondering "What could possibly go wrong?"

My oral examination in November 1982 was held at the Master's Lodge, Clare College, as my internal examiner was Professor Robin Matthews, who was the Master of Clare as well as Professor of Political Economy. Geoff Meeks told me that Matthews seemed a good fit for the task since he was "getting into institutional economics." I had been to the Master's Lodge at Clare once before, to a function that Matthews held to celebrate James Meade's success in being awarded the 1977 Nobel Memorial Prize in Economic Sciences. Otherwise, my only interaction with Matthews had been when he contacted me because of my reputation as a supervisor of undergraduates (all eighteen months of it!) to see whether I would be willing to take on a Clare student whom he felt was at risk of failing Part II due to over-indulging in student politics. He was probably impressed by what I did after taking on the task, for the student in question ended up with a lower-second. But I had no idea how my research would fare with him. Had I realized that Matthews was, with Hahn, on a mission to make Cambridge economics more orthodox (see Saith, 2022), I would have been very nervous indeed.

My external examiner was Professor John Pickering of the University of Manchester Institute of Science and Technology. He was one of very few suggestions that I had offered to Geoff Meeks about someone who might be right for the role. Pickering was a man of high integrity whose career was later blighted (as his Wikipedia entry explains at some length) by what happened when he acted as a whistle-blower against the Vice-Chancellor of the University of Portsmouth while serving as the latter's deputy. He was the only British economist that I could think of who was familiar with behavioral approaches to the firm as well as being interested in consumer behavior. In the latter context, his work focused on the demand for consumer durables with a Katona-like emphasis on the role of consumer sentiment.

However, although I had suggested Pickering, the thesis that I had submitted without knowing he would be my external examiner was not one that set out to cultivate his approval. It had two Pickering-related issues that had potential to have the reverse effect. One was that in my chapter on economists' choices I had critically commented on his contention that Andrews and Brunner's view of pricing was not "sufficiently general" in terms of the industries to which it might be applied. The other was that although my awareness of Pickering's work on consumer behavior came from seeing a review of his book *The Acquisition of Consumer Durables: A Cross-Sectional Investigation* (Pickering, 1977), I had forgotten to check it out and see how it related to my thesis. I very much doubt that either Pickering-related issue was decisive, but my advice to PhD students has always been to take careful account of the work of those that one nominates as potential examiners, and to be very careful not to get on the wrong side of them by challenging their work: not all academics will have the kind of integrity for which Pickering came to be known.

The hour-long grilling that Matthews and Pickering dispensed was very disconcerting, for they raised no issues about my original contributions; indeed, they barely commented on what I offered. Instead, it seemed as if all they were checking was my awareness of what they viewed as classic non-mainstream contributions on consumer behavior that might relate to what I was offering. These included Houthakker and Taylor (1970) (which I knew about from Ajit Singh mentioning it in my first Prelims supervision – in relation to the great importance of income effects relative to substitution effects as drivers of changes in the pattern of demand – but which I had never read) and the British market research pioneer Harry Henry's (1958) critique of linear demand functions. In asking about possible similarities between Andrews' methods and those of Wesley Clair Mitchell, Matthews provided evidence of his research direction that was consistent with what Geoff Meeks had said but also exposed a gap in my knowledge. My examiners thereby found my Achilles' heel: a lack of due diligence in developing my knowledge of the literature relevant to the thesis I had ended up submitting, a thesis on a very different topic from the areas on which I had read prodigiously and with scholarly determination in my first two years as a research student. I made no attempt to feign knowledge that I did not possess and eventually left Matthews's study without a strong sense of what the outcome would be.

Later, I realized that there were other cases where, as with Pickering's book, I had forgotten to take account of important sources of which I was aware. For example, during 1980, I discovered that Lutz and Lux (1979) and Bettman (1979) had recently analyzed, respectively, budgeting and product choices in non-compensatory terms. The former was inspired by Maslow's (1943, [1954] 1970) "hierarchy of needs;" the latter came from the marketing literature but was inspired by Simon's work on information processing with finite cognitive capacity. After the briefest of perusals, I made a mental note to read them one day. However, I then got diverted by the self-inflicted task of writing *Money Matters* with Sheila Dow after getting as far as buying a copy of Bettman's book on September 26, 1980. I did not bother to look at my copy of Bettman or at the library's copy of Lutz and Lux's book until at least three years later, when I was revising my thesis, having also failed to discuss them in *The Economic Imagination*. While revising my thesis, and in the years that followed, I discovered more contributions to a hierarchical view of choice, though never as many as Stirling PhD alumnus Stavros Drakopoulos. Readers who are interested in this field should consult the surveys provided by Drakopoulos (1994; Drakopoulos and Karayiannis, 2004).


## 4.11   REVISE AND RESUBMIT

Modern-day doctoral candidates are usually advised, at least informally, of the outcome of their thesis examination process on the day of their oral examination or within a few days of it. Detailed examiners' reports that include specific suggestions of any changes that should be made follow within a couple of weeks. In my case, by contrast, over two months passed before I received notification from Dr N. J. B. A. Branson, the Secretary of the Board of Graduate Studies in a form letter dated February 1, 1983. The letter explained that the Board had decided not to award me a PhD but to allow me to choose between revising and resubmitting my dissertation by January 1, 1985 or not doing that and instead being awarded the degree of MSc forthwith. The letter did not include any reports from my examiners to indicate the basis for the decision, but it informed me that if I replied to confirm that I was going to revise and resubmit, or that I was having difficulty deciding whether to do so, then my examiners would be contacted to ascertain which sections of their reports should be provided to me (though they would be sent to my supervisor) to assist me with the revision or my decision about whether to revise my dissertation. The letter then informed me, rather ominously, that I should not assume that I would be granted a PhD if I revised my dissertation along the lines suggested in the extracts from the examiners' reports, for a fresh examination process would begin when I resubmitted my dissertation and it would not necessarily involve the same examiners. The letter thus left me completely unclear about how much revision I might need to do and what my chances of success might be if I submitted a revised version of my dissertation. Yet it was clear that I needed to revise and resubmit, for as Neil Kay had said a year earlier, a PhD was my "travel ticket."

Finding out what the examiners thought of my work was not something that I needed to do with urgency. This was not merely because of the generous resubmission deadline but also because I knew that I was not going to be able to start work on the revision until the middle of the year. This was because I was about to begin my first sabbatical, the goal of which was to write *The Corporate Imagination*, which Edward Elgar had commissioned for Wheatsheaf Books in January 1982, only seven weeks after commissioning *The Economic Imagination*. At the time that the contract was drawn up, the plan was for me to deliver it at the end of the sabbatical that I expected to get, and I was determined to stick to this plan.

A week after the notification letter from Dr Branson, I received a more positively worded letter from Geoff Meeks, dated February 8, 1983. In contrast to the bureaucratic tone of the former, Geoff's letter showed concern about the impact such news might have on the morale of a research student. It read as follows:

Dear Peter,

I am sorry that your PhD was not completely straightforward. But I can confirm that both examiners said that you should be encouraged to resubmit and that the extra work should not be enormous. They also said many enthusiastic things.

They make the following suggestions:

'The things we should like to see are as follows. In the first place, more thorough treatment should be incorporated of the relevant empirical findings in the literature; this could be done either by means of a new chapter or by making insertions at appropriate places in the text. In the second place, a new chapter should be added giving a synoptic view of the theory of consumers' choice which the author is putting forward. In addition to these changes, the author will no doubt himself wish to make a number of alterations in the light of the evolution of his own thought.'

The examiners would also be willing for you to consult them informally if you need further clarification.

Although the resubmission is a minor inconvenience, therefore, there is no reason to be depressed about it.

With best wishes,

Yours sincerely,

G. Meeks

The news about the changes that were wanted invited reflection on how I had ended up writing a thesis that lacked both a literature review chapter (that included classic contributions to which I had not referred in the version originally submitted) and a concluding summary of what I had achieved? The absence of the chapters that my examiners wanted me to add was a consequence of the system in which I had been operating: there was no initial briefing about the necessity of (a) having a literature review chapter that established the shortcomings of, or a significant gap in, the existing literature, which the thesis was going to address; (b) that I could articulate what I had achieved and how I had achieved it; and (c) that I was able to acknowledge the work's limitations, practical implications and potential for further development. There had also been no supervisory discussions later in the process that could have drawn to my attention the limitations of the structure of my original thesis.

All that I had received in terms of supervisory feedback were brief comments written on draft chapters, and these comments were on matters of detail rather than basic issues. The limitations in my coverage of existing literature on consumer behavior might have been fewer if I had worked with a supervisory team of the modern kind, with one of the supervisors being a specialist in that area. However, what had happened was a combination of me not realizing that I needed to have a literature review chapter and the way the confirmation saga had unfolded. In my two years in Cambridge researching on firms and structural change, I had developed a very thorough knowledge of the literature via a "no stones left unturned" approach to scholarship. But I had lost this way of operating as I switched my focus to consumer behavior, where there was so much that was exciting and unfamiliar. With the clock ticking toward September 30, 1982, the key question became whether I had enough in this area that I could assemble as a synthesis that would be viewed as enough of an "original contribution to knowledge." In the process, I made the mistake of concentrating on what I was bringing together rather than on establishing the originality of what I was arguing. Supervisory comments had then concentrated on the former, i.e., on where small improvements might be made in what I had written rather than on what I was failing to do in basic terms.

The examiners' request in relation to relevant empirical literature were not at all surprising, given what had happened in the oral examination, and I realized that a synoptic chapter would be a good means for demonstrating my interpretation of my contribution to knowledge. It would also provide a means for ensuring that my examiners "got" what I had done. Seen thus, the examiners' two specific requests did indeed not look particularly onerous, so long as I could find a way of liberating space to implement them without breaching the 80,000-word constraint into which I had shoehorned the original thesis. However, about six weeks later, when the extracts from the examiners' reports arrived, I inferred that I would be wise to do a quite major rewrite and try to extract further economic implications from the clinical psychology perspectives that I had used. This seemed particularly necessary from the report of 'Examiner A', whom I inferred to be Pickering – both from the greater length of his report (of which I was sent more than four pages) and from him saying that he felt the structure of the arguments needed to be clearer to be readily grasped, for he had found the writing challenging despite the fact that he, 'at least, [had] considerable sympathy [with the behavioral approach].' In the extracts that I was sent, my examiners essentially described what I had done or had failed to do; they gave me little sense of whether they thought my departures from mainstream thinking were significant and had potential for empirical applications. I therefore felt I should find ways of developing my contribution in case they had not really warmed to what I was saying.

While working on *The Corporate Imagination*, I had many ideas about how I could improve my analysis and began to envisage what I wrote as *Lifestyle Economics* (Earl, 1986b) a couple of years later (see Section 5..3). With *The Corporate Imagination* finished on schedule, I began what I intended to be a major revision of my original dissertation. If I removed the chapter on the behavior of economists (a shorter version of which was now available in published form as Earl, 1983b), it would give me enough space to incorporate my new theoretical ideas and demonstrate their policy implications, as well as for adding the synoptic chapter and covering the literature that I had failed to review in the original version.

After I had been working on the revision for about three months, I was confident that I was writing a much more mature and carefully considered work than *The Economic Imagination*, whose subtitle *Toward a Behavioral Analysis of Choice* now seemed to have personal connotations, especially via its first word. But I then had to go down to Cambridge for an offshore interview for a job that I had applied for at the University of Tasmania (see Section 5.7). Naturally, I called in to see Geoff Meeks to assure him that I was well into the revision. When I told him that I was building in many new ideas that greatly improved my analysis, he almost seemed to levitate from his chair with alarm. He said, 'No, don't do this; they might not like the new material. All you really need to do is add a standard literature review chapter at the front and a conventional summary and conclusions chapter at the end. That's all they wanted; they liked your original work!' So, *that* was what he had been trying to convey in his letter of February 8, 1983, whereas I had thought I needed to do more, to be on the safe side, because of what I had read in the extracts in the examiners' reports.

As a result of this chain of events, the revised dissertation ended up as a kind of halfway house between *The Economic Imagination* and *Lifestyle Economics*. I told Geoff Meeks that one of the things I really wanted to include in the revision was a section in which I critically discussed text from motoring magazines in which the motoring journalists gave their summary rankings in multi-vehicle test reports. This was not merely an unusual empirical technique; it also provided a way of showing how non-compensatory decision heuristics could sometimes be readily identified as being used in practice. Geoff said it would be OK for me first to write to Robin Matthews about this idea to see whether he approved of it, and Matthews gave me encouragement to proceed.

In the end, it was fortuitous that I switched to the more modest revision plan, for early in January 1984 I accepted the job that, following the Cambridge interview, I had been offered at the University of Tasmania, with a starting date in early June. To give the examiners time to read the revised dissertation and, if necessary, also to run a further oral examination, I needed to be ready to submit the revision around mid-March.

On the morning that I accepted the Tasmanian job, it was snowing heavily in Stirling, so staff were advised to head home. Given the deadline that I now faced, I asked if I could take with me the departmental IBM golf-ball electric typewriter that I had been using. In the past, academic staff had not enjoyed a personal typewriter such as this, but I had been able to purloin it when word processors had been provided to more of the office staff. The weight of the typewriter made the journey out to my car rather hair-raising, as conditions had become very slippery by the time I set off into the snow.

I completed the revised dissertation on schedule and sent it to Cambridge on March 20, 1984. Soon after, my teaching timetable enabled me to take a few days' leave during which I visited music stores in London and Cambridge in search of a guitar that would serve as a suitable reward-to-self at the end of the PhD ordeal. In normal circumstances, I would have waited until I knew the outcome before doing this, but I was only a few weeks from having my possessions shipped to Hobart and I had discovered that guitars were much more expensive in Australia due to import tariffs. In London, I decided to walk from Kings Cross station to the guitar stores in the Charing Cross Road area (an obvious retailing example of a Marshallian business district) via the LSE bookstore.

One of the books that I bought there was a heavily discounted copy of Pickering's (1977) *Acquisition of Consumer Durables*. I had used a library copy when revising my thesis, but a personal copy seemed a fitting memento for the end of the PhD saga. Given what happened in the examination of my thesis, readers who are familiar with Clive James's famous poem "The Book of My Enemy Has Been Remaindered" may think it could provide a model for the kind of thoughts that were going through my head at the time I bought Pickering's book. Had I been buying the book a year or so earlier, such a conjecture might have been well-aimed. However, having gone through the revision process, I now had a much more mature perspective and fully appreciated the earlier verdict. The residual frustrations that I felt concerned the paucity of advice and limited feedback that I had received along the way. A few weeks after I arrived in Tasmania, I received a letter in which Sheila Dow sent her congratulations, saying that she had heard via Geoff Harcourt that the revised dissertation had passed. A couple of weeks after that, I received the news formally from the ever-leisurely Board of Graduate Studies.


## 4.12   SCHOLARLY SHORTCOMINGS AND MISSED OPPORTUNITIES

Although the revised thesis was good enough to satisfy my PhD examiners, it could readily have been a much better contribution to knowledge without me adding the material that, on the advice of Geoff Meeks, I refrained from including. That material would have taken my analysis in new directions that I pursued early in my time in Tasmania. But there were important things that I could have done that would have improved the areas that I explored in the thesis (and, earlier, in *The Economic Imagination*) if I had made more determined use of my imagination and critical thinking capacities and had operated with even more scholarly determination than I employed when working on the revised version.

*Failures of Imagination in Relation to the Non-Substitution Perspective*
There were several things I could readily have realized if I had asked myself whether viewing choices as based on intolerant rules linked up with other parts of the work that I was doing and whether it had wider implications than those that I was seeing in relation to non-price competition. Looking back, I am surprised that I did not do a better job of integrating this view of choice with personal construct psychology. In essence, the characteristic filtering view of choice can be viewed in terms of a stack of priority-ranked performance targets on personal construct axes that are either binary or scalar. The complete stack can be viewed as the decision-maker's personal construct for his or her "completely acceptable" vision of the product type to which it refers. As such, it is indeed a "template" against which contending products are assessed for their fit. However, although Kelly spoke of personal constructs as akin to templates, I failed to arrive at such a visualization until I read Grupp and Maital (2001) in 2006 in preparation for writing what was eventually published as Earl and Wakeley (2010b): Grupp and Maital's notion of a "technometric scale" was, in effect, a 90-degree rotation of a stack of constructs. I did not refer to Kelly in the Earl and Wakeley paper, but I did explicitly make the connection, and give an illustration in stack form, in Earl (2022, p. 102).

Clearly, having stacks of separate wants makes it cognitively much easier to rethink one's preferences than would be the case with convex preference sets of the kind that Lancaster (1966) assumed consumers have. A stack-based view of what one is looking for in a particular area thus aligns better with Kelly's "people are like scientists" perspective, for such a stack can be viewed as a basis for experimentation: if the results of applying it seem problematic, one can then use these results as a basis for re-prioritizing it and see whether it generates a better capacity to predict and control events. Moreover, new construct axes, with their respective experimental targets, can readily be slotted into such stacks.

It was also not until 2006 that I started to think seriously about the relevance of intolerant choices to the production side of the economy. The idea that there might be technical and human capability prerequisites and co-requisites should be obvious to any academic who works in an institution whose degree programs require students to satisfy prerequisite and/or co-requisite rules about sets of subjects that must be completed to qualify for graduation. Yet, around 1980–1981, as I failed to spot how mainstream production theory overlooks this kind of issue, my eventual partner, Annabelle Taylor, was studying to be a teacher and was taught about the prerequisites for learning to occur in a primary school classroom. Annabelle's education lecturers presented the idea in relation to Maslow's (1943, [1954] 1970) notion of a "hierarchy of needs," stressing that learning is not going to happen, regardless of the teacher's knowledge and ability to articulate it, if (a) children have not had breakfast, and (b) there is no classroom discipline. I was not aware of this in 2006 when I wrote a paper about the significance of capability prerequisites and co-requisites in production systems. The paper was dismissed as "merely an essay" by the referees of *Metroeconomica*, a journal that I had expected to be interested in this kind of perspective. It seemed as if the themes of the paper would only be taken seriously if expressed as a formal model of production. Many years passed before I wrote about the issue again (in section 3.8 of Earl, 2022), this time in relation to contributions to development economics by Rostow (1960) and Schumacher (1973).

*Missed Opportunities Due to Insufficiently Diligent Scholarship*
Very early in my time at Stirling, when I went to the library to consult further Kelly's (1955) *Psychology of Personal Constructs*, I happened to notice near to it a book called *The Sensory Order*. I was surprised to see that it had been written by Friedrich Hayek (1952). At the time, I took a brief look at it, suspecting that it might complement the subjectivist psychology that Kelly offered, but I soon re-shelved it. It looked like it was going to be even harder to digest than the books by Hayek that I had consulted a year earlier and referred to in the paper that I had sent to Brian Loasby before my interview trip to Stirling. Re-shelving *The Sensory Order* at that point in my career was a big mistake, for nearly thirty years later I found that my original hunch that it complemented personal construct psychology was right (see Section 7.5). Loasby, too, seemed to know of the book's existence back then, but the earliest that I have found him citing it is in Loasby (1996), with his first paper focused on it being Loasby (2004).

Secondly, there was my failure to give due attention to Ironmonger's (1972) *New Commodities and Consumer Behavior*. I do not recall reading Ironmonger's book until I was revising my PhD dissertation, after *The Economic Imagination* was published, even though the latter does refer (on pp. 52 and 63) to Ironmonger. There, I had relied on my memory of Ajit Singh having pointed me to the *Economic Journal* review by Prais (1973) of Ironmonger's book, around the time he introduced me to Lancaster's (1966) work. Ajit had said that in the review Prais had likened the spread of demand for new commodities to the process whereby a contagious disease spreads, and it was in that context that I had cited Ironmonger. What I had not remembered was that Prais had not said that Ironmonger had suggested the contagious disease parallel but that he *should* have raised it. Yet it turned out that my reference to Ironmonger in that context was correct because Prais had somehow failed to read Ironmonger's fourth chapter where the disease parallel is noted, along with relevant modeling methods. There was a lesson here about scholarship: always check your primary sources before you put anything into print, and, in case your memory lets you down, recheck them if you have already viewed them at first hand. It is possible that I did try to check what Ironmonger had written, for I can recall a couple of early attempts when I tried to find the library copy without success. I can also recall that when I did eventually get to look at it, the extent of mathematical content was rather intimidating, and I did little more than register that the diagrams presented a hierarchical, target-based view of wants and were similar to those that I had been drawing.

Despite having accidentally given the right impression in referring to Ironmonger without having checked his book, I really regret not having bothered to read Ironmonger's book before late 1983. By following his reference trail, I might have avoided having to revise and resubmit my PhD, and at the very least I could have referred to Ironmonger's failure to accommodate uncertainty in his hierarchical model as a gap that I was seeking to fill by integrating the priority-based view of choice with a satisficing version of Shackle's view of choice under uncertainty.

Ironmonger's emphasis on the role that the growth of knowledge played in the gradual adoption of new products also adds weight to the case for my attempts to integrate personal construct psychology into the economic analysis of consumer behavior. It was not until after I retired, when I was writing a retrospective assessment of Ironmonger's book (Earl, Markey-Towler and Coutts, 2022), that I looked carefully at the second part of it, where he sets out evidence on how long adoption processes can take before market saturation is reached. Much of his work entailed examining the adoption of new types of food and beverage products before World War II, many of which took three or more decades to achieve saturation, whereas I spent my career using the much shorter product lifecycles of modern electronics products as sources of inspiration. If I had been aware of the food-related analysis in Ironmonger's book when I was working in New Zealand during the 1990s, it might even have inspired me to consider potential for an agribusiness-related research grant application with some of my colleagues.

What Ironmonger discovered about the slow uptake of new types of food and beverage products seems also to apply to the spread of lifestyle practices, such as the uptake of vegetarian and vegan diets or "green" practices more generally, yet when I came to write about lifestyles shortly after leaving Stirling, my failure to give due attention beyond the first, theoretical part of Ironmonger's book meant that I was not primed to give much attention to long-term processes of lifestyle change. When I at last came to write anything about this issue (in Earl, 2017a), the inspiration came via Hayek's *Sensory Order*, not Ironmonger, for I still had not carefully read the second half of Ironmonger's book; indeed, I had not looked at it at all since about 1985. Things might have been different if I had bought a copy of it early in my career rather than just before I retired: availability biases favor the use of books in one's personal library, the more so the more one works from home rather than on campus and keeps one's library at home.

Thirdly, it is important to notice the shortcomings of my Shackle-related scholarship during my time at Stirling, even though what I did was enough to get me established as a Shackle authority. I have referred earlier in this chapter to my failure to track the genealogy of Shackle's writings on the theory of choice under uncertainty back to papers that he wrote before 1943. But I would have been wise also to look more carefully at how Shackle presented his critique of probabilistic thinking, how he engaged with probabilistic ideas after *Expectation in Economics* was published, and what adherents to probabilistic approaches themselves wrote.

In my enthusiasm for Shackle's view that actuarial risks entail knowledge, whereas genuine uncertainty entails a lack of knowledge, I failed to notice for three decades that Shackle failed to engage with the subjective approach to probability that emerged while he was developing and launching his theory. Via his skills in the rhetorical use of prose and my failure to study seriously subjective probability analysis (or even Keynes's (1921) *Treatise on Probability*), I ended up accepting Shackle's view that a range of mutually exclusive outcomes for a scheme of action may be viewed as "perfectly possible" with none of them being viewed as potential causes of surprise if they were to eventuate. This mattered, for it is the part of his analysis that causes problems if one tries to merge it with probabilistic approaches.

What Shackle had in mind as a "perfect possibility" is an event that seems to have no credible barrier to prevent it from taking place. While it is easy to view outcomes that are seen as sources of astonishment as having zero probability, we clearly cannot assign probabilities of one to more than one imagined outcome, and if we assign a probability of one to any outcome, we must assign probabilities of zero to all other imagined outcomes. From Shackle's standpoint, zero potential surprise thus should not be viewed as equivalent to certainty. However, his argument that *multiple* outcomes could seem perfectly possible becomes questionable if we take the view that it is illogical to view each member of a set of rival events as perfectly possible, since acceptance of rivalry must entail accepting that causal processes that favor one outcome serve as barriers to the eventuation of others.

The same argument applies against the notion of a *single* "perfectly possible" outcome if we are not ruling out that other outcomes could occur, even though at present we have reasons for doubting that any of them will occur. If we cannot rule out each of the latter potential outcomes altogether, because we can envisage scenarios in which they could occur (either specific causal chains and/or sets of conditions or "something I've not yet thought of or heard about") and whose eventuation would prevent an outcome at the supposed "perfectly possible" level, then it is illogical to classify the "perfectly possible" outcome as such even if, given the way things seem to be going, nothing currently seems to stand in its way.

Rejecting the "perfect possibility" aspect of Shackle's theory may make it legitimate to view Shackle's potential surprise scale as an inverted mapping to or from a subjective probability scale. This is the view that I have very belatedly come to take (see Earl, 2023b), but I think that it should not divert us from the merits of thinking about uncertainty in terms of the presence or absence of barriers to the eventuation of particular outcomes and thence to rate rival outcomes in terms of how surprised we would be if they occurred: it may be very useful to think about uncertainty by asking, "What could possibly go wrong or (be made to go) right?" However, perhaps we would be wiser to take a pluralistic view of how people think about uncertain prospects: some may indeed think as Shackle posited, rather than thinking in the deeper, more logical manner that I have just outlined; others may view rivalrous possibilities much as subjective probability theorists presume and perhaps some of this group "would not be at all surprised" by the eventuation of situations that they viewed merely as highly probable.

During my formative years in Stirling, I might have been more critical of Shackle, but also more able to use some of his ideas more constructively, if I had examined the relationship between Shackle's thinking and Kahneman and Tversky's (1979) prospect theory. However, although I became aware of prospect theory at an early stage, via Thaler (1980), I did not warm to it at that point. It seemed to me to be essentially a tweaked version of subjective expected utility theory, for although it portrayed decision-makers as considering separately the utility of gains and the disutility of losses, it remained a compensatory view of choice, with the net prospective change in utility being the criterion by which options are ranked. It had been developed in relation to choices between rival lotteries with simple payoff matrices, rather than via an attempt to find a plausible means of understanding how people deal with the cognitive challenges of choosing in situations where they face a wide range of choice between options that have many characteristics and uncertainty about what their options may deliver on some characteristic scales. Although Shackle's view of uncertainty had not been set out for such options, it seemed to be taking serious account of genuine uncertainty, and I had found a simple way of integrating it with a characteristics-space view of choice that took human cognitive limits seriously.

My failure to embrace prospect theory had a cascade of consequences for the contribution that I made to behavioral economics. I did not notice at this early stage that Shackle's theory can be viewed as a precursor to prospect theory, since both theories offer a reference-dependent view of risk-taking. Because of this, I failed to consider what benefits might come from seeing whether the two approaches could be blended. Had I attempted to do this, I would have had to address carefully which parts of Shackle's potential surprise approach to uncertainty could be reconciled with probabilistic thinking. Even if I had not ended up rejecting his perfect possibility notion, I might nonetheless have realized that, if one is willing to apply Shackle's analysis of focusing to a probabilistic view of rival outcomes, then one gets a view of how decision-makers might reduce choices over wide ranges of rival outcomes for rival schemes to the simple kinds of payoff matrices used in the experiments that underpinned prospect theory.

From there, I could have seen that, if one is applying the *S*-shaped utility function of prospect theory to situations where uncertainty is not an additional complicating factor (as Thaler was doing), then it might have much to offer for analyzing behavior where products are only viewed as presenting trade-offs between a pair of characteristics (instead of an overall gain and an overall loss), as opposed to a stack of many characteristics that would necessitate a non-compensatory approach or other means of simplifying decision-making. One implication of doing this would have been that, because of loss aversion, choices do not have the reversibility they seem to have, if changes in incentives are reversed, in Lancaster's (1966) characteristics-based model of choice. I also might have given the notion of loss aversion more attention and, having realized that it can readily be incorporated in Shackle's view of choice, I might have given earlier attention to how it might be understood in terms of the cognitive underpinnings of resistance to change.

My missed opportunities in relation to Hayek, Ironmonger, Shackle, Thaler, and Kahneman and Tversky in the early 1980s seem amenable to being characterized in behavioral terms: Hayek looked insufficiently engaging/too difficult to digest; Ironmonger's book was disadvantaged by (un)availability bias because I did not have a personal copy to keep delving into and thereby keep noticing more in it; I was overawed by Shackle; and prospect theory seemed unsatisfactory in some ways without giving me cause to question the synthesis I had been constructing. But I think my scholarly shortcomings also need to be viewed against the backdrop of the fact that, in the summer of 1980, I had started to find the process of writing, and the creative thinking that it led me to do, to be much more exciting than beavering away studying what others had written.

## 4.13  PROGRESS REVIEW

On the surface, it may appear that, despite the opportunities that I failed to notice and/or seize, I spent an academically successful four years and eleven months working at Stirling.[10] By the time of my departure at the end of May 1984, I had assembled an original view of consumer behavior that ranged far more widely than the one that Thaler (1980) offered, and along the way to completing my PhD, I had produced several books and papers. My enthusiasm for taking an interdisciplinary approach to economics had not gone unnoticed, for early in 1984 I was invited to attend a two-day "Workshop on Economic Beliefs" at the University of Bath, with all expenses paid by the Economic and Social Research Council. That event enabled me to meet all the senior figures and rising stars in the UK who took a similarly interdisciplinary approach, many of whom were involved with the recently established *Journal of Economic Psychology*. However, a deeper examination of my time at Stirling reveals that I had set myself on track to a career of under-achievement due to the strategic decisions that I made about how to get my ideas published. These decisions were very

---

[10] It was only after handing in my resignation that I began to investigate what my situation was in relation to my contributions to the UK universities' superannuation scheme and discovered that five years of service was required in order to remain a member and eventually be entitled to a pro-rata pension. By leaving one month too soon (to enable me to start my job in Tasmania at the start of the second term of its academic year), I was forced to withdraw my personal contributions and forfeited the contributions that Stirling had made.

different from those that Thaler made in respect of his more tightly focused contributions to knowledge.

The career track on which I put myself had much to do with both what I did and what I failed to do in the light of my own behavioral analysis of economists' behavior (Earl, 1983b). Instead of reflecting very carefully on what I might need to do to ensure that what I wrote got read and taken seriously by as many economists as possible, I began to operate as if it would be impossible for me to get traction with mainstream economists because I was rejecting the core of their research program, namely, the presumption that all choices should be viewed as acts that entail constrained optimization over utility functions that are built on the principle of gross substitution. If the economics profession had not even been willing to make the switch to doing such analysis in characteristics space, it surely would resist, or ignore, my more radical agenda for change.

This did not deter me from saying what I thought about the state of economics, but I took it as meaning that my audience was mainly going to consist of those who viewed themselves as "heterodox economists." That audience happened to work more from books than the mainstream did, and this aligned nicely with how much I had found I enjoyed working on books. But although my Cambridge education had left me with a good sense of the diverse range of heterodox factions, I failed to give much thought to the possibility that (a) many of them would not even be looking for alternative analysis of what drives choices, or that (b) if they came across my work, they would regard it as too much at odds with *their* ways of doing economics. If most of them were not particularly interested in microeconomics and wanted to focus on class struggle, imperialism and "monopoly capital," they would be unlikely to warm to microeconomics that drew heavily on psychology, marketing, and management, and which took competition seriously.

Although Mark Blaug had said that I had shown courage in writing *The Economic Imagination*, the reality was that, unlike Thaler, I was not prepared to run "the gauntlet" (see Thaler, 2015, chapter 6) that would have been inescapable in making a determined effort to package my ideas into a set of tightly focused papers and get them into journals that were revered by a wide audience, or (as with the case of the *Journal of Economic Behavior and Organization*) that I viewed as having the potential to attract a wide audience. Instead, after seeing the lack of enthusiasm for my first couple of papers, I began to focus on writing books. There were no tenure-related pressures to make me focus on writing articles, so I did not focus on doing so, even where I should have been able to recognize worthwhile opportunities to invest time in writing articles for journals.

For example, I did not make any attempt at a journal article that aimed at selling the idea of viewing people "as if they are scientists rather than utility seekers." Such a paper could have been positioned in relation to Skinner's (1979) paper about Adam Smith's way of looking at the history of astronomy and might at least have had a chance in the *Scottish Journal of Political Economy,* if not in a US-based economics journal. Even if economics journals rejected such a work, I might at least have been able to place it in the *Journal of Economic Psychology,* or in a marketing or philosophy journal.

There would also have been scope for trying to take the Olshavsky and Granbois (1979) paper as a starting point for arguing the case to economists that a "one size fits all" approach to the theory of choice may be unwise. But writing such articles and seeing whether I *could* get them past referees of economics journals was a process fraught with uncertainty about whether I was going to get them into print, in sharp contrast to the process of writing a book for which I had a contract. My focus on books probably contributed to me ultimately being able to get my PhD, given the tiny window within which it eventually had to be produced, but this focus would have dysfunctional consequences for me in the long run.

By contrast, Richard Thaler plodded away making the most of his narrower vision of how economics might be improved. He had obtained his doctorate (from the University of Rochester) six years before his seminal 1980 paper appeared. In the interim, as well as getting the ideas for that paper and initially receiving rejections for it, he had got on the treadmill of publishing two or three papers per year (with his early tally including articles in the *Journal of Public Economics* and *Economic Inquiry*). In trying to get his now-famous paper published, he may have seen no alternative to running the mainstream journals gauntlet. In the US context, it would have been key for dealing with the tenure track system and moving to a better job.

His mindset for the seminal paper seems to have been one that entailed taking seriously what mainstream economists said about economics being a positive science and therefore being open to evidence-based research that enhanced knowledge of how the economy works. He noticed anomalies and, via early access to Kahneman and Tversky's (1979) prospect theory, he offered an evidence-based theoretical perspective for making sense of them. His paper did not seem to be challenging the core of mainstream economics, even though he referred to Herbert Simon. He was not offering a satisficing approach; rather, the reference to Simon seemed merely intended as a bridge to bringing in Kahneman and Tversky's work on heuristics, on the basis that generally we should not be surprised to find people using heuristics if they have limited computational capacities. This was a gentle message, unlike the one that, via Loasby, I had drawn from Simon, namely, that decision-making that addresses open-ended problems logically *must* be rule- or heuristic-based, since optimization is only possible, even if there is no problem of information overload, after the boundaries of a problem have been determined. Thaler's use of anecdotes from minor, everyday experiences ensured that his work would resonate with referees as interesting but pertaining to the periphery rather than the core of mainstream economics. It looked like an optimization story with various minor twists, pitched in relation to positive economic methodology rather than as coming from a different school of thought. Although even this was too much for the mainstream journals in which Thaler tried to place his paper, his approach ultimately was something that mainstream economists could not resist.

# 5 University of Tasmania, Australia, 1984–1991

## 5.1 INTRODUCTION

My decision to move to the University of Tasmania (which henceforth I will normally abbreviate, in line with common practice, to UTAS) took me as far away from the UK as it was possible to go unless I moved, as I next moved, to the South Island of New Zealand. I applied for the job there, and accepted it, despite having virtually no knowledge of the island of Tasmania or of its capital city Hobart, where UTAS is located. There had been no "fly-out" interview trip. I also knew very little about the purchasing power of the salary that I was offered, though on a simple exchange rate conversion it appeared to be, and was, a big step up from UK pay. Taking up the job entailed exchanging my tenured position at Stirling for a three-year contract at UTAS, which I only accepted after being assured that two staff would be retiring before my contract expired and that there was every chance that I would then be offered one of the vacant continuing positions, as proved to be the case. That assurance aside, my move was very much an experimental "leap in the dark" and I had made no effort to research what life in Hobart might be like.

It was a choice that marketing theorists would naturally view as one of "high-involvement." Yet, for me, it did not feel like what Shackle would call a "crucial experiment," for I had rather few possessions to ship elsewhere in the event that I did not care for what I had got myself into, and I felt that, if the PhD revision worked out OK, I should be able to move on relatively easily. In any case, I did not expect that I would necessarily stay at UTAS in the long term even if I got a tenured position there, for I recognized that I might be able to ascend the academic ladder more rapidly by moving up to more senior jobs in other institutions rather than via internal promotion.

Life in Hobart proved very comfortable, with outdoor opportunities rather like those that Stirling had offered and cultural facilities that were, due to Hobart's state capital status, better than one might imagine for a city of about 180,000 people. The main surprise was that the banks' mortgage-to-income lending rules were tighter than in the UK, but houses were significantly cheaper. The meager deposit that remained after I sold my Stirling apartment did not prove a problem: I was able also to take out a loan from the Campus Credit Union at UTAS, thereby constructing what was known as a "mortgage cocktail" that amounted to just over one and a half times my gross annual income. After about six years there, I became mortgage-free, a feat that would be impossible for an equivalent UTAS academic in the 2020s, whose property value-to-income ratio would be around 5:1 (cf. Earl, 2019).

As far as the job was concerned, the teaching load was lower than I had been used to, and conference travel funds seemed incredibly generous, enabling me to attend conferences in the UK in 1987, 1988 and 1990 as well as to attend interstate conferences. Opportunities to present papers on mainland Australia or in New Zealand also arose due to job interview trips as I sought to move up the career ladder. The UTAS Department of Economics was much more mainstream than the one at Stirling had been, and it was not a place at which I developed any long-term research partnerships. My closest colleague was Michael Brooks, a public choice specialist who had done his PhD under the supervision of James Buchanan. Michael found the characteristic filtering view of choice interesting and together we explored ways of applying it to accommodate inferior goods and jointness in the characteristics that different goods offered. A short paper that we wrote on the latter topic (Brooks and Earl, 1987), which filled a gap in a model of hierarchical choice offered by Coursey (1985), was the only publication I had with a UTAS colleague. More significantly, in relation to what follows, it was also the only paper from my time at UTAS that appeared in a significant journal without being an invited submission and after going through a full refereeing process.

## 5.2    STRATEGIES FOR DEALING WITH UNCERTAINTY

Just as Neil Kay's work was much on my mind in the period immediately prior to my move to Stirling and early in my time there, so, too, it was at the center of my research focus just before I moved to Tasmania and early in my time there. Moreover, in both cases, what Neil had written about the behavior of firms proved relevant for thinking about consumer behavior.

Soon after I arrived at Stirling, Neil gave a presentation as a visiting speaker in which it became evident that the next stage of his non-reductionist thinking focused on the significance that complementarities between the things that firms develop, produce, and market have for the strength and vulnerability of these firms. Sharing investments between products is great for spreading fixed costs, but linkages between activities can result in a problem with one activity also afflicting the other activities to which it is linked. Diversification limits the risk of corporate failure from having "too many eggs in the same basket," but it comes at the cost of sacrificing economies of scale or potential for synergy. He developed this structuralist view of corporate strategy in his next books (Kay,

1982, 1984), also emphasizing the organizational challenges that linkages between activities pose as a firm grows: the cognitive limitations of managers necessitate the creation of organizational structures that compartmentalize activities.

I realized that these ideas, too, could be applied in the context of consumer behavior, in relation both to how resilient different kinds of lifestyles are and to differences in the resilience of the ways that people organize their ways of looking at the world. I arrived at this line of thinking in early 1984 while revising my PhD but, mindful of the forceful advice that Geoff Meeks had given me about the risks of introducing new material, I decided to limit the extent to which I included it in my thesis.

Just before leaving Stirling, with the thesis resubmitted, I began to pursue this theme in two ways. One is the subject of this section; the other is covered in section 5.3. The first way entailed beginning work with Neil on a joint paper in which we would explore the significance of strategic linkages for resilience in a world of disruptive surprises for firms and their employees. The paper was an invited contribution for a symposium organized by Frank Stephen. Frank worked in Glasgow at the University of Strathclyde, whence he edited the *Journal of Economic Studies*. He sometimes initiated symposia or special issues of invited contributions as a means of raising the profile of this journal and getting contributions from authors of higher standing. Neil and I were on a contributor list for a special issue on G. L. S. Shackle that included Professors John Hey, Brian Loasby, Jim Ford and Andrew Skinner. Neil and I mapped out our paper shortly before I left Stirling. Then, during my first term at UTAS, Neil's section arrived by airmail for me to stitch into what I had written. Our paper (Earl and Kay, 1985) was offered as a riposte to Coddington (1982) and Cross (1982), who had argued that adopting a Shacklean approach to economics has nihilistic implications for economics as a discipline since emphasizing potential for surprise and discontinuous/"kaleidic" change (as in Shackle, 1974) raises doubts about the value of building models aimed at predicting future economic outcomes.

Our defense of Shackle's view of the economic system was constructed mindful of Jefferson's (1983) account of why and how the Shell energy company engaged in scenario planning. We argued that a scenarios-based approach to dealing with uncertainty permits economists to offer policy insights even if the prediction of behavior is problematic due to its susceptibility to being affected by changes in the state of the news and by the tendency of people to take cues from each other when trying to deal with surprises and uncertainty.

Our contention was that the key thing that policymakers and individual decision-makers need to focus on is ensuring that they create systems that will be resilient if hit by shocks. However, we recognized that making systems shock-proof has costs, such as tying up resources in reserves and foregoing benefits that rivals may obtain from specialization and creating synergy links between activities. In environments where shocks are both rare and leave a residual market, those who pursue such benefits may be more able to survive shocks that force less committed players out of the game. Hence, as practitioners of scenario planning recognize, the key strategic issues to address are:

* How shock-prone are the environments between which one is choosing?
* What is the range of possible outcomes that warrant serious consideration for each variable of interest?
* Is it possible to implement a strategy that offers adequate shock-proofing as well as offering good prospects for survival and growth if present trends are maintained yet is flexible enough to enable one to grasp opportunities that one cannot yet imagine?

In other words, even if economic predictions are inherently unreliable, economists can contribute usefully to (a) assessing the costs and benefits of (not) being prepared for rival possible outcomes, and (b) imagining possible situations that could arise and assessing how seriously they deserve to be taken. This way of facing up to uncertainty underpinned much of my teaching at UTAS and both of the books (Earl, 1986b, 1990b) that I wrote while working there.


## 5.3   LIFESTYLE ECONOMICS

Shortly before I left the UK for Tasmania, I was invited to give a presentation at Birmingham Polytechnic. I used the occasion to signal that my work on consumer behavior was taking a strategic turn, and I alluded to the inspiration that I drew from Neil Kay's book *The Evolving Firm* by calling my presentation "The evolving consumer." The event in question was a double-header seminar that provided my first chance to meet the seminar convenor, John Pheby, with whom Sheila Dow and I had been corresponding about economic method, and the other speaker, Geoff Hodgson, whose 1982 book, *Capitalism, Value and Exploitation*, I had purchased a few months previously. It was clear from this book and his presentation that Geoff was moving in directions that complemented where my thinking was going. His subsequent work had a major influence on mine, even despite my inability to keep up with the extraordinary volume of his output.

As soon as the paper with Neil Kay was finished, I began substantially reworking my PhD into a book whose working title was the same as my Birmingham presentation. However, it was published as *Lifestyle Economics: Consumer Behavior in a Turbulent World* (Earl, 1986b). I suggested this title to Edward Elgar (who was still running the Wheatsheaf Books imprint of Harvester Press) in a letter that I wrote to him on September 14, 1984. Two weeks earlier, he had written to me about my proposal, saying that he did not think that "The Evolving Consumer" did justice to what I was trying to do in the book.

The phrase "The Evolving Consumer" was then relegated, with a bracketed numerical suffix, to a section header role in three chapters where parallels between business strategies and lifestyle choices were being discussed. As in Neil Kay's (1982) *The Evolving Firm*, these sections focused on the significance of linkages between activities, products and expectations. Consumers who specialize in developing their knowledge and capabilities in a few areas of interest, who seek to make the most of complementarities between the things they buy or do, and who build close ties with select bunches of social contacts, may enjoy deeply fulfilling lives, making the most of their resources without running into decreasing marginal returns. However, their narrow ranges of commitments also make them vulnerable if their key assumptions, assets or relationships fail. More diversified lifestyle strategies provide a way of insuring against this risk. However, the more diversified a person's life is, the more there is the risk of it proving unfulfilling due to superficiality that comes from a lack of in-depth commitment to anything or anyone, the result being that nothing seems to matter.

This view of lifestyles was not inspired merely by Neil Kay's work on corporate strategies. It also drew on things that I had picked up from my research on personal construct psychology and from my then-partner Sharon's clinical psychology books. The latter sources led me to argue that life is likely to prove problematic for those who try to cope with the world by building "ways" of living and "ways" of thinking that are so full of linkages that small disappointments tend to turn into cascades of difficulties (exemplified in the extremes of those afflicted by an obsessive–compulsive disorder), or who largely fail to build their lives around any organizing principles (the extreme clinical case of which is thought-disordered schizophrenia). Viewing lifestyles with a focus on complementarities, strategic specialization and linkage structures was very different from the conventional reductionist approach to the economics of consumer behavior that emphasized substitution at the margin and assumed linear household production functions and diminishing marginal utility, thereby excluding potential for patterns of spending to be affected by economies of scale or scope in consumption. My perspective complemented but went beyond the way that lifestyles were seen in marketing as sets of similar values that groups of people share (see Wells, 1975).

Given the novelty of the lifestyle concept, I could readily have focused the next stage of my career on work related to it, rather than leaving it merely as an aspect of a book that, despite its title, was mostly addressing the area of its subtitle by exploring – in a much more pluralistic way than in *The Economic Imagination* – ways of understanding how consumers cope with the decision-making challenges of a world of information overload, complexity, rapid change and uncertainty. A good first move, when I completed writing *Lifestyle Economics* in October 1985, would have been to write a theoretical article that focused on the lifestyle concept and its implications (including testable hypotheses) for research on the economics of consumer behavior. Empirical work could have followed, taking me into areas such as the economics of happiness, health and ageing, regional and urban development, the uptake of new technologies and transitions to sustainable living. But this was not what I wanted to do; after devoting about two-thirds of my research over the past six years to consumer behavior, I wanted to shift my research focus elsewhere, and I naively thought that *Lifestyle Economics* might be enough to trigger research on lifestyle-related issues by people whose applied research skills were already much better developed than mine.

## 5.4 THE IMPLICATIONS OF RESPONDING TO CHANGED INCENTIVES

While writing *Lifestyle Economics*, I wrote a related paper that also could have provided the basis for a research program. It was called "A behavioral analysis of demand elasticities" and was written rather in haste in March 1985 for the 14th Australian Conference of Economists. What I attempted to provide in it was a way of understanding why, in some cases, people switch to other products in response to very small changes in relative prices whereas, in other cases, they continue to buy products whose prices have increased sharply relative to other products. The key idea in the paper was that how attached people are to an established way of behaving depends on the net total of the number of positive and negative "implications" that they view as being associated with switching to something else. Having or not having a particular feature in a product matters to consumers because of the implications they see as contingent on its presence or absence. Furthermore, how much any individual implication matters depends on the net total of desired and undesired subsidiary implications that it is viewed as having.

On the surface, this may sound like nothing more than a Lancaster-style compensatory view of choice in which losses in respect of some characteristics are weighed against gains in respect of others. But it offers something deeper: a unit of analysis for which data can readily be obtained and which removes any need to refer to the more nebulous notion of utility. My thinking was inspired by the work of Dennis Hinkle ([1965] 2010), one of George Kelly's graduate students. Hinkle studied resistance to change with the aid of some new empirical techniques that he added to the "repertory grid technique" that Kelly had developed for eliciting the sets of construct axes that people employ to characterize particular kinds of events. In trying to understand resistance to change, Hinkle had focused on the significance of hierarchical relationships between construct axes.

While I was working on my PhD, one of Hinkle's novel techniques, "construct laddering," had been picked up by scholars in marketing (see, for example, Gutman, 1982, Reynolds and Gutman, 1984) as a means for digging deeper into the minds of consumers: by asking which pole of a construct axis (for example, "spicy" versus "bland") a consumer prefers, one may elicit a new layer of constructs (for example, "I prefer 'bland' because..."), to which the same process can be applied, and so on, until one gets to the stage at which the consumer says, "I prefer this because I do, period." But the marketing scholars had not taken up Hinkle's idea of an "implication" as being a change between the poles of a construct axis that a person's construct system requires if there is a polar change on another axis. Depending on the hierarchical rules that structure a person's construct system, switching to a different form of behavior might have few implications overall, or there could be many implications, skewed heavily in one direction. Sometimes, it would seem "crazy" not to switch, because of the net balance of negative implications of not switching, whereas in other cases a change might be seen as having a wide range of negative implications and few implications that are viewed positively, so change would be resisted. If constructs are viewed in simple dichotomous terms, an implication of change on one construct for where one will be on another construct is like throwing a switch, but one could do a somewhat more complex analysis for scalar constructs, in terms of how much movement on other constructs would be implied if a consumer moved between specific points on, say, a 1–10 scale.

In short, the desire or unwillingness of consumers to change their behavior will depend on how the features of the alternative forms of behavior matter due to the hierarchical webs of implications people attach to them. We can get a sense of this if we reflect upon how, if something goes awry with our plans, we experience a cascade of mental images of what this enforced switch means in terms of shattered expectations and new challenges. Hinkle had made a start in showing how patterns of implications and associated resistance to change can be mapped and measured empirically with the aid of what he called "implication grids" and "resistance to change grids." However, although his construct laddering technique revealed that people typically end up at the "I prefer this construct pole because I do, period" stage within six or fewer construct layers, Hinkle had only reported analysis via his innovative grids in terms of the initial set of constructs that he elicited from each of his subjects and a single layer of constructs laddered from them.

The implications of going down a Hinkle-style route in consumer research are, of course, dramatic, for researchers will need to engage closely with research subjects to peel back the layers of systems of personal constructs instead of focusing on differences between products in their "objective" characteristics in the way that Lancaster (1966) envisaged. I wrote my paper without even taking the time to develop a detailed example to illustrate what I had in mind and how a multi-level implications map could look, let alone waiting until I had an empirically based "proof of concept" demonstration to offer, and I never got as far as arriving at one. The complexity entailed in developing the idea further led me to appreciate the challenges that people could have in computing the overall implications of choices involving many dimensions of surface-level constructs that might affect constructs up to half a dozen layers away. Hence, I ended the paper on a pluralistic note by raising these computational issues and arguing that, when the mind runs into them, we should expect it to switch to non-compensatory ways of choosing.

Given the conceptual challenges that the implications-based view of choice entails and the limitations of my paper, it is not surprising that it failed to generate any feedback from my small audience at the conference, and it failed to generate any enthusiasm soon after when I submitted it to a marketing journal. Rather than filing it for future attention, I found an easy route to get it published as it stood. I had refereed a paper for the *Journal of Economic Studies* and when the editor, Frank Stephen wrote to thank me for my report, he mentioned that he would be interested to know what I had been working on after writing the invited paper with Neil Kay (Earl and Kay, 1985) for the Shackle symposium that he had organized a year earlier. I sent him a copy of the paper and, rather as I anticipated, he said he would like to take it for the *Journal* (where it was published as Earl, 1986a).

I should have declined Frank's offer of publication and should instead have worked on it further and then submitted it to the *Journal of Economic Psychology* or the *Journal of Economic Behavior and Organization*; that way, I might at least have got some decent feedback and been prodded to invest even more time in improving it. Instead, following Frank's acceptance of the paper, I did not return to its central idea until 35 years later when I was writing chapter 7 of my *Principles of Behavioral Economics* (Earl, 2022). At that point, I explored it further in theoretical terms, but it *still* awaits empirical investigation.


## 5.5    AN EDITORIAL EXPERIMENT WITH PSYCHOLOGICAL ECONOMICS

Less than six months after I arrived in Tasmania, and before I had got very far into writing *Lifestyle Economics*, I received a letter from Professor Warren Samuels, an eminent US historian of economic thought and contributor to the literature on economic method and institutional economics. The letter was an invitation for me to edit a book for Kluwer Academic Publishers (now part of the Springer group) under the title *Psychological Economics: Development, Tensions, Prospects*. It was an interesting concept: rather than aiming to offer a set of chapters that sought to present new research findings about economic issues that had been arrived at by applying concepts and methods from psychology, it would set out to identify areas with potential for economists to learn by employing psychological concepts and research methods. It would then explore the challenges that such an approach presented, mindful of the way that mainstream economics had distanced itself from psychology over the preceding half-century. I accepted the invitation after only a brief reflection on the kinds of chapters I might commission and whom to approach to write them, and after giving even less thought to how much of my time the book would consume.

The contract to proceed with the project was dated December 17, 1984. It was the first sign I had that *The Economic Imagination* had been taken seriously by a well-established North American economist. It also seemed to signify that, at 29, I was no longer and "early-career academic," for this sort of volume would normally be edited by someone much more senior than a mere lecturer (assistant professor).

All except for one scholar that I approached agreed to write a chapter for the book. The only psychologist among the contributors was Alan Lewis, whom I had got to know at the 1984 ESRC Workshop on Economic Beliefs and who provided a chapter on research methods that economists might borrow from psychology. I did not invite any other psychologists because I decided to see what would happen if I invited contributions from authors who mostly had no experience of engaging with psychology but whose areas of interest appeared to have potential to benefit from infusions of psychology. There was also a pluralistic agenda, for as well as getting John Hey to write a chapter about prospects for mathematical psychological economics, as a contrast to what Alan Lewis covered, I set out to see how economists from different schools of thought saw the potential for engaging with psychology. My three favorite chapters from the book were those by Malcolm Rutherford (an institutional economist, who examined differences between economists' and psychologists' views on expectation formation and rationality and the methodological challenges implied therein), my colleague Michael Brooks (who examined how psychologically-informed economics could help shed light on areas such as voting behavior and bargaining over resources) and Jochen Runde (who examined the compatibility of Austrian subjectivism and psychological methods).

The chapter that I wrote as the conclusion to the volume had the title "On being a psychological economist and winning the games economists play." It applied psychological perspectives on resistance to change, and ideas from business strategy, to illustrate why taking a psychological approach to economics was likely to be an uphill battle and how the career risks of taking such an approach might be managed. I also used experiences of some of the book's contributors to illustrate some of the difficulties of getting into this kind of research, such as the problems they faced in knowing how to get started with an unfamiliar discipline that, unlike economics, did not have a dominant unifying core.

The effort that I put into editing *Psychological Economics* (Earl, ed., 1988a) had only a small impact on my thinking as a behavioral economist. It is mainly evident via my use (in Earl, 1995a, pp.128–130) of Michael Brooks's (1988, pp. 171–2) adaptation of an Edgeworth box diagram into a principles-based satisficing view of bargaining, which I called the "Brooks box." Of all the papers in the book, Malcolm Rutherford's displayed the greatest willingness to go where economists had not previously gone in the literature of psychology. His impressive paper considered not only differences in the implications of the Kahneman and Tversky style of work on heuristics versus Simon's research program, but also drew on what he had gleaned from examining attribution theory. The contrasts that he drew between the fields that he surveyed led to a powerful discussion of methodological issues. Sadly, Rutherford's paper has not received the attention it deserves, not merely in terms of its methodological insights but also in terms of signaling the relevance of attribution theory.

However, editing the book enabled me to assuage a little the guilt I felt about not reading Hayek's *Sensory Order*. I achieved this by asking Jochen Runde to write a synopsis of it as an appendix to his chapter, given that Hayek is the only Austrian economist to have contributed to psychology. Runde's synopsis conveys how challenging the book is, while stressing the non-reductionist, context-based vision that Hayek has of the nature of cognition. However, the synopsis did not trigger the impact that Hayek's book had on me when I at last read it over two decades later (see Section 7.5). By the time that I read *The Sensory Order*, I had completely forgotten that I had commissioned the synopsis and what Runde had written for it, and hence I had to make my own sense of Hayek's theory. I only remembered the Runde appendix when reflecting on the process of editing the book for which he wrote it and the impact that the editorial role had on my research, with my failure to read Hayek's book during my years at Stirling already drawn back to my mind. This forgetting and remembering is, ironically, entirely consistent with Hayek's theory of the mind.

## 5.6   BEHAVIORAL ECONOMICS AS A SCHOOL OF THOUGHT

With *Psychological Economics* well into its production phase, I received an invitation to edit a different kind of book, a two-volume anthology of articles on behavioral economics for the "Schools of Thought in Economics" series that Edward Elgar planned to publish via the company that he had set up after leaving Harvester–Wheatsheaf. I was flattered to receive this invitation, for the general editor of the series was Mark Blaug and this was further confirmation that he took my work seriously. It was obvious that I should accept this invitation, for if the series were taken seriously, too, it would help establish my reputation as a behavioral economist. Better still, editing *Behavioral Economics* (Earl, ed., 1988b) might be a means through which I could try. to steer the field in directions where it could have significant impacts.

When one is preparing such a collection, the key question that must be addressed is the extent to which one should treat it as a research task versus the extent to which one should make selections based on the knowledge that one already has about the field in question. Nowadays, with Internet search engines, online databases, and Google Scholar to call upon, it would be both presumptuous and remiss of an editor simply to rely on his or her existing knowledge, for these technologies make it possible to check rapidly for significant contributions that one has not been aware of or considered including. Back in 1987, editing such a collection was much more a matter of considering whether one had a compelling enough list of sources already at hand from which to make the selection. If this were not the case, then one might spend time looking in likely journals to see if there were any papers that could fill the gaps that one had identified. This was how I put my proposed contents lists together for the two volumes, and I hoped that I could rely on Mark Blaug's legendary encyclopedic knowledge of the economics literature to kick in if there were any glaring omissions. I do not recall feeling that I did not have enough papers to give a good sense of what behavioral economics entailed and examples of where it had been employed. I knew that I had not read extensively in the US literature from psychology and management science on judgement and uncertainty to which some of the contributors to *Psychological Economics* had referred. However, this did not seem to matter since I included the superb survey of this field by Hogarth and Makridakis (1981) that organizes the findings in this literature around the various stages of a decision cycle.

With hindsight, I wish that I had included papers that Thaler had published between his seminal contribution on consumer choice (Thaler, 1980), which I did include, and the time I edited the book, such as his economic theory of self-control (Thaler and Shefrin, 1981) (which I had referred to in *Lifestyle Economics*), his paper on mental accounting (Thaler, 1985) (which I had noticed soon after it appeared but had forgotten to follow up) and the paper on fairness and profit-seeking behavior that Kahneman, Knetsch and Thaler (1986) had just published (but which I had not yet seen). I also regret not including Leff's (1985) paper on the realities of decision-making for planners in developing countries: he sent me a copy of it at some point in the late 1980s, and it is possible that this was before I was working on the collection and that I had at that time simply forgotten about it because I originally filed it with the letter that Leff had sent, rather than in the box files in which I kept photocopies of my favorite behavioral contributions. There are lessons here about giving better thought than I was in those days giving to the organization of one's filing system (for example, file copies in multiple places – something that, on environmental grounds, I had been reluctant to do in the days of hard copies) and developing routines about creating "to read" lists and working through them.

The introduction that I wrote has been a much bigger source of regret to me than deficiencies in the sets of articles that I included. I felt that anything I said about the nature of behavioral economics needed to be said in both volumes, for it was possible that prospective users of library copies would find that one of the volumes was out on loan. To stop the length of my introduction from ballooning out in either volume, I limited the extent of my commentaries on the papers in each volume more than I perhaps should have done, especially insofar as the volumes had a role to play in helping their readers make connections between the papers. However, my serious failure lies in the methodological analysis that the two volumes share. I suggested that there were four main sub-schools of thought within behavioral economics, and I tagged them as follows: via the institutions whose contributors exemplified them:

1. *The Carnegie School* – led by Cyert, March and Simon, drawing heavily on organizational analysis and simulation methods, and emphasizing finite human information processing capacities and the role of satisficing as a means for dealing with uncertainty and complexity.
2. *The Oxford School* – epitomized by the Oxford Economists' Research Group (especially the work of P. W. S. Andrews), Richardson and their graduate students, who studied actual business practices and were keen to understand how complex business processes were coordinated in the real world.
3. *The Michigan School* – led by Katona, that focused on the psychology of consumer behavior, especially the macroeconomic significance of shifting consumer sentiment.
4. *The Stirling School* – led by Loasby, that took a highly eclectic and inter-disciplinary approach that embraced elements from the other three approaches and focused on how decision-makers, in households as well as firms and other organizations, cope with problems of knowledge.

Significantly, I also drew attention to what I called "pseudo-behavioralists" and raised the possibility that contributions by these kinds of economists might lead to behavioral economics being absorbed into mainstream economics in a way that led to key insights being lost, rather in the way that Post Keynesian economists view as having happened with Keynes's ideas via the "neoclassical synthesis" that reduced Keynes's *General Theory* to the IS–LM diagram.

What I meant by the "pseudo-behavioral" approach was research that accepted some genuine behavioral lines of thinking but incorporated them into modes of analysis that were in other respects highly orthodox. I used the work of Kenneth Arrow (1974) and Oliver Williamson (1964, 1975, 1985) to illustrate what I had in mind. These eminent scholars accepted that the economics of organization and the organization of the economy were linked to human cognitive limitations, but their natural inclinations were to view choices in terms of constrained optimization with cognitive limitations coming in as an additional constraint.

I used Williamson's chapter in the original edition of Cyert and March's (1963) book *A Behavioral Theory of the Firm* as an illustration of pseudo-behavioral economic analysis. Williamson's chapter is in essence a potted version of his (1964) PhD-based book, and I argued that although it might seem to be behavioral, as it originated with the PhD that Williamson had done under the guidance of the Carnegie team, it was at odds with the methodology of the behavioral theory of the firm. Williamson saw managers as able to get away with operating in self-serving ways due to the bounded rationality of other corporate stakeholders, yet he used a constrained optimization model of how managers maximize their utility by only pursuing profits to a limited degree and making trade-offs between the pursuit of "pet projects" and perquisites. He did not offer a satisficing model and treated the rest of the firm's employees as if they perform in a way that minimizes the costs of doing what the managers ask them to do. Cyert and March (1992) seem implicitly to agree with this assessment, for they omitted Williamson's contribution from the second edition of their book.

My "pseudo-behavioral" label was perhaps too harsh when applied to Williamson's (1975, 1985) work, where he is rather vague about how managers and their subordinates take decisions. There, his focus is simply on how choices of transactions and organizational arrangements are likely to be affected by concerns that the other transacting party will behave guilefully if they enjoy an information advantage and believe that the reputational risk of being revealed as opportunists is worth taking. Such risks will seem small if, in the event of their opportunism being discovered, it will be difficult to replace them with a less devious trading partner. Bounded rationality is an issue in relation to the challenges of drawing up complex contracts and the capacity of managers to monitor how effectively their subordinates or contracted organizations are performing.

Williamson's analysis of how people deal with these issues can be read from a satisficing standpoint or envisaged in terms of transactors attempting to maximize utility under uncertainty. However, my concerns about where the contributions of Arrow and Williamson on the economics of organization might lead seem to have been well aimed, for the field did become dominated by the work of those who approached the problem from a constrained optimization standpoint. This was signaled by the award of the 2016 Nobel Memorial Prize in Economic Sciences to Bengt Holmström and Oliver Hart. Given what I had seen of Hart's way of thinking in my days as a Cambridge student, it was no surprise to me that he sought to offer an optimizing analysis of the design of incomplete contracts to deal with the contracting issues associated with the impossibility of specifying every possible eventuality in a contract.

The main cause of my regret in this area is that I failed to give enough thought to what, at the time, was only a small "elephant in the room" problem for my characterization of behavioral economics: where did Kahneman and Tversky (1979) and Thaler (1980) fit into my taxonomy? In hindsight, it seems obvious that I should have suggested that their work marked the beginning of a fifth behavioral school. I could also have noted, in my discussion of pseudo-behavioral contributions, that there was a risk that the kind of work they were doing could end up getting absorbed by the mainstream, since it seemed to entail ad hoc modifications to the mainstream rational choice model without setting out to offer a fundamentally different view of economics. I could have likened the situation to what happened in astronomy when the Ptolemaic view encountered empirical anomalies and was initially rescued via the ad hoc inclusion of orbital epicycles rather than by switching to the radically different Copernican view.

Before deciding how to position the work of Kahneman, Tversky and Thaler, I should have devoted more time to (a) carefully re-reading both papers, (b) working back along the genealogy of the works that they cited, and (c) checking via the Social Sciences Citation Index to discover where they were being cited and how they were being employed by their early adopters. In the case of Kahneman and Tversky's prospect theory article, serious reflection might have had a bigger payoff for me than merely putting me in a position to write a better introduction to the nature of behavioral economics: it could have resulted in me noticing what I had so far missed and did not notice until a quarter of a century later about areas of overlap between prospect theory and Shackle's potential surprise model of choice under uncertainty (see Earl and Littleboy, 2014, chapter 8), which would have provided the basis for a good journal article.

But I did none of these things. Instead, I simply did not give special attention to these two contributions. The issue that led me to do this was the organizing framework that I was using: there was no single geographical location to use as a tag: Kahneman and Tversky were West Coast psychologists, whereas Thaler seemed to be a lone-wolf East Coast economist who was, like me, trying to take a bounded rationality view of consumer behavior.

Thaler (1980, p. 40) had quoted Simon's (1957, p. 398) definition of bounded rationality in the introduction to his paper and seemed somehow to have latched on to Kahneman and Tversky's new heuristics-based prospect theory model as a fruitful way to make sense of what consumers do. Little did I then realize that, unlike me, Thaler was referring to Simon merely as an anchor for his paper; it was not a sign that he was an avid follower of Simon's perspective. In the absence of the story that Thaler (2015) tells of how he hooked up with Kahneman and Tversky, and with Thaler not using their theory with a focus on risk-taking and instead making novel use of its *S*-shaped utility function in a more general manner, I did not see what their connection was. Hence, I was not thinking of them as a research group. I had run into a similar issue when considering where to place Leibenstein's work on *X*-inefficiency, which he had commenced at Berkeley and continued at Harvard in what appeared to be a lone-wolf manner without connections to the Carnegie group.

I should have realized, from these classificatory problems, that perhaps I should not have been using a research centers-based way of identifying different behavioral approaches and should instead have grouped behavioral economists based on how they operated. I had got on to the centers-based organizing framework because I had already been tagged geographically by Cross (1984, p. 108) as being, with Brian Loasby, part of "the Stirling school." If I had been focusing on methods rather than centers, I might have identified a "heuristics and biases-focused" method there and then, and presented the papers by Kahneman and Tversky, and Thaler, as extensions of the research on judgment and decision-making that was surveyed in the Hogarth and Makridakis (1981) paper that I had included in the same section as Kahneman and Tversky's paper. I might then have used, say, "satisficing and simulations," "survey-driven," "growth of knowledge-focused" and "information processing-focused" as my other categories instead of the four center-based ones that I chose. If I had done this, I might even have tried to draw a Venn diagram to consider how researchers whose work was included in the collection could be located on it, with some of them working at the intersection of several of these approaches. Had I done this, the collection might have had a different and more substantial impact, and my own work on behavioral economics would have taken a rather different pathway.

There is an obvious irony here: I was very familiar with the idea that how people view things is constrained and shaped by the cognitive frames they employ for making sense of the world, yet I was not reflecting on how the frame that *I* was using was limiting the effectiveness of my characterization of behavioral economics. Nor was I arguing the case for considering the intersection between my "personal construct systems" view of cognition, the "attribution theory" view that Rutherford (1988) had included in his chapter in my *Psychological Economics* collection, and the heuristics-based view evident in the work of Hogarth, Makridakis, Kahneman and Tversky. At that point, I was unaware that Ross (1977) had already explored complementarities between these areas of psychology – despite Rutherford referring to Ross's paper in his chapter.

But the shortcomings of my work on the introduction to *Behavioural Economics* were also the result of me believing that what I had put together was good enough, coupled with my desire to move on to my next solo book project.

## 5.7  INTEGRATING BEHAVIORAL AND POST KEYNESIAN ECONOMICS

Very soon after arriving in Tasmania, before I had even signed the contract for *Lifestyle Economics*, I had raised with Edward Elgar the possibility of a book on banking and the theory of the firm. Such a book could go further than Minsky (1975) had done in modernizing Keynes's approach to macroeconomics, for it could explore the nature of financial intermediaries and competition between them from the standpoint of behavioral and institutional microeconomics. We kept this idea "on the back burner" while I was busy on the projects described above, during which my main teaching was on Money and Banking. The four iterations of this large class helped me toward organizing my thinking about the banking firm as I expanded my reading in that area to keep abreast of what was happening in financial markets that were being deregulated and populated by players who took a "greed is good" approach to their work. At the end of 1987, I emerged from my final stint of teaching Money and Banking with a clear idea of what I wanted to write, a thick wad of lecture summaries on which to build, and the prospect of a sabbatical in the second half of 1988 that would give me the opportunity to make rapid progress. I started to write it in March 1988. Nothing unexpected occurred to delay my writing and the book was finished around Easter 1989. I gave it the title *Monetary Scenarios: A Modern Approach to Financial Systems*. Instead of being a short book on the behavioral economics of banking, the project had morphed into a solo follow-up to *Money Matters*, with a lot more behavioral microeconomics and a systems-based evolutionary dimension concerned with potential for cascading consequences to result from seemingly minor trigger events (for example, bad weather causing completion delays in property developments) if the financial system's buffering had been depleted and growing interconnectedness had also sapped its resilience.

The manuscript was then reviewed for Edward Elgar by Mark Blaug and Victoria Chick, one of whom commented that its length might be a deterrent to publication but that it was hard to see how it could be pruned due to the lack of padding in how it had been written. However, to have the depth it should have had, it really needed to be quite a bit longer than it was, for I really should have used the sabbatical to increase my knowledge of primary sources rather than for writing the bulk of the book. Alternatively, I should have reverted to my original plan and written a shorter, tightly focused book on banking and the theory of the firm – after giving careful attention the relevant literature. But I felt I had a sufficiently original project to write up without investing in deeper reading. As a result, the book ended up being rather too close to what I had been teaching. This meant that it was written in an accessible style that in some places was more akin to that of financial journalists whose books I had used for case material for my classes. But despite the book being student-friendly, Elgar decided only to release it as a hardback.

The reason why I am including the work that I did for *Monetary Scenarios* as part of the story of how I evolved as a behavioral economist is that one of my main objectives in writing the book was to integrate, in a non-reductionist way, Post Keynesian macroeconomics and the kind of behavioral microeconomics that I had been doing for the past decade. In 1987, in a conference paper (published as Earl 1989a), I had argued the case for doing this. However, when I attempted to undertake such an integration in the book, I did not choose a title such as "Modern Monetary Economics: A Behavioral/Post Keynesian Synthesis" that would have made this goal evident. So, why did I fail to give the book a title that signaled that this was what I was trying to do?

The title and subtitle that I chose for the book reflected two other things that I was trying to do in writing it. The key words in this respect were "scenarios" and "systems," but their significance would have eluded the great majority of those that I hoped would find the book interesting. To have any sense of what I was trying to signal with this title, prospective readers would need to be familiar with the defense of "fundamentalist Keynesianism" that Neil Kay and I had offered in our joint paper (Earl and Kay, 1985) for the Shackle special issue in the *Journal of Economic Studies* – a journal not noted as an outlet for work by Post Keynesian or behavioral economists. From a scenarios standpoint, getting creative and critical in thinking about what could go wrong or could present opportunities that others fail to consider is central to designing policies. In the case of financial systems, policymakers need to ensure that the rules of the game (a) do not inhibit socially (and environmentally) desirable investments, and (b) limit systemic risks that come from the interlinked nature of individuals' balance sheets and limitations on the capacity of individual players to appreciate how their fortunes are linked to those of others.

From this standpoint, it seemed to me that there was an obvious link between the bounded rationality perspective of behavioral economics and the view of tidal shifts in systemic risk that is central to how Minsky extended Keynes's analysis to embrace the complex modern world of multi-layered financial structures and financial innovations. Here, a key issue is what can happen when new financial opportunities become available to those whose expertise and ways of taking financial decisions are not conducive to seeing the risks that come with seizing these opportunities. Bringing the two approaches together implies major roles for policies that entail prudential supervision of financial institutions and include measures aimed at improving financial literacy.

Unfortunately, I failed to illustrate the potential significance of these policies by presenting a scenario designed to show how some of the new financial instruments to which I referred, such as options and securitization, could be increasing systemic risk if they were being layered together in hard-to-fathom ways that gave the illusion that all risks were being insured against despite there being no guarantee that those at the end of the chain would be able to honour their commitments. Hence, I cannot say, "I told you so" ahead of the 2008 Global Financial Crisis.

I did a better job in applying my interest in slack and limits to substitution within firms or by consumers to the performance of the economy as a whole: the book's penultimate chapter is on "bottlenecks, slack and macroeconomic dynamics." Over three decades before the global economy was disrupted by the COVID-19 pandemic and Russia's invasion of Ukraine, my concern was with how the resilience of the supply side of the economic system to shocks depends on the extent to which the matrix of production is decomposable into modules (which also matters for the resilience of the nexus of financial balance sheets) rather than depending on supplies of what Sraffa (1960) called "basic commodities," i.e., commodities that are prerequisites for the production of everything. This perspective was inspired by Simon's (1962, 1969) writings on the evolutionary significance of system architecture for system resilience.

As with my failure at Stirling to read Hayek's (1952) book *The Sensory Order* despite briefly looking at it, I wrote *Monetary Scenarios* without reading a book that I believed might be relevant for the kind of work that I was doing. On this occasion, the book that I looked at briefly before re-shelving was Godley and Cripps's (1983) *Macroeconomics*, nowadays recognized as a bold pioneering contribution to "stock–flow–consistent" methods of macroeconomic modeling and the precursor to Godley and Lavoie's (2007) influential book *Monetary Economics: An Integrated Analysis of Credit, Money, Income, Production and Wealth.*

I decided not to read the Godley and Cripps book even though my brief examination of it revealed that, as I suspected, it might complement what I intended to write. I told myself that this scholarly shortcoming was acceptable because I knew that what I already had mapped out offered enough originality and was going to result in a significantly longer book than those that I had written before; moreover, I wanted to focus more on the role and impact of financial institutions than they seemed to be doing and to write a much less technical book than theirs. Godley and Cripps had tried to make their book accessible, too, by putting the more difficult mathematical material into appendices, but I could see that, despite having been published as an innocuous-looking Fontana paperback, it remained hard-going and that mastering it would hold me up significantly. (For an account of that book's background and its reception, see Shipman, 2010, chapter 11.)

My failure to read the Godley and Cripps book may look most peculiar, given that my attempt to conduct monetary and macroeconomic analysis in a non-reductionist manner (despite building on realistic micro-level foundations) was influenced by Godley and Cripps's earlier work with the Cambridge Economic Policy Group (CEPG). In chapters 3 to 6 of *Monetary Scenarios*, I analyzed, in turn, the household, business, government, and overseas sectors in terms of a blend of behavioral and Post Keynesian ideas. Then, in chapter 7 I examined how these sectors were interconnected in terms of their sources and uses of funds. What I wrote was inspired mainly by what I had learned as a Cambridge undergraduate from studying the CEPG's view of the UK economy with frequent reference to the "NAFA identity" which says that the sum of sectoral totals for net acquisitions of financial assets is necessarily equal to zero. When used in a flow of funds chart, the NAFA identity provided me with a means to highlight how the borrowing and (dis)saving decisions made in the various sectors intersect. This was useful for making sense of how, for example, low rates of domestic saving are connected to growing foreign indebtedness and growth in the monetary base and public sector borrowing. But it also raised the question that I explored in the next chapter, namely, what is the significance of the banking sector if, like its component financial institutions, it has a NAFA of zero? Once I had explored the economics of financial institutions (in chapter 8) and shown how they could make it problematic for reserve banks to control the size of monetary aggregates (in chapter 9), the impacts of financial institutions on sectoral NAFA compositions and totals seemed to require analysis in relation to how changes in lending by financial institutions impacted on output and employment and thereby generated multiplier effects. The latter were explored in chapter 10 of *Monetary Scenarios*, ahead of chapters on unemployment and inflation and financial instability.

In chapter 10 of *Monetary Scenarios*, I arrived at issues that I was only able to explore in terms of an unfolding process via a scenario with a simple numerical illustration, and I realized that I would need to make a major investment in developing my technical skills if I were to go any further. Getting to grips with Godley and Cripps (1983) would only have been the start of what I would have needed to do. In essence, the view that I had formed of what Post Keynesian economists needed to do was very similar to that which led Godley and Lavoie (2007) to produce their remarkable book.

After completing *Monetary Scenarios*, I did not go any further because I sensed from my brief look at Godley and Cripps's book that they were already "on the case." With modern computers, there seems enormous potential to model the macroeconomy in terms of micro-level behavior based on (a) simple behavioral rules regarding levels of spending, speculation, lending, borrowing, and saving, and (b) how these levels are affected by the operating rules that financial institutions and foreign currency traders use and that impact on the availability of loans and on interest rates and exchange rates. One can then apply a scenarios-based standpoint and explore how such a simulation model behaves in response to changes in the behavioral rules that are assumed to apply and in the rules of the game that constrain offers that can be made to potential borrowers.

The *Monetary Scenarios* project was very disappointing in terms of the ratio of hours invested in it to the number of citations that the book achieved. Very few people other than close contacts of mine have cited it. Furthermore, the fact that it was not released in paperback ensured that no one would ever build a course around it even though I wrote it with students in mind, hoping that it would be released as a paperback a couple of years after being published.

Marc Lavoie's name often comes to mind when I think about *Monetary Scenarios*. This is not merely in relation to his 2007 book with Wynne Godley but also because of two earlier connections. The first is that one of the reasons for wanting to write a sequel to *Money Matters* was that Lavoie (1985) had noted that book's lack of attention to the notion of endogenous money. This criticism was entirely justified and the embarrassment that I felt about it led me to be determined to show that I had developed a useful perspective on how monetary endogeneity arises. Secondly, the failure of *Monetary Scenarios* contrasts with the deservedly great success of Lavoie's (1992) *Foundations of Post-Keynesian Economic Analysis*. Lavoie's book is a far more substantial and thoroughly academic work that in many respects tries to do rather similar things to mine and generally does them better. Unlike me, he had taken the trouble to read Godley and Cripps (1983).

## 5.8   SURVEYING THE ROLE OF PSYCHOLOGY IN ECONOMICS

Early in November 1989, I received a letter from John Hey, who was then the editor of the *Economic Journal*, informing me that he had both good and bad news for me. The good news was that he wanted me to write a long survey article on economics and psychology; the bad news was that I would need to deliver my draft by the end of January 1990 and that I would also need to expect to have to find time in March to address referee reports, so that it could then be published in the September 1990 issue of the *Economic Journal* as one of the distinctive contributions Hey had in mind for its centenary year. The length of the paper was to be about forty of the *Journal's* pages.

Clearly, this was an invitation that I could not decline, and it had come my way despite me having shocked Hey by my sartorial misbehavior when I visited him at the University of York on an unusually hot August day in 1988. On that occasion, I showed up at his office, at the time we had arranged for a chat about his latest research, in bright yellow shorts and a "Viva La Wombat" T-shirt, looking as if I had just come from an Australian beach. By that point, I had known him for seven years, having first met him at the 1981 conference of the British Association for the Advancement of Science. In the interim, he had written reviews of *The Economic Imagination* (a perceptively critical part of a multi-book review article: see Hey, 1983) and *Lifestyle Economics* (a favorable review that noted how far the quality of my scholarship had improved in the years between the two books: see Hey, 1987), as well as contributing a chapter to the *Psychological Economics* volume. I liked his sense of humor as well as his interest in using psychology and experimental methods in economics. He was a good contact to have and proved to be a useful job-market referee for me after I did not disappoint him with the survey article – even though his reference for my professorial applications did cause some amusement via its reference to the yellow shorts. (At the start of my interview at Lincoln University in New Zealand, the chair of the panel welcomed me by saying, cheerily, that they had not been sure that I would show up in a suit, to which I replied, "I'll get John Hey for that!" Laughter ensued.)

The timing of John Hey's invitation to write the survey was perfect, for it came at the start of the summer research period, after I had finished writing *Monetary Scenarios*. The high-pressure deadline meant that it was not an ongoing distraction or diversion from research that I had been hoping to do. Although produced under time pressure, the survey article that I produced (Earl, 1990a) was properly researched – for example, I worked through all the extant issues of the *Journal of Economic Psychology* before writing it – and relatively few changes were required by the referees. It was the first time I had advanced my knowledge of the area beyond where I had arrived at while writing *Lifestyle Economics*.

According to Google Scholar, the paper is my third most-cited work, behind *The Economic Imagination* and *Lifestyle Economics*. However, analysis of the citations reveals a cautionary message about what a behavioral economist can achieve by publishing in a UK-based journal, even if it is the top-ranked UK-based journal. The contrast with Matthew Rabin's (1998) *Journal of Economic Literature* survey on economics and psychology is stark. As of February 15, 2026, Rabin's paper had 4729 Google Scholar citation hits, including many citing articles that are in top-tier mainstream journals and have been cited thousands of times. By contrast, my paper had a mere 305, barely a handful of which are in top-tier mainstream journals, with the most-cited works scoring citations in the hundreds rather than the thousands. Those who cite my paper are predominately heterodox economists (especially in evolutionary and institutional economics), economic psychologists and applied researchers (for example, in areas such as tourism); it has not found an audience among the modern behavioral economists whose eyes I had hoped it might open to a far wider psychology-related literature than they usually employ.


## 5.9    THE RESOLUTION OF COGNITIVE DISSONANCE

After the survey article was finished, I was free to work on another paper that focused on psychology. It was my first original contribution in the area since the paper discussed in section 5.4 that I wrote in 1985 (published as Earl, 1986a). Once again, it was an application of personal construct psychology. It was written for the 1990 conference of the International Association for Research in Economic Psychology (IAREP). The conference appealed to me because it was to take place at the University of Exeter, the main UK center for economic psychology aside from the University of Bath and not far from where my parents now lived. The paper that I wrote was published in revised form (Earl, 1992c) in a volume of papers selected from those that were presented at the conference, but it probably would have been much more widely read if I had declined to make it available for that book and instead found a place for it in a journal.

The Exeter paper explored the relationship between George Kelly's ideas and the famous theory of cognitive dissonance that Leon Festinger (1957) proposed a couple of years after Kelly's (1955) magnum opus appeared. These two works seemed potential complements because Festinger's theory essentially proposes that when people discover that their initial way of construing a situation results in a pair of constructs that clash, they resolve this dissonance by changing one of the constructs to make it compatible with the other one, with the change being justified by telling themselves a story about why the change is reasonable.

For example, suppose that a person who construes themself to be a diligent scholar is considering re-shelving a library book that they had initially construed as potentially relevant to the research that they are doing. The act that they are contemplating clashes with their self-construct. From a Kellian standpoint, the unease that this person feels is a manifestation of guilt, for the person is contemplating acting out of character. The person can remove the cognitive dissonance and guilt in several ways;

1. By downgrading their self-construct in respect of how diligent a scholar they view themself to be;
2. By relaxing somewhat how they construe what being a scholar entails;
3. By changing how they construe the potential value of the book to the research that they are doing'
4. By borrowing the book from the library and putting it on a shelf in their office, or on their desk, and telling themself that they will make time to read it during the period of the loan; or
5. By borrowing the book from the library and beginning to study it carefully as soon as they get back to their office, after playing down the importance of whatever it was that led them to consider not giving attention to the book.

To me, this set of scenarios begs the question of which construct will be twisted or, if several constructs are modified to some degree, what determines the extent to which they are modified. This question seemed not to be addressed by those who appealed to cognitive dissonance theory to make sense of behavior, and it was difficult to find an answer when I read Festinger's book.

From the standpoint of personal construct psychology, the obvious places to look for an answer were structural relationships between constructs and the idea that some constructs are assigned more of a "core" role than others in the predictive systems that people construct for coping with life. Hinkle's extension of Kelly's ideas seemed to be relevant once again: in his terms, it may not be possible to bend one construct without producing collateral implications for the viability of other constructs and hence for one's prospective capacity to predict and control events. This pointed to the conclusion that the processes that remove cognitive dissonance entail our minds selecting the way of re-construing the constructs in question that is least costly in terms of the cognitive effort that is required to deal with the wider implications of changing any of these constructs. In general, dissonance will be removed by changing the more peripheral construct while leaving unchanged the construct that is closer to the core of the person's way of thinking. In other words, I ended up viewing the mind as an economizing entity: changing how one sees things chews up mental energy but different ways of making changes differ in how burdensome they are because they entail different patterns of cognitive implications.

In relation to the first three options listed for the scenario above, we would expect the person to change how they see the potential relevance of the book, rather than change their self-construct as a scholar and how they construe the nature of scholarly activities, for changing the latter is more likely to raise all manner of questions about the kind of person they really are and how they are going to behave in future as a researcher. The cognitive effort of addressing these questions can be avoided by downplaying the significance of not bothering to read the book (such as by telling themself that, "Surely, others would be citing it in this area if it were worth taking seriously"). The fourth option provides a way of removing cognitive dissonance and feelings of guilt for the moment, but they will resurface if the book is allowed to sit unread in the person's office, especially if its nagging presence there comes to be seen as a selfish act that could be preventing others from noticing and/or reading the book.

The fifth option begs the question of why the person is considering not bothering to read the book in question, if the initial impression is that it warrants attention. One possibility is that putting off other tasks to make time available to read the book will have dissonant implications, but the answer could be that the idea of reading the book clashes with other constructs in their system (for example, due to the book looking too difficult), so reshelving it is a way of removing this dissonance, but it comes at the cost of creating other dissonance. For example, the person may already have written or planned a piece of work that seems to hold together perfectly well without needing to draw on the book in question, whereas reading the book and taking account of relevant material may delay publication of what is already seen as a prospective career-enhancing contribution that seems unlikely to be criticized for failing to take account of the book in question if no one in the field seems to refer to this book.

If its potential relevance is simply downplayed, the book can be re-shelved without any admission that lust for career progression has trumped scholarship. The scholarly self-construct can even be buttressed, by making a mental note to look carefully at the book – "just in case it has undeservedly been overlooked by others" – at some future point if one can find the time, despite denying its importance today. I did not use this scenario in the cognitive dissonance paper, but it seemed worth including here as a way of making sense of some of my own scholarly lapses.

For the final year of my stint in Tasmania, I tried to keep my scholarly standards to the post-*Monetary Scenarios* level that the survey article and cognitive dissonance paper had established. But I continued my tendency to write to order. First, I used a symposium invitation from Fred Lee as an opportunity to write a pluralistic paper that I had been wanting to write about pricing (Earl, 1991). Secondly, in mid-1990, Warren Samuels invited me to write a chapter on Tibor Scitovsky for a volume he was editing on leading economists who tried to take economics in new directions. However, in career terms, the Scitovsky chapter (Earl, 1992d) was not a good use of my time. It consumed all my research time from November 1990 to April 1991, for this was not a chapter that I could "come up with" merely by employing my existing knowledge of Scitovsky's work. That research did not have a significant impact on my subsequent work and the chapter only generated a few citations, albeit more than have been achieved by almost all the chapters that I have contributed to edited volumes. The chapter on Scitovsky would turn out to be the last work until 1999 that I based largely on fresh research as opposed to writing things that had been in my mind for a long while or "coming up with something" to serve a request from someone else.

## 5.10  PROGRESS REVIEW

As in my time at Stirling, I failed in my time at UTAS to concentrate on producing papers via my own initiative and doing whatever might be necessary to place them in journals that would be widely read. I did not bother to apply for, let alone win, competitive research grants, even though it would have been straightforward to build research proposals around the use of non-compensatory decision rules or using research tools from personal construct psychology to study lifestyle choices and resistance to change. Yet the output that I produced did deliver the career progress that I aimed to achieve. UTAS promoted me to senior lecturer from the start of 1987, even though I had not reached the top point on the lecturer scale, and in 1990 I was shortlisted for five full-professor positions. From those applications, I was offered, and accepted an established chair at Lincoln University, near Christchurch in New Zealand, the city that appealed to me most out of those where the institutions that shortlisted me were located. (The others were in Brisbane, Queensland [for a chair in marketing at Griffith University]; Bangor, North Wales [at what was then University College of North Wales, where my interview took place during a conference trip to the UK]; Sheffield, England [but I withdrew from the interview at the University of Sheffield due to its schedule clashing with the one at Lincoln University]; and Palmerston North, New Zealand [Massey University, but I withdrew before the interview due to accepting the offer from Lincoln University].)

Despite being ambitious and generally operating as a "young man in a hurry," I was positioning myself on the periphery, both geographically and in economics, rather than trying to find a way of getting closer to where my work might achieve a wide audience and/or positioning it to make it attractive to such an audience. I made no attempt to devise travel itineraries that permitted stopovers for North American conferences when I made trips to the UK that helped me to maintain my academic contacts there as well as see friends and family. I preferred to get the long trip between Tasmania and the UK over "in one hit," which ensured that my audience continued to consist of a small group of mainly Post Keynesian heterodox economists and economic psychologists.

A modern-day dean would not be impressed by the way I had been operating. Indeed, there might be doubts that any strategy underlay my research, for instead of establishing a research program based on applying the theoretical perspectives that I had studied on consumer behavior, I chose to write a book on monetary economics, and the last journal article that I wrote at UTAS was on pricing and the theory of the firm.

Yet my apparent dabbling in a wide range of areas, with sources from a similarly diverse set of schools of thought, belies the deeper kind of research program that I was pursuing. I was trying to find connecting principles between the fields in which I worked that might provide the basis for a coherent alternative to orthodox optimization- and equilibrium-focused ways of doing economics.

This wider mission meant that I simply was not operating with the mindset that is nowadays expected of an academic economist a few years on from being awarded a doctorate. To make the progress that would satisfy a modern-day dean, I should have sought to obtain research funding for empirical work on applying the personal constructs approach in economics. If I failed to win funds from a research council, I should have plodded away for as long as it took to do the empirical work without any research support. (Given that the research methods of personal construct psychology entail working with small samples of subjects but involve long sessions with each subject, time was the issue; I did not need to fund a major, large-sample research questionnaire.) Either way, I should then have written up the research meticulously, for submission to high-ranking journals. This was the road that Richard Thaler took with his approach to behavioral economics and in taking it he demonstrated that mainstream journals are much more open than heterodox economists seem to think to empirical work that challenges accepted ideas. I simply was not thinking of going down that road, and in the mid-1980s there was neither pressure to do so nor guidance of the kind that research-oriented universities in the 2020s offer their staff about how best to chase research funds.

A neat illustration of my failure to chase empirical opportunities concerns the issue of "rip-offs" and "bargains" in pricing. Thaler's well-known work in this area was based on the notion that people derive or lose utility when making transactions depending on where the price they (are being asked to) pay sits relative to what they have in mind as a reference price. In line with his general approach, he marketed his thinking via a simple empirical study whose findings rang true, namely, the "beer at the beach" study in which the research subjects were typically willing to pay significantly higher prices for beer brought to them at the beach by a friend if it were purchased at an upmarket beachside hotel than if it were purchased from a run-down convenience store nearby (Thaler, 1985, p. 206). Although the beer is consumed on the beach in both scenarios, the idea is that paying a higher price at the hotel is not a rip-off since the hotel supplies it with ambience-related advantages that could be enjoyed by consuming it at the point of purchase.

Around the time that Thaler was developing his ideas about pricing, I, too, wrote (Earl, 1986b, pp. 260–1) about the rip-off concept, arguing that consumers may resist buying things, despite wanting them and being able to pay the asking price, because they believe that the supplier has set a price that is unacceptably greater than the cost of producing the product and offering it in the market. Consumers may not know the full details of the production process, but we might think of them "as if" they can compute a hedonic price equation that predicts what relative prices should be based on knowledge of the products' features and quality of construction. This was a perfectly testable proposition (that I based on introspection) but I did not think for a moment of investigating it systematically with a view to building journal papers around it.

During my time at UTAS, my broad long-term goal was not to produce articles within a narrowly defined field for high-quality journals but to keep abreast of relevant literature across a broad front by successively coming back to consumer behavior, the theory of the firm/industry dynamics, and monetary theory/macroeconomics as each decade passed, and in the process gradually build a better and better alternative way of doing economics. Each circuit would involve writing a new book in each of these fields. In a sense, my research strategy was rather like that of a carmaker that offers three product lines that are synergistically related and successively revised, with each model having a decade-long product lifecycle. With *Lifestyle Economics* finished, I hoped next to make my second foray into monetary theory/macroeconomics before then spending several years working towards a sequel to *The Corporate Imagination* (rather in the way that Michael Porter followed his 1980 book *Competitive Strategy* in 1985 with *Competitive Advantage*). After that, I would return to consumer behavior for three or four years, and so on. The teaching that I was assigned had complemented this plan very well and, despite being diverted by work on the edited books, I got my money book finished by mid-1989 with four years of research and writing time remaining to produce my second theory of the firm book before I hit the tenth anniversary of completing *The Corporate Imagination*. However, sticking to the plan came at the cost of the money book being short-changed in terms of the research that went into it, which in turn affected how I wrote it. This would not have been obvious to selection committees in 1990 who saw *Monetary Scenarios* listed on my CV.

# 6 Lincoln University, New Zealand, 1991–2001

## 6.1    INTRODUCTION

Lincoln University (which I will henceforth usually refer to simply as "Lincoln") is located about ten miles west of Christchurch, the largest city on New Zealand's South Island. In terms of its facilities and cost of living, Christchurch itself proved to be as I expected based on my previous visits. However, very soon after I arrived, I discovered that in those days it had an unpleasant feature that no one had mentioned to me, namely a serious smog problem on wind-free winter nights. The hills on the south side of the city, where I chose to live to try to get above the smog layer, caused a temperature inversion that trapped smoke from the wood fires that many people used for heating their homes. The smog was completely at odds with New Zealand's clean, green image and could trigger asthma attacks, which I had hardly ever experienced in my earlier adult years. I was glad to have arrived in the winter and thereby discover the smog problem before choosing where to buy a house. However, even before I moved from temporary accommodation in a campus apartment to the large, electrically heated hillside property that I purchased, I began to realize that my new job came with many problems that I had not anticipated and about which my minder during the week-long interview visit had told me nothing.

In 1991, Lincoln was only in its second year as a university, but its future seemed bright, especially in the commerce and social sciences area. One of its attractions to me was that economics was not in a department of its own but part of the Department of Economics and Marketing, which also taught business management and organizational behavior and was located in a brand-new building with adjacent new lecture theaters with state-of-the-art audiovisual facilities. However, I soon discovered that the Vice-Chancellor, Professor Bruce Ross had hired me not merely with a view to my interest in marketing and management but also for my social science orientation. The social sciences staff were located mainly in the landscape architecture and tourism/recreation management departments. They proved to be those with whom I felt most at ease, for what I could achieve within the field of economics was severely constrained by the fact that Lincoln's heritage lay in the agricultural sciences.

Lincoln had originally been founded in 1878 as an agricultural college, the first to be established in the southern hemisphere, and prior to 1990 it had been part of the University of Canterbury. Even within the commerce area, there seemed to be a farm management "mafia" that included many Lincoln alumni who exerted disproportionate influence and ultimately foiled my attempts to embed behavioral economics within the curriculum. Lincoln's teaching timetable reflected its agricultural science heritage. In disciplines that were not taught in labs, there was an emphasis on lecturing at students rather than expectations that students would "read" extensively toward their degrees or that tutorial discussions were an important part of the learning process. Each subject was timetabled for five contact hours per week, which would fall on at least four different days (one of which would have a two-hour session) but often were on each day from Monday to Friday. This made it impossible to have research-only days during semester.

In my case, the challenge of getting research done was exacerbated by the absence of any formal equitable workload allocation formula. I was beset with administrative demands to participate in high-level working parties (on Lincoln's organizational structure, to create a degree program in social science, and to devise terms of reference for an ethics committee for research that involved human subjects, of which I then served for five years as the founding chair), academic board, hiring panels, convening PhD oral examinations for other disciplines, and so on. I would much rather have been given a stint as head of department and then both have greater leverage and be more resigned to the lack of research time, but the headship never came my way.


## 6.2    ADDING BEHAVIORAL ECONOMICS TO A CORE MICROECONOMICS SUBJECT

When I arrived at Lincoln my main teaching role was to run the large second-year undergraduate subject Microeconomics for Business and Marketing,[11] most of whose students were taking commerce degrees and would not go on to Advanced Microeconomics in their final year. I had been keen to get such a course, especially after my final four years in Tasmania had entailed using my behavioral expertise in teaching courses on marketing and organization behavior rather than any core courses in economics. The question of how I would teach a second-year microeconomics course had been raised in the UK summer of 1990 when I was being interviewed for a chair at the University College of North Wales, now the University of Bangor. What I proposed was essentially what I did at Lincoln a year later and continued to do for the next eight years. I explained to the Bangor interview panel that I would teach not just mainstream

---

[11] The subject that I had to teach alongside it was The New Zealand Economy, which of course required a lot of preparation, though I presume I had been assigned it as a means of ensuring that I developed my knowledge of New Zealand's economy and its economic history.

intermediate microeconomics but also an alternative synthesis built around behavioral concepts, and I would do so in a "horses for courses" way that emphasized the strengths and limitations of both approaches and the contexts in which they might serve as good analytical tools. My answer met with a mixed reception. The external assessors were Professors David Ulph (who had worked at Stirling before I did) and John Hey (who said "What, no shorts?" when he began chatting with me the previous evening at a social event for candidates). Their supplementary questions seemed to reflect genuine interest in the proposal. However, my minder for the interview visit had warned me to "Beware of the 'Taffia' representative." This was good advice, for the representative from the local council was concerned that, if I taught his daughter, her educational experience would be compromised since I would be "trying to cram a quart into a pint pot." How could I do what I promised while maintaining standards? Telling him that one of the ways that I would make space for new material would be to strip out mathematical content and work purely with graphs rather than calculus (as we had done at Stirling) did nothing to convince him that I would be safe to hire.

At Lincoln, my task was made easier by the timetable system having so many lecture slots per week for each subject. With this lecture-focused rather than reading-focused timetable, I would have enough time to do what I wanted without expecting the students to study material that was not covered in a standard intermediate microeconomics textbook by making extensive use of items on a reading list. However, several weeks into the lecture program, I realized that the students were getting very restive about what I was doing: they had not previously experienced pluralistic teaching and were unhappy that I was not following an established textbook "bible" that legitimized my approach, Moreover, they wanted to know what "the" way to think was in the areas that I was covering; they did not want to be given alternatives and debate which ones to use for analyzing problems focused on real-world cases rather than getting "the right answers" for numerical exercises. And, with no lecture recordings or PowerPoint slide handouts to use for revisiting material from the lectures, they were clearly in a vulnerable position in relation to the non-standard material that was not covered in the text (Douglas, 1987) that I recommended they should buy.

It was clear that they would have been far happier with a subject that merely covered orthodox microeconomics, even if it gave them a perspective that often would be of much more limited use. It was also clear that the two master's students who had been allocated to the subject as tutors were nervous about where things were heading, for they, too, only had an orthodox economics training. I knew that the tutor problem was one that I would have to weather by putting time into pre-tutorial training sessions for the first few years. Thereafter, I would be able to select tutors from the ranks of students who had studied with me (ideally in my own tutorial groups), and thus knew the subject content and how it worked. But how was I going to be able to keep my students from being restive for the rest of the semester and in future years?

I decided to start writing support material that summarized what had been covered in lectures and tutorials, much as I had done at the University of Tasmania when teaching Money and Banking. When this material began to appear, the mood of the class became much less restive. We survived to the end of the semester and by then I had decided that I was going to develop material from the subject into an innovative textbook that was not merely pluralistic but also brought together lecture material, tutorial cases and discussions of open-ended assignments or exam questions. The book was going to need these examples of how to apply the material and debate theoretical issues, for without this material, anyone who built a subject around the lectures would be likely to face an endless stream of students, each expecting a personal tutorial on how to do their assignments. I knew this from the experience I was having with my 250-strong class, few of whom seemed to have any experience of thinking for themselves in relation to the subjects they were studying, though some did tell me that, at last, they were experiencing what they had imagined studying at a university might be like.

The next three cohorts of students were able to buy versions of the in-progress textbook, at cost, that had been produced by Lincoln's printery. Having one's textbook produced only a couple of buildings away from my office proved fortuitous when enrolments shot up, for supplies could be expanded rapidly. One year, a total of 400 copies had to be produced, while I contemplated with dread what this level of enrolments was going to do to my workload, but numbers trended down thereafter.[12] Until it was finished in mid-1994, writing the textbook consumed almost all my research time and a lot of my leisure time, with the manuscript being finished on a winter vacation at a motel in Arrowtown while my then-partner enjoyed the nearby ski-fields.

---

[12] To ensure quality control in marking the final examinations, I did most or all the marking rather than having a lot of it done by the tutors. This made large enrolments especially terrifying, for the practice when timetabling examinations at Lincoln was to put the large classes at the end of the examination period in the hope of reducing the likelihood of students having parties in the halls of residence while others were still trying to study. The consequences of this policy for those who had to mark the scripts seemed to have been ignored.

*Microeconomics for Business and Marketing* (Earl, 1995a) did not short-change treatments of economic problems based on constrained optimization and in some cases went beyond what a mainstream text normally offered: for example, before moving from the dominant Hicks–Allen model of consumer choice to behavioral approaches, it presented a detailed graph-based account of Lancaster's (1966) characteristics-based view of choice. The chapter on uncertainty moved from expected utility theory to prospect theory and then to Shackle's potential surprise approach and his analysis of bargaining.

The students clearly enjoyed having "their own textbook." The production process meant that the published version was not available in time for the class of 1995, but Edward Elgar Publishing let me use the camera-ready copy in a final Lincoln printery version, which seemed to sustain the students' sense of ownership. When the class of 1996 were able to use the published version, some of the local students told me how delighted they were that its cover even had the black and red colors of the Canterbury rugby team, though the credit for this was due to Elgar's cover designer rather than any suggestion that I had made.

The effort that I put into making my pluralistic microeconomics subject work may have helped me stay at its helm for nine iterations, but it yielded no enduring legacy at Lincoln. As the years went by, my "for business and marketing" focus was staunchly opposed by Ralph Lattimore, who had a personal chair in economics and claimed that what I was doing was wrecking Lincoln's reputation in relation to the quality of its economics majors, the best of whom might hope to get jobs at the New Zealand Treasury or the Reserve Bank of New Zealand. This did not seem to be an evidence-based claim, for Lincoln's top students were now able to graduate not merely with the technical skills that were expected of them but also with much better skills in critical and creative thinking. Indeed, the reports that I received (e.g., when providing references over the phone) were that the latter skills were valued highly. However, Lattimore and others who took the orthodox line found a way to keep an orthodox subject in intermediate microeconomics alive, a way that would work well politically. This entailed having a second-year subject, Agricultural Economics, that was, in essence, intermediate microeconomics with agricultural examples and was usually taught via a standard microeconomics text.

Agricultural Economics played a major role in ensuring that my approach to teaching microeconomics had no legacy at Lincoln. Initially, it provided the benefit of reducing my teaching load in the second half of my decade at Lincoln, for as its enrolments grew, enrolments in Microeconomics for Business and Marketing decreased significantly where degree rules enabled substitution.

Given the choice, risk-averse students would naturally favor a non-pluralistic treatment of microeconomics whose assignments had "right" answers at which they might hope to arrive. However, in 2000, my time running Microeconomics for Business and Marketing came to an end, as I was assigned a subject on economic development.

Microeconomics for Business and Marketing was allocated to Lana Friesen, who was fresh from a mainstream PhD program at Simon Fraser University in Canada. As her career progressed, Lana proved herself to be open to behavioral economics (as will become evident in Section 7.4); indeed, she is now an associate editor of the *Journal of Economic Behavior and Organization*. However, when faced with the challenges of tooling up at Lincoln, she predictably decided to turn the subject into a standard intermediate microeconomics course and teach what she knew, rather than get herself familiar with my textbook and the material that I had been teaching. This meant that, in all but name, there were now two orthodox intermediate microeconomics subjects at Lincoln.

Given this situation, I decided to push for a different approach to pluralism in microeconomics. To me, the obvious thing to do was to come clean about what Lana had done and revamp the Lincoln University Calendar entry for ECON201 from "Microeconomics for Business and Marketing" to "Intermediate Microeconomics." With Agricultural Economics now offered with dual codes as Agricultural/Forestry Economics, the sensible thing to do would then be to offer a single set of intermediate microeconomics lectures under three different codes and offer tutorial streams for "economics," "agriculture" and "forestry." I was therefore happy to do the paperwork to address Lana's de-pluralization of the subject that I had taught, for rationalization of orthodox intermediate microeconomics teaching would then make it easier to argue the case for offering a new third-year subject on Behavioral and Evolutionary Economics. It would not displace the advanced microeconomics subject.

However, although my proposed new subject was approved for the 2001 Lincoln University Calendar, it did not get taught. Its approval had come without acceptance of what I envisaged for intermediate microeconomics, agricultural economics, and forestry economics. This proved problematic at the start of 2001 when pressures to cut costs led to a search for subjects to ax. Because of the political influence of the farm management group at Lincoln, any rationalization that entailed no longer offering a (supposedly) dedicated subject in agricultural economics was ruled out as if that subject were a kind of sacred cow. Instead, it was decided that Behavioral and Evolutionary

Economics could be canned. Given that I was soon to leave, there would have been no one to teach it from 2002.

## 6.3    A RESEARCH AWARD DESPITE VIRTUALLY NO ORIGINAL RESEARCH

As a result of my administrative load and the challenges of trying to teach at Lincoln in a pluralistic, non-deterministic manner, I produced very little original output as a behavioral economist from mid-1991 until I had settled into my study leave as a visiting professor at the University of Queensland in the second half of 1999. There was only one piece of work that I produced in those eight years that – if it had made it into print – would have been of the "right" kind in terms of the research audits that were starting to appear. This was "Economics and marketing: A survey," which I wrote in mid-1996 at the request of the *Cambridge Journal of Economics*. Although it was written around the mid-point of my decade at Lincoln, it was the first thing that I wrote at Lincoln that was based on extensive new reading. Finding the time to do this was not easy and because the library's collection of marketing journals was essentially confined to the "core" titles, I fully expected that the refereeing process would suggest that I considered papers that I had not come across.

However, despite being invited to revise the paper, I never did so. This was because one of the referees (who also claimed that my paper was written in a boring way) gave few clues to support his or her claim that there were many relevant marketing publications that I had neglected to consider. Trying to second-guess what this referee meant was not an attractive task, and no help was forthcoming when I asked the journal's managing editor to try to get the referee to be more specific. In this sort of situation, one might reasonably expect a third referee to be invited into the process – especially with an invited paper that crossed disciplinary boundaries. Given that I had spent a good chunk of vacation leave in the UK writing the paper rather than relaxing, the waste of my time was especially annoying.

The disaster with this paper was something that I knew I could ill afford in the new research audit-centered environment if I were to have any hope of escaping to the UK or, when research audits arrived Down Under, to another Australasian university. Yet, although Lincoln had adopted annual appraisal systems for its staff, its senior managers seemed to be asleep at the wheel in the face of the looming possibility that research audits would soon be introduced in New Zealand.

There was no effort to alert staff to the publication pressures that they could face in the future. No signals were provided about the volume and kinds of research output expected from staff in the Department of Economics and Marketing (later, part of the Commerce Division). If concerns were raised, during my annual performance appraisal meetings, about the volume of original research that I was producing, it was me who raised them. No one pulled me up for failing to publish output that embodied new ideas and fresh scholarship. In contrast to my ill-fated survey on the relationship between economics and marketing, the other research output that I produced in my first eight years at Lincoln was produced almost entirely with minimal new reading and entailed either writing up ideas that had been on my "to do" list for a long time or editing the work of others. At annual appraisals, I emphasized that this situation was not sustainable, and that building up new intellectual capital was hampered by the difficulties of finding big enough blocks of time to get immersed in research and by the limitations of Lincoln's library collection, which had to be worked around by finding time to visit the library at the University of Canterbury.

My early sense that senior management were not very fussy about the kind of output that was produced, so long as one did publish regularly, was reinforced in 1995 when the publication of my textbook *Microeconomics for Business and Marketing* was followed by me being given one of Lincoln's annual research awards. Yes, the book was innovative, unusually scholarly for a textbook, and had earned terrific pre-publication praise from Richard Cyert, Paul Ormerod and Herbert Simon. But it was not what I viewed as an original contribution to knowledge. The textbook aside, in my first four years at Lincoln, I had published the following:

- Three articles in obscure journals: Earl (1992a) was based on a guest lecture I had given to MBA students at the University of Canterbury, employing my existing knowledge of the car industry; Earl (1992b) was slightly modified from an old working paper (Earl, 1987); and Earl (1994) was the inaugural lecture that I had been asked to give after I had been at Lincoln for two years, where I explored the institutions and operation of the market for tertiary education services from the standpoint of the analysis of the nature of the firm proposed by Coase (1937).
- A co-edited collection of papers by P. W. S. Andrews (Lee and Earl, eds., 1993) to which my only scholarly input (as distinct from turning Fred Lee's digitized versions of Andrews's papers into typeset format) was the epilogue chapter (pp. 402-427) entitled "Whatever happened to P. W. S. Andrews' industrial economics?," originally written in 1985 as a job market paper for

an interview at the University of Auckland and subsequently presented at the 1987 conference of the History of Economic Thought Society of Australia.
- Five book chapters, of which the best two (Earl, 1992c, 1992d) had already been in press at the end of my time at UTAS.
- A review article, and three book reviews.

To me, this publication record did not warrant an award for research achievements.

In the year that followed the award for my "research," the struggle of trying to do the research for the economics and marketing survey helped to crystalize my sense that I needed to initiate action that would get me time to do genuine research rather than just "coming up with" publications based on my existing knowledge. Even before I started to write up the survey, I decided that my best hope for delivering the kind of research output that I knew I ought to be producing lay with a change in my employment arrangements. I therefore arranged a meeting with Paul Bradley, Lincoln's head of human resources, and the Vice-Chancellor, Professor Bruce Ross, at which I set out the difficulties I was having and what I had in mind. I requested a new contract in which I would work, and be paid, based on a 70 per cent load, with all of my coursework teaching to take place in one semester each year, leaving me to spend the second semester as if I were on sabbatical and with no requirement to be resident in New Zealand and able to visit the Lincoln campus during that semester, though I would supervise PhD students remotely as necessary. With my then-partner Sharon talking with increasing determination of her desire to move to Brisbane, such a contract would have made it possible for me each year to spend a semester there, too, and conduct my research with much better library facilities, possibly with a fractional appointment there.

The proposal went down well and a contract embodying it was drawn up before I set off for the UK to attend the tenth Malvern Political Economy Conference, spend a week in Scotland visiting the Dows and Neil Kay, and take some leave visiting my parents/writing the economics and marketing survey. By this point, however, it had been announced that Bruce Ross was moving on, to become New Zealand's Director-General of Agriculture. Bradley assured me that he would get Professor Ross to sign the contract before he left. Unfortunately, this did not happen, and I returned to discover that the Acting Vice-Chancellor, Professor Roger Field, refused to sign it. Field explained that Lincoln could not afford to have another "airport professor." He went on to explain that a similar kind of arrangement had been made with (if I recall correctly) a professor of agricultural engineering, who had then essentially used his university title to enable him to operate pretty much as a full-time consultant. Field was not prepared to saddle the next vice-chancellor with the risk that I would morph into that kind of operator – despite the fact that I had shown no interest in working as a consultant. He did not show any inclination to renegotiate the contract so that it could be terminated if I failed to meet specific research performance targets. So, I either had to move elsewhere, or find a way of making my job work. But with the rise of research audits, it had begun to appear that I would only be able to move to a chair elsewhere if I could first make my existing job work well enough to enable me to produce research outputs that ticked the right boxes. To succeed at that would probably be a five-year task, even if I were resolute in not allowing my time to be diverted into producing things that ticked the wrong boxes.

## 6.4    AN OVERDOSE OF EDITING

In the ensuing three years, up to my study leave at the University of Queensland, I failed to show such resolve. Almost all the research time that I could muster went into four co-edited books (Dow and Earl, eds., 1999a, 1999b; Earl and Kemp, eds., 1999; Earl and Frowen, eds., 2000). Working on these edited volumes was much less challenging than trying to do original research of my own would have been, as I could make progress with them by snatching a few hours here and there between teaching and administrative tasks; they did not require entire days to be regularly available to ensure that momentum was maintained. They also had the potential advantage of keeping me internationally visible and getting me better networked. Even so, I worked long hours on them, knowing that a research audit game player would not have got involved in any of them. So, why did I not play the game and single-mindedly seek instead to crank out at least one well-ranked paper per year? The answer lies in the nature of these books.

These four co-edited books were very different projects from *Management, Marketing and the Competitive Process* (Earl, ed., 1996a), which had been "in press" at the time of my attempt to obtain the fractional contract. That volume was completely initiated by me and consisted mainly of papers that others had sent to me and which I knew had not yet been placed elsewhere (including a chapter that David Harper[13] had cut from his PhD and which I reworked somewhat into a joint contribution on the growth of knowledge approach to the firm (Harper and Earl, 1996)), plus a few that I commissioned from close contacts, and one (Earl, 1996b, discussed further in Section 6.10) that I had been planning to write since 1990 and which required me to read little more than one book.

*Management, Marketing and the Competitive Process* did not chew up a lot of time and was something I wanted to put together as an interdisciplinary book on business as an exemplar of what a journal that brought economics, marketing and management together might look like. During my interview for the Lincoln chair, I had indicated that one of the things I hoped eventually to do was to set up such a journal. I never delivered on this, not just because I did not have the time to do so but also because *Industrial and Corporate Change*, first published in 1992, went a long way in the direction that I envisaged. With hindsight, I would have done better if I had not assembled this volume and had instead used my time simply to write my solo and joint chapters from it and place them with appropriate journals, where they would be more likely to be discovered by those who would find them interesting. (In the case of my solo paper "Contracts, coordination and the construction industry," the appropriate place might have been in a project management journal.) In terms of citations, the book had a very poor impact. Its main benefit to me seemed to be that it contributed to me being invited to become a founding member of the editorial board of a new journal, *Marketing Theory*. That role would hardly help my career in economics, though it might have helped facilitate an escape into a marketing department.

The two volumes that I edited with Sheila Dow were a consequence of my visit to Scotland in the UK summer of 1996, when Sheila and I discussed the idea of organizing a conference to honor Brian Loasby's contributions and celebrate his thirty-year association with the University of Stirling. These two volumes were based on papers from the conference, after I had put a lot of time

---

[13] David Harper is a New Zealander who did his PhD at the University of Reading, UK, under the supervision of Mark Casson. I got to know him while he was working on it and I provided many comments on drafts of it. This was an unexpected consequence of my job interview trip to the University of Auckland, New Zealand, in September 1985. There, I got to know Tony Endres, one of David's friends (and later one of his co-authors), who put David in touch with me. Like me, David was viewing human action as akin to scientific behavior. In David's case, inspiration had originally come from Popper rather than Kelly, Kuhn and Lakatos, and his focus was on entrepreneurs and venture capitalists and on the growth of knowledge that takes place as they experiment with new ventures. The excellent book (Harper, 1996) that was derived from the PhD opened the door for David to move from the New Zealand Treasury to New York University, where he is now a clinical professor of entrepreneurship.

into providing constructive feedback to their authors, with Sheila (who had played a bigger role on getting the conference facilities, etc., arranged) concentrating more on seeing the books through the production process.

My work on the Loasby festschrift volumes had an obligational basis, but initially I felt more of an obligation to help Sheila (given that many of the papers were likely to be about the theory of the firm and industrial dynamics, not monetary economics and methodology) rather than to honor Brian. This was the second time that I had been asked about editing a Loasby festschrift. Several years earlier, Edward Elgar had been the first to suggest such a project, but at that time there were three things that led me to decline. One was my disappointment over how little advice I had received from Loasby during my PhD. The second was what happened when he wrote me a reference for an externally advertised UTAS senior lectureship that I applied for shortly before being promoted to that level. When the senior lectureship was advertised at UTAS, I thought that it was worth applying as it might give me further interview practice and send some useful signals, even though it seemed very likely that it would go, as it did, to Harry Bloch, who had been visiting from Denver. I did get the interview practice, but I subsequently got something far more valuable: a member of the selection panel later privately said to me, in the strongest terms, "Do not use Loasby as a referee again." By the time that Elgar floated the festschrift idea, I had discovered that I was not the only former member of Stirling's Department of Economics to have been given that advice. I never discovered precisely what kind of unhelpful reference Loasby had written, but the following year he disappointed me in a third way by writing a rather unenthusiastic review of my *Lifestyle Economics* (see Loasby, 1987). His review had ended by remarking that the view of choice that I had presented implied that the book was unlikely to attract a wide following. He was, of course, right in his reflexive observation but he did not help the book's chances when he chose to end the review in that way, after perceptively summarizing the themes of the book without providing any praise for what I had done. I did my best not to let this affect my mood when I reviewed his book *The Mind and Method of the Economist*, which I viewed as a valuable contribution but not as significant as his *Choice, Complexity and Ignorance*: see Earl (1990c).

Ultimately, I was glad that I agreed to work with Sheila on the conference and post-conference books: the conference provided a platform from which to launch the career of my first PhD student in economics, Jason Potts (see Section 6.5), and it was great to see how touched Loasby was to be honored with the conference, during which his usual social awkwardness seemed to fall away.

While Sheila and I worked on the Loasby festschrift books, I was also working with Simon Kemp, a psychologist who ran a master's course in economic psychology at the University of Canterbury, on a much bigger task, namely getting about 100 authors to contribute to a reference book covering the intersection between consumer research in marketing, behavioral economics and economic psychology. When Edward Elgar floated the idea, I knew it would be crazy for me to edit it alone. However, with Simon sharing the task, I enjoyed working on it as an experience in project management and in the hope that it would provide a way for me to get back up to speed with the literature in this area. Although this book would not improve how my publications list looked from a research audit standpoint, I hoped that this editorial role might at least signal that I was well in touch with the latest literature in this area and hence that I was capable of getting back to making my own original contributions.

In late 1998, as soon as I had finished editing the books with Sheila and Simon, I began work on editing *Economics as an Art of Thought: Essays in Memory of G. L. S. Shackle* (Earl and Frowen, eds, 2000). I took on this task at my own initiative purely for obligational reasons, with the hope of ensuring that the book would be published while George Shackle's widow, Catherine, was still alive. In that respect, it was a great success, as Catherine, then in her 91st year, was clearly delighted when she attended an event that was held at UCL in the summer of 2000 to mark the book's publication.

The Shackle volume had a long and very odd history. It was originally set in motion around 1991, by John Pheby, Stefan Boehm and Stephen Frowen, as a volume to be presented to George Shackle on his 90th birthday in July 1993 but was turned into a memorial volume following Shackle's death at the age of 88 in March 1992. I had written a chapter on "Indeterminacy in the economics classroom' in which I used Shackle's inaugural lecture at the University of Liverpool, "What makes an economist?" (Shackle, 1953) as the starting point for a reflection on the challenges of teaching in a pluralistic manner and focusing on open-ended problems. I then examined the lessons that educational psychologist William Perry (1970) offered for those wishing to embrace these challenges. It had been a good means of organizing my thoughts after Lincoln's Director of Education, Neil Fleming had introduced Perry's work to me, and it turned out neatly to complement Brian Loasby's contribution, "How do we know?" I had submitted it on schedule, before using it as my presentation to the

1992 Australian Conference of Economists.[14] But things then went very quiet with the editorial process.

Routledge's representatives gave vague answers about its progress when I raised the issue with them at the 1994 and 1996 Malvern conferences, They eventually advised me that the manuscript had been lost in transit to their London office, and that Stefan Boehm was going to reconstruct it. But there continued to be no sign that the book was going to go into production. Brian Loasby was clearly as disappointed as I was about the situation, referring to the volume, in one of his dinner talks at the conference in his honor, as something which he hoped might be published in his own lifetime. I therefore asked him whether it might be a good idea if, with due consultation with Routledge, I hijacked the project and attempted to reconstruct the book. He supported the idea and hence that is what I did, after Routledge had explained my proposal to Boehm and given him a final deadline to deliver the completed manuscript.

After the manuscript again failed to arrive, I set to work on reconstructing the book. All I had to go on was the original tentative list of contributors, not all of whom I could locate. During the process of getting a copy of Victoria Chick's paper, she put me in touch with Stephen Frowen (1923–2007), who had, by this stage, become an honorary research fellow at UCL. Stephen's knowledge of how the original editorial team had failed to produce the volume was sketchy. In his own case, the story was especially bizarre: it involved him being diverted by having to nurse his wife after they had been lucky to escape alive from a house fire in Germany that resulted from a faulty Christmas tree light. He was keen to help me revive the project. I accepted his offer despite initially being somewhat nervous about how things might go, as I had noticed that the volume that he had edited based on a 1983 conference celebrating Shackle's 80th birthday had taken seven years to be published (Frowen, ed., 1990). He then

---

[14] I went on to present this paper in 1993 as a visiting speaker at the University of Lancaster, Leeds University Business School, Victoria University of Wellington, and the Department of Management at the University of Canterbury. The last of these could have been a disaster, and I hope that, in explaining why, I will not cause readers to have nightmares. So frantic had things been at Lincoln that I had forgotten all about the seminar until the day before, when I noticed in my diary a note saying "seminar, Canterbury." However, I thought that it referred to a seminar by someone else, as Alan Singer, a member of Canterbury's Department of Management, had, become a good friend after I got to know him via being an examiner of his PhD, and he sometimes invited me to seminars there. When I arrived and found the seminar room, it was fortuitous that, before going in and taking a seat, I decided to look at the notice on the door, to see who the speaker was going to be. I was shocked to find that it was me, and I realized that I would have to deliver it without any slides. Afterwards, Bob Hamilton – who had been a colleague at Stirling and was now a professor of management at Canterbury – came up to me and said, "That was a very good presentation, with no notes at all!' I then told him why I had not been using any notes.

played a key role in getting Stephen Littlechild to supply a brand-new chapter about the Shackle papers in Cambridge University Library. I enjoyed working with Stephen Frowen via many faxes and emails before eventually meeting him at the book's launch. However, I wish he had prevented me from a very embarrassing and out-of-character slip with the book. I will now end this section by recounting what it entailed.

The original sheet of paper that listed prospective contributors included a joint chapter by James Buchanan and Viktor Vanberg, but as Christmas 1998 approached, I had not been able to find email addresses for either of them, (It probably did not help that I was a few months away from discovering the wonders of Google.) I made a mental note to write an airmail letter to Buchanan in the New Year – which I then forgot to do amid other tasks on returning to campus in January 1999. The book was thus completed without a chapter by Buchanan and Vanberg, as Stephen Frowen did not remind me that there should have been one and neither did Routledge after I sent the typescript to them in camera-ready form, early in 2000. But, despite having provided me with no copies of early correspondence about the book, Routledge clearly did know that Buchanan was supposed to be one of the contributors, for soon after the book appeared, Buchanan wrote to me to say that Routledge had sent him a copy and he had been surprised to find that it did not contain his chapter with Vanberg. He was very pleasant about the matter when I explained what had happened, and he said he doubted there would be any difficulty publishing the paper elsewhere, even almost a decade after they had written it. Given that he was a Nobel Laureate, I had no reason to doubt his conjecture.


## 6.5    JASON POTTS AND COMPLEX ADAPTIVE SYSTEMS

My first experiences in supervising a PhD in economics came at Lincoln, a decade after I finished my own PhD. Given my difficult road to a doctorate, there was obviously potential for history to repeat itself when I began to supervise research. However, although I had not experienced styles of thesis supervision that I regarded as good role models, I had at least emerged from the process with a PhD and a sense of the kinds of mentoring that might have speeded up the process.

Jason Potts was my first start-to-finish doctoral student in economics, and he is now a Distinguished Professor of Economics at RMIT University in Melbourne. He had studied economics at the University of Otago and approached me after an economist at the University of Canterbury declined to be his PhD supervisor and suggested that, given Jason's area of interest, he might try me instead. However, when Jason approached me to ask if I would be willing to supervise him for a PhD that would develop an evolutionary analysis of entrepreneurship, my initial suggestion was that if he wanted to do a PhD in evolutionary economics, it would be better for him to do it at the University of Queensland in Australia, under the guidance of Professor John Foster. As luck would have it, some weeks later Jason came to my office to say that he *really* would like to work on his PhD under my supervision. The thesis that he eventually produced was a remarkably original piece of work, contributing to evolutionary economics in ways that went beyond the area of entrepreneurship. It was published, with an additional chapter, as *The New Evolutionary Microeconomics* (Potts, 2000) and it shared the 2000 J. A. Schumpeter Prize with Loasby's (1999) *Knowledge, Institutions and Evolution in Economics*.

Jason's PhD dissertation was a work that it is hard to envisage being produced via a doctoral program that is run along today's best-practice, managerialist lines with an emphasis on risk management and the expectation that students will produce, and be able to defend, rather tightly specified plans for what they are going to do. Jason was required to make a presentation and answer questions about it for his confirmation of candidature, but his proposal was far less thoroughly spelled out than today's best-practice demands. Indeed, the central ideas of Jason's thesis only came together much later, after I had given the thumbs-down to a succession of things that he had written, and after he had taken some time out having an overseas experience. Yet, before he arrived at the core of his thesis, it was clear to me that he was seriously bright and a very hard worker who had what it would take to get a PhD, so I was happy to sign off any progress reports. Then, one day, he came to my office and said, "I've got it: Graph Theory!" He proceeded to explain what Graph Theory was and its relevance to evolutionary economics and economics more generally.

Jason's central proposition was that conventional economics differs fundamentally from heterodox approaches in how it sees relationships between elements of the economy. The conventional approach is premised on a mathematical perspective that views every element as connected, to some degree, to every other element. In other words, the economic system is viewed much as the Universe is seen from the standpoint of Newtonian physics, where it is envisaged as a force field in which stars, planets, moons, and asteroids exert different degrees of gravitational pull on each other. General equilibrium models of economic systems are perhaps the most obvious parallel to the Newtonian view of how heavenly bodies all interact with each other to some degree, even if in many instances their pull on each other is tiny. In the general equilibrium view, a shock to the system in one market can trigger changes in relative prices, outputs and quantities consumed, to a greater or lesser degree, across the entire economy, as everything is seen as ultimately substitutable, to some degree, for everything else.

What Jason had picked up via Graph Theory was that an alternative to viewing the economy as if it is a force-field is to view it as a "complex adaptive system" whose elements only have connections with *some* other elements. Taking the latter view opens possibilities to which mainstream economists seem oblivious, such as:

- Purposive activities of entrepreneurs and consumers entail the creation of systems – such as new products, production systems and consumption lifestyles – with specific architectures of connections for how their elements go together.
- "Structural change" can occur, whereby innovations lead to changes in the connective architecture of the economy, with new patterns of economic connections being established and old ones ceasing to apply, rather than there being merely changes in relative prices and quantities via established links.
- The economic system may display "breaks in chains of substitution" that limit the effectiveness of policies designed to work by triggering a cascade of relative price changes, for there may be areas in which people are completely unwilling or unable to change their behavior in response to changes in relative prices.
- Some kinds of economic activities will not occur unless specific connections can be made; in other words, production or consumption may not be possible without complementary prerequisite or co-requisite assets or inputs.
- The strategic vulnerability of the economic system, or sub-systems within it, depends on the structure of linkages within the system or between systems.

In short, system architecture is a key concern if one does not employ the "field' perspective. Policymakers may need to focus on non-price drivers of economic behavior and performance, and policy interventions may need to focus on ensuring that necessary connections can be made and that dangerous connective structures do not emerge.

This system-based view was a way by which I could bring together the approaches to economics that appealed to me and get a clearer sense of what made my overall approach to economics different from that of the mainstream. It is a way of bringing together ideas as diverse as perspectives from institutional economics on the significance of social rules; the significance of patronage networks and discrimination in labor markets; and Keynes's "Chapter 17" view of money – as well as my long-standing interest in the significance of non-compensatory decision rules and the effects that the ways that people think have on their openness to change. However, it took me a while before I habitually thought explicitly from a connectionist perspective.

On that key day, I tried to soak up Jason's abstract central thesis by trying to relate it to concrete examples from economic systems and asking if I was getting the message correctly. This way of operating continued in successive meetings and the dissertation then started to come together quite rapidly. However, in 1997, well over a year before he submitted the thesis, I was nervous about what kind of reception his work might get. To ensure that Jason's ideas did not get examined without having been tried out on leading evolutionary economists, and to help his employment prospects, I told him that he should write a paper based on his key proposition and use his entire research fund allowance to buy a return ticket to attend the conference at the University of Stirling that I was organizing with Sheila Dow in honor of Brian Loasby, and that I would pay for his conference fee and accommodation.

On the final morning of the conference, Jason began his presentation by saying, "What I'm going to talk about may be important for evolutionary economics or may be mistaken, and I'm hoping you will be able to tell me which it is." His paper (published as Potts, 1999) rather stole the show, with Richard Day, co-founding editor of the *Journal of Economic Behavior and Organization*, leading the very positive reaction. John Foster was also in the audience, and he resolved that he was going to hire Jason, who duly joined the School of Economics at the University of Queensland at the start of 1999.[15]

---

[15] Lincoln University also provided the venue for my second role in supervising a PhD in economics, though, in this case, the project was not quite finished by the time I moved back to Australia, and it did not feed into my vision of behavioral economics. However, it is worth noting here because of the supervisory experience that it entailed. The PhD in question was by Greg Clydesdale, for whom it opened the door to an academic career in entrepreneurial studies and a base from which to contribute across a wide range of areas that intersect with behavioral and evolutionary economics. These areas have included the creative industries (Clydesdale, 2006, 2015) and the impact of culture on motivation (Clydesdale, 2021). Greg's thesis straddled behavioral, evolutionary and institutional economics, development economics and economic history, brought together via his focus on differences in operating systems between rival cultures and the effects of adherence to these system as they lost their effectiveness relative to those that regional rivals developed.

At the time that Greg started his PhD, he had a very clear vision of what he wanted to do: he wanted to write a book about the long-term dynamics of national rivalry and leadership in the shipping industry and its impact on economic growth. It was an ambitious idea, effectively an

## 6.6 PRODUCT SIGNATURES AND BRANDS AS SYSTEMS OF CONNECTIONS

While Jason was writing up his PhD, I got to know another very bright young New Zealander, Chris Hann, who was at that time in the early stages of doing a PhD in mathematics at the University of Canterbury (where these days he is an associate professor of electrical engineering). A mutual friend thought that I would enjoy meeting Chris not because of his PhD but because, like me, Chris was also a serious musician. In fact, he turned out to be a superb keyboard player and drummer and, bit by bit, in the ensuing couple of years, my home studio was the venue at which I served as his recording engineer for an album's worth of music on which he played all the instruments and supplied the vocals. One evening, when he came to do some recording, we talked about his upcoming PhD confirmation, and I discovered that his work had a connectionist dimension that intersected with what I was picking up from Jason's work.

Chris explained to me that the title of his confirmation presentation was going to be "When is a cat a cat?" and that he was exploring how object-recognition systems in engineering could use mathematical characterizations of objects as simple configurations of lines, curves and/or circles. The question was how simplified these characterizations could be and yet still capture the essence of the target object. In effect, it seemed to me that what he was doing was akin to the mathematics of the "jizz" concept in ornithology, but I rapidly realised that it related to other concepts in my approach to behavioral and evolutionary economics.

---

evolutionary and institutional analysis spanning many centuries. He already knew a lot of the relevant history, especially in relation to the rise and fall of India and China as leaders in shipping. After getting started, he showed great determination and resilience. But there was a problem that he had to overcome and which he is happy for me to share here, namely the fact that he wanted to write a book on this topic. Greg enjoys writing and writes very well but, in the early years of his work on the project, there was a clear danger that he would end up writing a book for a much wider audience, rather than the relentlessly analytical thesis that he needed to write for his PhD examiners. In a sense, he was in a zone that combined elements of where I had been in the period 1981–1982, and where Loasby's model-free research project in economic history was heading in the 1950s.

For a long while, almost all my effort as Greg's supervisor seemed to go into trying, repeatedly, to get across the message that the book would not work as a PhD. It was a frustrating but necessary experience for both of us, but in the end, Greg got the message and wrote a well-received PhD dissertation in the area of his chosen topic; it was only after his academic career was well established that a version aimed at a much wider audience was published (see Clydesdale, 2016).

Firstly, what Chris told me about his PhD helped me to start bringing together the birdwatcher's notion of "jizz," and Kelly's template-based view of personal constructs as templates for characterizing things. Next, it enabled me to link the "jizz" and cognitive template concepts to a term that I had often seen motoring journalists use, namely the idea that car brands or car models often have "signature" aspects of their designs that remain rather stable across successive generations of products. In the motor industry context, as with, say, instantly identifiable distinctive styles of some classical composers and rock bands, these signatures are essentially complex systems of connected features. The same can be said of the notion of a brand (see Harper and Endres, 2018). If we know the signature features of a particular producer's products, we can readily identify the maker or model of variants that we have not previously seen.

At the time, I thought that one day I might pursue these ideas in relation to marketing theory and try to study how the performance of firms is affected by the extent to which they employ product signatures. To date, I have not taken that research idea further, but thoughts about the intersection of the "jizz" notion and the challenge of programming object recognition systems would later prove very instructive when I was trying to get to grips with Hayek's (1952) book *The Sensory Order*, and I referred to some of Chris Hann's work in the first piece that I wrote in relation to this area of Hayek's work (Earl, 2010a).


## 6.7    INTERDISCIPLINARY DOCTORATES AND SIMON'S TRAVEL THEOREM

Although Jason Potts was my first start-to-finish PhD student, he was not the first PhD student that I worked with at Lincoln. At the time Jason commenced his work, I was already getting some experience as an associate supervisor for an interdisciplinary farm management doctorate by Ngenang Jangu (1997), who was studying how farmers made their decisions to adopt an innovative milking shed design. In a sense, this was a case study in behavioral/evolutionary agricultural economics, but I was invited to get involved because Ngenang's principal advisor knew of my interest in personal construct psychology (PCP) and Ngenang was using research tools from PCP to uncover differences in how adopters and non-adopters saw the innovation. Since he was probing towards the cores of his subjects' belief systems, this project had an ethical dimension that went beyond basic concerns about preserving the anonymity of his subjects: he had to be careful not to anger his subjects by trying to get them to articulate bases for things they said they believed "because I do, period."

Lincoln's PhD system ran in a way that had elements of both the Cambridge system that I had experienced and modern best-practice systems. Although students were required to give, and defend, an oral presentation as part of the process of having their PhD candidature confirmed, there seemed to be no other formal milestones prior to the submission of the thesis. If students failed to submit within eight years from commencing, their candidacy was terminated. In contrast to the rather casual approach to monitoring progress, the examination process was much more rigorous than the systems used in Australian universities, where there was no oral examination and examiners simply submitted their reports and outcome recommendations. Lincoln required its PhD students to be orally examined by a committee consisting of an external examiner from another New Zealand university, an overseas external examiner, and members of the student's advisory team. However, examiners submitted their reports and outcome recommendations prior to the oral. In the event of a dispute about the outcome, a further external examiner's opinion would be sought.[16] I felt that having the supervisors involved in the oral exam provided a good way for them (me included) to get some benchmarking experience relative to external assessors.

In Jason's case, the overseas external examiner, Stan Metcalfe, did not attend the oral and instead provided a set of questions to be asked on his behalf. This seemed to be the normal practice. However, in Ngenang's case a video conference was organized. The most obvious overseas expert for the task was Roy Murray-Prior, in Western Australia, another farm management scholar who had used PCP in his work. Although this was at an early time in the development of video-conferencing technology, the video link worked surprisingly well; indeed, it provided an effective illustration of Herbert Simon's (1991, p. 306) "travel theorem" whereby it is argued that if the only point of traveling is to gather information, then there should be no need to undertake the journey, since it should be possible to obtain the information locally via a good public library or remotely via telecommunications technology.

---

[16] In late 2009, over eight years after leaving Lincoln, I was invited to arbitrate in this way for an adventurous thesis on ecological economics. I attended the oral examination in person in January 2010 while on vacation in New Zealand. My next visit to this part of New Zealand was about six months after the February 2011 earthquake that caused major damage in Christchurch and the surrounding area, and significant aftershocks were still happening (there were three between 4.2 and 4.8 on the Richter scale on my final day there), Lincoln University had fared well during the earthquake, whereas. at the University of Canterbury, the Commerce Building was closed, and a large marquee had been erected nearby as a make-do substitute. The devastation in the center of Christchurch was horrific, with so many buildings having been removed that it was hard to get a sense of what one was looking at, through the cordon of steel fencing.

Ngenang's doctorate was neither the only interdisciplinary project in which I began to get experience as a PhD supervisor nor the only one that related to Simon's "travel theorem." While supervising Jason's work, I had another enjoyable associate supervisor role in a study by one of Lincoln's tourism lecturers, David Fisher (2000). David's project was an ethnographic study of differences between how tourism providers and tourists in a South Pacific destination viewed the attractiveness of that destination. This, too, could have involved the research tools of PCP, but David decided to adopt the anthropologist's approach of traveling to a community and embedding himself there for a significant period. I did not try to deter him from doing this by referring to Simon's travel theorem, for Simon only claimed it to apply for visits to a destination of less than six months.

The early phase of David's project provided a lesson that is relevant for all PhD confirmations, namely the need to have a "Plan B" in case the proposed project turns out not to be feasible. David's original plan was to do his research in Vanuatu, but the local volcano erupted, and we were not sure how long volcanic ash would continue to be a problem. He therefore decided instead to base himself in Levuka, the first western-style town to be built in the Pacific islands and the original capital of Fiji. The time that he spent embedded there enabled him to discover something important that he would have been much less likely to discover remotely: Levuka's visitors were attracted by its antiquity, whereas local entrepreneurs tended not to appreciate this and viewed modern development projects as the means to increase visitor numbers. Levuka was designated as a World Heritage site in 2013.

## 6.8   THE LEGACY OF HERBERT A. SIMON IN ECONOMIC ANALYSIS

When the opportunity arose to take six months of study leave in the second half of 1999, I was determined to make it a period in which I spent a lot of time refreshing my knowledge. My previous study leave had mostly been spent at Lincoln and had yielded very little, so it was clear to me that my upcoming leave should be spent somewhere else, somewhere that had a very good library. I spent it as a visiting professor at the University of Queensland, whose new head of school, John Foster, I had known for many years and who had recently hired Jason Potts. Spending my study leave in Brisbane also worked in domestic terms, for my then-partner Sharon had decided to move there with her recently adopted children: she would move permanently when I started my leave, and I would sample whether I fancied living in Brisbane in the long term if a job came up for me there. By the end of the study leave, I had concluded that the University of Queensland would be a much better place to work but that I much preferred Christchurch as a place to live. I hoped that, on returning to Christchurch, I could at last make the Lincoln job enjoyable.

The business plan for my study leave concentrated on my need for a world-class research library in order to extend my expertise in behavioral economics by editing, for Edward Elgar Publishing, a two-volume anthology of reprinted papers that would demonstrate the intellectual legacy of Herbert Simon in economics. This was to be a much more intensive exercise than my previous Elgar anthology on behavioral economics (Earl, ed., 1988b), for I intended to compile it with the aid of the Social Sciences Citation Index (SSCI). I had previously used the University of Queensland's hardcopy version of the SSCI when preparing my paper (Earl, 1998b) for a festschrift volume for George Richardson while visiting to attend the 1995 conference of the History of Economic Thought Society of Australia, but by July 1999 the online Web of Science version was available there. In the introduction that I wrote for the Simon volumes (Earl, ed., 2001b). I used the experience of trying to work with the SSCI as a way of introducing Simon's challenge to the notion of optimization: Simon's work was so extensively cited that I faced information overload when trying to consider which were the most significant economics-related works that cited his contributions – and this was despite Web of Science at that time running into difficulties displaying more than about the top 400 citing works for any of Simon's key contributions.

To deal with the information overload, I had to figure out a system of rules for deciding which papers to include. This entailed working with a plan for the structure of the two volumes and concentrating on recent papers unless I had other reasons for including earlier work. The focus on recent contributions seemed to be the best way – given the "legacy" theme – of getting a sense of where mainstream and behavioral views of bounded rationality had got to and of the range of applications of Simon-inspired analysis. In less than five months, I managed to decide which papers to include and to write detailed introductions to both volumes. I was very happy with the outcome: Simon-inspired behavioral or evolutionary economics seemed to have been making great progress over the past decade and Simon's legacy in economics seemed secure and significant.

This confident assessment was shattered a little over a year later, after Elgar had obtained all of the reprint permissions and the Simon Legacy volumes were about to go into production. Herbert Simon died unexpectedly on February 9, 2001. That news was bad enough, but two days later the *New York Times* published a pair of articles about the emergence of a new field called behavioral economics, one of which focused on the work of Richard Thaler (Lowenstein, 2001), with the other spotlighting David Laibson, a younger rising star of whom I had not previously been aware (Uchitelle, 2001). Neither article mentioned the work of Simon, let alone his passing, or the work of Cyert and March on the behavioral theory of the firm. I was bewildered by this turn of events: it was as if Simon and others who had pioneered the behavioral approach before Thaler's (1980) initial contribution – indeed, even before Laibson's birth in 1966 – had been airbrushed from the history of economic thought at precisely the time when Simon's impact in economics ought to have been acknowledged. Six years would pass before I came to understand what was happening to behavioral economics (see Section 7.3).


## 6.9   EDITING THE *JOURNAL OF ECONOMIC PSYCHOLOGY*

Shortly after I finished my work on *The Legacy of Herbert A. Simon in Economic Analysis*, psychologist Simon Kemp got back in touch with me. He suggested that our respective areas of expertise, and our success in getting the *Elgar Companion to Consumer Research and Economic Psychology* to fruition in a timely manner, could be seen as implying that he and I would be a credible team if we put in a bid to become editors of the *Journal of Economic Psychology* for the period 2000–2005. I agreed to join him in such a bid, and his hypothesis was confirmed. The fact that I agreed to participate may seem odd, given that I had been keen to leave editorial tasks behind me on completing the Simon Legacy anthology. Why did I not decline, pleading my need to get my own research back on a strong footing and prove that I could deliver a steady stream of papers in well-ranked journals?

I imagine that some people might see my behavior as implying that I had got addicted to editing, that I saw the editor role in terms of power, status and control, and/or that I had developed some kind of aversion to doing original research and going through the refereeing gauntlet. But this was not the case. This is evidenced by the fact that I resigned from the role early in 2004 when I experienced a major problem with my eyesight. I was not sure how long the problem was going to last, and it was making my work very challenging, so I decided that I needed to put myself first and concentrate on my own writing, though I felt guilty about letting Simon down. He was most understanding and did not try to get me back into the role a few months later after my vision had recovered, and he served out the rest of his term without enlisting anyone else to share the editor-in-chief role.

A major part of the reason that I agreed to pitch for the role was that I had decided that one of the things I wanted to do in my academic career was experience as many as possible of the different tasks that academics undertake, and thereby find out what each kind of task entails and whether I was capable of performing them successfully. My teaching and administrative loads at Lincoln had lately become much less demanding, so I felt that editing a journal, especially jointly with Simon Kemp and with a team of associate editors, would be feasible without preventing me from getting my own original research happening again. However, Simon and I soon found that the task was initially going to consume a lot more of our time than we had imagined.

If incoming journal editors are to apply their quality aspirations from the outset, the key thing they need to inherit from the outgoing editors is a buffer of accepted papers to fill the first few issues – ideally, the first volume. However, with the previous editorial team having overseen the switch from four issues per year to six issues per year, the buffer had ended up being rather limited. This was despite the growing interest in behavioral economics, for the *Journal* still seemed mainly to be attracting papers from those in the old European tradition in economic psychology. This was not surprising, given the adjective–noun relationship in the *Journal's* title did not signal it to be a forum for psychological economics. The latter seems to me to be a good alternative phrase to behavioral economics, whereas I took economic psychology as pertaining to the use of economic perspectives in psychological analysis (which was essentially what I had done in my analysis of cognitive dissonance management by viewing the brain as attempting to minimize the extent to which it had to restructure itself in order to remove clashes between cognitions).

To rebuild a buffer of accepted papers without lowering our sights for the quality of regular articles, we needed rapidly to attract papers and get them refereed promptly. This could be done by calling for papers for special issues and/or commissioning survey papers or obituary articles or using particular articles as bases for creating symposia by inviting responses or complementary papers from scholars whom we believed were likely to be able rapidly to deliver good copy. Some further pages to meet the publisher's required annual total could also be achieved by running more book reviews.

By these kinds of measures, we managed to satisfy Elsevier and create a buffer. But it was very challenging being initially, for we had to find a couple of replacement associate editors and engage in damage control after analyzing the progress on getting submissions refereed and discovering that some of the associate editors that we had inherited had been allowing turnaround times to drag badly. We also had to look for a new book review editor (with me taking over the role in the interim), after discovering that this section of the journal was on the verge of collapsing, and that publishers were not amused by how few of the books they sent actually got reviewed in a timely manner, or at all.

Amid these recovery activities, we sought to signal openness to behavioral economics papers from North American authors by enlisting some big-name US behavioral economists for the editorial board, making clear that their duties would be very limited. To our delight, Richard Thaler accepted, whereas Matthew Rabin declined, saying that if he got involved with the *Journal* it might have adverse consequences for his mission to get psychology into the core generalist economic journals. The fact that Rabin had been succeeding in his mission should have provided a signal to me to take a close look at the kind of behavioral economics that was proving acceptable in these journals, but I was too busy in my editorial role, and in getting back into my own work, for this to register at the time.


## 6.10  USING TEXT AND INTROSPECTION IN BEHAVIORAL ECONOMICS

One of the contributions that I hoped to make in behavioral economics when I moved to Lincoln was to explore further the use of published text in economic analysis. This seemed to be a potentially powerful extension to what Thaler (1980) had been doing by starting to deploy anecdotes in his work. By definition, his anecdotes could not each constitute a statistical sample, yet they could sound warning bells insofar as they rang true in relation to everyday experience in ways that were anomalous for the established economic wisdom. Better still, they might also point toward alternative testable hypotheses. My first steps in this direction had been in the revised version of my PhD and in *Lifestyle Economics* where I dissected the conclusions that motoring journalist wrote to multi-vehicle test reports. Often, but not always, their verdicts appeared to be based on non-compensatory decision rules, as when they referred to a particular car as having an "Achilles heel" that limited how highly it was ranked.

My decision to take a text-based approach further was a belated result of meeting Charlotte Phelps at the 1990 IAREP conference at Exeter, where I seemed to be about the only person at her session who appreciated her bold effort (Phelps, 1990) to explore labor supply choices by examining how Arthur Miller had presented such choices in his play *The Price* (Miller, 1972). Phelps seemed to have offered a "proof-of-concept" contribution and very soon I saw on television some of a five-episode Channel 4/PBS documentary series about the construction of the One Worldwide Plaza skyscraper complex in New York that was a ready source of material for exploring the behavioral economics of industrial organization. I did not try to obtain a video recording of the series despite immediately realizing its potential when I stumbled into an episode; instead, I obtained a copy of the book that the producer/narrator, Karl Sabbagh (1989) had written to accompany the series. However, it was not until 1995 that I managed to find time to write the paper that I envisaged (Earl, 1996b).

From the standpoint of Williamson's (1975, 1985) transaction cost-based view of industrial organization, building a skyscraper might look like a context in which major hold-up potential would result in a highly vertically integrated construction process being used to deter opportunism. However, the actual system was more like a kind of virtual firm that took the form of a hierarchy of specialized contractors and subcontractors, with a construction management firm at its head. Pressure to get work done in a timely manner flowed down from the top but contractors generally did not behave with opportunism because getting a reputation for doing so would be disastrous for winning contracts on subsequent building projects. Hold-ups did occur but they resulted from unforeseen problems that were inevitable given the complexity of the project, especially given that upper floors were being designed while lower ones were being built. Even though there were concerns that some remote contractors (suppliers of bricks and marble) might not be telling the truth about whether they were going to be able to deliver on schedule (which led to them being visited by representatives of the construction management company), Sabbagh's text was much more in line with Richardson's (1972) capabilities-based view of the boundaries of firms.

Another text-based idea that I had was to explore the view of human behavior offered by Marcel Proust in his seven-volume novel *À la Recherche du Temps Perdu* (Proust, 1913–1927; in English: *Remembrance of Things Past*, or *In Search of Lost Time*), which I suspected would be fertile territory for a view of behavior that largely reflected habits and social norms. But the scale of such a study ruled it out, given how pressed I was for time. Instead, I tried something much more modest, in a book chapter on "Consumer goals as journeys into the unknown" (Earl 1998a).

This paper was written in late 1995, a few weeks after my then-partner Sharon and I attended a performance of the Stephen Sondheim and James Lapine musical *Into the Woods* at Christchurch Town Hall. It seemed fitting to begin the paper by referring to the musical before proceeding to explore why bold ventures are prone to go awry. By this point, Sharon had gone "into the woods" by heading off to Paraguay to undertake an inter-country adoption of a four-year-old boy, a Kafkaesque mission whose difficulties began almost as soon as she arrived there and kept her from bringing Daniel to start his life in New Zealand for over six months. The problems were only resolved after I asked our local Member of Parliament to lobby the Minister of Immigration to provide the right kind of visa. Some of my paper's analysis of "the problem of arriving" drew from the autobiography of a New Zealand property developer who made and lost a fortune in New Zealand's Minsky-style mid-1980s episode of financial instability. But the paper also drew implicitly on my own reflections about how, by giving too much attention to the task of winning the job at Lincoln, I had failed to glean enough intelligence about what I could be getting into. After I completed this experimental chapter, four years passed before I found time to write a paper that was entirely and explicitly based on introspective methods.

The classic discussion of the use that economists can legitimately make of introspection is in Hutchison's (1938) *The Significance and Basic Postulates of Economic Theory*. I had a copy of this book, and I knew of its relevance in this area, but it was not what led me to make a serious and explicit effort to bring introspective methods into behavioral economics, for I had barely looked inside since purchasing it in April 1979. Rather, the inspiration for my introspective turn came from the work of Morris Holbrook, a professor of marketing at Columbia University who has often allowed his love of jazz into his writing on consumer behavior. While considering whether to revise and resubmit my survey paper on economics and marketing, I came across Holbrook's (1995a) then-new paper on the commodification of marketing education, and it was this paper's reference to the difficulty that he had experienced trying to publish an unorthodox book on consumer behavior via a "big textbook publisher" that led me to discover that he had written an entire book on introspective consumer research (Holbrook, 1995b). I obtained a copy of it in late 1997 and read it during the ensuing summer vacation. If I could think of a way of doing something similar in economics, it would certainly be at risk of being viewed disapprovingly by those who conflated introspection and *a priorism* and who, like Hutchison, wanted economics to be an empirical science based on applying statistics to falsifiable hypotheses. However, I discovered that Hutchison had not made such a conflation and that he did acknowledge a role for introspection in economics, namely as a disruptive tool for questioning empirical claims and suggesting alternative lines of theorizing that might yield testable hypotheses.

The challenge was to find an area in which I could use introspective methods in this way, and toward the end of my 1999 study leave I found a perfect opportunity. Like Holbrook's examples, it involved music, though in my case it was not jazz but the question of whether I should attend a concert by the classically influenced Swedish heavy-metal guitar virtuoso Yngwie J. Malmsteen. His playing had been inspirational to me during the preceding two years. However, for several weeks after discovering that he was going to be performing in Brisbane, I reminded myself why I had given up going to rock concerts and that if I took Simon's travel theorem seriously, there was no point in going since I already had all of Malmsteen's albums, along with several videos of him playing live, and note-by-note transcriptions of much of his music. My then-partner Sharon could not believe I was resisting getting a ticket on this basis. Ultimately, I felt I really should go to the concert, and we got some tickets. Sure enough, the concert made no sense in terms of gathering information about Malmsteen's playing, and it came with downsides, most notably the dangerously loud volume level (even though I was armed with shooters' earplugs), exactly as I had anticipated. But it did not refute Simon's travel theorem, for via introspection, I realized that a recorded concert does not enable one to meet some objectives that a fan may be able to meet by attending a live show. One such motivation is to pay homage to a performer that one admires, the musical equivalent of making a religious pilgrimage to Mecca.

After drafting my Holbrook-inspired paper on the demand for live music (eventually published in revised form, including some feedback from Holbrook, as Earl, 2001a), I spent the last couple of weeks of my study leave writing an autobiographical account of my car-buying decisions over the preceding twenty years. This was an exploration in a more Proustian style of introspective economics, but I then put it aside until 2010, when I updated it and found myself with a "much too long" 50,000-word tale of "Remembrance of Cars Past" (available as Earl, 2010b) that set out thirty years of learning about what I really wanted in a car and the limits to what I was prepared to pay to get it, with intolerant decision criteria repeatedly shaping the choices that I made. I attempted to capture the essence of this experiential analysis of automotive consumption in Earl (2012a), my contribution to a dual special issue of the *Journal of Business Research* on introspective methods. Around the time it was in press, another of my papers surveyed, with illustrative examples, the methodological case for, and scope for using, introspection and text in behavioral economic analysis: see Earl (2011). I am tempted to bring the "much too long version" of the motoring paper up to date – and intro the age of electric vehicles – and extend it into a book on the behavioral economics of motoring.

## 6.11   THE MARKET FOR PREFERENCES

When I returned to Lincoln at the start of 2000, my teaching and administrative loads turned out to be much lower than I had ever experienced there. By the time of Herbert Simon's passing, and as the result of a couple of trips back to the University of Queensland to maintain contact with Jason Potts, I had a pair of related papers in process. The first (published as Earl and Potts, 2000, though it did not appear until well into 2001) examined how shopping malls are designed to promote browsing behavior rather than to minimize the search costs of busy shoppers. A significant volume of purchasing decisions may thus arise contingently depending on the success of attempts to manage the attention of shoppers, rather than emerging as shoppers find what they went out to purchase or succeed in solving the problems they went out hoping to solve. Some years later, we discovered that what we had been writing about is known in marketing as "The Gruen Transfer," after Victor Gruen, the pioneering designer of modern shopping malls. Our paper can be read as complementary to the dominant behavioral view that real-world consumers, unlike idealized "econs," are susceptible to making suboptimal choices due to the choice architecture that they are presented with being designed to nudge them in directions that favor supplier interests. However, what we wrote next offered a more upbeat view of the quality of choices that people make.

The second paper (eventually published, after a typically leisurely *Cambridge Journal of Economics* refereeing process, as Earl and Potts, 2004a) was the last and the most significant that I worked on in my decade at Lincoln. It takes a less cynical view of the role of shopping malls, viewing retailers as one category among a variety of types of market institutions that enable inexperienced, boundedly rational consumers to outsource their preferences to those who have specialist knowledge about the sets of product characteristics that it is wise to obtain in a particular context, and which products match these templates. This view of consumer behavior entails a multi-level view of preferences, for when another party (e.g., a salesperson at a retail site, a service consultant such as an interior design specialist, an online recommendation, or a member of one's social network who appears to have the requisite expertise) suggests what we should want or buy, we are not obliged to "buy" their suggestion.

Jason and I coined the term "the market for preferences" to denote the set of institutions that make it possible partially to outsource one's preferences. Clearly, it is not a market in which transactions necessarily involve payments for the preferences that one takes on board. Sometimes we do pay money for our outsourced preferences, as when we pay a premium price if we choose to shop at a full-service retailer, or purchase something to give to a social contact as a token of our appreciation for their help in discovering what we need. But sometimes we spend less money by using the market for preferences, as when we, in effect, let Aldi shop for groceries for us by presenting us with a very limited range of choice of products that offer excellent value for money due to Aldi concentrating its buying power on products whose attribute mixes will serve most customers well.

This perspective takes the division of labor notion into new territory, emphasizing that economic actors typically are operating in a social context that makes it possible for them to benefit from the superior knowledge of others and to contribute their expertise to the decision-making of others. This is a very Hayekian view of how markets function to enhance the rationality of buyers (cf. Dekker and Remic, 2024) and its "extended mind" aspect implicitly brings it in to the category of what is known as "enactivist rationality" (see Frolov, 2024; Viale, 2024). Behavioral economists need to embrace and study the potential for enactivist rationality processes to enhance consumer wellbeing. But they, and Austrian economists, also need to recognize that the market for preferences can fail if people lack the expertise to make effective choices about how to outsource aspects of their choices. For example, it takes skill to discern the honesty of a financial advisor or whether a product review has been posted by a wise customer or an agent of the supplier of the product.


6.12   PROGRESS REVIEW

Moving from UTAS to Lincoln certainly delivered the sort of material outcomes that I had hoped a full professor position would bring, but it was a disastrous career move. It was by far the least productive part of my career in terms of the extent to which I made original contributions to knowledge. Moreover, my bemusement when I read the *New York Times* articles by Lowenstein (2001) and Uchitelle (2001) reflected the fact that my decade at Lincoln was also problematic in terms of the growth of my knowledge of what others were doing, implicitly or explicitly, under the banner of behavioral economics. Both these progress shortfalls reflected the impact of Lincoln's operating system, and how I tried to deal with it, on the time that I had for research and the use that I made of it.

A key factor in what happened was my complete unwillingness to do what a typical academic would have done if asked to teach Lincoln's Microeconomics for Business and Marketing, namely, follow closely a conventional intermediate microeconomics or managerial economics text and build tutorials and assessment tasks around technical problem sets that had definitive answers and could be marked rapidly. My behavioral economics knowledge meant that I could not teach that course with a clear conscience unless I presented students with the best perspective that I had available for addressing problems that orthodox economics was ill-suited for addressing. And I was not willing to ignore the knowledge problems that often make it difficult to arrive a clear-cut answers to economic questions. This led me to saddle myself with a lot more teaching-related work than would have been involved if I had "taught from a standard textbook" – not merely in terms of the time that was consumed by writing a substantial textbook of my own but also in running tutorials, marking, and consultations with students. The latter were necessary due to the tiny tutoring budget (one hour per student, to cover contact time, marking and consultations) that I had for hiring postgraduates at tutors.

My experiment with trying to rewrite intermediate microeconomics to include the kind of behavioral perspective that I had developed was a proof-of-concept exercise that had the potential to make it a lot easier for others to move away from teaching merely orthodox constrained optimization microeconomics. In other words, the textbook that I produced (Earl, 1995a) had a role that went far beyond keeping the Lincoln students from being restive: I saw it as a means for teaching other microeconomics teachers about a behavioral approach that was infused with evolutionary and institutional aspects, with copious referencing to enable them to go back to the prime sources on which I based my teaching. Thereby, they might also shift their research ideas in those directions. But it was not the sort of textbook that would have interested a typical "big textbook publisher," so I continued my association with Edward Elgar Publishing. I suspect that most readers of the present book will previously have been completely unaware of *Microeconomics for Business and Marketing*, especially if they are based in North America. It had some fans and adoptions on the other side of the Atlantic but not enough to take it beyond the original edition (which is still in print). Its fate is a sign of just how hard it is to subvert core ways of doing economics even if the potential deal-breaker of the lack of a suitable textbook is removed.

If I had been willing to "bite my tongue" and just teach orthodox microeconomics from a standard text, then I might have done some original research in my first four years at Lincoln. This could have entailed developing ideas from *Lifestyle Economics* into empirical research for which I might have been able to win a research grant from the New Zealand Government's Marsden

Fund. I could even have devised such a research program at Lincoln after finishing the textbook if I had been absolutely determined to do so amid administrative demands at Lincoln and invitations to provide chapters for edited volumes or to serve in editorial roles. Doing this would have required me to decline those invitations and have multiple years in which I published nothing, and there was always the risk of not being successful in winning research funds due to my lack of knowledge of how to play the fund-chasing game. So, once again, I did not develop a tightly defined research program and continued on the track of producing outputs for which I had upfront requests. It was only once I had a desk free of contracted work, after completing the Simon Legacy anthology, that I began to focus on doing something original again and concentrated on consumer behavior. But even this was not the product of strategic thinking on my part; indeed, the ideas for the two papers with Jason Potts simply emerged by chance in conversations we were having.

The main areas in which I had expanded my knowledge were marketing theory, consumer behavior research produced by marketing scholars, and economic psychology. These areas helped to inform my view of behavioral economics but – except for taking note of papers on economics and psychology by Lewin (1996) and Rabin (1998) – I largely lost track of what was produced during the 1990s that might be labeled as behavioral economics. When I arrived at Lincoln, I had hoped to keep up with what was going on by regularly browsing the *Journal of Economic Behavior and Organization*, and Lincoln's library started subscribing to it at my request. However, we soon discovered that the journal was much more expensive than its initial expensive per volume price had seemed, because Elsevier started offering multiple volumes per year. Given this, and the difficulty I was having in getting time to browse new journal issues, I agreed to the termination of the subscription and hoped that I would somehow make time to read it at the library of the University of Canterbury. Another issue was that I had stopped browsing in the main generalist journals: even if I had the time to look at them, I would not have expected to find them, in the 1990s, publishing papers that violated core orthodox axioms.

My editorial roles certainly helped me maintain and expand my network of international contacts, but here, too, this was not in relation to those in North America who were following Thaler's lead in relation to how to take a behavioral approach to economics. The only US-based behavioral scholars with whom I corresponded were Mie-Sophie Augior and Esther-Mirjam Sent, who were then research students whose work, like mine, focused on Simon-style behavioral economics with an eye to its intersections with Austrian, evolutionary and institutional approaches. The letters that I wrote to invite

Thaler and Rabin to join the editorial board of the *Journal of Economic Psychology* were the only attempts that I made to initiate contact with the post-Simon generation of behavioral contributors except for getting Daneil Kahneman and Eldar Shafir to contribute an entry to the *Elgar Companion to Consumer Research and Economics Psychology*. Similarly, I did not attempt to make myself better known in North America and meet behavioral scholars by attending conferences there. Just as in my time at UTAS, I confined my conference travel to events in Australia and the UK.

The way that I operated increasingly became all wrong for putting myself in a position where I could move to a chair with better research prospects in an institution that could attract better students, on average, than Lincoln was able to attract. Such mobility required a track record of recent articles in well-ranked journals, success in competing for research grants and, possibly, in attracting consultancy work.

Given all this, the way to a better academic future without compromising my real income turned out to be to return to the top of the Australian senior lecturer scale, which was where I had been at the time that I left UTAS to move to Lincoln. New Zealand's academic pay had stagnated during the time I was at Lincoln, whereas there had been substantial real income gains for Australian academics. Moreover, although I had returned to Lincoln from my study leave at the University of Queensland hoping that I could find a better way to make progress, it had been hard to maintain that resolve after returning to a much more poorly resourced institution where there were pressures to fit student grade distributions to prescribed templates rather than use criteria-based grading of the kind that the University of Queensland employed. So, I was excited when, in mid-2000. John Foster told me that the University of Queensland's School of Economics would shortly be advertising four positions at the lecturer/senior lecturer level and that he hoped I would consider applying for one of them.

# 7 University of Queensland, Australia, 2001–2020

## 7.1    INTRODUCTION

My move to a senior lectureship at the University of Queensland (henceforth normally referred to simply as "UQ") in mid-2001 might seem to imply that I had an intransitive system of preferences, for in late 1987 I had declined a job there at that level. But UQ had changed a lot in the interim. For a start, the School of Economics (henceforth normally referred to as the "SOE") was now located in an air-conditioned building, so working there in the hot, humid subtropical summer months no longer seemed to be an unpleasant prospect. There had also been a major advance in UQ's size and standing, just as there had been for Brisbane. Instead of joining a rather grand provincial university in a city that many viewed in the mid-1980s merely as an overgrown country town, I joined a massive institution that was well on the way to being ranked in the middle of the top 100 universities globally, located in a city whose facilities have made it an attractive venue for globally significant events: it hosted the 2014 G20 World Leaders Summit, and is scheduled to host the 2032 Summer Olympic Games. The SOE had grown considerably, too, and it was very open to alternative perspectives under the headship of evolutionary economist John Foster.

In my early years at UQ, it was mainly my business economics expertise that was in demand for teaching, at both undergraduate and MBA levels. However, toward the end of his decade as the SOE's head, John Foster invited me to get the paperwork done for a new subject in Behavioral and Evolutionary Economics. Except for 2008, the first year in which it was offered, I taught it under his more mainstream successors (2009–2010, 2014–2019) during which enrolments grew steadily, eventually necessitating three tutors being assigned each year to work with me in running tutorials and/or marking. This was such a contrast to the resistance and poor resourcing I had faced in trying to make behavioral economics an enduring part of the curriculum at Lincoln.

It was clear that John Foster and the Dean of the Faculty of Business Economics and Law, Ian Zimmer, were keen to deter me from looking for positions elsewhere, as I was given a new contract, at the associate professor level, from the beginning of 2004. The arrival of this new contract in my pigeonhole in the SOE's mailroom had not been foreshadowed and it appeared to be their way of dealing with the fact that, a few months earlier, UQ's promotions committee had rather unsurprisingly decided not to grant me promotion based on my first two years' performance at UQ. By that stage, all that I could point to as evidence that I was making a serious effort to focus on making high-quality original contributions were two rather hastily prepared and unsuccessful applications with Jason Potts for Australian Research Council (ARC) Discovery Grants.

This was after I had mistakenly spent my first six months at UQ putting together *Information, Opportunism and Economic Coordination* (Earl, 2002), a book consisting of somewhat reworked papers from my Lincoln decade, which I mistakenly hoped would bring this work to a wider audience. I would have been wiser to spend those months catching up with the literature of behavioral economics. The ARC application experience had then shown me how important it was to have a strong recent track record of journal articles and I felt that I had been a liability for Jason due being written off by one of the referees for my failure to live up to my earlier signs of potential. I would have to wait until I had got my research standing on track by other means before I applied again for a large ARC grant.

In the meantime, it was heartening to know that John Foster and Ian Zimmer were confident that I would deliver research outputs of high quality now that I was free of the impediments that I had experienced at Lincoln. However, their confidence might seem questionable given that the main project that I was working on at the time that the new contract was sent to me was rather like the one that had consumed much of my time a decade earlier, namely, a pluralistic business economics textbook (published as Earl and Wakeley, 2005); there was only one completely fresh potential journal article in the pipeline and it was not until I was on study leave in the first half of 2006 that I drafted any others. This was despite the work on the new textbook leaving me enough time to "come up with" three written-to-order book chapters (Earl, 2003, 2004, Earl and Potts 2004b).


## 7.2    APPLYING THE CONNECTIONIST PERSPECTIVE

Contrary to how things initially might seem, my ways of operating in my early years at UQ went beyond what had happened a decade earlier at Lincoln. The two unsuccessful ARC grant applications and three of the the four publications to which I have just referred had a shared new thread that could have blossomed into a major research program if funding had been forthcoming. What I hoped to do was explore the practical significance of Jason Potts's PhD-based book (Potts, 2000) by viewing human action with a focus on the building of complex connective structures and their adaptation as circumstances changed. The two ARC applications were for projects that would have mapped the evolving connective structure of Australia's media and entertainment industry with a view to understanding the significance of its changing architecture for policymakers and consumers. The Earl and Potts (2004b) book chapter was similarly focused on the importance of the architecture of connections, for it was written for a book of essays in memory of Herbert Simon and we decided to pay tribute to Simon by bringing out the impact that his pioneering work (Simon, 1962, 1969) on the evolutionary significance of system architecture had for our economic thinking. When I was asked to contribute a chapter to an edited volume on entrepreneurship in the annual refereed book series *Advances in Austrian Economics*, the paper that I wrote characterized the essence of entrepreneurship in terms of making new connections – as when a new technology is arrived at by integrating elements from existing technologies, or a product range is expanded by bringing together new combinations of parts, many of which are from other products that are already offered.

The Earl and Wakeley (2005) textbook *Business Economics: A Contemporary Approach* extended these connectionist lines of thought, with a view to taking Jason's perspective into the economics classroom. Tim Wakeley, a business economics lecturer at the University of Bath, had brought together evolutionary thinking and behavioral ideas on pricing in a book based on his PhD (Wakeley, 1997). Around the time that his book came out, he started corresponding with me after making use of my earlier (Earl, 1995a) textbook. It became clear from these exchanges, and from meeting face-to-face when I visited the UK, that we were "on a similar wavelength" and I subsequently asked him to write a review article on Potts (2000) for the *Journal of Economic Psychology* (Wakeley, 2002). Shortly after this was published, McGraw-Hill invited him to pitch a proposal for a business economics textbook that would appeal to lecturers who wanted to go beyond mainstream material. Tim asked if I would like to work with him on such a project and I replied positively, for I could not resist the idea of seeing how far I could take the connectionist perspective in this context. Our proposal for a pluralistic text that contrasted mainstream and evolutionary thinking led McGraw-Hill to offer us a contract.

We structured the book around the issues that needed to be addressed to get a firm started and grow it into a large, diversified, global business, beginning with the idea of the entrepreneur being a constructor of connections. We then extended the connections perspective into the role of goodwill relationships between firms and customers, supply chains and vertical integration decisions, and into the drivers of Minsky-style episodes of financial instability in the firm's external environment. There was extensive coverage of problems of knowledge and their ties to rule-based decision-making and corporate capabilities. We also supplied the usual modern teaching aids such as PowerPoint lecture slides and extensive case study material for tutorials, and (rather to our surprise) the publisher commissioned multiple-choice questions from a third party.

But, like the radical textbook that Robinson and Eatwell (1973) wrote for McGraw-Hill three decades earlier, our book was a commercial flop (for the story of the Robinson and Eatwell book, see King and Millmow, 2003). The availability of a textbook may be a necessary condition for taking new approaches into the curriculum, but it is not sufficient. Lecturers may be unwilling to change what they are used to doing, even if they are skeptical of its value, for even a comprehensive package of instructors' materials still leaves them with the costs of "getting their heads around" new material and training their tutors. Tim and I also suspected that McGraw-Hill may have been misled by market research data from which they had inferred there was a large potential market for a "heterodox" business economics text; we wondered whether they understood how factionalized the world of non-mainstream economists is or that those with political inclinations toward the radical left might not warm to a book that concentrated on how large, successful capitalist enterprises might be built.

Instead of writing the book, Tim and I should have simply started work earlier on two of the papers whose first drafts I wrote during my 2006 study leave, while Tim prepared to move to Brisbane to a senior lectureship at Griffith University. Both of these papers were not published until 2010 due to multiple sources of delay. Tim had a more challenging teaching load than me, spread between three campuses on the Gold Coast and in Brisbane, and from the beginning of 2007 my research was disrupted for about eighteen months by my need to get to grips with the role of coordinator of the SOE's PhD program. The delays were compounded by slow refereeing processes. One of these papers (Earl and Wakeley, 2010a, which was published online on May 12, 2009) could particularly have done without the delay: the point of writing it was to show the practical significance of Jason's book (Potts, 2000), which was almost a decade old by the time our paper appeared. In this paper, we set out, armed with a couple of dozen examples, to show how thinking in terms of choices about the construction or modification of preferred sets of connections produced very different perspectives from those derived from the conventional field-based method of analysis, and we did so in the contexts of both consumer behavior and industrial change. We considered connective structures in terms of what was chosen (for example, to fit in with prior lifestyle choices) and inter-agent connections (for example, how choices are affected by the social networks consumers create or goodwill relationships with past suppliers), and we explored the significance of system-based choices for complementarity and barriers to substitution. The other much-delayed paper (Earl and Wakeley, 2010b) carefully explored the implications of widespread use of similar non-compensatory decision rules (for example, "must have at least a four-star energy rating") for the uptake trajectories of new products, the impact of rising aspiration levels on sales of established products, and what all this implied for product development strategies. It was a paper in a high-tier journal that I should have been able to write in the mid 1980s if I had put my mind to it.

The experience of working with Jason and Tim illustrates both the importance of being able to maintain regular interactions for the processes that generate knowledge and how the growth of knowledge depends on social connections in a path-dependent way. When Tim moved to Brisbane, we had hoped that we would keep working together in the long term, but after five years Tim decided to return to the UK and took a break from academia; he eventually returned to the University of Bath but by that point I was involved in other collaborative work (see Sections 7.4 and 7.6). This new work was not with Jason, for he had moved to RMIT University in Melbourne and hence we no longer had frequent spontaneous in-conversation opportunities for making new conceptual connections. Much of the rest of this chapter would probably have been very different if Tim and Jason had both stayed in Brisbane and we had continued working together. Fortunately, although Jason, Tim and I did not continue working together on developing the connectionist approach, two of my other long-standing contacts, Tony Endres and David Harper, applied it to the theory of capital and capability formation, economic development, and brands: see Endres and Harper (2012, 2020) and Harper and Endres (2010, 2012, 2017).


## 7.3    OLD AND NEW BEHAVIORAL ECONOMICS

The sole journal article that I wrote while working on the textbook with Tim Wakeley was "Economics and psychology in the twenty-first century," which was eventually published in revised form as Earl (2005a). It was yet another written-to-order piece – this time, for a plenary presentation at the September 2003 conference organized by the *Cambridge Journal of Economics* to celebrate the centenary of the Cambridge Economics Tripos. Instead of concentrating mainly on where things seemed to be heading, the paper that I came up with was devoted primarily to my personal, normative view of how economics should embrace psychology. I devoted the third section of this paper to an attempt to characterize psychological economics as a Lakatos (1970)-inspired scientific research program consisting of sets of hard-core axioms and "do" and "don't" heuristics for conducting research. Because I adopted this writing strategy, I remained as bemused about what was going on in behavioral economics as I had been in February 2001 on seeing behavioral economics being hailed in the *New York Times* as a new field of economics, without any reference to Herbert Simon's contributions and Nobel award.

In 2007, I at last started to realize that my work as a behavioral economist, and the work that inspired it, differed from mainstream economics in an important way that the contributions that were gaining traction did not. Coming to this realization was an unexpected consequence of my colleague Bruce Littleboy and I organizing the annual conference of the History of Economic Thought Society of Australia. Rather than offering a regular paper, I used a gap in the program to give a short, unscripted talk about the need to be careful with search terms when using Google in work on the history of economic thought. I illustrated my theme by noting that, if one were studying behavioral economics, the search results that Google displayed differed considerably depending on whether one typed in "behavioral" or "behavioral." I then wondered aloud about whether the lack of impact of my work among the latest generation of behavioral economists was because it was written in UK English rather than US English and was therefore being disadvantaged in Google searches conducted by those who used the US spelling of "behavioral." My argument was part of a bigger concern about the consequences of academics employing a variant of the hubristic "not-invented-here" (NIH) elimination heuristic that I had come across in 1983 when researching for my book *The Corporate* Imagination. I wondered how many US academics were confining themselves to articles in US-based journals, for virtually none of them had cited my *Economic Journal* survey article on economics and psychology (Earl, 1990a): if they presumed that US journals were better and hence were happy to rely on Rabin's (1998) survey in the *Journal of Economic Literature*, they would fail to discover the different sources that I had considered.

In other words, I was trying to make sense of how behavioral economics was evolving as if it were the product of cumulating satisficing processes that were driven by differences in the search rules that scholars were using. The discussion that my talk provoked led a participant from Western Australia (Greg Moore, if I recall correctly) to ask if I had come across Esther-Mirjam Sent's (2004) article in *History of Political Economy* on how psychology was being readmitted to economics in a rather limited way. Although Sent and I had been corresponding a few years before she wrote her (2004) paper, we had then fallen out of touch and I had not previously known of this paper. As soon as the conference was over, I read Sent's article and realized that I was working in the tradition of what she called "old behavioral economics," which was different from the approach of those who practiced what she called "new behavioral economics."

My view of how the economy functions began with the problems of information and knowledge that real-world agents have to deal with, and I considered how people operate when facing these problems. Such ways of operating range from highly effective systems of rules and shortcuts, through to operating systems that can lead decision-makers to end up with outcomes that are much worse than they might readily have obtained if they were using different rules that other people used and/or advocated.

What fascinated me were the differences in functionality of the different systems of rules that people use, how people come to use the systems of rules that make them the individuals they are, and why they differ in their willingness to embrace new rules if their existing ones are no longer serving them well or new kinds of behavior become possible. I saw some rules as being inherited as part of human nature, some as acquired socially, and others as personal creations, with the structural relationships that people assign between the rules they have in their repertoires determining how clashes between rules are resolved and the admissibility they assign to potential additions to their repertoires of rules. These systems of rules also determine the extent to which people seek to employ the knowledge and/or heuristics of others when making decisions, and whose knowledge they call upon. However, I had recently realized (see Earl, Peng and Potts, 2007) that it could also be important to be mindful that the quality of knowledge and decision rules that people pick up from others may get degraded in the process of being transmitted and received, as per the notion of "getting lost in translation" or what happens in a game of "Chinese whispers."

I applied this rule-based view of human action to what people believe and view as problems that are worth trying to solve, to the processes by which people go about gathering information, and to how they choose, given the information they have obtained and the inferences that they draw from this information. It implies a growth of knowledge view of human action, in which the quality of choices is limited by what the decision-maker currently knows but can improve as the knowledge possessed by the decision-maker and anyone from whom he or she seeks decision-making inputs grows via the formation of new connections and/or as the decision-maker acquires better-functioning heuristics for handling complex situations.

Mindful of this, I had come to focus on current best-practice in the context in question as the benchmark by which one should assess the decision-making competence of consumers, much in the way that Leibenstein (1966, 1976) seemed to think about the efficiency of firms. Indeed, in a training session on behavioral economics that I provided in Wellington for the New Zealand Ministry of Economic Development and Ministry of Consumer Affairs in September 2005, and in a chapter for a volume in memory of Leibenstein, I explored parallels between the reasons that Leibenstein identified for the failure of firms to attain best-practice levels of productivity and efficiency, and reasons why consumers may under-achieve. In other words, Leibenstein's "X-inefficiency" concept should be extended to the analysis of consumer welfare (see Earl, 2005b, 2007).

With this way of doing behavioral economics, I had essentially abandoned the orthodox normative view of rational choice: after noting its inapplicability in many situations, I began afresh, employing psychology that began with the problem of coping with a problematic world rather than by assuming that people were trying to optimize in terms of a given objective function. From my Loasby (1976)-inspired vantage point, real-world choice problems first had to be recognized as such by decision-makers, were usually open-ended, and had to be closed by applying rules to avoid decision paralysis.

Via Sent's (2004) paper, I came to realize that "new" behavioral economics was essentially a set of ad hoc modifications to the established view of choice in closed settings. The modifications had been derived by studying behavior experimentally in close-choice settings (such as lottery choice experiments). These experiments had been used to infer that humans have evolved to use a set of heuristics to cope with real-world cognitive challenges – heuristics that a "fully rational" economic agent would not need to use. Real people therefore are predicted to behave in systematically different ways from how rational choice theory says they should behave. In other words, the heuristics that are part of human nature "bias" behavior away from what an "econ" would do, with the "bias" being conceptualized with reference to "fully rational" behavior, given a pre-specified view of the situation being analyzed, rather than using current best-practice behavior as the point of reference.

I thereby realized the "new" behavioral economics is much more conservative than the "old" approach. My kind of behavioral economics readily embraces heuristics that appear to be part of human nature and capable of driving predictable departures of behavior *from best-practice ways of behaving that some people have figured out by going beyond human nature*. I had never really bought into the "full rationality" reference point even as a second-year undergraduate, and my practice-based perspective began early in 1977 during my Part II undergraduate year in Cambridge when I read Leibenstein's (1966) first paper on *X*-efficiency. It was from that best-practice standpoint that I had always viewed references to heuristics and biases. By contrast, those who adhere to the "new' behavioral economics will need to shake off the habit of using the full-rationality reference point if they are to embrace the perspective that has driven the work of "old" behavioral economists such as myself.

With its focus on a repertoire of heuristics that are part of human nature, the "new" approach also does not clash with the orthodox economists' preference for building models based on representative agents, whereas in the "old' approach, as in marketing, one is interested in individuals or, at least, groups of individuals with similar ways of operating. It is thus not surprising that the "new" behavioral economics has been much easier to sell to orthodox economists, especially by those armed, as Thaler and his colleagues have been, with evidence of "anomalies" (in terms of orthodoxy) that could be explained with reference to specific heuristics.


## 7.4    MARKET-ASSISTED CHOICES IN A CONFUSOPOLY

Toward the end of 2008, Lana Friesen and I started discussing ideas for possible grant-funded projects. Lana had joined the UQ SOE in 2007, giving up a Lincoln University senior lectureship for a UQ lectureship and a much-improved teaching and research environment. As mentioned in Section 6.2, Lana inherited Microeconomics for Business and Marketing from me at Lincoln and proceeded to turn it into a mainstream intermediate microeconomics subject. However, by 2007, she had evolved from specializing in environmental economics into a "new" behavioral economist and had developed expertise in experimental economics. We reckoned that we could now make a good research team for a project in applied behavioral economics, with my wider knowledge of behavioral economics and its research methods being complemented by Lana's knowledge of conventional experimental economics methods and her statistical expertise. The key challenge was to find an original project for which we could readily make a case to the Australian Research Council (ARC) and its referees.

My initial suggestion was that we might study resistance of commuters to switching to transport modes that would enhance their physical fitness and reduce their environmental impacts. I had recently coauthored a book chapter with Tim Wakeley (Earl and Wakeley, 2009) that included some theoretical analysis of this issue, and I could readily imagine exploring it empirically via a large-sample survey and a small-sample application of repertory grid and construct laddering methods from personal construct psychology. However, this field was already well-researched, and it did not seem to be well-suited for applying experimental methods. We therefore decided to go with Lana's suggestion, namely, a study of how, and how well, consumers cope with the challenges of trying to choose connection service plans for their cell phones (in Australia, mobile phones) without ending up wasting money and having nasty "bill shock" surprises. The risk of error seemed enormous as there were many providers, most of whom offered a wide range of plans that came with a mass of contractual "fine print." The market for cell phone connection services plans thus appeared to be a "confusopoly."[17]

We then set about the task of writing our research proposal as if we were conducting research for an article to submit to a top journal. It was crucial that we could demonstrate we knew the existing literature, had identified a significant gap to fill, and were familiar with best-practice in terms of the research methods that we intended to employ. The process of researching the project consumed much of the 2008–2009 summer. To me, it seemed rather like getting a PhD project into shape to glide through a confirmation process, whereas the unsuccessful ARC Discovery Grant applications that Jason Potts and I had made in my first few years at UQ were assembled without such rigor. I hoped that this time around, unlike with the first effort with Jason, I would not be written off by referees as "someone who has not lived up to his initial promise."

It was an easy project to justify based on its prospective benefits to the Australian population: the project would pay for itself even if it only resulted in the average Australian resident saving a few cents on their spending on cell phone connection services. Late in 2009, we were informed that our application had been successful and that we had been awarded AUD394,000 over the period 2010–2013. However, it took much longer than this to deploy the funds that we had been awarded.

---

[17] It was the second "confusopoly" project that I was involved with in my time at UQ. The first was the PhD of Joseph Clark (2007) for which I served as principal advisor. Joseph is the grandson of the noted British/Australian economist Colin Clark, whose unusual life story has been told by Millmow (2021) and in whose honor the building that houses the UQ SOE is named. Joseph's dissertation was an experimental study of the difficulties of taking rational choices about which retirement savings fund to use, given the presence of complex fee structures, contractual fine print and costs of switching between rival funds. The challenges presented by this context were such that even the seasoned financial advisors who participated in his study found it difficult to make efficient switching choices.

It is possible that the project has had a positive return based purely on consumers reading the three blog posts that I wrote about cell phone service contracts while we were working on it. By September 2022, these blog posts had only had a total of 2773 views. Yet, if each viewer had on average saved about AUD125.00, they would have matched the ARC's AUD349,000 investment in the project. It is not inconceivable that this could have happened, for such savings could accumulate, in just two years, even if the viewers of the blog posts on average only saved AUD5.00 per month by taking note of what I had written about how to calculate the costs of using one's phone, how different kinds of contracts arrive at their monthly charges in different ways, and on the economics of buying an iPhone outright versus via a monthly cell phone service contract.

These calculations make me feel rather happier about the returns to the project than I felt at the time we realized that the first phase of the project had largely failed after consuming over a third of our research budget. We had hoped to find out how much Australian consumers were spending on their cell phone service contracts beyond what they needed to spend to get the services that they used. To do this, we used our research resources in two ways.

First, we designed a questionnaire that was completed online by a representative sample of over 1,000 cell phone users. This was administered by a market research company, and to reduce the risk of respondent fatigue, we followed the company's advice to limit our questionnaire to what could be answered in about 25 minutes. The questionnaire sought responses about which connection service offers our respondents were using, their rates of use of the various services (calls, SMS, data) and how they had chosen the offers they had taken up. We also asked respondents to answer several call-cost and bill-cost calculation questions, and to supply standard demographic information.

Secondly, we employed a full-time research assistant for two years, with her primary task being the construction of an Excel database covering the cell phone plans that were offered in Australia at the time the online survey was conducted (which numbered over 800, from over 50 providers, even without also taking account of plans that included handsets). This was to be programmed to serve as a calculating engine to find the least-cost way of obtaining each respondent's mix of service usage. In our research proposal we suggested that, once constructed and working reliably, our Excel spreadsheet and calculating engine could be made publicly available to help consumers make more cost-effective choices of cell phone service offers. We indicated that we hoped to keep the spreadsheet and calculating engine up to date as the project progressed and that, on completion of the project, it might then be handed over to a public agency for ongoing updating.

The ARC's referees did not suggest that our hopes of ongoing updating were wildly optimistic, but we soon realized that this was the case: the cell phone service sector was characterized by frequent changes in the menus of offers, and we happened to be running our investigation of the sector at the time at which the adoption of smartphones led to a major shift of service plans toward a focus on data. That shift eventually made choices of cell phone service plans rather more straightforward for many customers, with even the offers that only included a few gigabytes of data commonly allowing unlimited national calls and SMS usage. In a sense, then, our study was a contribution to economic history.

However, the failure of our attempt to use the survey and calculating engine to find out how much money Australian consumers were wasting on their cell phone connection service contracts had nothing to do with whether we could keep updating the information we had about the set of available service offers. We were only trying to answer that question in respect of a point in time (late 2010) and we had archived all the relevant pages from the 50+ providers' websites while the online survey was running. Rather, our attempt to answer this question arose from the problem of bounded rationality that provided the study's rationale. It impinged on both the online survey and the Excel programming.

The programming involved different challenges for "pre-paid" and "post-paid" types of service offers. The former often caused complications by having credit expiry periods that were not based on calendar months, or by having credit carry-forward between months due to credit top-ups needing to be purchased part-way through a month, whereas the latter entailed monthly bills but multi-tier pricing. When our first research assistant resigned (without notice, on the day she was scheduled to move to a part-time contract after two years on a full-time contract), the Excel programming remained incomplete. However, enough of it had been completed and tested for Lana to begin to use it to test the quality of the usage data that our online respondents had supplied. She discovered that, in many cases, the responses given for usage rates and typical monthly outlays for the offers that our subjects claimed to have taken up were significantly at odds with the amounts the Excel calculating engine said they should have been having to spend per month. The implication was that, if our survey respondents had correctly recalled the plans they were using, many of them had a poor idea of their usage patterns and/or monthly outlays. Our big mistake had been that when we tested our questionnaire with a small sample/focus group before submitting it to the market research company, we had focused on whether the wording of our questions made sense to the focus group subjects and whether they could complete the questionnaire within 25 minutes; we did not check whether their usage data and claimed monthly outlays were consistent with the outlays that the plans they were using implied, given their usage data.

Clearly, we could have continued this part of the project after removing the roughly two-thirds of subjects whose data seemed to be blighted by defective recall, but this could have left us with a less representative sample. Moreover, there remained the problem of getting the programming completed and we were unsure about how much more of the budget this might consume. Computing the per-capita needless overspending of Australians on cell phone service contracts seemed less important to study than which types of plans were especially problematic for consumers to assess, how the ways that consumers took these kinds of decisions affected the quality of the outcomes, and the relative effectiveness of feasible policies aimed at ensuring consumers reduce the extent to which they waste money on needlessly expensive cell phone service plans.

These were issues that we had proposed to study in the second and third phases of the project, via very different research methods. The second phase employed a pair of conventional multi-treatment economic experiments, both of which used stylized cell phone service contracts in computer laboratory settings. Both experiments went largely as originally envisaged. The only problem was that we had significant delays in getting to run them. The delay started because the program that the original research assistant had written for the lab failed to save the data and there was a significant hiatus before we were able to find a new research assistant on whom we felt we could rely.

The first experiment, reported in Friesen and Earl (2015), explored the impact that service plan formats and usage uncertainty had on the quality of plan choices. The choice environment was artificial, with probabilistic usage variability, easy switching between plans, and only seven plans between which to choose. But it showed the significant adverse impact that two-tier pricing schemes had on the costs that our subjects incurred, especially for those who had to contend periodically with usage spikes, even if they were free to experiment and learn by switching between service offers as the experimental "months" passed. The second experiment, written up in Friesen and Earl (2020), tested the impact of a variety of policies – something that it is difficult for regulatory authorities to do via randomized or geographically segmented trials where products are being purchased online.

We designed the cell phone service plans in these experiments with a view to seeing whether initial choices could be explained in terms of the use of plausible simple rules, such as "try first the plan with the lowest cost for a two-minute call." Otherwise, however, we deferred until the third phase the task of studying how research subjects went about choosing among rival plans.

In the grant application, we had envisaged that the project's third phase would employ the MOUSELAB software developed for research by Payne, Bettman and Johnson (1993) whereby subjects are presented with a multi-layered search environment that provides opportunities for them to click for different kinds of information. MOUSELAB automatically records the clicks that they make as they search within this environment. However, when the project was underway, I devised a much more naturalistic way of gathering information: we would set our research subjects the task of finding, among real plans, the cheapest pre-paid phone plan to service a particular usage remit, with our subjects each being given an hour to undertake the task and being required to think aloud as they did so. As in a conventional economics experiment, subjects would be rewarded according to how well they performed.

The third phase was thus an application of the verbal protocol analysis method set out in Ericsson and Simon (1993), but with some original twists. First, instead of working with short and relatively simple tasks, we would use a complicated, hour-long task that was very likely to prove cognitively exhausting.[18] Our subjects did indeed become cognitively exhausted, and it was at times difficult to keep prodding them to "keep talking" without seeming to harass them. Fortunately, I had realized that, if we were prepared to invest time in dealing with non-automated data collection, we could supplement verbal data with a screen-capture movie that recorded everything each subject did on the computer screen: Apple's Quicktime app made this very easy to do. These movies made it much easier to understand how decisions were arrived at and to see how mistakes were made (for example, when scrolling too fast to notice information that was being sought, or failing, while slowly studying a screen, to

---

[18] While working on this phase of the project, I served as an associate advisor on a law and economics PhD by Peter Macmillan (2015) that also used verbal protocol analysis in the context of extended, complex decision-making. It was originally hosted by UQ's Law School but was ultimately submitted to Bond University as the principal advisor moved to a law chair at Bond while Peter's research was in progress. Peter's dissertation was a study of differences in the thinking styles of experienced and recently qualified competition lawyers. I had no doubts that it was going to be the impressive piece of work that it turned out to be, as Peter had performed very well as one of my students at UTAS and had gone on to have a very successful career as a Hong Kong-based competition lawyer. His success as a lawyer had enabled him to retire very early and his PhD was his way of beginning to put something back into the legal profession to help with the training of competition lawyers. There were indeed significant differences between seasoned and rookie competition lawyers in how they thought aloud as they each spent 45 minutes perusing summaries of several in-process cases that were before the Australian Competition and Consumer Commission and considered which of them would be likely to be taken to court.

acknowledge cues that should have been useful). But with 41 subjects, transcribing nearly 41 hours of "thinking aloud" soundtracks and forensically analyzing and categorizing what happened on the screen in our Quicktime movies took a *very* long time.

This phase of our project implicitly offered an empirical study of the "extended mind" concept that Austrian economist (such as Dekker and Remic, 2024) have lately been using to challenge the emphasis in "new" behavioral economics on the shortcomings of real-world decision-makers. The subjects in the third-phase experiment were divided into offline and online groups. The offline subjects searched within clones of provider websites that we had created from the webpages that we had archived at the end of 2010, whereas the online subjects were allowed to operate like real consumers. Subjects in the offline group were provided with a home page that contained an alphabetical list of links to each archived provider website, whereas the online subjects were simply given a Google search page as their starting point. The offline setting was clearly unusual, despite entailing real service contract offers, but the point of using it was to see how well subjects were able to choose, and how they went about the task, if forced to operate in a totally self-reliant manner (aside from us having provided the homepage list of links and letting subjects use the Apple laptop's calculator). This enabled us to get a picture of the difference that online market institutions – i.e., Google, discussion boards and product comparison websites – made to the quality of choices and how decisions were reached. The difference between what I decided to call "self-reliant choices" and "market-assisted choices" was the focus of the first paper from this part of the study (Earl, Friesen and Shadforth, 2017).

A second paper (Earl, Friesen and Shadforth, 2019) used the data from the Quicktime movies of the online subjects to explore what constituted "procedural rationality," i.e., "appropriate deliberation" (Simon, 1976) in this setting. This was done by compiling a list of 51 types of behavior (divided into five groups) that we had observed some subjects to engage in and which we hypothesized were procedurally rational to use. We noted the incidence of each of these kinds of behavior among our sample, and the cost of the plan that each subject selected, and we then explored the relationship between them via non-parametric statistics. This was thus a statistical, practice-based analysis of procedural rationality. It was much more likely to yield useful lessons about how to cope in this kind of environment than we would have obtained by simply trying to generalize from the behavior of those who selected the cheapest or second-cheapest plan for serving the specific remit that we had presented to our subjects. Even those who had performed very well in the experiment had achieved their rewards partly by luck, after making mistakes that could have produced very different results if the remit or set of available plans had been somewhat different.


## 7.5    HAYEK'S THEORY OF THE MIND

While Lana and I were beginning the collaboration just described, I was taking my solo research into territory that I should have ventured into nearly thirty years earlier, namely, finding out what I could learn from Hayek's (1952) book *The Sensory Order*. I had purchased a copy of the paperback in March 2008, hoping that I would soon get the demands of my PhD administration role under control and get time to find out what Hayek had to say. Coincidentally, around the time I got to that point, William Butos invited me to write a chapter for the 2010 edition of the annual book series *Advances in Austrian Economics*, which was going to be devoted to papers on *The Sensory Order*. I soon realized that, if I had read Hayek's book in 1979, I would have had a different view of why he had been a participant at the 1968 Alpbach Symposium that had yielded the volume *Beyond Reductionism* (Koestler and Smythies, 1969) that did not include a paper by him. Hayek presents in *The Sensory Order* his theory of how the mind works. He had originally worked out its core ideas in the early 1920s and it complements his subjectivist view of economic action and his extended rationality perspective in which individuals help each other to cope with the world by sharing their knowledge (see further, Dekker and Remic, 2024).

Hayek's theory does indeed go "beyond reductionism," not merely via its extended rationality aspect but also because it sees cognitive processes as working by finding *patterns* in incoming stimuli that match events that we have previously encountered, and which have been stored by our brains as memories in terms of networks of neural connections. As Hayek emphasizes, it is not by registering in our minds the individual tesserae in a Roman mosaic that we figure out what kind of mosaic it is; rather, it is the overall configuration of the tesserae – the structure of the spatial relationship between the tesserae – that is of interest to us. If a set of tesserae has been laid out in a way that matches the configuration we have memorized as "a swan," then we know we are looking at a mosaic "of a swan."

I found Hayek's theory very helpful in understanding how people deal with unfamiliar products and situations (Earl, 2010a, 2013). On these occasions, we may struggle to find any patterns in incoming stimuli that match something we have memorized. To avoid cognitive paralysis, we must ignore, dismiss or remove the incomprehensible stimuli, or we must be able to arrive at an interpretation that we view as a satisfactory basis for going forward. We may be able to do the latter by finding sub-patterns within the flow of stimuli that each match a different item in our memory. If we can do this, we can then classify the situation as a hybrid construct and store it as a new set of neural connections. These connections will be activated next time we think about that situation or next time we are in a situation where we find that the incoming stimuli have the same pattern.

However, in some situations we may end up making dysfunctional or comical categorizations because the stimuli are incomplete or somewhat scrambled. Thus, for example, if I talk about Phyllis Deane to someone who is unfamiliar with the female first name Phyllis, I run the risk of being viewed as talking about someone who operates like a Philistine. I might even be viewed as if I am referring, with rather poor diction, to someone who is known via the unfortunate nickname of "Syphilis Deane." This is, of course, the kind of process that results in "mondegreen" misinterpretations of song lyrics, as when a person hears Jimi Hendrix as singing "Excuse me while I kiss this guy" in his song "Purple Haze" and ABBA as opening their song "Chiquitita" by singing "Take your teeth out, tickle my toes."

Sometimes, we may get completely the wrong match initially, but then find the right one seconds later. I vividly recall experiencing this in Sydney in 1987 when I met up with one of my Cambridge friends (coincidentally, another member of the supervision group that included the friend who sent me the "Philistine" card). Before she introduced me to her fiancé, she took me aside and said, "Please don't tell him about my 2:2." Initially, I was bewildered, as what I thought she had said was, "Please don't tell him about my tutu" and I had no recollection of having ever talked about ballet attire with her. But then I realized what she meant: I now remembered that, to my surprise and her disappointment, she had only achieved a lower second in Part II of the Cambridge Economics Tripos, and I could see that, as a merchant banker with an economist/banker as her fiancé, she might be embarrassed if this came up in conversation. I had not thought about her degree class in the intervening years: she always came to mind as someone whose career was going really well, not as someone whose degree class had been a bit disappointing. But ballet had been on the agenda when my then-partner Sharon and I met up with her in Sydney a year earlier, for on that trip Sharon and I saw the ballet version of "The Sentimental Bloke" at Sydney Opera House.

When I read *The Sensory* Order, it brought to mind my disconcerting "tutu" cognitive experience, and the memories that I associate with it, for they aligned well with another key aspect of Hayek's analysis. To appreciate this aspect, it is helpful to recognize that the brain's problem when forming cognitions is rather like that of a locksmith who has a vast collection of keys and is trying to open a lock: the brain has a huge array of memories to try as templates to find a pattern in each set of stimuli. Hayek's theory of how the mind does this does not presume it tries all memories at once (hence the "tutu" experience). Instead, his analysis complements Herbert Simon's view of how cognition works.

Simon emphasizes the scope for hierarchical filtering to narrow down the set of conjectures about what we are looking at: i.e., we begin by defining a context, which puts boundaries on the set of things we may normally expect to find; we keep adding more detail and reducing the set of contending possibilities until we arrive at a position where one option seems a good enough solution. In Hayek's analysis, our brains examine how good a fit we get with the first memory that comes to mind, moving on to a second if the first seems problematic, and so on. He argues that the probability of a memory being used to try to find a match with incoming stimuli is a joint function of how frequently and how recently we have called that memory to mind in that context.

This implies that our minds are dynamic entities: the set of neural connections that is first used as a template to find a pattern in a new set of stimuli will have an increased probability of being used in that kind of context in future, relative to other stored sets of connections that might have been fired up. When memories that have been most recently/frequently activated do not lead to the discovery of a matching pattern, we "wrack our brains," successively trying other memories that come to mind until we get a satisfactory fit. In the latter case, things we have not thought about for ages and/or rarely think about at all will become more likely to come to mind in future, as they have now been "recently activated." What we expect to see in a particular context can thus change as we accumulate a changing set of memories of what we have encountered. Over time, then, things that we once viewed as normal and acceptable can come to seem abnormal and unacceptable, and vice versa. (This applies particularly obviously with changing social norms, but it is also relevant in relation to transitions to greener lifestyles: see Earl, 2017a.) However, if we do not operate in environments that involve diversity in the sets of stimuli that we need to make sense of, we are unlikely to develop new sets of neural connections, with the result that our thinking appears to be close-minded and driven by a limited range of stereotypes.

Hayek's *Sensory* Order is a remarkably prescient book that now comes to my mind any time that I am thinking about problems of coordination and change. His memory-based view of how cognition works prefigures Kahneman's (2011) view of the role of "associative memory" and tacit pattern recognition in what is commonly referred to as "expert intuition." Hayek's probabilistic analysis of the process of using memories as means for categorizing things also complements Tversky's (1972) "elimination by aspects" view of choice and is a precursor to the modern neuroscience notion of "brain plasticity," whereby each act of thinking changes how we think (see further Doidge, 2007). As such, it points toward a path-dependent view of consumer preferences insofar as consumers reflect on their consumption experiences and observe each other's behavior.

## 7.6 REVISITING SHACKLE'S THEORY OF CHOICE UNDER UNCERTAINTY

Soon after Kahneman's (2011) *Thinking, Fast and Slow* appeared, Stuart Macdonald,[19] the new editor of the interdisciplinary journal *Prometheus*, invited me to write a review article giving an economist's view of the book. The similarities of some of Kahneman's analysis with Hayek's *Sensory Order* were not the only areas of the book that grabbed my attention in relation to earlier contributions. It was evident that Kahneman had a tendency to use endnotes as a means of both showing he was aware of, and burying, major contributions that some might view as challenging his work. He did this with Simon's work, which he only highlighted in respect to what Simon had done on the behavior of expert chess players, and with Gigerenzer's positive view of the role that heuristics can play as "fast and frugal" means for reaching smart decisions. But what he said about how he and Tversky (1979) had arrived at their prospect theory view of risk-taking called to mind the "potential surprise" theory of choice under uncertainty that Shackle had devised three decades ahead of prospect theory.

Kahneman emphasized that, when he and Tversky started to consider the implications of their experiments for the theory of risk-taking, they realized that it was much easier for people to focus on prospective gains and losses relative to a reference point rather than in relation to the impacts that rival outcomes might have on their total wealth. Hence, Kahneman and Tversky built their

---

[19] Stuart Macdonald has taken this role very seriously: for example, on Christmas Day 2020, he wrote to let me know that referees of a submission to *Prometheus* by Chidambaran Iyer had found that Iyer had plagiarized material from one of my papers (Earl, 2003). Further investigation had led to the discovery that Iyer had previously got away with doing the same thing with another journal. Stuart's message included a copy of the letter he had sent to Iyer's head of department about this misconduct.

theory around a reference-dependent view of utility. Shackle's (1949, 1969) theory had already offered a view of choice centered on gains and losses relative to a reference point – which he called the "neutral outcome" – but in his case, he was thinking of the reference point as the entrepreneur's view of the safest alternative to undertaking an investment, relative to which prospective gains would provide hope and prospective losses would seem worrying.

Shackle's model predicts that, for each scheme of action that is under consideration, the decision-maker will focus on the most attention-arresting prospective gain and the most attention-arresting loss, via an "ascendancy function" in which the attention-arresting power of an imagined outcome is an increasing function of its distance from the reference point and a decreasing function of how potentially surprising it seems in prospect. Focusing on these pairs of possible outcomes reduces the cognitive demands of weighing up one's options, thereby sidestepping an issue that prospect theory runs into if applied to choices that involve payoff matrices that are more complex than those that Kahneman and Tversky employed in their experiments. In Shackle's analysis, rival schemes are viewed as if they are ranked via the decision-maker's "gambler preference map" on which each focal gain/loss pair reduces to a single point on an indifference map whose axes essentially represent the degree of excitement/hope that the decision-maker associates with focal gains, versus the degree of nervousness/fear associated with focal losses. (I say "essentially" because Shackle's own way of explaining how focal gains and losses come to be weighed up removes the psychology of hope and fear and instead is needlessly convoluted and entails the conversion of "primary" focus gains/losses into "standardized" focus gains/losses – i.e., gains/losses that would be just as attention-arresting if they were viewed as perfectly possible – with gambler preferences being expressed in terms of the latter.)

Rather than merely writing my review article (Earl 2012b) on *Thinking, Fast and Slow*, I also wrote a paper entitled "Kahneman's *Thinking, Fast and Slow* from the standpoint of old behavioral economics" (Earl, 2012c), which I presented at the History of Economic Thought Society of Australia (HETSA) conference held in Melbourne in July 2012. I explored there the relationship between Kahneman's views and the work of Simon and Shackle. However, I never turned the paper into a journal article. Instead, I developed ideas from it into a chapter on Shackle and behavioral economics for a book about Shackle that I had started to write with my UQ colleague Bruce Littleboy (published as Earl and Littleboy, 2014).

The Shackle book was not one that I had planned to write, but I was not surprised to find myself working on it. I was Bruce's supervisor and he needed to get his research on the history of economic thought happening again after a long period focused on textbook writing. I had suggested to him that he might try to build a study leave plan around spending time in Cambridge as a Shackle Fellow at St Edmund's College and exploring the Shackle papers in Cambridge University Library. He followed my suggestion and had a very productive study leave in Cambridge, so writing a book on Shackle for Palgrave's "Great Thinkers in Economics" series seemed the logical next step. He had been keen to take that step, so long as he could concentrate on Shackle's philosophical perspective and approach to macroeconomics, with me coming in as co-author to write the chapters on Shackle's potential surprise view of choice. I was happy to do this, since there seemed to be time to get the book finished before I had to focus on the data from the third phase of the cell phone service contracts project and write papers based on that data. We also managed to get Michael Jefferson, whom I had not seen since the British Association conference at York in 1981, to write a chapter about the relationship between Shackle's work and the use of scenario planning at Shell. As Shell's former chief economist, Michael was far better placed to do this than Bruce or myself.

The Shackle book project was a very enjoyable task, but as far as my own research was concerned, it would likely have been better if I had merely written the chapter on "Shackle and Behavioral Economics" as an article for a well-ranked journal, for that would probably have attracted the attention of a wider audience and chewed up much less time. The chapter went beyond the HETSA paper by showing that, if excitement/hope and nervousness/fear are viewed, respectively as proxies for prospective utility and disutility, then some versions of Shackle's theory imply an $S$-shaped utility function, while he sometimes drew the gambler preference map in a way that implies loss aversion, as well as with a limit to acceptable levels of risk.

My main regret about the Shackle book was that, yet again, I had not invested time in developing my knowledge of Keynes's (1921) *Treatise on Probability* and the emergence of subjective expected utility theory. In a sense, this meant that I repeated Shackle's own shortcomings by failing adequately to consider (a) how decision-makers make inductive use of evidence in forming conjectures, rather than operating in a purely deductive manner, and (b) the extent to which the subjective probability perspective is immune from Shackle's critique of probabilistic thinking in the context of individual decision-makers who are taking one-off decisions. To some degree, I have attempted to make amends in this area in Earl (2023b).

## 7.7    PRINCIPLES OF BEHAVIORAL ECONOMICS

As the thirtieth anniversary of the publication of my (1983a) book *The Economic Imagination* approached, Edward Elgar began to encourage me to think about writing a new edition of it to take account of how my thinking as a behavioral economist had evolved in the interim. To facilitate this, he secured the return to me of the book's copyright and, for good measure, the copyrights of *The Corporate Imagination* and *Lifestyle Economics* from Pearson Publishing, into whose ownership they had come following a series of acquisitions in the publishing sector.

With the commencement of the cell phone service contracts project, I thought it more realistic to aim to mark instead the thirtieth anniversary of the 1986 publication of *Lifestyle Economics* by preparing a combined update of it and *The Economic Imagination*, under the title of *Consumer Lifestyles and the Economic Imagination*. To get this project started, I worked with a digital copy of *Lifestyle Economics* created via an optical character recognition app, but I soon realized that I really wanted to write the book from scratch rather than by word-processing material from the old books. Given the need to prioritize writing up and publishing findings from the cell phone project, it was clear that I was not going to be able to get the book ready for publication in 2016 even though, by the end of 2013, the Shackle book was out of the way. Having held off from getting as far as a contract with Edward Elgar, I decided to put the book on hold until I was free from other commitments.

The publication of Richard Thaler's *Misbehaving* in 2015 left me with very mixed feelings. I greatly enjoyed Thaler's account of how his ideas had originated and evolved, but I was appalled by the way that his book gave the impression that he had created behavioral economics pretty much from scratch. To be sure, he had done a wonderful job in garnering interest in the "new" behavioral economics to which he had made seminal contributions, but his scholarship was mostly woeful in terms of giving due credit to "old" behavioral economics – whose evolution I was in the process of surveying just before Thaler's book appeared (see Earl, 2016). It was not that Thaler was unaware of Herbert Simon, for he noted that Simon had coined the term "bounded rationality." But Thaler (2015, loc. 527) had then made the extraordinary claim that Simon "had not done much to flesh out how boundedly rational people differ from fully rational ones." He had then portrayed Simon as merely one of those who had tried unsuccessfully to take economics in a somewhat different direction. Specifically, he pointed to Baumol's (1962) contribution to the literature on "new theories of the firm," oblivious to the fact that Baumol's model is, as Loasby (1989, chapter 7) had emphasized, a conventional deterministic model of optimizing behavior, except that it uses imperfections in product and capital markets as the pretext for modeling managers as maximizing the growth of turnover rather than profits.

Some Simon scholars might wonder whether this way of brushing aside Simon's contributions to the analysis of decision-making in organizations – the basis for Simon receiving the 1978 Nobel Memorial Prize in Economic Sciences – was designed to deter his readers from exploring Simon's contributions, rather than merely a reflection of poor scholarship. Whatever it was, it made me want to write a book in which I presented where I had got to as a behavioral economist not merely in relation to consumer behavior but also in relation to firms and other organizations – territory on which the "old" behavioral economists had mainly focused but which the "new" behavioral economists mostly ignored.

Such a book would be much bigger than the one that I had been discussing with Edward Elgar; in effect, it would be my magnum opus, a legacy volume that set out where I had got to as a behavioral economist with a much wider range of influences than were deployed by those like Thaler who were getting so much attention while those that had inspired me were being left unappreciated.

The final impetus for me to write it came in January 2017 when Sanjit Dhami sent me an email to draw my attention to his recently published book *The Foundations of Behavioral Economics* and an online video of his book-launch presentation about it. Dhami's (2016) book is a remarkable contribution that runs to 1764 pages. Yet it is essentially an encyclopedia only of "new" behavioral economics. Someone needed to set the record straight in a constructive manner, so in July 2017 I began writing the book that was published five years later as *Principles of Behavioral Economics: Bringing Together Old, New and Evolutionary Approaches* (Earl, 2022). Less than six months into the project, I put it on hold for several months so that I could write an invited paper (published as Earl, 2018) that critically surveyed Richard Thaler's contributions in the light of him being awarded the 2017 Nobel Memorial Prize in Economic Sciences. This small delay was worthwhile, for my article was given an open access release and, by January 24, 2026, it had been viewed 42,330 times. Progress on the book was rapid until the end of 2018, by which point I had half of it in draft form, but it then dried up completely when I was given a second stint as coordinator of the UQ SOE's PhD program. I was not able to resume work on the book until July 2020. I eventually finished it a year later, the process being facilitated by my retirement into an honorary role at UQ at the end of 2020, after I had escaped a final semester of PhD administration by using up my long service leave balance and spending it writing rather than on recreation. With Oxford University Press having published Dhami's book, and the long road to my book having started in Cambridge, it seemed appropriate to see whether Cambridge University Press would be interested in being its publisher.

After the book had gone to press, I noticed that I had written it oblivious to the potential for an acronym that lay in its subtitle: I could have called the synthesis that I had written the "ONE behavioral" approach. I was able to use the acronym in an invited paper for a special issue of the *Journal of Consumer Behavior* (Earl, 2023a) in which I set out where I had arrived at in methodological terms as a behavioral economist.

## 7.8   PROGRESS REVIEW

At the time that I retired, I was still merely an associate professor, for although my research-related achievements steadily began to look more like what had become the currency for being promoted to a full professorship, I failed to publish frequently enough in journals of A*-rank on the list produced by the Australian Business Deans' Council. The ARC-funded project's output included two such papers, but it had taken far longer to complete than we had planned, which would have been seen as an impediment to getting further grants if I had wanted to apply for them. Also – and this was of much greater concern to me personally than not getting promoted, given the very comfortable standard of living that I enjoyed – I was unable to demonstrate evidence of a steadily (let alone exponentially) growing impact trajectory. My Google Scholar citation rate peaked in 2013 but since then has averaged roughly the same as it was in the period 2005–2010, despite the significant growth in both the quantity and, in terms of modern metrics, the average quality of my publications. This was despite behavioral economics surging in popularity: it appears that very few "new" behavioral economists have been coming across my work and finding it interesting and that younger generations of those who brand themselves as "heterodox" economists have not been latching on to it in the way that their predecessors did.

The impact situation may largely be a consequence of other behavioral or heterodox economists asking research questions that relate to popular areas within narrowly defined visions of the realms of the kinds of economics that they practice, but which are questions that I have not tried to answer or have reflected on in works whose titles have not signaled their relevance to these issues. My lack of impact may also be due to me spending too much time producing publications and too little time trying to market them, and to me continuing to consort mainly with stalwarts of the History of Economic Thought Society of Australia or those who branded themselves as "heterodox" economists (via the 2005, 2006, 2009 and 2013 conferences of the Association for Heterodox Economics) rather than getting involved with, say, the Society for the Advancement of Behavioral Economics. After 2013, I decided completely to give up traveling to conferences, because I did not see the environmental impact of such travel as being justifiable given how small the audiences for my conference papers seemed to be. In hindsight, I should have invested time in putting my work on ResearchGate long before I did so, for having made that investment shortly after retiring, I can see that it generates a far bigger audience than my conference presentations ever did. I could have made time to use this and other networking systems if I declined to write some of the rarely cited works that I wrote for edited books and special issues of journals.

My work at UQ ultimately had no legacy for the teaching of behavioral economics there. Instead, what happened after my final stint running Behavioral and Evolutionary Economics was depressingly similar to what happened at Lincoln a decade earlier following my final stint with Microeconomics for Business and Marketing. In both cases, what I had taught had been consistent with the latest version of the course descriptions that had been formally approved based on paperwork that I had prepared; and in both cases, my successors merely paid lip-service to the formal course descriptions and taught what they were familiar with, regardless of me offering to make available all of my teaching material (including, in the UQ case, as much of the draft of *Principles of Behavioral Economics* as I had completed). Thus, in 2020, to the surprise of some students, Behavioral and Evolutionary Economics suddenly became a conventional "new" behavioral economics subject, taught with assessments focused on weekly exercises and examinations consisting of short-answer questions (latterly, a couple of computerized tests and a "research proposal") rather than essays and authentic report-writing tasks. "Old" behavioral content vanished completely, as did evolutionary material from Marshal and Veblen to Nelson and Winter. After seeing that students were not going to have the kind of behavioral economics unit that I had provided, I acted collegially to help ensure that they would not be surprised by the changes and to give them as much value as possible for their investments in the subject. I proactively filled out the paperwork to rename Behavioral and Evolutionary Economics as, simply, Behavioral Economics. I had been thinking of doing this anyway as, toward the end of my time as the course's coordinator, I discovered that the student records system abbreviated the original title to Evolutionary

Economics on student transcripts, which probably made them seem a bit less valuable to prospective employers than they might have seemed when behavioral economics became widely known as a field of study. But the point of the long title had been to ensure that the subject was taught in a way that went beyond "new" behavioral economics.

# 8 A Wider Vision of Behavioral Economics

## 8.1    INTRODUCTION

In this final chapter, I summarize the vision of behavioral economics that I arrived at via my unusual journey as a behavioral economist. Most of my key ideas were in place as long ago as 1985, when I was writing my post-PhD book *Lifestyle Economics*. However, in the decades that followed, these ideas failed to gain traction with the vast majority of those who came to regard themselves as behavioral economists, and my post-*Lifestyle Economics* contributions fared similarly. It therefore seems appropriate, after summarizing my vision for a more powerful way of doing behavioral economics, for me to conclude this chapter by offering some reflections on why my work failed to have much of an impact.

This chapter does not attempt to summarize the contributions that I made. Rather, it is about my vision of how behavioral economists should try to see their field of research and the catalogue of opportunities available to those who are open to taking a wider view of behavioral economics. These opportunities lie in the following broad areas: the range of research methods that can be used to study economic behavior; extending the motivational underpinnings of behavior; the "ways" in which people identify problems and address them; the kinds of policy approaches that warrant consideration; and the ranges of areas within which these opportunities can be found and contributions to knowledge can be made. However, it is useful first to set out the issue that brings these elements together in a non-reductionist way, namely, the co-evolutionary nature of human agents, economic and social institutions, and the wider economic environment. What follows in Section 8.2 should be kept in mind when reading subsequent sections.

## 8.2    ECONOMIC AGENTS AND THE SOCIO-ECONOMIC SYSTEM

In the popular narrow vision of behavioral economics, the focus is on behavior in situations where stimuli from the external environment are not employed in the way that a fully rational "econ" would employ them: real-world economic agents use repertoires of heuristics to simplify the process of forming expectations and selecting actions. However, although modern behavioral economists have shown considerable interest in social behavior, in areas such as behavioral game theory and "in-group" and "out-group" behavior, they cast economic agents in cognitively complex situations as self-sufficient users of heuristics. The analytical focus is on the use of heuristics that people in general are prone to use, as if these heuristics are part of human nature, and it seems to be assumed that the only way that others impact on the choices that individuals make is by shaping the flow of stimuli with which they are presented (such as when corporations and governments seek to shape the architecture of choice to nudge people to behave in a particular way). Otherwise, rather like Robinson Crusoe before he encounters Friday on his desert island, people are presented as if they choose alone and as if their environment is something that they simply take as given.

This simple vision has yielded powerful results, but richer research opportunities and potential for new findings are to be found via the more complex perspective at which I gradually arrived. It was not until this book was close to completion that I discovered that the ways that I had come to view human action implicitly embodied what cognitive scientists call "enactivism" (see Frolov, 2024; Viale, 2024). This entails not merely accepting John Donne's famous 1624 poetic line that "No man is an island, entire of itself." It also entails a co-evolutionary view of humans and their socio-economic environment: we affect each other's ways of thinking and behavior, while the ways in which we think and behave are affected by the contexts in which we operate, with our own behavior potentially also affecting the nature of the choice environment in which we and others operate.

The following are among the implicitly enactivist ingredients that I picked up from my environment over the decades and which became part of my way of thinking, or that I have been involved in contributing:

- Market coordination processes are enhanced to the extent that disaffected customers "voice" their concerns to suppliers rather than simply making an "exit" without explaining why, though even better outcomes may eventuate if the provision of feedback is combined with a display of "loyalty" that helps suppliers stay in business and effect changes (Hirschman, 1970). Those who meekly "put up with" mediocre products and accept "rip-off" prices will help to ensure that such deals continued to be offered.
- In dealing with uncertainty about what levels of attainment they should aim to achieve, people commonly use the behavior and/or achievements of others as reference points (Loasby, 1976). Hence, their attainments will depend on whether they use local or more global (for example, 'world-class') reference points. External reference standards also have vital roles to play when figuring out how bold to be when taking financial risks (Minsky,

1975a, 1982a) or engaging in creative/innovative behavior (Earl and Potts, 2013, 2016), and tidal shifts in boldness can result from competitive responses to what others are doing. This can result in the ratcheting up of boldness to the point of over-reach.

- Innovative ways in which consumers use or combine products sometimes run ahead of, and inform, the behavior of established entrepreneurs. (A classic example of demand-side innovation is the mountain bike: see Buenstorf, 2003.)

- A significant amount of spending is fashion-related rather than based on personal preferences (Foley, 1893; Fullbrook, 1998; Andreozzi and Bianchi, 2007). People who view themselves as fashion leaders have to keep experimenting with different ways of consuming to maintain their differentiation from those who imitate their behavior (Chai, Earl and Potts, 2007).

- The uptake trajectories of new products resemble how contagious diseases spread (Ironmonger, 1972; Prais, 1973).

- To a significant degree, expectations and behaviour are based on norms that are socially acquired through repeated exposure to patterns of stimuli that get increasingly memorized (without necessarily even being consciously processed) as probable features of particular contexts (Hodgson, 2003). However, changes in the relative frequency of exposure to rival patterns of behavior can affect what a person views as normal, leading to changes in that person's behavior that, in turn, affect the norms of other people (Hayek, 1952; Earl, 2017a).

- Some of the decision rules in a person's repertoire are acquired socially, though they may be incompletely acquired or improved upon by the recipient (Earl, Peng and Potts, 2007).

- People may develop knowledge about effective ways of allocating resources in a particular environment as a result of their preferred strategies being blocked by institutional factors, for such contexts are conducive to more extensive searching for solutions to problems (Loasby, 1967a).

- Most of our wants arise via cultural processes rather than purely from in-built preferences; moreover, although firms may intend their advertising to serve as a tool for manipulating choices, it can also provide "food for thought," i.e., ideas for consumers to consider in areas where they do not have well defined preferences (Hayek, 1961).

- Individuals commonly form their cognitions about the relative efficacy of rival products and/or suppliers as means toward particular ends, and about which ends they should attempt to pursue, not on their own but with the aid of other individuals and institutions that comprise the "market for preferences" (Earl and Potts, 2004a). In such situations, their choices are "market-assisted" rather than "self-reliant" (Earl, Friesen and Shadforth, 2017). However, the possibilities to which they are exposed, and which ones are presented as credible (or "thinkable"), will depend on the social contexts and networks within which their lives are embedded (Granovetter, 1985) and the extent to which "their hands are tied" by prior lifestyle choices (Earl, 1986b, 2017a; Thompson, 1996).

- Decision-makers' attitudes toward a potential course of action are not based purely on how they see the possible consequences of selecting it but also on how they imagine their social referents would view such a choice, and how willing they are to comply with the views of their social referents (Fishbein and Ajzen, 1975).

This way of viewing decision-makers in relation to their economic and social surroundings intersects to some degree with Dekker and Remic's (2024) "extended mind" characterization of Hayek's approach to rationality, and with institutionalist perspectives that Frolov (2024) sees, with behavioral and Austrian thinking, as ingredients of an enactivist approach to economics. It offers ingredients for analyzing whether and when the social side of cognition facilitates much better decisions than we might expect from a heuristics and biases standpoint, or whether it merely drives "echo-chamber" processes that feed conspiracy theories and foster dysfunctional behavior.


## 8.3    RESEARCH METHODS

At its core, behavioral economics involves analysis that is informed by studying how people behave, rather than analysis that is arrived at by making assumptions based on a view of how resource allocation decisions should ideally be made. Much of the knowledge that behavioral economists have hitherto deployed or have sought to generate has used experiments as means of studying behavior. This method is commonly employed in computer laboratories that enable researchers to isolate the drivers of behavior by setting the experiment in a stripped-down environment and running alternative treatments and a control group. However, the experimental method typically creates closed problems that research subjects are prevented from trying (or have no need to try) to address by using some of the means they would employ when trying to solve supposedly similar problems in real-world counterparts of the kinds of context on which the experiments focus. Economics experiments also require research funds for paying performance-based rewards to subjects. Other ways of studying behavior may be less costly and may at least yield ideas that can be fed into the design of experiments even if they point to plural modes of behavior rather than attesting to the truth or lack of truth of a specific hypothesis. Hence, I hope that readers will consider the following research methods:

- *Using research tools from personal construct psychology* – such as repertory grid technique (Kelly, 1955), construct laddering, implication grids and resistance to change grids (Hinkle, [1965] 2010) – to uncover (a) how people view their options as bundles of characteristics, (b) the deeper ends that these characteristics serve or compromise (Gutman, 1982; Reynolds and Gutman, 1984), (c) ideal and tolerable options, and (d) determinants of responsiveness to changes in incentives (Earl, 1986a, 2022, chapter 7).

- *Asking people how they behave in the context of interest, or (if observations are already available) why they behaved as they did.* Questionnaires and focus groups may not be completely reliable, but researchers can reflect on what the incentive might be not to tell the truth or how answers might be affected by how research subjects manage cognitive dissonance, and whether more reliable answers can be achieved by having more open-ended questions and/or asking subjects about how they believe people (rather than themselves) make decisions in the context in question. These kinds of research methods have advanced considerably since the days when Robinson (1939) and Machlup (1946) reacted with hostility toward, respectively, behavioral research conducted by the Oxford Economists' Research Group in the 1930s and Lester's (1946) study of whether employers based their use of labor on marginalist principles.

- *Conducting ethnographic research by embedding oneself among decision-makers in the area of interest.* Even during the Lester–Machlup debate, Machlup was prepared to consider whether embedded researchers might get deeper insights into behavior than a brief interaction with research subjects might reveal (see Lavoie, 1990). Moreover, it should not be forgotten that the use of embedded researchers can pay dividends (a) when research subjects know much more about the research context than the researchers do (as with the study of New York bond traders by Abolofia, 1996, 1998) or (b) by having more general implications, as with the embedded research that led psychologist Robert Cialdini (1984, 2009) to his influential analysis of the process of persuasion.

- *Using published text* – such as product reviews by lay consumers and professionals, case studies of business history, passages from novels, plays and screenplays, and transcripts of parliamentary proceedings and public inquiries (cf. Mosley, 1981), minutes of board meetings, and so on, as sources of information about behavior or lay theories of behavior (see further, Earl, 2011). At the very least, you can be confident that such sources will not have been authored with a view to impressing or helping behavioral economists. Even if you cannot create a statistical sample by such means, you may find anomalies or ideas from which to build testable hypotheses. Introspection may serve a similar role (Earl, 2001a, 2012a).

- *Using computerized simulation models* to explore whether observed behavior is consistent with what is predicted by building and calibrating models based on simple decision rules. This method was pioneered by Cyert and March (1963) in the early days of computers and has been widely used by researchers in the "old/evolutionary" behavioral tradition.

Those who intend to conduct economic experiments should consider building in verbal protocol analysis (Ericsson and Simon, 1993), supplemented with screen capture movies (Earl, Friesen and Shadforth, 2017, 2019) as means for analyzing how subjects arrive at their decisions in naturalistic on-screen decision-making settings.


## 8.4  HUMAN OBJECTIVES AND THE IMPLICATIONS OF CHOICES AND CHANGES IN CIRCUMSTANCES

If we want to know what people are trying to achieve and how they see their options in a particular context, we can readily find out by using repertory grid technique (Kelly, 1955) and construct laddering (Hinkle, [1965] 2010) to undertake "means–end chain" analysis (Gutman, 1982). This makes it possible to peel back from how people view the surface-level characteristics of their options to the psychological connotations of having or not having these characteristics. This does not of itself explain how decision-makers rank their options based on such psychological connotations, but it certainly signals potential for behavioral economists to move beyond the conventional economists' practice of modeling economic agents "as if" they maximize utility.

This opportunity has not been seized with gusto by "new" behavioral economists. Although they emphasize that humans are not "econs," they still model people essentially as utility maximizers – utility-maximizers whose choices are systematically and therefore predictably different from those that an "econ" would make. We have Kahneman and Tversky's (1979) prospect theory to blame for this: knowledge of bias-inducing heuristics is used to infer that probabilities are not incorporated in the way that a skilled statistician would take account of them, while the utility function is reference-dependent and $S$-shaped, with its inflexion point at the reference point and displays loss aversion. It is essentially a modified version of the orthodox expected utility maximization model: the heuristics that it embodies only play the role of generating predictable biases relative to what an "econ" would do; they are not procedures or simple decision rules that play the role of ranking the options at hand. This is rather ironic, for one example of the latter type of heuristic is "elimination by aspects," an earlier contribution by Tversky (1972) himself. (Another example of the latter kind of heuristic, which addresses uncertainty, too, is what I labeled "characteristic filtering" in Earl, 1980a, 1983a, 1986b.)

Prospect theory may indeed be the best tool available for explaining how financial gambles are taken (see Barberis, 2013), and it might deal even more plausibly with bounded rationality if behavioral economists follow my suggestion (in Earl, 2023b) that Shackle's "ascendancy function" view of focus gains and focus losses could be bolted on to it to show how investors might remove the complexities of distributions of (adjusted) probabilities. However, in ultimately reducing choice to a form of utility maximization, it sits rather uneasily alongside "old" behavioral thinking in terms of satisficing with respect to multiple objectives (where conflicts are dodged by giving sequential attention to goals, as in Cyert and March, 1963, or via ranking goals hierarchically, as in Ironmonger, 1972). Unlike Tversky's (1972) analysis, prospect theory does not even serve implicitly as a behavioral reworking of Lancaster's (1966) characteristics-space model of consumer behavior, which is constructed using orthodox tools except for abandoning the Hicksian goods-space view of preferences. Kahneman and Tversky's theory readily accommodates prospective financial gains and losses of rival ventures, for these are all expressed in monetary terms. However, when rival options are seen in terms of multiple dimensions, it seems to require that the decision-maker reduces gains and losses on these dimensions to a single scale of measurement. Clearly, that scale cannot pertain to the utility/disutility of the various types of gains/losses, for this would result in a circular argument: the $S$-shaped value function is supposed to show how utility/disutility is a function of gain/loss.

My wider view of behavioral economics offers a way of escaping from that looming circularity, namely, the "implications-based" approach that I proposed (in Earl, 1986a, 2022, chapter 7), based on work by Hinkle ([1965] 2010) in personal construct psychology. It takes means–end chain analysis further and its practical implementation similarly involves one-on-one sessions with research subjects to elicit the multilayer networks of positive and negative implications that they see as being associated with particular changes in their behavior or arising from changes in their external environment. Scores for the sum of positive implications can then be tallied, and likewise for negative implications. Some changes, even from pole to pole, on a characteristic scale will carry very few implications of either kind, so we are "indifferent" between facing them or their reference point counterparts. But other changes may seem to have many subsidiary implications fanning out from them and, in some cases, they may be skewed in a negative or positive direction. If so, the changes "matter" to us and we are in what marketers call a "high involvement" situation (see the Hinkle-inspired work of Laaksonen, 1994). If this perspective is bolted on to prospect theory, non-financial gains and losses can be quantified in terms of numbers of positive and negative implications rather than numbers of dollars gained or lost.

I hope that behavioral economists will share my sense of the empirical relevance of cascading webs of implications for understanding how people feel as they think about alternative prospects from those they were using as their reference points: to me, it captures well the sinking feeling we get as we identify the wider consequences of giving up something that we already have, or the excitement that comes as we perceive the opportunities that will come from getting something we do not have right now, whether the "something" is a good or a feature of a good. But I think there is much more for behavioral economists to take from this perspective if they do not focus purely on employing it as a complement to utility-maximization perspectives.

For one thing, it makes very clear the demands that are placed on short-term memory capacity if people attempt to compute the overall implications of selecting rival options that have many dimensions, differ from each other in many ways, and have complex webs of perceived implications. In such situations, computational overload is likely to lead to ranking errors, so it will be wise to simplify the decision-making process by using a decision rule that does not entail the computation of relative overall values for the options under consideration. Overall values seem likely only to be computed, if they are computed at all, after non-compensatory, checklist-style rules have been used to arrive at shortlists of options that are deemed acceptable.

Where the absence of (enough of) a particular feature is viewed broadly (i.e., without formally counting implications while one mentally scrolls through them) as having, on balance, the greatest excess of negative implications, one might simply make the presence of (enough of) that feature a high priority and reject any option that seems unlikely to meet it, before then examining the remaining options in terms of the characteristic whose absence broadly seems likely, on balance, to have the next-biggest excess of undesirable implications, and so on. If only one option, or none of the options "ticks all the boxes," a verdict can be arrived at without weighing together all the positive and negative implications for any of the options: in other words, the choice is arrived at in a procedural manner without reference to a utility function, *S*-shaped or otherwise.

Such considerations favor taking a pluralistic, context-focused view of how decision-makers operate, rather than assuming that any individual approaches each occasion for choice in the same way. Sometimes, people may be open to making trade-offs and can usefully be viewed as assessing prospects in terms of total scores for desirable and undesirable implications, with these prospective pairings of gains and losses being ranked along the lines envisaged in prospect theory. But we need to recognize that, in other situations, people will approach choices in a less open manner: for example, they may simply have in mind a set of templates that specify what they "ideally" would like to get, and a set templates for what "acceptable" options should offer if ideal ones are not available, with priority rankings or rules for further search being called upon if nothing fully conforms to their "acceptable" specification. In my wider vision, then, behavior can be viewed as resulting from the application of repertoires of rules for selecting actions, with these repertoires including procedures that determine which rules are selected as decision-making aids as particular contingencies arise. Hence, for decades, I have not felt any need to think of behavior as consequent on the desire to maximize utility.

This is not to say that I advocate viewing humans as doing nothing more than applying rules, for seeing them as applying rules – whether compensatory or non-compensatory – to patterns of implications that they infer by applying cognitive rules begs an important question: in relation to *what* are implications being deemed as good or bad, or as representing gains or losses in the decision-maker's wellbeing? Here, the view that I arrived at via Adam Smith's ([1795] 1980) study of the history of astronomy, and George Kelly's (1955) psychology of personal constructs, is that we can learn more about why people do what they do if we view them as if they are, like scientists, trying to predict and control the world in which they find themselves, than if we view them as utility maximizers. So, a perceived implication of an event or choice is viewed positively (negatively) because it is seen as enhancing (reducing) the capacity of the person in question to predict and control events. This capacity is central to the role of the mind as a device for enhancing the fitness of a person to survive in challenging environments and not be at the mercy of events. Where possible, people do not "go there" if they do not expect to be able to fathom what they encounter and/or damage to their predictive systems seems likely, whereas people become fascinated with aspects of the world that they do not yet fully understand but which they believe they will be able to fathom by using, and thereby enhancing, their predictive system. In short, what motivates people is potential to enhance – or, at least, limit any withering of – the capacities of their predictive systems.

On this view of human motivation, a person's predictive system, like a scientific paradigm or research program, is itself rule-based. The sets of implications that a person sees as associated with a choice or change in the external environment are arrived at by applying a personal set of rules for theorizing and determining what constitutes knowledge and when a conjecture has been refuted or supported. Depending on the system's rules, the abandonment of one hypothesis may have wider implications due to the hypothesis in question having been used as a foundation for other expectations, without which the person may have little or no idea of how to be in control in the areas in question. Those whose personal predictive systems are resilient will typically have built systems that resist changing core constructs that are used as foundations for many other expectations about the world, with this resistance being upheld by twisting more peripheral aspects of their systems (including denial of evidence that conflicts with core ideas) to remove cognitive dissonance.

In other words, in this wider vision of behavioral economics, economic agents are viewed fundamentally as slaves of their predictive systems rather than as utility seekers. Their predictive systems are organized systems of rules and heuristics. However, their heuristics include not merely those that "new" behavioral economists presume all humans tend to use, but also those that they have worked out for themselves or picked up from others. People thus have some freedom to use their imaginative capacities and successively modify their personal predictive systems during their lives, rather in the way that purveyors of operating systems for computers design system upgrades. However, people can only assess potential changes to what they do, and to their predictive systems, from the standpoint of their existing predictive systems. Some actions and potential new ways of trying to predict and control events may be ruled out because their existing systems deem them to be unthinkable/inadmissible.

Even if behavioral economists do not employ research methods from personal construct psychology that were developed by Kelly (1955) and Hinkle ([1965] 2010), they have great potential for forming conjectures about the kinds of events that people with well-functioning predictive systems will find appealing or be keen to avoid. (Note that people may avoid some activities not because these activities seem beyond the scope of their predictive systems but for the opposite reason, namely because they construe them as offering nothing new and/or unexpected to make sense of and hence no prospect of enhancing their predictive capacities.) This view of motivation also opens opportunities to make sense of dysfunctional, emotional behavior, such as hoarding, compulsive shopping, getting into personal debt crises, domestic violence, reclusive lifestyles, and aversions to technologies that most of the population use to get more out of their lives.

From this Kelly-inspired standpoint, it seems likely that dysfunctional behavior patterns are manifestations of at least one of the following:

(a) *Anxiety*, i.e., people attempt to avoid any situation that has potential for unpredictability (including uncertainty about how one might cope with it);

(b) *Guilt*, i.e., people try to avoid forms of behavior that they see as being at odds with how they see themselves, with departures from their self-construct having major implications for the capacity of their predictive systems.

(c) *Threat*, i.e., behavior is a means of heading off a change in social standing, a position that the threatened person uses as an assumptive foundation for how they see themselves and try to cope with life.

(d) *Hostility*, i.e., efforts to extort evidence consistent with what is predicted by the person's system when other people appear to be challenging their core predictions.

As with many new ways of looking at the world, this Smith- and Kelly-inspired way of viewing human motivation may initially seem daunting to those who have not practiced trying to use it. The good news is that there is a simple way to avoid anxiety that taking it up will bring a period in which one suffers diminished capacity to make sense of economic behavior: try it initially as if it signifies a switch into a pluralistic way of understanding motivation, in which it can be tried as an alternative to utility-based thinking without requiring that one immediately jettisons any model based on utility maximization.


## 8.5    FINDING AND ADDRESSING PROBLEMS

One of the payoffs to thinking about people in general as scientists is awareness of the impact of their predictive systems on which problems they notice and deem worthy of attention, as well as on how they seek to address them. Problems do not speak for themselves, and what I see as a problem may not be something you even notice, let alone deem worthy of attention, and vice versa. The problem identification issue is not centerstage in "new" behavioral economics. Moreover, because of the centrality of cognitive shortcomings to that way of thinking, instances in which problem recognition is addressed are prone to focus on how such shortcomings affect whether a problem is identified: an obvious example here is Thaler's (2015, p. 32) reference to how, due to threshold effects in the processing of stimuli, a person may mistakenly believe that both headlights on his or her car have failed together when what has really happened is that the person in question has been driving around previously with no awareness that one headlight has failed and then notices there is a problem when the second one fails, causing the road to become too hard to see and prompting a check of the headlights.

Behavioral economists need to be alert to the possibility that *their* methods may affect which problems *they* notice. Because prospect theory emerged via research on lottery-style choices, its focus on gains and losses has resulted in the theory not being conducive to recognizing the lack of attention that economists have traditionally given to the information-processing challenges posed by a perceived need to choose between products that have many different characteristics, especially if there are many products between which to choose. But because the classic studies on which prospect theory was based presented the research subjects with pre-specified problems and payoff matrices, they were also not conducive to noticing that real-world decision problems are often open-ended: having identified a problem (not necessarily the best problem to work on given the goal(s) being pursued), the decision-maker then needs to identify and assess potential solutions in order to arrive at a payoff matrix.

Issues associated with identifying problems and solutions became a key part of my wider vision of behavioral economics via the work of Loasby (1967a, 1973, 1976), who became aware of them by studying behavior in the real world, not in psychology laboratories (see Section 3.3). These issues are important elements of a wider view of behavioral economics, not merely in relation to policy design (see Section 8.9) but also in relation to the need to take seriously work on decision-making from "old" behavioral economics rather than focusing primarily on the impacts of bias-inducing heuristics on utility-maximization. If people have to choose how to allocate their attention and are dealing with open-ended problems, behavioral economists need to view decision-making as a process that in some contexts may be protracted but may be brief in other contexts; either way, it ultimately must be underpinned by rules that enable the decision-maker to circumvent several problems of infinite regress.

Such problems arise because the process of dealing with an open-ended problem entails a set of problems, each of which raises their own problems, and so on, such as the following (see also Earl, 2023c):

- The problem of knowing where problems lie and which of them deserve attention.
- The potential to discover better solutions to problems if one can find better ways of searching for them.
- The problem of knowing what might happen that could facilitate or prevent other things from happening, including things that might be possible and which might play facilitating or blocking roles in relation to desired events.
- The normative question about which preferences one should prefer in the context in question, or how to decide which decision rule or heuristic to apply to make a choice and proceed to try to implement it.

Choices that entail these kinds of issues cannot be addressed as optimization problems until they have been turned into closed problems by using rules or heuristics to stop the infinite regress spiral, and the rules or heuristics that people use to close problems-within-problems may in some cases be ones that proceed directly to solutions without first applying optimization techniques to closed-off versions of open-ended problems. So, for example, after using rules to define where problems exist and which ones are worthy of attention, and after using rules to limit search for solutions and conduct appraisals of them, the set of remaining options may be ranked via a simple rule (for example, a non-compensatory checklist-based rule) rather than their overall performance in terms of some kind of utility function.

Ultimately, then, in the wider vision of behavioral economics, all choices are wholly or partly arrived at by applying rules-based procedures, which may include satisficing processes (as argued by Simon, 1947, 1957, 1959) and "fast and frugal" heuristics that may perform even better than attempts to apply optimizing procedures (Gigerenzer *et al.*, 1999). In saying this, I am not attempting to claim that prospect theory should be discarded as an analytical tool within a wider vision of behavioral economics; on the contrary, it may, as Thaler and others have demonstrated, be a powerful source of insight for understanding how people behave once they have arrived at closed problems that are computationally simple enough to address in a manner akin to that envisaged in the theory. Indeed, prospect theory could be relevant to some of the earlier sub-problems within a decision cycle (e.g., when choosing between alternative search strategies) even if it seems implausible at the ultimate ranking stage. What I *am* saying is that, if one adopts the wider vision of behavioral economics, the "ways" by which people identify and go about closing open-ended problems become research problems that are themselves worthy of attention from those who regard themselves as behavioral economists.

## 8.6    EVOLUTIONARY PROCESSES VERSUS EQUILIBRIUM STATES

Instead of studying how people find and attempt to deal with problems, economists usually engage in comparative static equilibrium analysis, focusing on how people change their behavior to adapt optimally to changes in their external environment. Analysis begins with the representative agent in a state of equilibrium, which is then disturbed by a change in the agent's external environment. The representative agent adapts to the new external environment as an "econ" would and settles at a new equilibrium, pending any further shock.

This is such an ingrained part of a typical economist's predictive system that it prevents economists from considering the possibility that life is an ongoing process of trying to cope with problems and challenges rather than a succession of equilibrium states. Disequilibrium analysis therefore comes to entail studying what happens when transactions are made at prices that are out of line with what they ought to be, given the underlying fundamentals of supply and demand. This mindset has predictable consequences when behavioral economics is practiced by using knowledge of heuristics and biases to address the predictive shortcomings of conventional economics: the act of making a choice in the context being analyzed will be viewed as an endpoint, a form of equilibrium but not the equilibrium at which an "econ" would arrive.

This truncated approach to thinking about behavior can generate useful results and is convenient for those who want to stick as far as possible with conventional formal modeling tools and pursue what Berg and Gigerenzer (2010) call "'as if' behavioral economics." However, "old/evolutionary behavioral economics" opens a wide range of additional analytical opportunities by taking account of aspects of real life that are at odds with the equilibrium-focused way of thinking. They include the following:

- The capacities of the systems that people use to predict and control events are finite: they may employ false assumptions and mistaken inferences; they may fail to include relevant dimensions in terms of which possibilities could usefully be construed; and limitations of imagination, memory and computational capacity may prevent appropriate consideration of relevant issues. So, even if there are no disturbances in the external environment, choices tend to result in the generation and/or identification of further problems, rather than the attainment of full control. This is easily appreciated via the example that Loasby (1976, pp. 85–6) drew from Miller (1963) regarding what happened after the Briggs Manufacturing Company chose to diversify into making steel bathtubs when it found it had spare capacity at the presses that it normally used for making steel panels for the complete car bodies that it supplied to automakers: the diversification triggered a major learning experience that unexpectedly necessitated additional investments – which eventually included the purchase of new presses, as the existing ones proved unreliable when it came to making bathtubs.

- People who acknowledge the limitations of their predictive systems will make their choices in a tentative manner and will expect to adjust what they do after seeing what happens as a result of their choices. Those who do not acknowledge the limitations of their predictive systems will be prone to encounter surprises. Insofar as the latter's predictive systems are at least partly permeable to these surprises, they will rethink their behavior to improve their control over their lives. Those whose predictive systems are dysfunctional to such a degree that they cannot see the need to change how they think are also likely not to behave as if they are settled after they have made choices: things that most people would view as minor surprises can be viewed with alarm by those with obsessive–compulsive disorders, while new purchases may fail to set compulsive shoppers' minds sufficiently at ease to result in them exploring fully what they can get from what they have just bought; instead, the latter are likely to start to dwell on what they might buy next. (Musicians frequently exhibit this behavior, which Steely Dan bandmember Walter Becker famously called "gear acquisition syndrome." For many guitarists, the answer to the question, "How many guitars are enough?" is always, "One more.") And those who cannot control their spending will sooner or later be forced by their creditors to change their behavior.

- As Schumpeter (1943) recognized, we live in a world of "creative destruction" in which established order is continually being disrupted due to entrepreneurs experimenting with new sets of connections, such as new products, new production processes, new sources of supply and new methods of organizing and managing how they do business. These entrepreneurial experiments have the potential both to render some existing systems obsolete and to provide a basis from which better systems can be developed. The innovation and adjustment processes play out through time, reflecting the fact that the creative capacities of the human imagination are finite at any point in time and they work by creating new combinations based on extending or hybridising existing concepts.

So, within a wider view of behavioral economics, the processes by which knowledge grows take centerstage and the process of problem solving is viewed as entailing the ongoing development or (for, say, ageing consumers who feel they are being left behind as the world around them changes) the shoring up of personal predictive systems. Therefore, these systems at any point should be viewed as works in progress rather than as in temporary equilibrium. Sometimes, these processes may entail revolutionary shifts in how people view the world and in how they behave, but for much of the time what we need to be studying is the relentless evolution of people's predictive systems and the consequent gradual changes in their lifestyles as they incorporate new ways of meeting their goals and abandon older ways as they do so. The "micro–meso–macro" analytical framework proposed by Dopfer, Foster and Potts (2004) provides a very good means for viewing such evolutionary processes, with the "meso" level pertaining to the changing popularity of a generic way of doing things (e.g. the smartphone meso, as distinct from a micro-level aspect of it, such as the product lifecycle of a particular model of an Apple iPhone). I have provided an extended behavioral discussion of the micro–meso–macro perspective on structural change in Earl (2022, pp. 355–75).

## 8.7 HUMAN PRACTICES AND PROCEDURAL RATIONALITY

The wide range of research methods available to behavioral economists is fortuitous, given the challenges of assessing the quality of behavior outside experimental laboratory settings and the hopes that we might have of designing effective policies for improving wellbeing. To design such policies, it is necessary to understand where organizations and consumers could be doing better than they are and what is causing them to do less well than they should be able to do, given their resources. Here, we run into the question of what the reference point should be against which we measure under-achievement. To a "new" behavioral economist, the automatic answer is that it should be what an idealized "econ" would achieve. This may be reasonable if the goals of decision-makers and optimal means of reaching them can readily be identified. In such situations, we can specify what Herbert Simon (1976) called "substantively rational" solutions to the choice problems in question. However, there are many situations in which optimal strategies cannot readily be identified, even if we can ascertain what the decision-makers are trying to do. In such situations, we need to look at rationality in a different way to assess the quality of decision-making.

My colleague Lana Friesen and I ran into this issue when studying how effectively Australian consumers were choosing their cell phone connection services in the early 2010s. We found that it was indeed possible to calculate which would be the cheapest offer to serve a well-specified usage remit from among a given set of over 800 offers. But it took many hours of research time to do this, and it became evident that many consumers had a rather poor idea of their usage patterns, even when asked merely to specify them as typical values rather than in terms of probability distributions. Moreover, the set of offers kept changing, adding scope for them to reduce costs by taking up offers that did not entail contractual lock-in: there would then be no penalty if the consumer wanted to switch to a new deal that appeared after initially choosing such a contract. Offers that provided this option value typically did so at a price. However, if a seemingly better deal with subsequently offered, it might have a contractual lock-in period. Taking up such an offer would be problematic if even better new plans were offered within the lock-in period, and so on. It was unclear how rational expectations might be formed about the stream of new plans that might appear within the duration of contracts that might be accepted for existing plans. This was especially the case at the time of our study, which was during a period of radical changes due to the uptake of smartphones, which might themselves affect usage patterns.

By the end of that research project, I concluded that behavioral economists (and economists in general) should be open to taking a practice-based view of the extent (if any) to which decision-makers should be characterized as under-achieving in a particular area and how they might do better. In other words, we need to devote more attention to studying practices and the outcomes they yield among research entities or individuals whose situations are rather similar but whose practices and attainments differ – for example, how practices and productivity levels differ between firms who produce the same, or similar, products, or between households with similar compositions who live in similar geographical areas but differ in their spending on, say, public utilities or meeting nutritional needs. Then, even if we cannot specify substantively rational choices for the subjects of our research, we can at least take best-practice behavior as our reference point and analyze what it is about best-practice ways of operating that contributes to superior outcomes. We might also use our skills as economists to suggest practices that could beat observed best-practice ways of choosing, without any need to spend significantly more time on addressing the choice in question, or which could serve as "fast and frugal" heuristics that could deliver best-practice outcomes more rapidly. (For example, Lana Friesen and I were correct to predict that the research subjects in the naturalistic experiment in the third phase of our cell phone service contract study could in many cases have achieved far better rewards by applying the heuristic "First, examine plans offered by providers whose websites mention that they are 'award-winning' providers.")

In the past, behavioral economists have left practice-focused research to sociologists and social anthropologists. (A good place to start to get a sense of such work is via the Google Scholar profile page of Professor Elizabeth Shove, a University of Lancaster sociologist who is one of the foremost practitioners of practice-focused research. Much of her work has a dynamic aspect, seeking to address the processes by which practices change, as in transitions to more sustainable lifestyles.) If we catalogue the habits, heuristics, and rules that different people use, and the results that these ways of operating deliver, we can then take a statistical view of the ingredients of good practice in the context of interest (see, for the cell phone connection service plan case, Earl, Friesen and Shadforth, 2019). In other words, by studying the behavior of people who differ in the quality of their ways of making decisions, we can arrive at a context-specific view of what Herbert Simon (1976) called "procedural rationality," which he defined in terms of "appropriate deliberation."

A practice-based approach to the quality of behavior would make behavioral economics less susceptible to the claim that Mehta (2013) has leveled at "new" behavioral economics, namely, that the heuristics and biases-based perspective "pathologizes" consumers in general. The approach may put us in a position to do something akin to what schoolteachers routinely do in respect of their students, namely, categorize users of different operating systems as "High achievers," or "In the normal range" or "Having special needs for improving their ways of operating."

## 8.8    UNDERPINNINGS OF UNDER-ACHIEVEMENT

From the standpoint of "new" behavioral economics, under-achievement by organizations and individuals is viewed as resulting essentially from decisions being made with the aid of heuristics that generate biased probability judgments and/or behavior such as procrastination and giving weight to sunk costs and other "supposedly irrelevant factors" that a "fully rational 'econ'" would ignore. I do not dispute the potential value of viewing these factors as contributing to under-achievement by human decision-makers, but I think that it can be useful for behavioral economists also to have other perspectives at their disposal. For example, if we observe consumers seemingly paying the so-called "lazy tax" due to not bothering to shop around, we might be wise to consider whether they do this because they have set their aspirations needlessly low and are not searching because the prices that they can already see are acceptable (an "old" behavioral satisficing perspective) rather than inferring that their behavior is a manifestation of, say, the default bias.

As part of a wider view of why attainments fall short of the best that can be identified as feasible, or, at least, what current best-practice ways of operating can deliver, behavioral economists could profit by adopting Leibenstein's (1966, 1976) notion of $X$-inefficiency and his "old" behavioral perspective on why it arises. He introduced the $X$-inefficiency term to denote the extent to which an organization incurs needlessly high costs for reasons other than some of the prices of factors of production being kept above those that would prevail in markets that were not afflicted by monopolistic behavior (such as wage costs that trade unions have inflated) or policy-driven distortions (such as tariffs on imported machinery). But we can also apply the $X$-inefficiency term to the extent to which consumers pay more than they need to pay for reasons that pertain to the choices they make rather than because some market prices are higher than those that would prevail in a competitive market. I think we are likely to arrive at a better understanding, and better policies for improving attainments, if we undertake analysis in this area mindful of the consumption $X$-inefficiency equivalents of the four causes that Leibenstein identified for organizational $X$-inefficiency (see also Earl, 2005b, 2007):

- *Organizations and consumers may lack knowledge of best-practice methods for minimizing the costs of achieving what they are trying to achieve.*
  Such knowledge will be hard to keep pace with when technological change is rapid, but it may also be problematic in relatively slow-changing markets for products that are only sought infrequently, or where products are complex to use, offer multiple outputs and there is a wide range of choice. This knowledge pertains to organizational and household production functions, both in engineering terms (i.e., the feasible outputs of products or production systems or characteristics that can be obtained from alternative combinations of inputs) and the cheapest ways of sourcing alternative sets of inputs. In other words, compared with those who achieve best-practice

performance, some people may purchase inferior combinations of inputs and/or pay too much for their inputs and/or use ineptly the inputs that they purchase.

- *The deals that organizations and households make with those who supply products and services to them commonly do not completely specify what is going to be supplied.*

In the case of employment contracts, this fuzziness is key to enabling adaptation in light of new information and changed circumstances (Coase, 1937); it is a potential issue for purchasers of anything that is not a "search good" in the purest sense of one whose qualities can be fully ascertained before a purchase agreement is made, and in reality most purchases involve "experience good" and/or "credence good" aspects. When labor services are contracted at an hourly rate, the quality and quantity of work undertaken will depend on the skills that workers have and how industriously they apply them. Payment-by-results contracts may guard to some degree against opportunistic behavior by workers, but it is often problematic (a) to specify fully what is to be produced and (b) to obtain redress in the event of a dispute about the quality of what is delivered. Where physical products are purchased, their specifications may be incomplete or misleading. So, organizations and households can both end up with needlessly high costs due to their suppliers behaving opportunistically in respect of vague aspects of contracts. Supplier opportunism may arise even in respect of what the contracts have specified if they believe that their clients will face significant enforcement costs and cannot inflict reputational damage on them. However, poor value for money spent on experience goods and credence goods is not always the result of supplier opportunism; it may also arise when dealing with suppliers who act in good faith but are not as competent as they believe themselves to be.

- *Organizations and consumers may face barriers to elevating their achievements toward best-practice levels by developing or efficiently outsourcing the requisite capabilities.*

In principle, it may be possible and worthwhile to invest in obtaining knowledge of the relevant production function and associated know-how for (a) extracting output from well-chosen sets of inputs, (b) shopping for supplies and negotiating deals, (c) motivating and managing suppliers of labor inputs, and (d) obtaining redress on occasions where there are shortfalls in the standard of what is supplied. However, those who need to develop or outsource such capabilities must first recognize their need for them and then have the capacity to source them efficiently. It is possible that personal pride, self-reliance ethics and/or lack of awareness of the potential relevance of the "it takes one to know one" problem will result in such needs being denied rather than admitted. Clearly, there is also scope for failures in markets for such capabilities due to difficulties in judging which of those who profess to have the desired capabilities actually possess them and will not behave in an opportunistic manner. A further complication (emphasized in the work of Nelson and Winter, 1982) is that some of the knowledge that is sought may be of the "tacit" variety that cannot be fully articulated in words and can only be acquired (if at all) by experimenting, armed only with incomplete instructions, until one stumbles upon the necessary knack.

- *If organizations and consumers operate in environments where competitive pressures are weak, they are less likely to seek to find ways of reducing the costs of what they do or improving its quality.*
  This may seem obvious enough for firms in which internal competition is limited due to social pressures among workers not to break productivity norms. It may likewise apply with firms that operate in markets where there are significant entry barriers, trade policies that provide protection from imports, and customers whose demands are not challenging due to them not habitually being careful to search for lower prices and having modest non-price aspirations. But consumers, in varying degrees, may likewise feel they are under pressure to shop and use purchased items efficiently. Households differ in the extent of internal competition for resources – for example, because of the size of the household relative to its budget or because members of households differ in how adept they are at bargaining for resources. (There are parallels here with the underpinnings of organizational slack in the behavioral theory of the firm proposed by Cyert and March, 1963.) External competitive pressures will be present to the extent that consumers are status seekers who set out to demonstrate their place in society via conspicuous consumption. If one is not a status seeker, there is less to be gained from, say, getting one's weekly groceries more cheaply than there is for a status seeker. The latter will be able to finance more daring acts of conspicuous consumption if it is possible to find ways of economizing when buying less discretionary products that are not chosen for their status signaling capacities.

The last of these four factors aligns well with a demand-side laziness-based perspective on under-achievement (or even one formally based on search for cost savings being repeatedly postponed due to present-bias/quasi-hyperbolic discounting). That perspective encourages behavioral economists to focus on failures to gather information about cheaper supply sources, or failures to switch to cheaper sources so long as old habits deliver adequate outcomes. However, the *X*-inefficiency perspective is otherwise conducive to taking account of shortfalls in capabilities for making the most of one's budget. Note, too, that knowledge deficiencies in relation to household production functions may not relate merely to areas such as how to make tasty, nutritious meals more cheaply but also to combinations of activities that can make people happy. There may be plenty of sources of information about what these combinations might be, but many of the activities in question may yield payoffs only to those who are prepared to persist with them until they develop the requisite capabilities. People who underestimate their capacity to learn and who expect that failure to acquire new capabilities will result in losses in their self- and/or social-esteem will be prone to waste funds if they get as far as experimenting with such activities – instead of ramping up their commitment to any of them when things start to prove challenging, they are likely merely to dabble with them in succession before abandoning them. If they were more susceptible to sunk-cost bias, they might be able to do rather better.


## 8.9    POLICIES FOR IMPROVING PRODUCTIVITY AND WELLBEING

One year before Thaler and Sunstein's (2008) book *Nudge* appeared, nudge-style policies were used successfully by my local water services utility to ensure that a severe drought in Queensland did not result in the water levels in local dams becoming dangerously low. Instead of raising unit prices for water, the utility sent out water bills that compared the addressee's water usage with usage rates in their suburb as well as in previous periods and made it known that those with abnormally high usage rates would be sent "please explain" letters. Those who thereby felt that they ought to try to reduce their water consumption could readily find ideas on how to do this via a newsletter that accompanied the water bills. The strategy achieved its goal in a very equitable manner, whereas following the conventional economic wisdom would have made it harder for Brisbane's poorer residents to meet their basic needs while the rich would have been without non-price pressure to reduce the extent to which they continued watering their lawns.

What my local utility did went beyond the nudge concept, for its policy for reducing the demand for water did not merely try to induce change by getting customers to think about their use relative to others and by imposing what are sometimes called "frown costs" on heavy users; it also tried to educate water users about how they might be wasting water. It was thus better aligned with the wider policy philosophy that is implied by the wider, knowledge-focused view of behavioral economics explored in this book and which is central to the extended $X$-inefficiency perspective offered in the previous section.

In contexts where under-achievement results from poor knowledge and inadequately developed capabilities, it is important for designers of economic policies to understand the extent to which these shortfalls result from limited opportunities to acquire knowledge and develop capabilities, or from people using predictive systems that are not conducive to them taking up opportunities to learn and develop their capabilities. Insofar as the latter is the issue, policy designers need to focus on bringing about changes in how people view the process of acquiring the relevant knowledge or capabilities.

Suppose, for example, that the barrier to people learning how to do better is that the very thought that they need to develop their decision-making capacity in the area in question conflicts with their self-images as capable people, and they do not want to show others how little they know about the area in question. They may in any case not want to present themselves as people who need to find out how little they really need to spend on a product that would suit their requirements (if only they knew what these should be). The result of such thinking may be that they make uninformed purchases of "default option" products. In such a case, the use of an attainment-limiting heuristic has more complex foundations than the "heuristics and biases" approach to behavioral economics considers, and policies for improving attainments may fail unless they take account of these issues.

So, members of "behavioral insights teams" should not merely view themselves as working for "nudge units." Rather, they should recognize that they will be able to contribute more to policy design if they keep the following issues and possibilities in mind:

*Boosting Decision-Making Capabilities*
In essence, nudge-based policies apply knowledge of commonly used heuristics to steer people to make choices that will enhance their wellbeing or to help the policy instigators (government agencies, not-for-profit organizations, and firms) toward meeting their objectives. The policy measures entail changing the choice architecture – i.e., how options are presented to the target audience – rather than changing prices and/or product characteristics. An alternative, potentially complementary approach is to supply people with better heuristics and knowledge about decision-making to "boost" their capabilities (see Gigerenzer, 2015; Grüne-Yanoff and Hertwig, 2016; Hertwig, 2017). This is essentially

what management education programs in business schools aim to achieve, but behavioral insights teams have roles to play in advocating and helping to design programs that will enable consumers to limit the extent to which they are susceptible to using dysfunctional heuristics. Such programs could be particularly effective as parts of school curricula – for example, to develop better generic statistical thinking to apply to the problems of everyday life, or more context-specific knowledge such as in matters of financial literacy. To reduce risks that people will succumb to nudge-based policies and persuasive techniques that run counter to their own interests, education can be provided in how these techniques work, while assertiveness training is a way toward ensuring that people can get treated fairly and obtain outcomes to which they are entitled.

Those on the political right who have warmed to the libertarian side of Thaler and Sunstein's "libertarian paternalism" will doubtless object to "boost" programs that aim to change the repertoires of heuristics that people use, on the basis that such programs could be the start of a slippery slope from "nanny state" interventions to more sinister attempts to brainwash people to think in particular ways. They might question the need for such policies by pointing to the ready availability of helpful websites and moderately priced self-help books – such as Cialdini (1984, 2009) on techniques of persuasion, Alberti and Emmors (2008) on assertiveness training, and Belsky and Gilovich (1999) on financial decision-making – that have sold in huge quantities. From an enactivist view of cognition, there is clearly something in this market-based perspective. However, it has a key limitation, namely, that shortcomings in people's predictive systems and/or decision-making processes may prevent them from acknowledging that they would be wise to invest in aids to improving their decision-making (an "old/evolutionary" behavioral perspective). Moreover, even if people recognize that they have such shortcomings, they may repeatedly defer any action in that direction because they are susceptible to present-bias and/or quasi-hyperbolic discounting (a "new" behavioral perspective).

*Making it Easier to Gather Information and Switch to New Providers and Practices*

The wider view of behavioral economics acknowledges that there is also a role for policies that aim to foster higher attainments by making it easier for people engaged in problem-solving activities to gather relevant information, draw reliable inferences from it, and, if they wish, change their behavior. This vision of what needs to be made easy is wider than what is often observed in "new" behavioral contributions because it includes a role for policies that make it easy to find options and evaluate them, rather than merely for policies that make it easy to implement a change of behavior.

For example, we might indeed anticipate that consumers will be more likely to fail to switch to cheaper providers of electricity if they face a system in which they are required to contact both their existing and their new providers to initiate the handover. This hurdle can be removed by a policy intervention that requires the new provider to liaise with the old one once the consumer has clicked acceptance of the new offer. But first the consumer needs to be able to ascertain which provider and plan to select. Making it easy in this area could require a government-sponsored website that pulls together all the necessary information about how each plan works, along with the customer's past bills that detail usage history and solar-generated feed-in (or even, if required by regulations, fine-grained time-of-day-and-month consumption and feed-in information from smart-meters), and which can calculate prospective costs for all the plans and thereby rank them. A policy that addresses consumers' cognitive needs by creating such an institution is what naturally comes to mind if one takes an enactivist view of cognition, though it would, of course, need to be complemented by one that made it easy to implement changes of provider. The cognitive institution that this policy example entails would require a much greater investment in programming and would no doubt be met with much more resistance from providers, than half-baked state-provided websites that only go as far as making comparisons against typical usage patterns and fail properly to adjust for the effects of solar systems on electricity bills. However, it would remove the need to "boost" customer expertise in respect of complex tariffs with time- and grid usage-dependent pricing.

*Consumer and Worker Protection*
Regulation- and tribunals-based consumer and worker protection and arbitration policies warrant consideration in contexts where:

- There is good reason to believe, or evidence that, appropriate decision-making capabilities and knowledge are uncommon and hence consumers and workers are at risk of being nudged or otherwise persuaded to accept offers that serve them far less well than offers they could have discovered if they had such capabilities – including capabilities required for obtaining redress if suppliers or employers engage in unethical behavior toward them.
- Effective "boost" policies prove impossible to design or are precluded by political opposition, or if they end up entailing programs in which participation is (like buying and reading self-help books) not compulsory.

- Competitive pressures are neither strong enough to promote ethically appropriate behavior by suppliers, nor so strong (for example, due to extremely low entry barriers – cf. Richardson, 1960) as to put suppliers in a position in which they are so desperate to survive that they resort to unethical practices.

The third point implies that market deregulation may be unhelpful if it goes as far as some libertarians wish (as was recognized at an early stage by Etzioni, 1988). However, it is also important to recognize that there are two reasons why it may not take a particularly high proportion of skilled and diligent shoppers to deter suppliers from engaging in "rip-off" pricing and other forms of ethically questionable behavior that come under Akerlof and Shiller's (2015) umbrella term of "phishing for phools." One reason comes via the enactivist view of cognition: canny shoppers may play an active role as sources of knowledge for those who lack shopping expertise or time to engage in gathering information in the market in question. Secondly, there is what is known as the "Ward-Perkins point" by those who, like Loasby and I, have been influenced by the work of Andrews (1964, p. 102). Neville Ward-Perkins, one of Andrews's students at Oxford, argued that it may only require a small percentage of customers to be canny shoppers for incumbent players to be concerned about deterring new entry. What concerns potential entrants to a market will be whether there are enough canny shoppers who would switch to a new player that offered a better deal than the incumbent suppliers. If the minimum efficient scale of production in a market is small relative to the total volume of goods sold in the market, and if canny shoppers can be expected to give their goodwill to an entrant who offers a better deal even if the deal is later matched by the incumbents, the incumbent suppliers may take the threat of entry very seriously and seek to deter it by neither engaging in greedy pricing nor trimming quality.

*Promoting Constructive Criticism to Facilitate Experimentation and Learning*
In situations where other people's predictive systems enable them to see actual or potential problems that have not been noticed by a decision-maker, scope for the latter to avoid under-achievement will be reduced if the former are reluctant to raise the issues in question, even in a constructive manner, because they fear that this will be seen as a personal affront and elicit a hostile reaction. The "shooting the messenger" reactions that whistleblowers commonly face are but one indication of the need to design systems for drawing attention to problems and ensuring that what is said will be taken seriously. Such systems could, in the case of households, play significant roles in reducing domestic violence, while

they could have a major role to play in helping organizations to terminate or rethink projects that are heading for disaster and likely to lead to sunk-cost bias and escalation of commitment. There is enormous potential for behavioral insights teams to offer consultancy services in this area if they can uncover effective operating principles for making fearlessly offered and gratefully received constructive criticism a routine feature of how organizations function.

If we are viewing people in general as if they are scientists, an obvious starting point in thinking about what these kinds of principles might look like is to reflect on academic best-practice methods for promoting the growth of knowledge and avoiding misallocation of research resources. However, given the application of modern divide-and-rule methods to universities in recent decades, current practice seems less conducive to a healthy, constructively critical work environment than the kinds of operating principles that Ed Catmull (2014) and his colleagues developed to ensure the success of the Pixar animated movie firm.

Pixar's operating system is very much in line with enactivist views of cognition rather than the individual-centered perspective that dominates in mainstream and "new behavioral" economics. If applied in academia, it implies that staff should be discouraged from taking pride in operating alone (which they may otherwise do to make their originating roles clear in what they publish), and they should not seek to maximize their promotion prospects by contributing nothing to their colleagues. Those who recognize the benefits of social inputs in cognition and who therefore operate in a collegial, collaborative manner will facilitate each other's intellectual growth in a cumulative manner. They will appreciate being expected to air their latest thinking at least once a year at departmental workshops, share drafts with each other and provide feedback, and work collaboratively. By such means, their research outputs should be closer to being publication-ready by the time they submit them than otherwise would have been the case.

When it comes to hiring new colleagues, such academics will strive to secure people whose potential to contribute to collegial knowledge-generation exceeds their own by the widest margin; existing staff should not be fearful that brilliant new colleagues who are highly collegial and therefore pleasant to work with could make them look less valuable than hitherto. The academics to avoid are those who are arrogant, self-absorbed and who have prima-donna tendencies, however capable they are of writing papers for top-tier journals single-handedly or as part of a narrow clique; those who fancy themselves are likely to contribute as little as possible in collegial terms and to focus instead on moving onward and upward to higher-status organizations before their deficiencies become elements of their international reputations.

Secondly, it is vital that research grant allocations and research outputs are peer-reviewed in a civil and constructive manner, in which referees write their reports on the work of others in the way that they would like to see others report on their own work. The current norm is to use double-blind refereeing to promote frank criticism of submissions and ensure that grant proposals and submitted works are assessed based on their scholarly merits rather than who submitted them. However, the anonymity of referees is not as conducive to civil and diligent conduct as would be a system in which referees were not anonymous (see also, Holbrook, 1995a). If referee reports were signed by referees, with dates of when the reports were invited and received, and if they were published as supplements to the works in question, authors could be more confident of getting worthwhile reports, written in a civil style, and delivered in a timely manner. This would have the added benefit of providing an incentive for authors to address referee comments assiduously rather than trying to grind down the resolve of referees and journal editors by merely paying lip-service to what the reports say. Indeed, the knowledge generation process might be improved further if it became standard practice for journals to signal the quality of their processes by requiring authors to allow them to post rejected submissions and accompanying referee reports on the journal websites. Such a transparent process would surely concentrate wonderfully the minds of researchers on getting collegial feedback on their works before submitting them for publication.

*Providing Role-Models of Ambition and Practice*
Insofar as under-achievement results from people setting their aspirations needlessly low and therefore not searching as far as they might have done before choosing, an obvious policy remedy is to provide role-models of what can be achieved and of the practices that can make it possible. I first came across this kind of policy as a second-year undergraduate when studying the development of Japan in the late 19th century: efforts to raise agricultural productivity were built around demonstrating what was being achieved by best-practice "model farms" that farmers from the surrounding areas could visit. Other elements of what I later discovered was called "agricultural extension" include farmer-focused newspapers, magazines and, more recently, radio and television programs, as well as visits from roving farm advisors to spread awareness about innovations and improvements in practice. Such initiatives need not come from governments; they may also be market institutions and benchmarking services

that result from entrepreneurial activities or trade associations. These include bodies such as the UK-based Centre For Inter-Firm Comparisons that are set up to collect performance data of rival firms on an anonymous basis and which then provide their members with details of their rankings and the productivity levels of the best and median firm attainments.

*Using Regulatory Constraints to Induce Search and Learning*
Where policies based on nudges, boosts and exemplars are impractical or prove ineffectual as means to trigger search and learning about ways of raising achievements, those who have a wider vision of behavioral economics should consider how regulatory constraints may be used to generate search activities that will result in better choices. Clearly, one can attempt to ensure that people and organizations perform better than they otherwise would have done by imposing regulations that, in effect, force them to meet required levels of performance, as with making it illegal to drive a car without supervision if one has not passed a driving test, or reducing vehicle emissions by requiring carmakers to comply with combined average fuel economy (CAFE) standards that are progressively tightened.

We might even envisage regulations that prevent consumers from purchasing products if they have not first engaged in due diligence in terms of developing a basic appreciation of how the charges they will incur are calculated – for example, requiring them to take a financial literacy test before they are allowed to sign a loan contract, or to demonstrate that they can do a multi-tier pricing calculation before they sign up for, say, electricity supply or cell phone service products that involve such pricing systems. Internet technology makes it feasible to require that prospective customers are diverted to official websites that provide training material and test whether the concepts have been understood, before purchasing decisions can be actioned. The imposition of such requirements might also prod service providers to offer products whose price structures are simpler, more transparent, and easier to compare with those of rivals.

However, policy designers should also be mindful of potential for efficiency enhancing consequences of attempts to circumvent regulations. This is a lesson that comes from Loasby's study of the impact of UK location policies in the late 1950s and early 1960s that made it difficult for firms to meet their growth objectives by moving to larger premises unless these were in new towns or depressed areas (see Loasby, 1967a, 1973). Loasby emphasizes that when firms did expand their operations by moving to areas where Industrial Development Certificates could readily be obtained, they searched for ways of overcoming the disadvantages of these locations and were often successful in finding solutions – often, things they could have done long ago in their original locations. However, in some cases, managers thought creatively about ways in which they might grow in their present area without needing to obtain Industrial Development Certificates - i.e., they sought to find a way of getting round the regulations. For example (though not one provided by Loasby), the Jaguar car company solved its need for more capacity in the Birmingham area by taking over Daimler, its ailing local rival, which enabled it to get Daimler's factory and to get economies of scope by creating a new smaller Daimler sedan by putting Daimler's small V8 engine into a Daimler-badged variant of the Jaguar Mark II.

*Reducing Human Environmental Impacts*
Behavioral economics who start to view consumers as if they are scientist rather than compromised utility maximizers will have a wider range of opportunities to contribute to policies aimed at reducing human impacts on the natural environment. Implied in the Adam Smith/George Kelly view of human action is a view of human wellbeing that only depends on consuming more and more insofar as people view this as their preferred way of enhancing their abilities to predict and control events. So, behavioral economists should be mindful of how they might contribute to the design of policies that present acceptable cases for people to rethink, in environmentally more sustainable ways, how they should go about trying to improve, or prevent reductions in, their capacities to predict and control events.

Such policies can take many forms. For example, if people prefer private cars to public transport because they view the latter as having high probabilities of not adhering to their timetables, then policies could focus on making public transport journey times more predictable (for example, via the introduction of bus lanes) and/or making journey times in private cars more unpredictable (for example, by reducing the availability of parking spaces, thereby making it hard to find somewhere to park, or by limiting road space for cars via creating bus lanes). If cars are seen as devices for upholding how people see themselves relative to others, the policy role could be in promoting different ways of viewing social standing or in dealing with issues that contribute to the use of alternative means of transport being viewed as signifying low status. Attention could also be given to promoting greener views of which kinds of people and behavior are to be valued in society. To the extent that motoring enthusiasts are fascinated by cars because they view them as engineering marvels, then perhaps it could be demonstrated to them that smaller, thriftier vehicles require much more creative design engineering and/or that there are plenty of other things at which to marvel that entail smaller environmental footprints, and so on.

## 8.10   WIDER OPPORTUNITIES FOR BEHAVIORAL ECONOMISTS

Behavioral economists would be wise not to view themselves as confined to analyzing the behavior of consumers and how firms and government agencies can seek to manipulate consumers. They should be mindful that, before Thaler came along, behavioral economics focused mainly on firms and other organizations. Much of that work in the early post-World War II decades paid rather little attention to the potential for external pressures to deter employees from pursuing personal sub-goals, and this may have left economists with the impression that satisficing behavior, organizational slack, and $X$-inefficiency were only of interest where competitive pressures were limited. Internal competitive pressures increased from the mid-1960s in large firms that switched to profit-centers-based (M-form) organizational structures. Then, from around 1980, competitive pressures both inside and outside organizations were cranked up following the political success of neo-conservatives/neo-liberals that drove the transition to the modern world of managerialism, deregulation, privatization, and globalization. But despite today's pressures for members of firms and other organizations to raise their productivity, optimal choices remain elusive. Understanding differences in the "ways" that organizations work and how they deal with changing situations is not something that economists should view as the preserve of management scholars; it should be part of behavioral economics, just as it used to be.

Behavioral labor economics (surveyed by Berg, 2015) is arguably the main area in which modern behavioral economics has embraced issues relating to firms and other organizations, such as the effort that workers put into their jobs and the impact of social norms on productivity. Yet it is also a good example of a field in which "old/evolutionary" ideas are under-applied. This is evident in areas related to labor supply behavior, such as educational choices, career orientation and management, choosing when to quit or which jobs to apply for, willingness to move geographically and the extent to which this is affected by non-price and emotional factors, and so on. On the demand side of the labor market, the processes by which workers get matched with jobs is one that seems to align perfectly with the use of non-compensatory decision rules for shortlisting, even if final choices are made in terms of trade-offs in a compensatory manner. From an "old/evolutionary" behavioral standpoint, the "even if" condition seems rather unlikely to apply where the capabilities of workers are key to getting a competitive edge. A case in point appears to be how academic positions are filled in today's world of research audits and university league table rankings, where it appears that disjunctive or lexicographic decision rules are used to rank shortlisted applicants: so long as applicants are viewed as adequate in research and teaching, their research potential may be the dominant criterion, with teaching capabilities only referred to if there is a tie for the best researcher.

But labor economics is just one area in which it helps to think with a wider vision of behavioral economics. Here, I will list just +three others. First, consider development economics, which captured my attention at an early stage via the attempts of Bauer (1971) to argue that economic development depended on attitudes and motivation rather than ready access to natural resources. Information overload associated with a surfeit of options may be less of a driver to the use of simplifying decision rules in less developed countries than in advanced industrial economies, but that does not mean there are few gains to be had from understanding the operating systems that people in developing countries develop for surviving or trying to get ahead amid challenges posed by cultural traditions, corruption, and other institutional factors.

Secondly, consider applying "old/evolutionary" behavioral economics to the field of international trade – not merely in relation to the possible significance of non-compensatory decision rules for understanding non-price drivers of trade, but also the search strategies that exporters use to solve problems caused by external changes that reduce their access to established markets, the pricing strategies that exporters use for dealing with currency fluctuations, how would-be exporters develop the knowledge they need to become credible competitors in foreign markets, and how customers go about judging the quality of unfamiliar foreign products.

Finally, consider ecological economics and the transition to a sustainable future. For me, when writing an entry (Earl, 2017b) on the theory of the firm for a handbook on ecological economics, it was natural to consider how the behavioral theory of the firm might be useful for understanding how firms can end up behaving in ways that damage both the environment and their reputations (as with Volkswagen's "dieselgate scandal"). If I were studying, say, the uptake of electric cars, I would certainly find Thaler's (1985) work on mental accounting relevant: insofar as buyer resistance comes from such vehicles being much more expensive than what people are used to paying, then a potential solution is to offer cars on a "battery not included" basis and then lease the battery separately, especially if this can be done for a monthly fee less than what people budget for fuel and servicing. But I would also consider non-price dimensions that may be deal-breakers, as where, say, vehicles have inadequate range, touch-screen controls that require menu-diving operations, batteries that contain nickel and cobalt mined by questionable means and/or that cannot be charged at home from rooftop solar due to the would-be buyer living in an apartment or other lifestyle constraints, are made in politically repressive countries such as China and/or by a firm in which Elon Musk has a major interest, and so on.

Taking a wider view of behavioral economics also has potential to enable behavioral economists to contribute more readily to other disciplines, especially if they work with co-authors from these areas. These disciplines include not merely marketing and finance, both of which were early adopters of Thaler's work, but also fields such as:

- Business history.
- Corporate culture.
- Criminology (for food for thought, see the Google Scholar profile of Professor Mandeep Dhami).
- Entrepreneurial studies.
- Health policy (cf. Foster, Earl, Haines and Mitchell, 2010).
- International business.
- Organizational behavior.
- Project management.
- Strategic management.

Indeed, rather than merely making contributions to such fields, those who have wide-ranging behavioral economics expertise may even find it relatively easy to advance their careers by defecting from departments of economics to positions in these areas. I explored such possibilities during my career and had no trouble getting shortlisted up to full professor level in marketing or strategic management. What limited my determination to pursue such opportunities and ultimately kept me in economics were concerns that I had about being able to continue doing work that would be recognized as economics and, in doing so, would help to promote behavioral economics (as I saw it) as an alternative to conventional economics. I was probably mistaken in having these concerns, especially given the mistakes I was making in trying, as an economist, to generate interest in the behavioral alternative that I was pursuing.

## 8.11   CONCLUDING REFLECTIONS

For almost five decades, I have been trying to build on behavioral contributions that existed before Thaler's (1980) seminal article was published, and on extensions of those contributions on which I was then working at the time Thaler's article appeared. But even in 1980, I could see that interest in what I viewed as behavioral economics was waning. I sought to understand what was going on by applying behavioral ideas to the behavior of economists (Earl, 1980b, 1983b). Given what was happening, I did not entertain thoughts that my work would enable me to become an academic superstar; I merely hoped that it would win some converts and enable me to work among congenial colleagues and enjoy a comfortable lifestyle. I similarly did not imagine that Thaler would become an academic superstar and have a profound effect on what behavioral economics was viewed as constituting. I enjoyed his 1980 paper and was among the first to cite it, even though it seemed a bit odd relative to the behavioral contributions that inspired me: although it began by referring to the notion of bounded rationality, I was unable to find any way in which it claimed to offer a satisficing analysis of consumer behavior, whereas that was what I was busily engaged in trying to develop. It did not occur to me that what I found odd about Thaler's paper might ultimately help it to win (by February 18, 2026) well over twice the number of citations that my entire output had achieved (10313 on Google Scholar, from Thaler's 230,786 total, versus my far from terrible total of 4212).

But despite the misgivings that I came to have about Thaler's way of doing behavioral economics, I was delighted when he won the 2017 Nobel Memorial Prize in Economic Sciences (see Earl, 2018): the sight of so many economists working with a Thaler-inspired way of doing behavioral economics is, to me, far better than would have been the sight of just a few scholars such as myself claiming to be doing behavioral economics and winning very few converts to the field. Because of what Thaler kickstarted, there are now vastly more scholars than there would have been who might be open to stepping from the narrow view of behavioral economics to the wider one that I have been canvassing here.

I do not regard the difference between the spectacularly greater interest that there has been in "new" behavioral economics than in work in "old/evolutionary" behavioral economics as a sign that my wider vision of the field is based on flawed thinking and/or a deluded sense of its potential to be applied. Rather, as I have sought to show in the Progress Review sections of earlier chapters of this book, I probably have myself in large part to blame for my behavioral perspective not being widely known and/or adopted. In essence, the problem was that I operated as if it would be impossible to interest most economists in the ideas that excited me, because these ideas clashed with the core axioms and operating rules of the conventional research program in economics. Hence, I mainly consorted with historians of economic thought, economic psychologists, and self-styled "heterodox" economists whose core ways of thinking and doing research should have made them open to the kind of behavioral approach that I was pursuing.

With hindsight, I believe that I should have treated mainstream economists as being true to their words when they preached the methodology of positive economics. This was what Thaler did in his seminal 1980 paper, and his strategy thereafter was to emphasize phenomena that were anomalous for conventional economics but which he could explain with his behavioral analysis. My mistake was to view positivistic preaching as a disingenuous smokescreen and to think that the reality was that mainstream economic theorists were not open, no matter what empirical claims were being made, to contributions that did not seek to conduct analysis with the aid of formal mathematical models and did not seek to do economic analysis as if choices were always acts of constrained optimization. Hence, I mostly did not focus on making systematic empirical contributions. Instead, I sought to build a better theoretical picture of the economic system by drawing on behavioral principles. I illustrated it with reference to real-world examples, instead of testing it, one hypothesis after another, by applying statistical methods.

My cynicism about how open economists really were to empirical critiques of their core ideas had been considerably reinforced when I noticed how Rabin and Thaler (2001, p. 230) seemed to be exasperated by attempts to cling to expected utility theory despite evidence that risk aversion was widespread: they conveyed how they felt by likening the behavior of those who would not face up to this evidence to the behavior of the pet-shop manager in the legendary "Dead Parrot Sketch" from the television comedy series *Monty Python's Flying Circus* – except that they noted how, after making farcical attempts to deny that the parrot he had sold was dead, the manager of the pet-shop did eventually concede that it was indeed dead. But, despite their exasperation, Rabin and Thaler did not abandon their attempts to win over the mainstream and (perhaps partly because of what they had said) the tide soon turned in their favor: their 2001 paper appeared in the same winter as the *New York Times* articles on behavioral economics by Lowenstein (2001) and Uchitelle (2001).[20] I had never even started trying to do what they were doing.

In a sense, what I did was perhaps an unfortunate result of being blessed at an early stage with an economics education that gave me an unusually good sense of the existence of alternatives to the mainstream approach to economics and how they were faring: if I had been unaware of all this, I might have viewed my only hope as being to play the long game via a systematic Thaler-like evidence-based strategy.

My way of operating was by no means a complete failure, but it ensured that almost all interest in my behavioral approach came from outside the mainstream and not from "new" behavioral economists. It led to a stream of invitations for me to produce works (many of which are not cited in this book) whose forms (for example, book chapters and papers in lower-tier journals) often guaranteed that they would have less impact than it might have been possible for me to achieve if I had instead concentrated on producing fewer outputs but ones that concentrated on providing proof-of-concept demonstrations of how my ideas could be implemented and/or demonstrations of why the ideas were important for policy design.

---

[20] It is possible that Rabin's impact had much to do with his demonstrations that psychological factors can be incorporated in formal models, for this may have led growing numbers of technically skilled mainstream economists to engage in what Berg and Gigerenzer (2010) call "as-if behavioral economics." By contrast, the uptake of Thaler's heuristics and biases-driven approach is consistent with mainstream economics being what Lakatos (1970) calls a "degenerating research program." Thaler-style behavioral economics could be accepted as a way of dealing with anomalies in areas where they were identified, while enabling conventional economics to continue to be practiced, with no change to its hard-core axioms and operating heuristics, in the areas that remained unscathed.

# References


Abolafia, M. Y. (1996). *Making Markets: Opportunism and Restraint on Wall Street*. Cambridge, MA: Harvard University Press.

Abolafia, M. Y. (1998). Markets as cultures: An ethnographic approach. *Sociological Review, 46*(May), 69–85.

Ackley, G. (1961). *Macroeconomic Theory*. New York: Collier Macmillan.

Adams, T. F. N., & Kobayashi, N. (1969). *The World of Japanese Business*. London: Ward Lock.

Akerlof, G. A., & Shiller, R. J. (2009). *Animal Spirits: How Human Psychology Drives the Economy, and Why It Matters for Global Capitalism*. Princeton, NJ: Princeton University Press.

Akerlof, G. A., & Shiller, R. J. (2015). *Phishing for Phools: The Economics of Manipulation and Deception*. Princeton, NJ and Oxford: Princeton University Press.

Akerlof, G. A., & Yellen, J. L. (eds) (1986). *Efficiency Wage Models of the Labor Market*. Cambridge: Cambridge University Press.

Alberti, R. E,, & Emmors, M. L. (2008). *Your Perfect Right: Assertiveness and Equality in Life and Relationships* (9th edn). St Luis Obispo, CA: Impact Publishers.

Alchian, A. A., & Allen, W. R. (1967). *University Economics* (2nd edn). Belmont, CA: Wadsworth Publishing.

Allen, G. C. ([1939] 1970). *British Industries and Their Organization*. London: George Allen & Unwin (5th edition, 1970, London: Longman).

Allen, G. C. (1968). *Monopoly and Restrictive Practices*. London: George Allen & Unwin (reprinted 2003, London: Routledge).

Andreozzi, L., & Bianchi, M. (2007). Fashion: Why people like it and theorists do not. In M. Bianchi (ed.), *The Evolution of Consumption: Theories and Practices. Advances in Austrian Economics, Volume10* (pp. 209–229). Oxford: Elsevier.

Andrews, P. W. S. (1949). *Manufacturing Business*. London: Macmillan.

Andrews, P. W. S. (1958). Competition in the modern economy. In G. Sell, ed., *Competitive Aspects of Oil Operations*, London: Institute of Petroleum. Reprinted in F. S. Lee and P. E. Earl (eds) (1993), *The Economics of Competitive Enterprise* (pp. 323–362). Aldershot: Edward Elgar.

Andrews, P. W. S. (1964). *On Competition in Economic Theory*. London: Macmillan.

Andrews, P. W. S., & Brunner, E. (1951) *Capital Development in Steel*. Oxford: Basil Blackwell.

Andrews, P. W. S., & Brunner, E. (1975). *Studies in Pricing*. London: Macmillan.

Archibald, G. C. (ed.) (1971). *The Theory of the Firm*. Harmondsworth: Penguin.

Arrow, K. J. (1974). *The Limits of Organization*. New York: W. W. Norton.

Baddeley, M. (2010). Herding, social influence and economic decision-making: Socio-psychological and neuroscientific analysis. *Philosophical Transactions: Biological Sciences, 365*(1538, Jan. 27), 281–290.

Baddeley, M. (2013). *Behavioral Economics and Finance*. London and New York: Routledge.

Baddeley, M. (2017). Keynes' psychology and behavioral macroeconomics. *Economic and Labor Relations Review, 28*(2):177–196.

Barberis, N. C. (2013). Thirty years of Prospect Theory in economic: A review and assessment. *Journal of Economic Perspectives, 27*(1): 173–196.

Barnard, C. I. (1938). *The Functions of the Executive*. Cambridge, MA: Harvard University Press.

Barro, R. J., & Grossman, H. I., (1976). *Money, Employment and Inflation*. Cambridge: Cambridge University Press.

Bauer, P. T. (1971). *Dissent on Development*. London: Weidenfeld & Nicolson.

Baumol, W. J. (1959). *Business Behavior, Value and Growth*. New York: Macmillan.

Baumol, W. J. (1962). On the theory of the expansion of the firm. *American Economic Review, 52*(5): 1079–1087.

Baumol, W. J. (1972). *Economic Theory and Operations Analysis* (3$^{rd}$ edition). London: Prentice-Hall International.

Belsky, G., & Gilovich, T. (1999). *Why Smart People Make Big Money Mistakes and How to Avoid Them*. New York: Simon and Schuster.

Berg, N. (2015). Behavioral labor economics. In M. Altman (ed.) *Handbook of Contemporary Behavioral Economics* (pp. 479–500). London and New York: Routledge.

Berg, N., & Gigerenzer, G. (2010). As-if behavioral economics: Neoclassical economics in disguise? *History of Economic Ideas, 18*(1), 133–166.

Bettman, J. R. (1979). *An Information-Processing Theory of Consumer Choice*. Reading, MA: Addison-Wesley.

Brooks, M. A. (1988). Toward a behavioral analysis of public economics. In P. E. Earl (ed.), *Psychological Economics: Development, Tensions, Prospects* (pp. 169–188). Boston, MA: Kluwer Academic Publishing.

Brooks, M. A., & Earl, P. E. (1987). On the implications of jointness in a normative model of behavior based on an activity hierarchy. *Journal of Consumer Research, 14*(3): 445–448.

Buchanan, J. M., & Thirlby, G. (eds) (1973). *LSE Essays on Cost*. London: Weidenfeld and Nicolson.

Buenstorf, G. (2003). Designing clunkers: Demand-side innovation and the early history of the mountain bike, In U. Cantner and J. S. Metcalfe (eds), *Change, Transformation and Development* (pp. 53–7,0) Heidelberg: Physica.

Catmull, E. (2014). *Creativity, Inc.* New York: Random House.

Chai, A., Earl, P. E., & Potts, J. (2007). Fashion, growth and welfare: An evolutionary approach. In M. Bianchi (ed.), *The Evolution of Consumption: Theories and Practices (Advances in Austrian Economics, Volume 10)* (pp. 187–207). Oxford: Elsevier.

Chandler, A. D. (1962). *Strategy and Structure: Chapters in the History of the American Industrial Enterprise*. Cambridge, MA: MIT Press.

Channon, D. F. (1973). *The Strategy and Structure of British Enterprise*. London: Macmillan.

Chick, V. (1983). *Macroeconomics After Keynes*. Deddington: Philip Allan.

Christensen, C. (1997). *The Innovator's Dilemma: When New Technologies Cause Great Firms to Fail*. Boston, MA: Harvard Business Review Press.

Cialdini, R. B. (1984). *Influence: The Psychology of Persuasion*. New York: William Morrow & Company.

Cialdini, R. B. (2009). *Influence: Science and Practice* (5th edn). Boston: Pearson Education.

Clark, J. (2007). Essays on Complexity, Choice and Competition in the Market for Retirement Funds. PhD dissertation, University of Queensland.

Clower, R. W. (1965). The Keynesian counter-revolution: A theoretical appraisal. In F. H. Hahn and F. P. R. Brechling (eds), *The Theory of Interest Rates*. London: Macmillan.

Clower, R. W. (1967). A reconsideration of the microfoundations of monetary theory. *Western Economic Journal* (now *Economic Inquiry*), 6(1): 1–8.

Clower, R. W. (ed.) (1969). *Monetary Theory*. Harmondswoth: Penguin.

Clydesdale, G. (2006). Creativity and competition: The Beatles. *Creativity Research Journal, 18*(2): 129–139.

Clydesdale, G. (2015). Capabilities and industrial policy: Lesson from the New Zealand movie industry. *Industrial and Corporate Change, 24*(5): 1149–1171.

Clydesdale, G. (2016). *Waves of Prosperity: India, China and the West – How Global Trade Transformed the World*. London: Robinson.

Clydesdale, G. (2021). *Reducing Inter-generational Ethnic Poverty: Economics, Psychology and Culture*. Abingdon and New York: Routledge.

Coase, R. H. (1937). The nature of the firm. *Economica, 4 (new series)* (16): 386–405.

Coddington, A. (1976). Keynesian economics: The search for first principles. *Journal of Economics Literature, 14*(4): 1258– 1273.

Coddington, A. (1982). Deficient foresight: A troublesome theme in Keynesian economics. *American Economics Review, 72*(3): 480-487.

Coursey, D. K. (1985), A normative model of behavior based upon an activity hierarchy. *Journal of Consumer Research, 12*(1): 64–73.

Cripps, T. F., & Tarling, R. J. (1973). *Growth in Advanced Capitalist Economies, 1960–1970 (Department of Applied Economics Occasional Papers, No. 40)*. Cambridge: Cambridge University Press.

Cross, R. (1982). *Economic Theory and Policy in the UK*. Oxford: Martin Robertson.

Cross, R. (1984). Methodology in economics. *Scottish Journal of Political Economy, 31*(1): 100–110.

Csikszentmihalyi, M. (1990). *Flow: The Psychology of Optimal Experience*. New York: Harper & Row.

Cyert, R. M., & March, J. G. (1963). *A Behavioral Theory of the Firm*. Englewood Cliffs, NJ Prentice-Hall.

Cyert, R. M., & March, J. G. (1992). *A Behavioral Theory of the Firm*. (2nd edition) Malden, MA and Oxford: Blackwell.

Darby, M. R., &. Karni, E. (1973). Free competition and the optimal amount of fraud. *Journal of Law & Economics, 16*(1): 67–88.

Dekker, E., & Remic, B. (2024). Hayek's extended mind: on the (im)possibility of Austrian behavioral economics. *Journal of Institutional Economics*, published online and open access, March 7, 2024, e19, 1–19 doi:10.1017/S1744137424000055. ,

Denison, E. F. (1967). *Why Growth Rates Differ: Postwar Experience in Nine Western Countries*. Washington, DC: Brookings Institutions.

Dewey, J. (1910). *How We Think*. New York: D. C. Heath.

Dhami, S. (2016). *The Foundations of Behavioral Economics*. Oxford: Oxford University Press.

Doidge, N. (2007). *The Brain that Changes Itself: Stories of Personal Triumph from the Frontiers of Brain Science*. New York: Viking Penguin.

Dopfer, K., Foster, J., & Potts, J. (2004). Micro-meso-macro. *Journal of Evolutionary Economics, 14*(3), 263-279.

Douglas, E. J. (1987). *Managerial Economics: Analysis and Strategy* (3rd edn). Englewood Cliffs, NJ: Prentice-Hall.

Dow, S. C., & Earl, P. E. (1982). *Money Matters: A Keynesian Approach to Monetary Economics*. Oxford: Martin Robertson.

Dow, S. C., & Earl, P. E. (eds) (1999a). *Economic Organization and Economic Knowledge: Essays in Honour of Brian J. Loasby, Volume I*. Cheltenham: Edward Elgar.

Dow, S. C., & Earl, P. E. (eds) (1999b). *Contingency, Complexity and the Theory of the Firm: Essays in Honour of Brian J. Loasby, Volume II*. Cheltenham: Edward Elgar.

Downie, J. (1958). *The Competitive Process*. London: Duckworth.

Drakopoulos, S. A. (1994). Hierarchical choice in economics. *Journal of Economic Surveys, 8*(2): 33–153.

Drakopoulos, S. (2021). "The marginalization of absolute and relative income hypotheses of consumption and the role of fiscal policy. *European Journal of the History of Economic Thought, 28*(6): 965–998.

Drakopoulos, S. A., & Karayiannis, A. D. (2004). The historical development of hierarchical behavior in economic thought. *Journal of the History of Economic Thought, 26*(3): 363–378.

Duesenberry, J. S. (1949). *Income, Saving and the Theory of Consumer Behavior*. Cambridge, MA: Harvard University Press.

Earl, P. E. (1980a). Characteristic Filtering: Towards a Behavioral Theory of Individual Choice. University of Stirling Discussion Papers in Economics, Finance, and Investment, No. 84, August.

Earl, P. E. (1980b). A Behavioral Theory of Economists' Behavior and the Lack of Success of Behavioral Economics. University of Stirling Discussion Papers in Economics, Finance, and Investment, No. 85, August.

Earl, P. E. (1983a). *The Economic Imagination: Towards a Behavioral Analysis of Choice*. Brighton: Wheatsheaf Books/Armonk, NY: M. E. Sharpe, Inc.

Earl, P. E. (1983b). A behavioral theory of economists' behavior. In A. S. Eichner (ed.), *Why Economics is not yet a Science* (pp. 90–125). London: Macmillan/Armonk, NY: M.E. Sharpe, Inc.

Earl, P. E. (1983c). The consumer in his/her social setting: A subjectivist view. In J. Wiseman (ed.), *Beyond Positive Economics? (Papers presented to Section F of the British Association for the Advancement of Science, York, 1981)* (pp, 176–191). London: Macmillan.

Earl, P. E. (1984). *The Corporate Imagination: How Big Companies Make Mistakes*, Brighton: Wheatsheaf Books/Armonk, NY: M. E. Sharpe, Inc.

Earl, P. E. (1986a). A behavioral analysis of demand elasticities. *Journal of Economic Studies*, *13*(3): 20–37.

Earl, P. E. (1986b). *Lifestyle Economics: Consumer Behavior in a Turbulent World*. Brighton: Wheatsheaf Books/New York: St Martin's Press.

Earl. P. E. (1987e). Scientific Research Programs, Corporate Strategies and the Theory of the Firms. Information Research Unit Occasional Paper, University of Queensland.

Earl, P. E. (ed.) (1988a). *Psychological Economics: Development, Tensions, Prospects*. Boston, MA: Kluwer Academic Publishers.

Earl, P. E. (ed.) (1988b). *Behavioral Economics*. Aldershot: Edward Elgar.

Earl, P. E. (1989a). Bounded rationality, psychology and financial evolution: Some behavioral perspectives on Post Keynesian monetary analysis. In J. Pheby (ed.), *New Directions in Post Keynesian Economics* (165–189). Aldershot: Edward Elgar.

Earl, P. E. (1990a). Economics and psychology: A survey. *Economic Journal*, *100*(402): 718–755.

Earl, P. E. (1990b). *Monetary Scenarios: A Modern Approach to Financial Systems*. Aldershot, Edward Elgar.

Earl, P. E. (1990c) Book review: *The Mind and Method of the Economist*, by B. J. Loasby. *Economic Journal, 100*(401): 642–644.

Earl, P. E. (1991). Normal cost versus marginalist approaches to pricing: A behavioral perspective. *Journal of Post Keynesian Economics, 13*(2): 264–281.

Earl, P. E. (1992a). The evolution of cooperative strategies: Three automotive industry case studies. *Human Systems Management, 11*(2): 89–100.

Earl, P. E. (1992b). Scientific research programs and the prediction of corporate behavior *Cyprus Journal of Economics*, 5(2): 75–95.

Earl, P. E. (1992c). On the complementarity of economic applications of cognitive dissonance theory and personal construct psychology. In S. E. G. Lea, P. Webley, & B. Young (eds), *New Directions in Economic Psychology* (pp. 49–65). Aldershot: Edward Elgar.

Earl, P. E. (1992d). Tibor Scitovsky. In W. J. Samuels (ed), *New Horizons in Economic Thought: An Appraisal of Ten Leading Economists* (pp. 265–293). Aldershot: Edward Elgar Publishing Ltd.

Earl, P. E. (1992e). Shearnur on subjectivism. In S. Boehm& B. Caldwell (eds), *Austrian Economics: Tensions and New Developments* (pp. 129–135). Boston, MA: Kluwer Academic Publishers.

Earl, P. E. (1994). The economic rationale of universities: A reconsideration. *Prometheus, 12*(2): 131–151.

Earl, P. E. (1995a). *Microeconomics for Business and Marketing: Lectures, Cases and Worked Essays*. Aldershot: Edward Elgar.

Earl, P. E. (1995b). Coordination problems in tertiary education and research. Paper presented at the G. B. Richardson Colloquium, St John's College, Oxford, 4–6 January. Available for downloading at: https://shredecon.files.wordpress.com/2010/12/cep-richardson-colloquium.pdf.

Earl, P. E. (ed.) (1996a). *Management, Marketing and the Competitive Process*. Cheltenham: Edward Elgar.

Earl, P. E. (1996b). Contracts, coordination and the construction industry. In P. E. Earl (ed.) *Management, Marketing and the Competitive Process* (pp. 149–171). Cheltenham: Edward Elgar.

Earl, P. E. (1998a). Consumer goals as journeys into the unknown. In M. Bianchi (ed.), *The Active Consumer: Novelty and Surprise in Consumer Choice* (pp. 122–139). London: Routledge.

Earl, P. E. (1998b). George Richardson's career and the literature of economics. In N. J. Foss & B. J. Loasby (eds), *Economic Organization, Capabilities and Coordination: Essays in Honour of G. B. Richardson* (pp. 14–43). London: Routledge.

Earl, P. E. (2001a). Simon's travel theorem and the demand for live music. *Journal of Economic Psychology*, 22(3): 335–358.

Earl, P. E. (ed.) (2001b). *The Legacy of Herbert A. Simon in Economic Analysis*. Cheltenham: Edward Elgar

Earl, P. E. (2002). *Information, Opportunism and Economic Coordination*. Cheltenham: Edward Elgar.

Earl, P. E. (2003). The entrepreneur as a constructor of connections. In R. Koppl (ed.), *Austrian Economics and Entrepreneurial Studies – Advances in Austrian Economics, Volume 6* (pp. 117–134). Oxford, JAI/Elsevier.

Earl, P. E. (2004). How economists model choice, versus how we behave, and why it matters. In E. Fullbrook. (ed.), *A Guide to What's Wrong with Economics* (pp. 95–105). London: Anthem.

Earl, P. E. (2005a). Economics and psychology in the twenty-first century. *Cambridge Journal of Economics, 29*(6): 909-926.

Earl, P. E. (2005b) Behavioral Economics and the Economics of Regulation. Briefing Paper for the New Zealand Ministry of Economic Development and Ministry of Consumer Affairs. Available at: https://espace.library.uq.edu.au/view/UQ:8811.

Earl, P. E. (2007). Consumption X-inefficiency and the problem of market regulation. In R. Frantz (ed.), *Renaissance in Behavioral Economics: Essays in Memory of Harvey Leibenstein* (pp. 176–193). London: Routledge.

Earl, P. E. (2010a). The sensory order, the economic imagination and the tacit dimension. In W. Butos (ed.), *The Social Science of The Sensory Order: Advances in Austrian Economics, Volume 13* (pp. 211–236). Bradford: Emerald.

Earl, P. E. (2010b). Remembrance of Cars Past: An Experiential Analysis of Automotive Consumption (The Much Too Long Version). Available at: https://shredecon.files.wordpress.com/2023/05/earl-motoring_much-too-long-version.docx.

Earl, P. E. (2011). From anecdotes to novels: Reflective inputs for behavioral economics. *New Zealand Economic Papers, 45*(1/2): 5–27.

Earl, P. E. (2012a). Experiential analysis of automotive consumption. *Journal of Business Research, 65*(7): 1067–1072.

Earl, P. E (2012b). On Kahneman's *Thinking, Fast and Slow*: What you see is not all there is. *Prometheus, 30*(4): 449–455.

Earl, P. E. (2012c). Kahneman's *Thinking, Fast and Slow* from the standpoint of old behavioral economics. Paper presented to HETSA conference, Melbourne, July. Available at: https://shredecon.files.wordpress.com/2012/06/hetsa-2012-earl.pdf.

Earl, P. E. (2013). Satisficing and cognition: Complementarities between Simon and Hayek. In R. Frantz & R. Leeson (eds), *Hayek and Behavioral Economics* (pp. 278–300). Basingstoke and New York: Palgrave.

Earl, P. E. (2016). The evolution of behavioral economics. In R. Frantz, S.-H. Chen, K. Dopfer, F. Heukelom, & S. Mousavi (eds), *Routledge Handbook of Behavioral Economics* (pp. 5–17). London: Routledge.

Earl, P. E. (2017a). Lifestyle changes and the lifestyle selection process. *Journal of Bioeconomics, 19*(1): 97–114.

Earl, P. E. (2017b). Theory of the firm. In C. L. Spash (ed.), *Routledge Handbook of Ecological Economics* (pp. 194–202). London and New York: Routledge.

Earl, P. E. (2018). Richard H. Thaler: A Nobel Prize for behavioral economics. *Review of Political Economy, 30*(2): 107–125.

Earl, P. E. (2022). *Principles of Behavioral Economics: Bringing Together Old, New and Evolutionary Approaches*. Cambridge: Cambridge University Press.

Earl, P. E. (2023a). Rules all the way down: Consumer behavior from the standpoint of the "ONE behavioral" research program. *Journal of Consumer Behavior, 22*(3): 531–546.

Earl, P. E. (2023b). Shackle's analysis of choice under uncertainty: Its strengths, weaknesses and potential synergies with rival approaches. *Journal of Post Keynesian Economics, 46*(3): 400–419.

Earl, P. E. (2023c). Infinite regress problems and the methodologies of behavioural economics, In I. Negru & P. Hawkins (eds) *Economic Methodology, History and Pluralism* (pp. 94–107). London and New York: Routledge.

Earl, P. E. (2023d). A Comprehensive Bibliography of the Works of Brian J. Loasby. School of Economics, University of Queensland (available via ResearchGate, DOI: 10.13140/RG.2.2.35301.37608).

Earl, P. E., Friesen, L., & Shadforth, C. (2017). The efficiency of market-assisted choices: An experimental analysis of mobile phone connection service recommendations. *Journal of Institutional Economics, 13*(4): 849–873.

Earl, P. E., Friesen, L., & Shadforth, C. (2019). Elusive optima: A process-tracing analysis of procedural rationality in mobile phone connection plan choices. *Journal of Economic Behavior and Organization, 161*: 303–322.

Earl, P. E., & Frowen, S. F. (eds) (2000). *Economics as an Art of Thought: Essays in Memory of G. L. S. Shackle*. London, Routledge.

Earl, P. E., & Glaister, K. W. (1979). Wage Stickiness From the Demand Side. University of Stirling Discussion Papers in Economics, Finance, and Investment, No. 78, December.

Earl, P. E., & Kay, N. M. (1985). How economists can accept Shackle's critique of economic doctrines without arguing themselves out of their jobs. *Journal of Economic Studies, 12*(1/2), 34-48.

Earl, P. E., & Kemp, S. (eds) (1999). *The Elgar Companion to Consumer Research and Economic Psychology*. Cheltenham: Edward Elgar.

Earl, P. E., & Littleboy, B. (2014). *G.L.S. Shackle (Great Thinkers in Economics Series)*. Basingstoke and London: Palgrave.

Earl, P. E., Markey-Towler, B., & Coutts, K. (2022). 50 Years Ago: Duncan Ironmonger's *New Commodities and Consumer Behavior* and its relationship with Lancaster's "New Approach' to Consumer Behavior. *History of Economics Review, 83*(1): 40–67.

Earl, P. E., & Peng, T.-C. (2011). Home improvements. In S. Cameron (ed.), *Handbook of the Economics of Leisure* (pp. 197–220). Cheltenham: Edward Elgar.

Earl, P. E., & Peng, T.-C. (2012). Brands of economics and the Trojan horse of pluralism. *Review of Political Economy, 24*(3): 451–467.

Earl, P. E., Peng, T. C., & Potts, J. (2007). Decision-rule cascades and the dynamics of speculative bubbles. *Journal of Economic Psychology, 28*(3): 351–364.

Earl, P. E., & Potts, J. (2000). Latent demand and the browsing shopper. *Managerial and Decision Economics, 21*(3–4): 11–22.

Earl, P. E., & Potts, J. (2004a). The market for preferences. *Cambridge Journal of Economics, 28*(4): 619–633.

Earl, P. E., & Potts, J. (2004b). Bounded rationality and decomposability: The basis for integrating cognitive and evolutionary economics. In M. Augier & J. G. March (eds), *Models of a Man: Essays in Memory of Herbert A. Simon* (pp. 317–333). Cambridge, MA, MIT Press.

Earl, P. E., & Potts, J. (2013). The creative instability hypothesis. *Journal of Cultural Economics, 37*(2): 153–173.

Earl, P. E., & Potts, J. (2016). The management of creative vision and the economics of creative cycles. *Managerial and Decision Economics, 37*(7): 474–484.

Earl, P. E., & Wakeley, T. (2005). *Business Economics: A Contemporary Approach.* Maidenhead: McGraw-Hill.

Earl, P. E., and Wakeley, T. (2009. Price-based versus standards-based approaches to reducing car addiction and other environmentally destructive activities. In R. P. Holt, S. Pressman, & C. L. Spash (eds), *Post Keynesian and Ecological Economics* (pp. 158–177). Cheltenham: Edward Elgar.

Earl, P. E., & Wakeley, T. (2010a). Alternative perspectives on connections in economic systems. *Journal of Evolutionary Economics, 20*(2): 163-183.

Earl, P. E., & Wakeley, T. (2010b). Economic perspectives on the development of complex products for increasingly demanding customers. *Research Policy, 39(8):* 1122–1132.

Eichner, A. S. (ed.) (1979). *A Guie3 to Post-Keynesian Economics.* London: Macmillan/White Plains, NY: M.E. Sharpe, Inc.

Eichner, A. S. (ed.) (1983). *Why Economics is Not Yet a Science.* London: Macmillan/Armonk, NY: M.E. Sharpe, Inc.

Endres, A. M., & Harper, D. A. (2012). The kinetics of capital formation and economic organisation. *Cambridge Journal of Economics, 36*(4), 963–980.

Endres, A. M., & Harper, D. A. (2020). Economic development and complexity: the role of recombinant capital. *Cambridge Journal of Economics, 44*(1, January), 157–180.

Engel, J. F., Blackwell, R. D., & Kollat, D. T. (1978). *Consumer Behavior* (3rd edition). Hinsdale, IL: Dryden Press.

Engel, J. F., & Blackwell, R. D. (1982). *Consumer Behavior* (4th edition). Hinsdale, IL: Dryden Press.

Engel, J. F., Kollat, D. T., & Blackwell, R. D. (1968). *Consumer Behavior*. New York: Holt, Rinehart & Winston.

Ericsson, K. A., & Simon, H. A. (1993). *Protocol Analysis: Verbal Reports as Data* (2nd edition). Cambridge, MA: MIT Press.

Etzioni, A. (1988). *The Moral Dimension: Toward a New Economics*. New York: Free Press.

Farrell, M. J. (1959). The new theories of the consumption function. *Economic Journal, 69*(276): 678–696.

Festinger, L. (1957). *A Theory of Cognitive Dissonance*. New York: Harper & Row.

Feyerabend, P. K. (1975). *Against Method: Outline of an Anarchistic Theory of Knowledge*. London: Verso Books

Fishbein, M., & Ajzen, I. (1975). *Belief, Attitude, Intention, and Behavior*. Reading, MA: Addison-Wesley.

Fisher, D. (2000). The Socio-Economic Consequences of Tourism in Levuka, Fiji. PhD dissertation, Lincoln University, New Zealand.

Foley, C. A. (1893). Fashion. *Economic Journal, 3*(11, September), 458–474.

Foster, M. M., Earl, P. E., Haines, T. P., & Mitchell, G. K. (2010). Unravelling the concept of consumer preference: Implications for health policy and optimal planning in primary care. *Health Policy, 97*(2–3): 105-112.

Friedman, M. (1968). The role of monetary policy. *American Economic Review, 58*(1): 1–17.

Friesen, L., & Earl, P. E. (2015). Multipart tariffs and bounded rationality: An experimental analysis of mobile phone plan choices. *Journal of Economic Behavior and Organization, 116*: 239–253.

Friesen, L., & Earl, P. E. (2020). An experimental analysis of regulatory interventions for complex pricing. *Southern Economic Journal, 86*(3): 1241–1266.

Frolov, D. (2024). The economics of cognitive institutions: mapping debates, looking ahead. *Journal of Institutional Economics*. 20: e28. doi:10.1017/S174413742400016X.

Frowen, S. F. (ed.) (1990). *Unknowledge and Choices in Economics*. Basingstoke: Macmillan.

Fullbrook, E. (1998). Caroline Foley and the theory of intersubjective demand. *Journal of Economic Issues, 32*(3), 709–731.

Galbraith, J. K. (1958). *The Affluent Society*. London: Hamish Hamilton.

Garfinkel, H. (1967). *Studies in Ethnomethodology*. Englewood Cliffs, NJ: Prentice-Hall.

Gigerenzer, G. (2015). On the supposed evidence for libertarian paternalism. *Review of Philosophy and Psychology, 6*(3): 361–383.

Gigerenzer, G., & Goldstein, D. G. (1996). Reasoning the fast and frugal way: Models of bounded rationality. *Psychological Review, 103*(4): 650–669.

Gigerenzer, G., Todd, P. M., & The ABC Research Group (1999). *Simple Heuristics that Make Us Smart*. New York: Oxford University Press.

Godley, W., & Cripps, F. (1983). *Macroeconomics*. London: Fontana.

Godley, W., & Lavoie, M. (2007). *Monetary Economics: An Integrated Approach to Credit, Money, Income, Production and Wealth*. Basingstoke: Palgrave.

Goodhart, C. A. E. (1975). *Money, Information and Uncertainty*. London: Macmillan.

Gouldner, A. W. (1954). *Patterns of Industrial Bureaucracy*. Glencoe, IL: Free Press.

Granovetter, M. (1985). Economic action and social structure: The problem of embeddedness. *American Journal of Sociology, 91*(3, November), 481–510.

Grüne-Yanoff, T., & Hertwig, R. (2016). Nudge versus Boost: How Coherence are policy and theory. *Minds and Machines, 26*(1–2). 149–183.

Grupp, H., & Maital, S. (2001). *Managing New Product Development and Innovation: A Microeconomic Toolbox*. Cheltenham: Edward Elgar.

Gutman, J. (1982). A means–end chain model based on consumer categorization processes. *Journal of Marketing, 46*(2): 60–72.

Harper, D. A. (1996). *Entrepreneurship and the Market Process: An Enquiry into the Growth of Knolwedge*. London and New York: Routledge.

Harper, D. A., & Earl, P. E. (1996). Growth of Knoewledge perspectives on business behaviour. In P. E. Earl (ed.) *Management, Marketing and the Compeititve Process* (pp. 306–328). Cheltenham: Edward Elgar.

Harper, D. A., & Endres, A. M. (2010). Capital as a layer cake: A systems approach to capital and its multi-level structure. *Journal of Economic Behavior & Organization, 74*(1), 30–41.

Harper, D. A., & Endres, A. M. (2012). The anatomy of emergence, with a focus upon capital formation. *Journal of Economic Behavior & Organization, 82*(2), 352–367.

Harper, D. A., & Endres, A. M. (2018). From Quaker Oats to Virgin Bridge: Band capital as a complex adaptive system. *Journal of Institutional Economics, 14*(6), 1071–1096.

Hayek, F. A. (1952). *The Sensory Order: An Inquiry into the Foundations of Theoretical Psychology*. Chicago, IL: University of Chicago Press.

Hayek, F. A. (1961). The non sequitur of the "dependence effect." *Southern Economic Journal, 27*(4): 346:348.

Hedges, M. R. (2010). Tertiary Education Choices in New Zealand: A Pluralistic Investigation. PhD dissertation, University of Queensland.

Henry, H. (!958). *Motivation Research: Its Practice and Uses for Advertising, Marketing and Other Business Purposes*. London: Crosby Lockwood.

Hertwig, R. (2017). When to consider boosting: Some rules for policy-makers. *Behavioral Public Policy, 1*(3): 143–162.

Hey, J. D. (1983). Unshackling economics. *Scottish Journal of Political Economy, 37*(2): 202–208.

Hey, J. D. (1987). Book review: *Lifestyle Economics*, by P. E. Earl. *Manchester School, 55*(1): 101–102.

Hicks, J. R. ([1939] 1946). *Value and Capital: An Inquiry into Some Fundamental Principles of Economic Theory* (2$^{nd}$ edition, 1946). Oxford: Clarendon Press.

Hicks, J. R. (1976). Some questions of time in economics. In A. M. Tang, F. M Westfield and J. S. Worley (eds), *Evolution, Welfar and Time in Economics: Essays in Honor of Nicholas Georgescu-Roegen*. Lexington, MA: Lexington Books.

Hicks, J. R., & Allen, R. G. D. (1934a). A reconsideration of the theory of value (Part I). *Economica (New Series), 1*(1, February), 52–76.

Hicks, J. R., & Allen, R. G. D. (1934b). A reconsieration of the theory of value (Part II). *Economica (New Series), 1*(2, May), 196–219.

Hinkle, D. N. ([1965] 2010). The change of personal constructs from the viewpoint of a theory of construct implications. [PhD dissertation, Ohio State University, 1965]. *Personal Construct Theory and Practice, 7*(Supp. No. 1), 1–61.

Hirschman, A. O. (1970). *Exit, Voice and Loyalty*. Cambridge, MA: Harvard University Press.

Hodgson G. M. (1982). *Capitalism, Value and Exploitation*. Oxford: Martin Robertson.

Hodgson, G. M. (1988). *Economics and Institutions: A Manifesto for a Modern Institutional Economics*. Cambridge: Polity Press.

Hodgson, G. M. (1997). The ubiquity of habits and rules. *Cambridge Journal of Economics, 21*(6): 663–684.

Hodgson, G. M. (2003). The hidden persuaders: Institutions and individuals in economic theory. *Cambridge Journal of Economics, 27*(2), 159–175.

Hofstadter, D. R. (1979). *Gödel, Escher, Bach: An Eternal Golden Braid.* Hassocks, Sussex: Harvester Press.

Hogarth, R. M., & Makridakis, S. (1981). Planning and forecasting: An evaluation. *Management Science, 27*(2): 115–138.

Holbrook, M. B. (1995a). The four faces of commodification in the development of marketing knowledge. *Journal of Marketing Management, 11*(7): 641–654.

Holbrook, M. B. (1995b). *Consumer Research: Introspective Essays on the Study of Consumption.* Thousand Oaks, CA: Sage.

Houthakker, H. S., & Taylor, L. D. (1970). *Consumer Demand in the United States: Analysis and Projections.* Cambridge, MA: Harvard University Press.

Hutchison, T. W. (1938). *The Significance and Basic Postulates of Economic Theory.* London: Macmillan (reprinted 1965, New York: Augustus M. Kelley).

Hutchison, T. W. (1977). *Knowledge and Ignorance in Economics.* Oxford: Basil Blackwell.

Ironmonger, D. S. (1972). *New Commodities and Consumer Behavior.* Cambridge: Cambridge University Press.

Irving, J. (1978). P. W. S. Andrews and the Unsuccessful Revolution. Ph.D. dissertation, University of Wollongong, NSW.

Jackson, D., Turner, H. A., & Wilkinson, F. (1972). *Do Trade Unions Cause Inflation? (University of Cambridge Department of Applied Economics Occasional Paper 36).* Cambridge: Cambridge University Press.

Jangu, N. (1997). Decision-Processes of Adopters and Non-Adopters of an Innovation. PhD dissertation, Lincoln University, New Zealand.

Jefferson, M. (1983). Economic uncertainty and business decision- making. In J. Wiseman (ed.), *Beyond Positive Economics? Proceedings of Section F (Economics) of the British Association for the Advancement of Science, York, 1981* (pp. 132–159). London: Macmillan.

Kahneman, D. (2011). *Thinking, Fast and Slow.* New York: Farrar, Strauss and Giroux.

Kahneman, D., Knetsch, J. L., & Thaler, R. H. (1986). Fairness as a constraint on profit seeking entitlements in the market. *American Economic Review, 76*(4): 728–741.

Kahneman, D., & Tversky, A. (1979). Prospect theory: An analysis of decision under risk. *Econometrica, 47*(2): 263–291.

Katona, G. A. (1960). *The Powerful Consumer: Psychological Studies of the American Economy.* New York: McGraw-Hill.

Kay, N. M. (1979). *The Innovating Firm: A Behavioural Theory of Corporate R&D*. London: Macmillan

Kay, N. M. (1982). *The Evolving Firm: Strategy and Structure in Industrial Organization*. London: Macmillan.

Kay, N. M. (1984). *The Emergent Firm: Knowledge, Ignorance and Surprise in Economic Organization*. London: Macmillan.

Kelly, G. A. (1955). T*he Psychology of Personal Constructs*. New York: W. W. Norton.

Kelly, G. A. (1963). *A Theory of Personality*. New York: W. W. Norton.

Kemp, S., & Wall, G. (2013). *Economic Psychology and Experimental Economics*. Abingdon and New York: Routledge.

Keynes, J. M. (1921). *A Treatise on Probability*. London: Macmillan.

Keynes, J. M. (1936). *The General Theory of Employment, Interest and Money*. London: Macmillan

Keynes, J. M. (1937). The general theory of employment. *Quarterly Journal of Economics, 51*(2): 209–223.

Keynes, J. M. (1971). *The Collected Writings of John Maynard Keynes, Volume 5: A Treatise on Money, Volume 1: The Pure Theory ofd Money*. London: Macmillan/Royal Economic Society.

Keynes, J. M. (1979). *The Collected Writings of John Maynard Keynes, Volume 29: The General Theory and After: A Supplement*. London: Macmillan/Royal Economic Society.

King, J. E. (2016). Katona and Keynes. *History of Economics Review, 64*(1), 64–75.

King, J. E., & Millmow, A. (2003). Death of a revolutionary textbook. *History of Political Economy, 35*(1): 105–134.

Koestler, A., & Smythies, J. R (eds) (1969). *Beyond Reductionism: New Perspectives in the Life Sciences*. London: Hutchinson.

Kornai, J. (1971). *Anti-Equilibrium: On Economic Systems Theory and the Tasks of Research*. Amsterdam: North-Holland.

Kuhn, T. S. (1962). *The Structure of Scientific Revolutions*. Chicago, IL: University of Chicago Press.

Laaksonen, P. (1994). *Consumer Involvement: Concepts and Research. London: Routledge.*

Lafferty, G., and Fleming, J. (2000). The restructuring of academic work in Australia: Power, management and gender. *British Journal of Sociology of Education, 21*(2): 257–267.

Lakatos, I. (1970). Falsification and the methodology of scientific research programs. In I. Lakatos & A. Musgrave (eds), *Criticism and the Growth of Knowledge* (pp. 91–196). London, Cambridge University Press.

Lancaster, K. J. (1966). A new approach to consumer theory. *Journal of Political Economy, 75*(2): 132–157.

Latsis, S. J. (1972). Situational determinism in economics. *British Journal for the Philosophy of Science, 23*(3): 207–245.

Latsis, S. J. (ed.) (1976). *Method and Appraisal in Economics.* Cambridge: Cambridge University Press.

Lavoie, D. (1990). Hermeneutics, subjectivity and the Lester/Machlup debate: Towards a more anthropological approach to empirical economics. In W. J. Samuels (ed.), *Economics as Discourse: An Analysis of the Language of Economics* (pp. 167–184). New York: Springer.

Lavoie, M. (1985). Credits and money: The dynamic circuit, overdraft economics, and Post-Keynesian economics. In M. Jarsulic (ed.), *Money and Macro Policy* (pp. 68–84). Dordrecht: Springer

Lavoie, M. (1992). *Foundations of Post-Keynesian Economic Analysis.* Aldershot: Edward Elgar.

Lee., F. S., & Earl, P. E. (eds) (1993), *The Economics of Competitive Enterprise: Selected Essays of P. W. S. Andrews.* Aldershot: Edward Elgar.

Leff, N. H. (1985). Optimal investment choice for developing countries: Rational theory and rational decision-making. *Journal of Development Economics, 18*(2–3): 335–360.

Leibenstein, H. (1966). Allocative efficiency vs. "X-efficiency." *American Economic Review, 56*(3): 392–414.

Leibenstein, H. (1976). *Beyond Economic Man: A New Foundation for Economics.* Cambridge, MA: Harvard University Press.

Leijonhufvud, A. (1968). *On Keynesian Economics and the Economics of Keynes.* New York: Oxford University Press.

Leijonhufvud, A. (1969). *Keynes and the Classics.* London: Institution of Economic Affairs.

Leijonhufvud, A. (1973). Effective demand failures. *Swedish Journal of Economics, 75*(1): 27–48.

Lenton, A. P., & Stewart, A. (2008). Changing her ways: The number of options and mate-standard strength impact mate choice strategy and satisfaction. *Judgment and Decision Making, 3*(7): 501–511.

Lester, R. A. (1946). Shortcomings of marginal analysis for wage-unemployment problems. *American Economic Review, 36*i(1): 63–82.

Lewin, S. B. (1996). Economics and psychology: Lessons for our own day from the early twentieth century. *Journal of Economic Literature, 34*(3): 1293–1323.

Lipsey, R. G. (1966), *An Introduction to Positive Economics* (2nd edition), London: Weidenfeld & Nicolson..

Loasby, B. J. (1967a). Making location policy work. *Lloyds Bank Review*, No. 83, 34–47; reprinted in P. E. Earl (ed.) *Behavioural Economics, Volume II*, Aldershot, Edward Elgar, 1988: 264–277.

Loasby, B. J. (1967b). Management economics and the theory of the firm. *Journal of Industrial Economics, 15*(3): 165–176.

Loasby, B. J. (1973). *The Swindon Project*. Lonson: Pitman.

Loasby, B. J. (1976). *Choice, Complexity and Ignorance*. Cambridge: Cambridge University Press.

Loasby, B. J. (1977). On imperfections and adjustments, University of Stirling Discussion Papers in Economics, Finance, and Investment, No. 50.

Loasby, B. J. (1978). Whatever happened to Marshall's theory of value? *Scottish Journal of Political Economy, 25*(1): 1–12.

Loasby, B. J. (1983). Knowledge, learning and enterprise. In J. Wiseman (ed.), *Beyond Positive Economics? Proceedings of Section F (Economics) of the British Association for the Advancement of Science, York, 1981* (pp. 104–121). London: Macmillan.

Loasby, B. J. (1987). Book review: *Lifestyle Economics. Consumer-Behavior in a Turbulent World*, by P. E. Earl. *Scottish Journal of Political Economy*, 34(4): 420.

Loasby, B. J. (1989). *The Mind and Method of the Economist*. Aldershot: Edward Elgar.

Loasby, B. J. (1991). *Equilibrium and Evolution. An Exploration of Connecting Principles in Economics*. Manchester and New York: Manchester University Press.

Loasby, B. J. (1996). The division of labor. *History of Economic Ideas*, 4(1–2), 299–323.

Loasby, B. J. (1999). *Knowledge, Institutions and Evolution in Economics*. London and New York: Routledge.

Loasby, B. J. (2004). Hayek's theory of the mind. In R. Koppl (ed.), *Evolutionary Psychology and Economic Theory:Advances in Austrian Economics, Volume 7* (pp. 101–134). Oxford: Elsevier.

Lodge, D. (1989). *Nice Work*. Harmondsworth: Penguin.

Lowenstein, R. (2001). Exuberance is rational. *New York Times Magazine*, 11 February.

Lutz, M. A., & Lux, K. (1979). *The Challenge of Humanistic Economics*. Menlo Park, CA: Benjamin–Cummings Publishing.

Lutz, V. (1969). *Central Planning for the Market Economy: An Analysis of the French Theory and Experience*. Harlow: Longman, for the Institute of Economic Affairs.

Machlup, F. (1946). Marginal analysis and empirical research. *American Economic Review, 36*(4): 519–554.

Machlup, F. (1967). Theories of the firm: Marginalist, behavioral, managerial. *American Economic Review, 57*(1): 1–33.

Macmillan, P. J. (2015). Thinking Like an Expert Lawyer: Measuring Specialist Legal Expertise Through Think-Aloud Problem Solving and Verbal Protocol Analysis. PhD dissertation, Bond University, QLD.

Marris, R. L. (1964). *The Economic Theory of "Managerial" Capitalism*. London: Macmillan.

Marshall, A. (18900. *Principles of Economics*. London: Macmillan.

Maslow, A. H. (1943). A theory of human motivation. *Psychological Review, 50*(4): 370–396.

Maslow, A. H. ([1954] 1970). *Motivation and Personality* (2nd edition, 1970). New York: Harper & Row.

Mason, R. (2000). The social significance of consumption: James Duesenberry's contribution to consumer theory. *Journal of Economic Issues,* 34(3): 553–572.

Meeks, G. (1977). *Disappointing Marriage: A Study of the Gains from Merger*. Cambridge: Cambridge University Press.

Mehta, J. (2013). The discourse of bounded rationality in academic and policy arenas: Pathologizing the errant consumer. *Cambridge Journal of Economics, 37*(6): 1243–1261.

Miller, A. (1972). *The Price*. New York: Bantam Books.

Miller, S. S. (1963). *The Management Problems of Diversification*. New York: Wiley.

Millmow, A. (2021). *The Gypsy Economist. The Life and Times of Colin Clark*. Singapore: Palgrave Macmillan.

Minsky, H. P. (1975a). *John Maynard Keynes*. New York: Columbia University Press (London: Macmillan, 1976).

Minsky, H. P. (1975b). The Sky Did Not Fall. *Hyman P. Minsky Archive.* 174. https://digitalcommons.bard.edu/hm_archive/174

Minsky, H. P. (1982a). *Can "It" Happen Again? Essays on Instability and Finance*. Armonk, NY: M. E. Sharpe (Published in the UK as *Inflation, Recession and Economic Recovery*. Brighton: Wheatsheaf, 1982).

Minsky, H. P. (1982b). The financial instability hypothesis: A restatement. In P. Arestis & T. Skouras (eds.), *Post Keynesian Economic Theory* (pp. 24–55). Brighton: Wheatsheaf/Armonk, NY: M.E. Sharpe.

Minsky, H. P. (1986). *Stabilizing an Unstable Economy*. New Haven, CT: Yale University Press

Mosley, P. (1976). Towards a "satisficing" theory of economic policy. *Economic Journal, 86*(341): 59–72.

Mosley, P. (1981). The Treasury Committee and the making of economic policy. *Political Quarterly, 52*(3): 348–355.

Mosley, P. (1984). *The Making of Economic Policy: Theory and Evidence from Britain and the United States since 1945*. Brighton: Wheatsheaf.

Myrdal, G. (1957). *Economic Theory and Underdeveloped Areas*. London: Gerald Duckworth.

Nelson, R. R., & Winter, S. G. (1982). *An Evolutionary Theory of Economic Change*. Cambridge, MA, Belknap Press of Harvard University Press.

Nicosia, F. M. (1966). *Consumer Decision Processes: Marketing and Advertising Implications*. Englewood Cliffs, NJ: Prentice–Hall.

Nightingale, J. (1994). Situational determinism revisited: Scientific research programs in economics twenty years on. *Journal of Economic Methodology, 1*(2): 233–252.

Nightingale, J. (1997). Anticipating Nelson and Winter: Jack Downie's theory of evolutionary economic change. *Journal of Evolutionary Economics, 7*(1): 147–167.

Nightingale, J. (1998). Jack Downie's Competitive Process: The first articulated population ecological model in economics. *History of Political Economy, 30*(3): 369–412.

Nisbett, R. E., & Ross, L. (1980). *Human Inference: Strategies and Shortcomings of Social Judgment*. Englewood Cliffs, NJ: Prentice-Hall.

Olshavsky, R. W., & Granbois, D. H. (1979). Consumer decision-making – Fact or fiction? *Journal of Consumer Research, 6*(2): 93–100.

Paish, F. (1964). *Benhan's Economics*. London: Isaac Pitman & Co.

Payne, J. W., Bettman, J. R., & Johnson, E. J. (1993). *The Adaptive Decision Maker*. Cambridge: Cambridge University Press.

Pech, W., & Milan, M. (2009). Behavioral economics and the economics of Keynes. *Journal of Socio-Economics, 38*(6): 891–902

Peng, T.-C. (2009). A Pluralistic Analysis of Housing Renovation Choices in Brisbane. PhD dissertation, University of Queensland.

Penrose, E. (1959). *The Theory of the Growth of the Firm*. Oxford: Blackwell.

Perry, W. G. (1970). *Forms of Intellectual and Ethical Development in the College Years: A Schema*. New York: Holt, Rinehart and Winston.

Phelps, C. (1990). Motivational determinate of occupational choice in Arthur Miller's "The Price." In S. Lea, P. Webley, & B. Young (eds), *Applied Economic Psychology in the 1990s: Papers Presented to the 15th Annual Colloquium of the International Association for Research in Economic Psychology* (pp. 411–427). Exeter: Washington Singer Press.

Pickering, J. F. (1976). Book review: *Studies in Pricing*, by P. W. S. Andrews and E. Brunner. *Economic Journal, 86*(343): 621–622,

Pickering, J. F. (1977). *The Acquisition of Consumer Durables: A Cross Sectional Investigation*. London: Associated Business Programs.

Porter, M. E. (1980). *Competitive Strategy: Techniques for Analyzing Industries and Competitors*. New York: Free Press.

Porter, M. E. (1985). *Competitive Advantage*. New York: Free Press.

Posner, M. V. (1978). Wages, prices and the exchange rate. In M. J. Artis & A. R. Nobay (eds), *Contemporary Economic Analysis*. London: Croom Helm.

Potts, J. (1999). Choice, complexity and connections. In S. C. Dow and P. E. Earl (eds), *Contingency, Complexity and the Theory of the Firm" Essays in Honour of Brian J. Loasby, Volume II* (pp. 287–305). Cheltenham: Edward Elgar.

Potts, J. (2000). *The New Evolutionary Microeconomics: Complexity, Competition and Adaptive Behavior*. Cheltenham: Edward Elgar.

Pounds, W. F. (1969). The process of problem finding. *Industrial Management Review, 11*(1): 1–19.

Prais, S. J. (1973). Book Review: *New Commodities and Consumer Behavior*, by D. S. Ironmonger. *Economic Journal* 83 (330): 578–580.

Prest, A. R., & Coppock, D. J. (eds) (1972). *The UK Economy: A Manual of Applied Economics* (4th edition). London: Weidenfeld & Nicolson.

Proust, M. (1913–1927). *À la Recherche du Temps Perdu*. Paris: Éditions Grasset

Rabin, M. (1998). Psychology and economics. *Journal of Economic Literature, 36*(1): 11–46.

Rabin, M., & Thaler, R. H. (2001): Anomalies: Risk aversion. *Journal of Economic Perspectives, 15*(1): 219–232.

Reid, G. C. (1981). *The Kinked Demand Curve Analysis of Oligopoly*. Edinburgh: Edinburgh University Press.

Remenyi, J. V. (1979). Core demi-core interactions: Toward a general theory of disciplinary and subdisciplinary growth. *History of Political Economy, 11*(1): 30–63.

Reynolds, T. J., & Gutman, J. (1984). Laddering: extending the repertory grid methodology to attribute–consequence–value hierarchies. In R. E. Pitts & A. G. Woodside (eds.), *Personal Values and Consumer Psychology* (pp. 155–167). Lexington, MA: D. C. Heath.

Ricardo, D. (1951). *The Works and Correspondence of David Ricardo, Volume I: On the Principles of Political Economy and Taxation*(edited by P. Sraffa). Cambridge: Cambridge University Press.

Richardson, G. B. (1960). *Information and Investment.* Oxford: Oxford University Press.

Richardson, G. B. (1972). The organisation of industry. *Economic Journal, 82*(327): 883–896.

Robinson, E. A. G. (1939). Review article on *Oxford Economic Papers. Economic Journal, 49*(September): 538–543.

Robinson, J. (1933). *The Economics of Imperfect Competition.* London: Macmillan.

Robinson, J. (1964). *Economic Philosophy.* Harmondsworth: Penguin.

Robinson, J. (1977). What are the questions? *Journal of Economic Literature, 15*(4): 1318–1339.

Robinson, J., & Eatwell, J. (1973). *An Introduction to Modern Economics.* London: McGraw-Hill.

Ross, L. (1977). The intuitive psychologist and his shortcomings: Distortions in the attribution process. *Advances in Experimental Social Psychology, 10*: 173–220.

Rostow, W. W. (1960). *The Stages of Economic Growth: A Non-Communist Manifesto.* Cambridge: Cambridge University Press.

Rotheim, R. J. (1981). Keynes' monetary theory of value. *Journal of Post Keynesian Economics, 3*(4): 568–585.

Rothschild, Lord (1982). *An Inquiry into the Social Science Research Council.* London: HMSO

Rutherford, M. (1988). Learning and decision-making in economics and psychology: A methodological perspective. In P. E. Earl (ed.), *Psychological Economics: Development, Tensions, Prospects* (pp. 35–54). Boston, MA: Kluwer Academic Publishing.

Sabbagh, K. (1989). *Skyscraper: The Making of a Building.* New York: Viking Penguin.

Saith, A. (2019). *Ajit Singh of Cambridge and Chandigarh: An Intellectual Biography of the Radical Sikh Economist* (Palgrave Studies in the History of Economic Thought). Cham: Springer International Publishing.

Saith, A. (2022). *Cambridge Economics in the Post-Keynesian Era: The Eclipsing of Heterodox Traditions* (Palgrave Studies in the History of Economic Thought). Cham: Springer International Publishing.

Salter, W. E. G. (1966). *Productivity and Technical Change* (2nd edition). Cambridge: Cambridge University Press.

Scherer. F. M. (2017). Ajit Singh (1940–2015). In R. Cord (ed.) *The Palgrave Companion to Cambridge Economics* (Volume II, pp. 1113–1130). London: Palgrave Macmillan.

Schettkat, R.. (2022). *The Behavioral Economics of John Maynard Keynes: Microfoundations for the World We Live In*. Cheltenham: Edward Elgar.

Schoenberger, E. (1997). *The Cultural Crisis of the Firm*. Oxford, Blackwell.

Schuetz, A. (1943). The problem of rationality in the social world. *Economica, 10* (38): 130–149.

Schumacher, E. F. (1973). *Small is Beautiful: A Study of Economics as if People Mattered*. London: Blond and Briggs.

Schumpeter, J. A. (1943). *Capitalism, Socialism and Democracy*. London: George Allen & Unwin (new edition, 1992, London and New York, Routledge).

Selznick, P. (1957). *Leadership in Administration*. Evanston, IL: Harper & Row.

Sent, E.-M. (2004). Behavioral economics: How psychology made its (limited) way back into economics. *History of Political Economy, 36*(4): 735–760.

Shackle, G. L. S. (1940). The nature of the inducement to invest. *Review of Economic Studies, 8* (1): 44–48.

Shackle, G. L. S. (1941). A means of promoting investment. *Economic Journal, 51* (202/203): 249–260.

Shackle, G. L. S. (1943). The expectational dynamics of the individual. *Economica, 10* (38): 99–129.

Shackle, G. L. S. (1949). *Expectation in Economics*. Cambridge: Cambridge University Press.

Shackle, G. L. S. (1953). *What Makes an Economist?* Liverpool: Liverpool University Press (reprinted in Shackle, G. L. S. (1990). *Time, Expectations and Uncertainty in Economics* (edited by J. L. Ford). Aldershot: Edward Elgar).

Shackle, G. L. S. (1958). *Tine in Economics*. Amsterdam: North-Holland.

Shackle, G. L. S. (1967). *The Years of High Theory: Invention & Tradition in Economic Thought, 1926–1939*. Cambridge: Cambridge University Press.

Shackle, G. L. S. (1969). *Decision, Order and Time in Human Affairs* (2nd edition). Cambridge: Cambridge University Press.

Shackle, G. L. S. (1974). *Keynesian Kaleidics*. Edinburgh: Edinburgh University Press.

Shackle, G. L. S. (1979). *Imagination and the Nature of Choice*. Edinburgh: Edinburgh University Press.

Shackle, G. L. S. (1982). Means and meaning in economic theory. *Scottish Journal of Political Economy 29*(3): 223–234.

Shipman, A. (2019). *Wynne Godley: A Biography*. Cham: Springer.

Silberston, A. (1970); Surveys of applied economics: Price behavior of firms. *Economic Journal, 80*(319): 511–582.

Simon, H. A. (1947). *Administrative Behavior*. New York: Macmillan (3rd edition 1976. New York: Free Press).

Simon, H. A. (1951). A formal theory of the employment relationship. *Econometrica, 19*(3), 293–305.

Simon, H. A. (1957). *Models of Man*. New York: Wiley.

Simon, H. A. (1959). Theories of decision-making in economics and behavioral science. *American Economic Review, 49*(3): 253– 283.

Simon, H. A. (1962). The architecture of complexity. *Proceedings of the American Philosophical Society, 106*(6): 467–482.

Simon, H. A. (1969). *The Sciences of the Artificial*. Cambridge, MA: MIT Press.

Simon, H. A. (1976). From substantive to procedural rationality. In S. J. Latsis (ed.), *Method and Appraisal in Economics* (pp. 129–148). Cambridge: Cambridge University Press.

Simon, H. A. (1991). *Models of My Life*. New York, NY: Basic Books.

Singh, A. (1977). UK industry and the world economy: A case of de-industrialisation? *Cambridge Journal of Economics, 1*(2)): 113–136.

Skinner, A. S. (1979). Adam Smith: An aspect of modern economics? *Scottish Journal of Political Economy, 26*(2): 109–125.

Smith, A. ([1795] 1980). The principles which lead and direct philosophical enquiries; illustrated by the history of astronomy. In W. P. D. Wightman (ed.), *Essays on Philosophical Subjects* (pp. 33–105). Oxford: Oxford University Press.

Smith, R. P. (1975). *Consumer Demand for Cars in the USA (University of Cambridge Department of Applied Economics Occasional Paper No. 44*. Cambridge: Cambridge University Press.

Sraffa, P. (1960). *Production of Commodities by Means of Commodities*. Cambridge: Cambridge University Press.

Stanlake, G. F. (1967). *Introductory Economics*. London: Longman.

Steer, P. S., & Cable, J. R. (1978). Internal organization and profit: An empirical analysis of large companies. *Journal of Industrial Economics, 27*(1): 13–30

Steinbruner, J. D. (1974). *The Cybernetic Theory of Decision: New Dimensions of Political Analysis*. Princeton, NJ: Princeton University Press.

Stewart, M. (1967). *Keynes and After*. Harmondsworth, Penguin.

Stoneman, P. (1976). *Technological Diffusion and the Computer Revolution: The UK Experience*. Cambridge: Cambridge University Press.

Stout, D. K. (1977). *International Price Competitiveness, Non-Price Factors and Export Performance*. London: National Economic Development Office.

Strotz, R. H. (1957). The empirical implications of a utility tree. *Econometrica, 25*(2)): 269–280.

Swinnerton-Dyer, P. (1982). *Report of the Working Party on Postgraduate Education*. London: HMSO.

Thaler, R. H. (1980). Toward a positive theory of consumer choice. *Journal of Economic Behavior and Organization*, 1(1): 39–60.

Thaler, R. H. (1985). Mental accounting and consumer choice. *Marketing Science, 4*(3): 199–214.

Thaler, R. H. (2015). *Misbehaving: The Making of Behavioral Economics*. New York: W. W. Norton.

Thaler, R. H., & Shefrin, H. M. (1981). An economic theory of self-control. *Journal of Political Economy, 89*(2): 392–406.

Thaler, R. H., & Sunstein, C. R. (2008). *Nudge: Improving Decisions About Health, Welfare and Happiness*. New Haven, CT: Yale University Press.

Thompson, C. J. (1996). Caring consumers: Gendered consumption meanings and the juggling lifestyle. *Journal of Consumer Research, 22*(4): 388–407.

Townshend, H. (1937). Liquidity premium and the theory of value. *Economic Journal, 47*(185): 157–169.

Trevithick, J. (1978). Recent developments in the theory of employment. *Sottish Journal of Political Economy, 25*(1): 107–118.

Tuck, M. (1976). *How Do We Choose? A Study in Consumer Behavior*. London: Methuen.

Tversky, A. (1972). Elimination by aspects: A theory of choice. *Psychological Review, 79*(4): 281–299.

Uchitelle, L. (2001). Some economists call behavior a key. *New York Times*, Business section, 11 February.

Veblen, T. B. (1899). *The Theory of the Leisure Class: An Economic Study of Institutions*. New York: Macmillan.

Viale, R. (2024). Enactive problem-solving: An alternative to the limits of decision making. In G. Gigerenzer (ed.), *The Elgar Companion to Herbert Simon* (pp. 198–227). Cheltenham: Edward Elgar.

Vickerman, A. (1985). *The Fate of the Peasantry: Premature "Transition to Socialism" in the Democratic Republic of Vietnam*. New Haven, CT: Yale University Press.

Wakeley, T. (1997). *Innovation, Welfare and Industrial Structure: An Evolutionary Analysis*. Aldershot: Avebury.

Wakeley, T. (2002) Book review: *The New Evolutionary Microeconomics: Complexity, Competence and Adaptive Behaviour*, by Jason Potts. *Journal of Economic Psychology, 23*(2): 279–286.

Wärneryd, K.-E. (1982). The life and work of George Katona. *Journal of Economic Psychology, 2*(1), 1–31.

Wärneryd, K.-E. (1999). *The Psychology of Saving: A Study on Economic Psychology*, Cheltenham: Edward Elgar

Wells, W. D. (1975). Psychographics: A critical review. *Journal of Marketing Research, 12*(2): 196–213.

Williamson, O. E. (1964). *The Economics of Discretionary Behavior: Managerial Objectives in a Theory of the Firm*. Englewood Cliffs, NJ: Prentice-Hall.

Williamson, O. E. (1975). *Markets and Hierarchies: Analysis and Anti-Trust Implications*. New York: Free Press.

Williamson, O. E. (1985). *The Economic Institutions of Capitalism: Firms, Markets and Relational Contracting*. New York; Free Press.

Williamson, O. E., Wachter, M. L., & Harris, J. E. (1975). Understanding the employment relation: The analysis of idiosyncratic exchange. *Bell Journal of Economics, 6*(1), 250–278.

Williamson, O. E., Wachter, M. L., & Harris, J. E. (1975). Understanding the employment relation: The analysis of idiosyncratic exchange. *Bell Journal of Economics, 6*(1), 250–278.

Woodward, J. (1965). *Industrial Organization: Theory and Practice*. London: Oxford University Press.

# Index